The Air Pilot's **Manual**

Volume 4
The Aeroplane – Technical

Trevor Thom

Airlife England

Copyright © 1997 Aviation Theory Centre

ISBN 1 85310 928 2

First edition published 1987
Second edition 1988
Reprinted with amendments 1989, 1991, 1993 and 1994
Reprinted 1995, 1996
This third revised edition published 1997
Reprinted 1998

Origination by Bookworks Ltd, Ireland.

Printed in England by Livesey Ltd, Shrewsbury, England.

A Technical Aviation Publications Ltd title
under licence by

Airlife Publishing Ltd
101 Longden Road, Shrewsbury SY3 9EB, Shropshire, England.

The Air Pilot's **Manual**

Volume 4

Contents

Section Three – Flight Instruments

Section Four – Airworthiness and Performance

Appendix 1

Exercises and Answers

Index

Editorial Team

Trevor Thom

A Boeing 757 and 767 Training Captain, Trevor has also flown the Airbus A320, Boeing 727, McDonnell Douglas DC-9 and Fokker F-27. He has been active in the International Federation of Airline Pilots' Associations (IFALPA), based in London, and was a member of the IFALPA Aeroplane Design and Operations Group. He also served as IFALPA representative to the Society of Automotive Engineers (SAE) S7 Flight-Deck Design Committee, a body which makes recommendations to the aviation industry, especially the manufacturers. Prior to his airline career Trevor was a Lecturer in Mathematics and Physics, and an Aviation Ground Instructor and Flying Instructor. He is a double degree graduate from the University of Melbourne and also holds a Diploma of Education.

Peter Godwin

Chief Instructor at Bonus Aviation, Cranfield (formerly Leavesden Flight Centre) Peter has amassed over 13,000 instructional flying hours as a fixed-wing and helicopter instructor. As a member of the CAA Panel of Examiners, he is a CAA Authorised Examiner (AE), Instrument Rating and Type Examiner, and is currently training flying instructors and candidates for the Basic Commercial Pilot's Licence and Instrument Rating. Previously he was Chief Pilot for an air charter company and Chief Instructor for the Cabair group of companies based at Denham and Elstree.

John Fenton

A Flying Instructor for over 20 years, John was joint proprietor and assistant CFI of Yorkshire Flying Services at Leeds/Bradford, a PPL examiner, and has received the Bronze Medal from the Royal Aero Club for his achievements and contributions to air rallying. John has made considerable contributions to the field of flying instruction in this country and pioneered the use of audio tapes for training.

Jim Hitchcock

Former Supervisor of Pilot Technical Training, Oxford Air Training School, Jim joined the RAF as an apprentice, was later commissioned as a navigator, and served in Coastal and Flying Training Commands, and on Photo Reconnaissance. On leaving the RAF he joined CSE, Oxford.

vi

Ronald Smith

A senior aviation ground instructor, Ron's 25 years in aviation include considerable time as a Flying Instructor, specialised flying in remote areas, fish-spotting, and a period operating his own Air Taxi Service. He is an active member of *International Wheelchair Aviators* and holds a Commercial Pilot's Licence.

Robert Johnson

Bob produced the two editions of this manual. His aviation experience includes flying a Cessna Citation II-SP executive jet, a DC-3 (Dakota) and light aircraft as Chief Pilot for an international university based in Switzerland, and seven years on Fokker F27, Lockheed Electra and McDonnell Douglas DC-9 airliners. Prior to this he was an Air Taxi Pilot and also gained technical experience as a Draughtsman on airborne mineral survey work in Australia.

Warren Yeates

Warren has been involved with editing, indexing, desktop publishing and printing Trevor Thom manuals since 1988 for UK, US and Australian markets. He currently runs a publishing services company in Ireland.

Acknowledgements

The Civil Aviation Authority; Cessna, Gulfstream American, Lycoming, Piper and Slingsby for technical material; Airtour International Ltd, Ralph Bryder, Graeme Carne, Derek Davidson, Edward Pape, Ola Rustenberg, Steve Storey, and the many other instructors and students whose comments have helped to improve this manual.

Introduction

An aeroplane is a man-made device designed to use natural forces to enable motion through the air, or to enable *flight*.

Air is that mixture of gases which surrounds the earth. If any slight pressure is applied to air, it will flow and change its shape, hence it may be classified as a fluid.

Aerodynamics studies the motion of a body through the air or, if you like, the flow of air past a body. It is concerned with the relative motion of air and a body. The basic principles of aerodynamics relevant to the motion of an aeroplane through the air come under the name *principles of flight*.

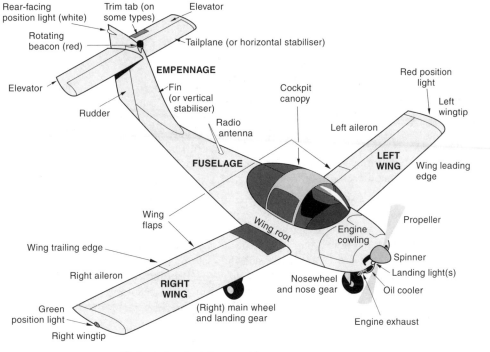

■ *A modern training aeroplane*

In order to control an aeroplane safely and to make correct decisions during the course of a flight, you must understand the principles of flight. When actually in flight you do not have time to analyse in detail the effect of everything that you do, or are about to do, or fail to do, but you should be aware of the fundamentals.

The purpose of *The Air Pilot's Manual* is to give you the understanding and knowledge to be a safe and competent pilot, and to pass the exams. These books will remain useful reference books and should be retained throughout your flying career.

To be a good pilot you must have a sound understanding of the principles of flight, the operation of aircraft, and the performance capabilities of your particular aircraft type.

The Aircraft (General) Examination

This volume is designed to prepare you for the UK Private Pilot's Licence (Aeroplanes) Examination in Aircraft (General). You take this examination at your flight training organisation. Our course on Aircraft (General) is divided into five main sections:

1. **Principles of Flight.**
2. **Airframe, Engines and Systems.**
3. **Flight Instruments.**
4. **Airworthiness and Performance.**
5. **Safety, First Aid and Survival,** covering the aeromedical items in the Aircraft (General) syllabus. This subject is contained in Vol. 6 of this series – *Human Factors and Pilot Performance.*

EMERGENCIES. It is required that you be familiar with the general procedures for handling basic aircraft emergencies on the ground and in the air. These are covered in the relevant chapters in this volume (15, 16 & 17) as well as in the first chapter of Vol. 1, *Flying Training.* Fire extinguishers and their use is covered in the *Safety, First Aid and Survival* section of Vol. 6.

GENERAL AVIATION SAFETY SENSE. A series of CAA *General Aviation Safety Sense* leaflets is available covering various important subjects, such as use of Mogas, aeroplane performance, weight and balance, and piston engine icing. You should be familiar with these leaflets, which are found at most flying schools and aero clubs. They are also obtainable by writing to CAA Printing And Publication Services at Cheltenham. Information contained in these leaflets is sometimes used for PPL exam questions.

AIRCRAFT TYPE. At the end of this volume is an appendix containing information designed to prepare you for the ground examination: Aircraft (Type). This is normally an oral examination that is confined to the type of aeroplane in which you are flight tested. It is usually conducted at the same time as your Private Pilot's Licence flight test.

Exercises

Exercises and answers for all the chapters in this book (Sections 1 to 4) are at the end of the book. Exercises on *Safety, First Aid and Survival* are in Vol. 6.

Section **One**

Principles of Flight

The Forces Acting on an Aeroplane

L ike all things, an aeroplane has **weight,** the force of gravity, which acts through the centre of the aeroplane in a vertical direction towards the centre of the earth.

While the aeroplane is on the ground, its weight is balanced by the reaction force of the ground on the aeroplane, which acts upwards through the wheels.

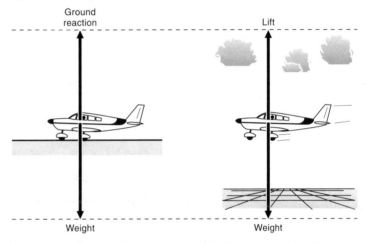

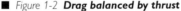

■ *Figure 1-1* **The aeroplane is supported by the ground, or by lift**

While in level flight, the weight of the aeroplane is balanced by the **lift** force, which is generated aerodynamically by the flow of air over the wings. In addition, as the aeroplane moves through the air it will experience a retarding force known as **drag,** which, unless counteracted (or balanced), will cause the aeroplane to decelerate, i.e. to lose speed.

■ *Figure 1-2* **Drag balanced by thrust**

In steady straight and level flight, the drag (or retarding force) is balanced by the **thrust,** which is produced by the engine-propeller combination in most smaller aircraft. (In pure jet aircraft the thrust is produced by the turbine engines without the need for a propeller.)

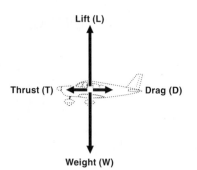

■ *Figure 1-3* **The four main forces in balance**

As the forces in Figure 1-3 are in balance, the resultant force acting on the aeroplane is zero, and it will neither accelerate nor decelerate. In this situation the aeroplane is said to be in a state of equilibrium. In this case (steady straight and level flight):

The four main forces are in equilibrium during unaccelerated flight.

■ **weight** is balanced by **lift**; and
■ **drag** is balanced by **thrust**.

The aeroplane will continue flying at the same velocity, i.e. at the same speed and in the same direction, unless, for example, the pilot or a gust of wind alters this situation.

For the type of aeroplane that you are likely to be flying during your training (and indeed as a licensed PPL pilot) the magnitude (size) of the lift (and therefore the weight) during cruising flight will be approximately 10 times greater than the drag (and thrust). This relationship of lift to drag is very important and is referred to as the **lift/drag ratio**. The L/D ratio is in this case 10 to 1, i.e. the lift (to balance the weight) is 10 times greater than the drag (which is balanced by the thrust).

In this section (principles of flight), we will look at each of the four basic forces in turn:

1. Weight.

2. Lift.

3. Drag.

4. Thrust.

Our plan of attack is to discuss **weight** first of all, because the aeroplane is subject to this force at all times, both in flight and on the ground. This takes only a page or two.

Then we will examine the **aerofoil** and the production of **lift** and **drag**. Lift is produced by the wings, and drag is produced by the wings and most other parts of the aeroplane, as the entire flying machine moves through the air.

Next we discuss how the **propeller** produces the **thrust** which moves the aeroplane along.

Straight and level flight at a steady airspeed is a fairly simple situation, covered in Chapter 10. Other phases of flight such as accelerating, decelerating, climbing, descending, gliding, turning, stalling, taking off and landing are slightly more complicated and are considered in detail later in this section.

Now complete **Exercises 1 – The Forces Acting on an Aeroplane.**
Exercises and Answers are at the back of the book.

Weight

G ravity is the downward force attracting all bodies vertically towards the centre of the earth. The name given to the gravitational force is **weight** and for our purposes in this study of principles of flight it is the total weight of the loaded aeroplane. This weight may be considered to act as a single force through the **centre of gravity (CG)**.

The CG is the point of balance and its position depends on the weight and position of all the individual parts of the aeroplane and the load that it is carrying. If the aeroplane was suspended by a rope attached to its centre of gravity, the aeroplane would balance.

> The centre of gravity is the point through which the weight of a body (object) acts.

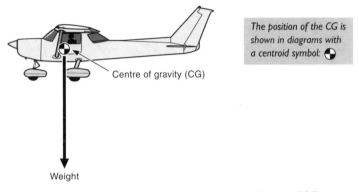

> The position of the CG is shown in diagrams with a centroid symbol: ◓

Centre of gravity (CG)

Weight

■ *Figure 2-1* **Weight acts down through the centre of gravity (CG)**

The magnitude of the weight is important and there are certain limitations placed on it, e.g. a maximum take-off weight (MTOW) will be specified for the aircraft. Weight limitations depend on the structural strength of the components making up the aircraft and the operational requirements that the aircraft is designed to meet.

The balance point (centre of gravity – CG) is very important during flight because of its effect on the stability and performance of the aeroplane. It must remain within carefully defined limits at all stages of the flight.

The location of the CG depends on the weight and the location of the load placed in the aeroplane. The CG will move if the distribution of the load changes, e.g. by passengers moving about or by transferring fuel from one tank to another. The CG may move as the weight changes by fuel burning off or by parachutists leaping out. It is usual for the all-up weight to decrease as the flight progresses.

Both of these aspects, weight and balance, must be considered by the pilot prior to flight. If any limitation is exceeded at any point in the flight, safety will be compromised. **Weight and balance** is covered in Section Four, *Airworthiness and Performance.*

A useful means of describing the load that the wings carry in straight and level flight (when the lift from the wings supports the weight of the aeroplane) is wing loading, which is simply the weight supported per unit area of wing.

$$Wing\ loading\ =\ \frac{Weight\ of\ the\ aeroplane}{Wing\ area}$$

EXAMPLE 1 An aeroplane has a maximum certificated weight of 1,220 kg and a wing area of 20 square metres. What is its wing loading?

$$Wing\ loading\ =\ \frac{Weight\ of\ the\ aeroplane}{Wing\ area}$$

$$=\ \frac{1,220}{20}$$

$$=\ 61\ \text{kg square/metre}$$

Now complete **Exercises 2 – Weight.**

Aerofoil Lift

Pressure Distribution and Airflow around an Aerofoil

An aerofoil is a surface designed to help in lifting, controlling or propelling an aircraft by making use of the airflow. Some well-known aerofoils are the wing, the tailplane (or horizontal stabiliser), the fin (or vertical stabiliser), and the propeller blades.

Control surfaces such as ailerons, elevators and rudders form part of the various aerofoils. You can move these to vary the shape of the aerofoil and the forces generated by the airflow over it. This enables you to manoeuvre the aircraft and control it in flight.

The wing shape can also be changed by extending and lowering flaps to provide better low-speed aerofoil characteristics for take-off and landing.

The production of the lift force by an aerofoil is explained by **Bernoulli's principle** ('high flow velocity gives a low static pressure' − also known as the *venturi effect*). Daniel Bernoulli (1700–1782) was a Swiss scientist who discovered this effect.

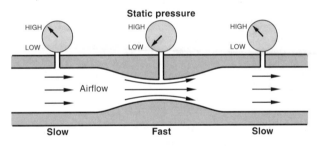

■ *Figure 3-1* **The venturi – high flow velocity, low static pressure**

At Private Pilot Licence (PPL) level we are mainly concerned with aircraft that fly at 200 knots and below. At higher speeds, even well before the speed of sound is reached, there is the complication of the compressibility of air − this is considered at commercial pilot level.

Airflow around an Aeroplane

The pattern of the airflow past an aeroplane depends mainly on the shape of the aeroplane and its attitude relative to the freestream airflow. It is the *relative velocity* of the aeroplane and the airflow that matters, not whether it is the aeroplane moving through the air or the air flowing past the aeroplane. Either approach gives us the same answers.

The most important part of the aeroplane is the aerofoil. Airflow past the main aerofoils (wings) generates the lift force that enables the aeroplane to fly. The airflow around an aerofoil may be likened to the airflow through a venturi.

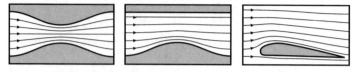

■ *Figure 3-2* ***The airflow around an aerofoil resembles a venturi***

Some other factors apart from the speed of the air past the aerofoil are involved. The size of the aeroplane, the shape of the wings, the density and viscosity (stickiness) of the air — each of these plays a role in determining the characteristics of the airflow around the aeroplane.

The behaviour of the airflow nearest the surface of the aerofoil is most important, and this layer of air is referred to as the **boundary layer.** Friction between a surface and the air flowing over it slows down the layers of air nearest to the surface. The air actually in contact with the surface may in fact have a relative velocity of zero. The thickness of this boundary layer, in which the relative velocity is reduced, is typically several millimetres.

At some point on the surface the airflow within the laminar boundary layer becomes turbulent and the layer thickens significantly. This is known as the **transition point.**

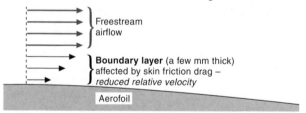

■ *Figure 3-3* **Boundary layer**

Streamline Flow

If succeeding molecules follow the same steady path in a flow, then this path can be represented by a streamline. There will be no flow across the streamlines, only along them.

■ *Figure 3-4* **Streamline flow**

At any fixed point on the streamline, each air molecule will experience the same velocity and static pressure as the preceding molecules when they passed that point. These values of velocity and pressure may change from point to point along the streamline.

A reduction in the velocity of streamline flow is indicated by wider spacing of the streamlines, while increased velocity is indicated by decreased spacing of the streamlines.

Any molecules following a streamline will experience the same velocities and pressures as the preceding molecules.

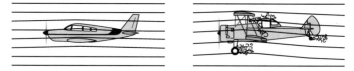

■ *Figure 3-5* **Streamline flow is desirable around an aircraft**

Turbulent Flow

In turbulent flow, succeeding molecules do not follow a streamlined flow pattern. Succeeding molecules may travel a path quite different to the preceding molecules. This turbulent flow is an undesirable feature in most phases of flight, and is why the wings should be free of contamination.

Steady streamline flow is desirable in most phases of flight, and turbulent flow is best avoided. The point where the boundary layer separates from the surface of an aerofoil, causing the main airflow to break away and become turbulent, is known as the **separation point**. This is covered in more detail later in Chapter 14, *Stalling*.

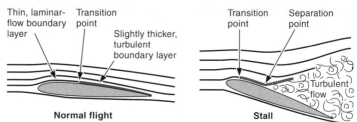

■ *Figure 3-6* **Streamline flow is preferable to turbulent flow**

Bernoulli's Principle

A fluid in steady motion has energy:
- ☐ **static pressure energy**; and
- ☐ **dynamic pressure energy** (kinetic energy due to motion).

Total energy in a steady streamline flow remains constant.

Air is a fluid, and if we assume it to be incompressible, it behaves as a so-called 'ideal' fluid. Daniel Bernoulli showed that for an ideal fluid, total energy in a steady streamline flow remains constant. Therefore:

Pressure energy + kinetic energy = constant total energy
   (static)   (dynamic)

The energy can change from one form to the other, but the total energy content will remain the same. If the pressure energy decreases (lower static pressure) then the kinetic energy must increase (higher velocity of flow), i.e. a *venturi effect.*

The **static pressure** at any point in a fluid acts equally in all directions. Static pressure of the atmosphere is being exerted at all points on your hand right now.

The energy of motion is called **kinetic energy** and is expressed as:

■ *Figure 3-7* **Static pressure acts in all directions**

Kinetic energy = ½ × Mass × Velocity-squared (V^2)

The kinetic energy of a parcel of air in motion relative to an object allows it to exert a force on the object. This force, when calculated per unit surface area, is called **dynamic pressure** and is expressed as:

Dynamic pressure = ½ × rho × Velocity-squared, or ½ρV^2

Dynamic pressure involves air density (*rho*) which is mass per unit volume (rather than just *mass* which is used in the formula for kinetic energy). Dynamic pressure is a more useful quantity than kinetic energy when discussing aerodynamics.

If you hold your hand up in a strong wind or out of the window of a moving car, then wind pressure or moving pressure is felt because of the air striking your hand and flowing around it. This pressure is called dynamic pressure, i.e. pressure due to relative movement between your hand and the air. Just how strong this dynamic pressure is depends on two things:

1. **The speed of the body relative to the air** – the faster the car drives or the stronger the wind blows, then the stronger the dynamic pressure that you feel on your hand. This is because more air molecules per second strike your hand.

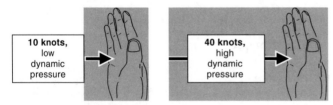

■ *Figure 3-8* **Dynamic pressure increases with airspeed**

2. **The density of the air** – at the same speed, the denser the air, the more air molecules per second that will strike you and so the greater the dynamic pressure.

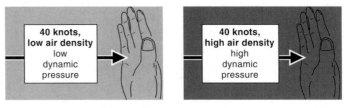

■ *Figure 3-9* **Dynamic pressure is greater in dense air**

Since dynamic pressure equals ½ × *rho* × *V-squared,* our equation can now be written:

> **Static pressure + dynamic pressure = constant total pressure**
> $(rho$ or $\rho)$ $(^1\!/_2 \times rho \times V\text{-squared})$

The term ½ × *rho* × *V-squared* is one of the most important in aerodynamics. There must be dynamic pressure for an aerofoil to produce lift. Dynamic pressure is also important when we consider other aerodynamic items such as drag and indicated airspeed.

We know that static pressure plus dynamic pressure equals constant total pressure. If the speed *V* of the airflow increases, the dynamic pressure increases – this means that the static pressure must decrease (Bernoulli's principle.)

> *Increased velocity means decreased static pressure.*

Conversely, if the velocity (and therefore the dynamic pressure) decreases, the static pressure must increase.

> *Decreased velocity means increased static pressure.*

The Aerofoil and Bernoulli's Principle

All parts of an aircraft contribute towards both lift and drag, but it is the aerofoil, or wing, that is specifically designed to provide the lift force to support the whole of the aircraft.

A study of the variation of static pressure and velocity around the aerofoil, using Bernoulli's principle, is the easiest non-mathematical way to understand the production of lift and drag.

A thin flat plate placed in an airflow at **zero angle of attack** (aligned with the airflow) causes virtually no alteration of the airflow and consequently experiences no reaction (force). **Angle of attack** is the angle at which the plate is presented to the airflow, see Figure 3-10.

If the angle of attack is altered, however, the flat plate experiences a reaction that tends both to lift it and to drag it back – the same effect you feel with your hand out of a car window. The amount of reaction depends on the speed and the angle of attack between the flat plate and the relative airflow.

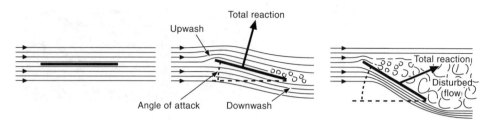

■ *Figure 3-10* **Airflow can lift a flat plate**

Because of the angle of attack, the straight-line streamline flow is disturbed. A slight **upwash** is created in front of the plate causing the air to flow through a more constricted area, almost as if there was an invisible venturi above the plate. The air, as it passes through this constricted area, speeds up.

> *The velocity increase causes a decrease in static pressure (Bernoulli's principle).*

The static pressure above the plate is lower than the static pressure beneath the plate, causing a net upwards reaction. After passing the plate there is a **downwash** of the airstream.

The total reaction on the plate caused by it disturbing the airflow has two components – one at right angles to the relative airflow known as **lift,** and one parallel to the relative airflow, and opposing the relative motion, known as **drag.**

■ *Figure 3-11* **Downwash behind the flat plate**

Aerofoil Shapes

Most aeroplanes do not have flat plates for wings. A flat plate is not the ideal aerofoil for a number of reasons – it breaks up the streamline flow, causing eddying (turbulence), with a great increase in drag. It is also difficult to construct a thin, flat wing.

A curved aerofoil surface not only generates more lift and less drag compared to a flat plate, it is also easier to construct in terms of structural strength.

An aerofoil can have many cross-sectional shapes. Aircraft designers choose the shape which has the best aerodynamic characteristics for their purposes. Although most low-speed aerofoils are similar in shape, each section (cross-section) is designed to give certain specific aerodynamic characteristics.

Our discussion will be only in broad terms that can be generally applied to most aerofoils.

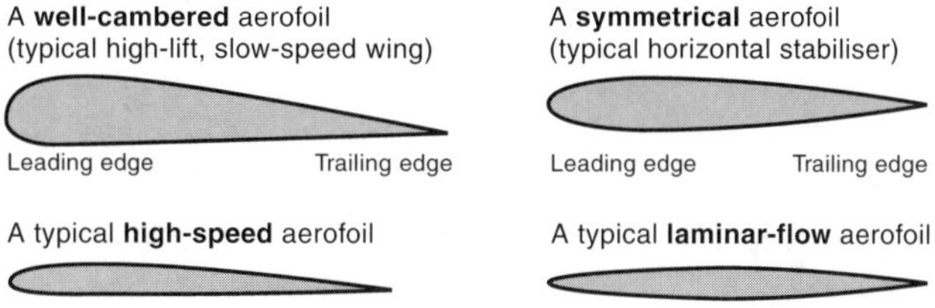

A **well-cambered** aerofoil
(typical high-lift, slow-speed wing)

Leading edge   Trailing edge

A **symmetrical** aerofoil
(typical horizontal stabiliser)

Leading edge   Trailing edge

A typical **high-speed** aerofoil

A typical **laminar-flow** aerofoil

■ *Figure 3-12* **Various aerofoil cross-sections**

Camber

Camber is curvature.

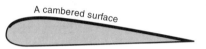
A cambered surface

■ *Figure 3-13* **Aerofoil camber**

Increasing the camber on the upper surface causes the airflow over it to accelerate more and to generate more lift at the same angle of attack (since a higher velocity means a lower static pressure).

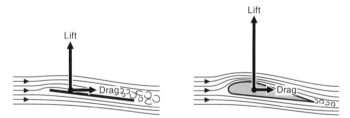

Lift

Lift

Drag

Drag

■ *Figure 3-14* **More camber – more lift**

Wings with a large camber give a good lift, making them suitable for low-speed flight and carrying heavy loads. The position of greatest camber is usually about 30% of the chord back from the leading edge.

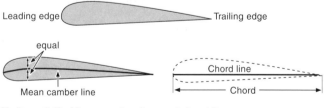

Leading edge   Trailing edge

equal

Mean camber line

Chord line

Chord

■ *Figure 3-15* **Mean camber line and chord line**

*The **mean camber line** is the line drawn halfway between the upper and lower surfaces.*

The mean camber line gives a picture of the average curvature of the aerofoil.

The chord line is the straight line joining the leading edge and the trailing edge of the aerofoil. Another way of saying this is:

*The **chord line** is the straight line joining the ends of the (curved) mean camber line. The length of the chord line is called the **chord**.*

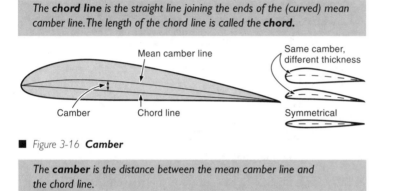

■ *Figure 3-16* **Camber**

*The **camber** is the distance between the mean camber line and the chord line.*

The shape of the mean camber line is extremely important in determining the aerodynamic characteristics of the aerofoil section. The magnitude and position of the maximum camber relative to the chord of the aerofoil help to define the shape of the mean camber line and are usually expressed as a percentage of the chord.

NOTE that a highly cambered wing may be thick or thin and that a symmetrical aerofoil has zero camber.

*The **thickness** of an aerofoil is the greatest distance between the upper and lower surfaces.*

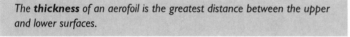

■ *Figure 3-17* **Thickness**

A thick wing with a well-cambered upper surface is ideal for producing high lift at low speeds. Short take-off and landing (STOL) aircraft, which are designed for take-off and landing on short fields and rough or unprepared strips, are most likely to have well-cambered and thick wings, e.g. *de Havilland Canada Dash 7, Beaver* and *Twin Otter, Pilatus Porter* and *Maule Rocket* series.

Also, as mentioned earlier, a thick wing is easier to construct than a thin wing as there is more room for structural parts such as

spars. A thick wing is also advantageous when it comes to installing fuel tanks.

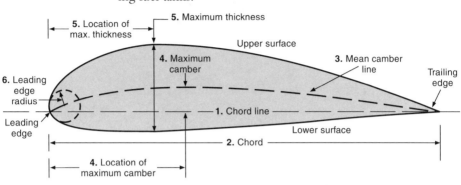

■ *Figure 3-18* **Summary of aerofoil terminology**

A Typical Low-Speed, Well-Cambered Wing

At the small positive angles of attack common in normal flight,
the static pressure over much of the top surface of the aerofoil is
slightly reduced when compared to the normal static pressure of
the free airstream well away from the aerofoil. The static pressure
beneath much of the lower surface of the aerofoil is slightly
greater than that on the upper surface.

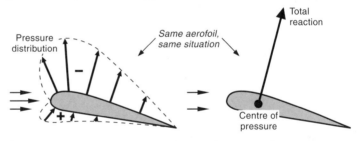

■ *Figure 3-19* **Total reaction acts through the centre of pressure**

This pressure difference is the origin of the total reaction force
exerted on the aerofoil, the greatest contribution coming from
the upper surface. In the same way that the total weight can be
considered to act through a point called the centre of gravity, the
total reaction of the aerodynamic forces on the aerofoil can be
considered to act through the **centre of pressure.**

It is convenient for us to consider this **total reaction (TR)** in
its two components: lift and drag.

> **Lift** is the component of the total reaction at right-angles, or
> perpendicular, to the relative airflow.
> **Drag** is the component of the total reaction parallel to the relative airflow
> and opposing motion.

> **Relative airflow** refers to the relative motion between a body and the remote airflow, i.e. the airflow far enough away from the body not to be disturbed by it.

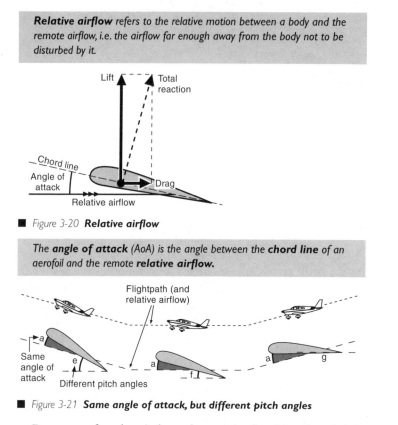

■ Figure 3-20 **Relative airflow**

> The **angle of attack** (AoA) is the angle between the **chord line** of an aerofoil and the remote **relative airflow**.

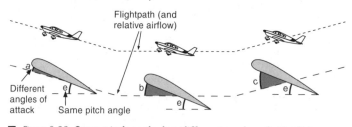

■ Figure 3-21 **Same angle of attack, but different pitch angles**

Do not confuse the **pitch angle** or **attitude** of the aircraft (relative to the horizontal) with the *angle of attack* of the aerofoil (relative to the remote airflow).

■ Figure 3-22 **Same pitch angle, but different angles of attack**

Do not confuse *angle of attack* (relative to the remote airflow) with **angle of incidence,** the angle at which the wing is fixed to the airframe relative to the longitudinal axis. The angle of incidence is fixed, but the angle of attack changes in flight.

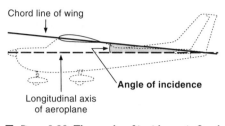

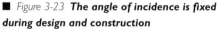

■ *Figure 3-23* **The angle of incidence is fixed
during design and construction**

Bernoulli's principle associates a decrease in static pressure with an increase in velocity, i.e. a decreasing static pressure goes hand in hand with an accelerating airflow. The shape of the aerofoil and its angle of attack determine the distribution of velocity and therefore the distribution of the static pressures over the surface.

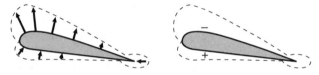

■ *Figure 3-24* **Distribution of static pressure around an aerofoil**

As a means of illustrating different static pressures, we will use an arrow away from the aerofoil to indicate a pressure less than the free airstream static pressure (a 'suction') and an arrow towards the surface to indicate a static pressure greater than that of the free airstream. Elsewhere you may see a '−' to indicate a lower static pressure and '+' to indicate a higher static pressure.

At the leading edge of the wing, the airflow actually comes to rest relative to the wing – this point is called the leading edge **stagnation point.** There is also a trailing edge stagnation point.

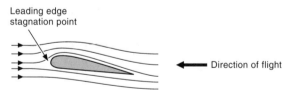

■ *Figure 3-25* **Leading edge stagnation point**

At the leading edge stagnation point the airflow divides to pass over and under the aerofoil section. The positive angle of attack causes an increased velocity on the upper surface and therefore a decreased static pressure (Bernoulli). If the profile produces a continuous acceleration there will be a continuous static pressure reduction.

At other points on the aerofoil the airflow must slow down and this will be accompanied by a corresponding rise in static pressure (Bernoulli). A smoothly contoured surface will produce a smoothly changing pressure distribution.

Pressure Distribution Changes with Angle of Attack

It is interesting to consider the pressure distribution around a particular aerofoil as the angle of attack is varied (Figure 3-26).

In normal flight, the airflow accelerates over the leading edge of the aerofoil – the rate of acceleration being greater at greater angles of attack. As the velocity increases, the static pressure decreases (Bernoulli) and at the point of highest velocity, the static pressure is least. The airflow under the aerofoil accelerates much less rapidly than that above and so the static pressure decreases much more slowly. It may or may not decrease to a value less than the static pressure of the free airstream, depending on the angle of attack.

At small angles of attack there are static pressure reductions over both the upper and lower surfaces, with the lift force being generated by the pressure differential. The static pressure is reduced to a lower value on the upper surface compared to the static pressure on the lower surface at small angles of attack.

At a small negative angle of attack, about –4° (minus four degrees) for this aerofoil, pressure reductions are about equal and therefore no lift force results.

At high angles of attack the lift is due to the decreased pressure on the upper surface and the slightly increased pressure on the lower surface.

Beyond the stalling angle of attack, the streamline flow over the upper surface is reduced, with a consequent weakening of the low-pressure area due to the formation of eddies. (Bernoulli's principle only applies to streamline flow.) What little lift is left is due mainly to the pressure increase on the lower surface.

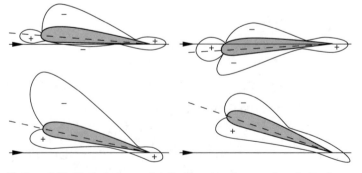

■ Figure 3-26 **Static pressure distribution at various angles of attack**

The Centre of Pressure

Rather than have all these complicated pressure plots it is easier to show the overall effect of these changes in static pressure using the single aerodynamic force **total reaction** acting at a single point on the chord line – the **centre of pressure (CP)**.

As the angle of attack is increased in normal flight two important things happen:

1. The lifting ability of the wing (coefficient of lift) increases, allowing the wing to produce the same lift (required to balance the weight) at a lower airspeed.

2. The centre of pressure moves forward.

At normal cruising speeds (about 4° angle of attack), the centre of pressure is back towards the centre of the wing. As the angle of attack is increased and the airspeed decreased, the centre of pressure moves forward. The furthest forward that it moves is to about ⅕ of the chord (20%) aft of the leading edge.

Past the stalling angle of attack (about 16° angle of attack), the streamline flow over the upper surfaces breaks down, and the lower static pressures on the upper surface are not created. The total reaction (especially the lift component) is reduced and the centre of pressure moves back along the chord.

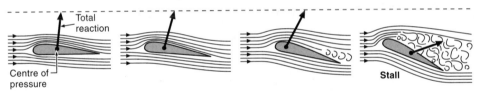

■ *Figure 3-27* **The total reaction changes size and the centre of pressure moves as the angle of attack changes. At the stall, the wing loses lift, the (previously smooth) airflow becomes turbulent, and the centre of pressure moves rearwards.**

Lift from a Typical Wing

The lift force is perpendicular to the relative airflow. The total reaction (also known as total aerodynamic force) is resolved into two components: the **drag force,** which opposes motion and acts parallel to the relative airflow; and the **lift force,** which is perpendicular to the relative airflow and the flightpath of the aeroplane.

Experimentally it can be shown that the total reaction, and therefore the lift, depends on:

☐ **wing shape;**
☐ **angle of attack;**
☐ **air density (*rho*);**
☐ **freestream velocity (V-squared);**
☐ **wing surface area (S)**

The lift (and drag) produced by a wing follows natural laws. We can simplify our understanding of this marvellous natural effect by describing it in a fairly simple formula (one of the very few you need to remember).

Velocity of the airflow and air density (*rho*) combine in the expression for dynamic pressure ½ × *rho* × *V-squared*. (The Greek letter *rho* is symbolised as ρ.)

Putting this together with the wing surface area (S), we obtain:

Lift = (some factor) × ½ × rho × V-squared × S

We use 'some factor' to cover the other variables, especially the wing shape and the angle of attack (i.e. the profile that the wing presents to the airflow). This factor is given the more technical name **coefficient of lift** (C_{Lift} or C_L) which is really the 'lifting ability' of the wing at that angle of attack. Therefore: *Lift = C_{Lift} × ½ × rho × V-squared × S.*

Lift = C_L ½ ρ V^2 S

Since the wing shape is fixed by the designer, any changes in C_{Lift} must be due to changes in angle of attack. If the C_{Lift} (lifting ability) of the wing is high at a particular angle of attack, then the same lift force (L) to off-set the weight can be generated at a lower speed. This inter-relationship between angle of attack (C_{Lift}) and airspeed is important for the pilot.

Lift depends on the angle of attack and indicated airspeed.

By using the formula: $L = C_{Lift}$ × ½ × *rho* × *V-squared* × S and measuring L, V, *rho* and S, we can calculate C_{Lift} and develop a graph or curve of C_{Lift} as angle of attack, known as the **lift curve** (Figure 3-28).

For a given wing, the angle of attack is the major controlling factor in the distribution of the static pressure around the wing. This determines the lift force that is generated. The actual value of C_{Lift} will therefore differ according to the angle of attack.

Each aerofoil shape has its own particular lift curve which relates its C_{Lift} to angle of attack. We will consider an average cambered wing like that found on a typical training aircraft such as a *Cessna 172*.

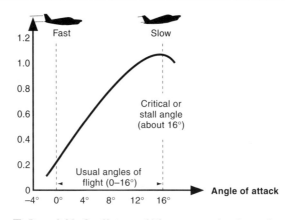

■ *Figure 3-28* **Coefficient of lift versus angle of attack.**
Each angle of attack produces a particular C_{lift} value.

At zero degrees angle of attack, *the cambered aerofoil creates some lift and has a positive C_{Lift}.*
At about –4° angle of attack *the lift is zero and $C_{Lift} = 0$. The aeroplane is rarely flown at the zero lift angle of attack, which occurs in a vertical climb or vertical dive.*
As the angle of attack increases, *the C_{Lift} increases proportionally up to about 12° or 13° angle of attack.*

At higher angles of attack the curve starts to lean over, until at the stalling angle of attack (about 16° in this case) there is a significant drop in C_{Lift} and the ability of the wing to produce Lift. This occurs when the airflow is unable to remain streamlined over the upper surface, separates and breaks up into eddies. This is called **stalling** of the aerofoil. Notice that the maximum C_{Lift} (the maximum lift capability of the wing) occurs just prior to the stall.

The lift force acts through the centre of pressure. At 4° angle of attack the location of the centre of pressure is about 40% of the chord back from the leading edge, and moves further forwards to about 20% as the angle of attack is increased through the normal flight range (from about 4° used in the cruise and glide, up to 16° near the stalling angle).

At the stalling angle of attack *the centre of pressure is at the furthest point forward.*
Beyond the stalling angle of attack *the centre of pressure moves rearwards.*

As the magnitude of the lift force and the location of the centre of pressure change, there will be a different moment or turning effect in the pitching plane of the aircraft. The turning effect (moment) generated by the lift force depends on both its magnitude (size) and the distance between the centre of pressure and the centre of gravity. You can balance this turning moment, and prevent the aircraft pitching nose-up or nose-down, by varying the amount of the aerodynamic force generated by the **tailplane**. You do this by fore and aft movement of the control column, which controls the elevators. (More of this later).

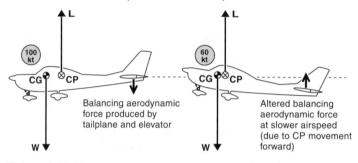

■ *Figure 3-29* **The tailplane keeps the aeroplane in balance**

Lift from a Symmetrical Aerofoil

Typical symmetrical aerofoils are the rudder and some tailplanes. The mean camber line of a symmetrical aerofoil is a straight line because of the identical curvature of the upper and lower wing surfaces. Therefore the chord line and mean camber line are identical.

The lift curve for a symmetrical aerofoil will give a $C_{Lift} = 0$ (and zero lift) at $0°$ angle of attack.

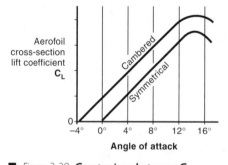

■ *Figure 3-30* **Comparison between C_{Lift} of cambered and symmetrical aerofoils**

The Laminar Flow Wing

A wing with low curvature allows the air to retain laminar (streamline) flow over more of the surface. The location of maximum thickness is usually about 50% back.

A laminar flow wing produces the same lift in the cruising speed range for less drag, when compared to a thicker wing. Laminar flow wings are found on some high-speed aircraft like the *Mustang* WW II fighter and on some training aircraft like the *Piper Cherokee/Warrior* series.

A typical laminar flow aerofoil   A typical cambered aerofoil

■ *Figure 3-31* **Comparison of aerofoil cross-section**

There are some disadvantages of a laminar flow wing. The behaviour near the stall is not as good as a normal aerofoil. The lower value of $C_{Lift\ max}$ means that the stalling speeds are higher.

To produce the required lift (to balance the weight) the stalling angle of attack (about 15–16°) is reached at a higher indicated airspeed than with a well-cambered wing. The $C_{Lift\ max}$ for the aerofoil occurs near the stalling angle, but it is a lower value than the $C_{Lift\ max}$ for a well-cambered aerofoil.

Now complete **Exercises 3 – Aerofoil Lift.**

Drag

While in flight, each and every part of the aircraft exposed to the airflow will produce an aerodynamic force – some aiding flight, such as lift, and some opposing flight, such as drag.

Drag is the aeronautical term for the air resistance experienced by the aeroplane as it moves relative to the air. It acts in the opposite direction to the motion through the air, i.e. it opposes the motion and acts parallel to, and in the same direction as, the relative airflow.

Drag is the enemy of high-speed flight. Streamlining of shapes, flush riveting, polishing of surfaces and many design features are all attempts to reduce the drag force.

The main function of the powerplant-produced thrust is to overcome drag. The lower the drag, the less the thrust required to balance it. The advantages of a lower thrust requirement are obvious: smaller (and possibly fewer) engines, lower fuel flows, less strain on the engine(s) and associated structures, and lower operating costs.

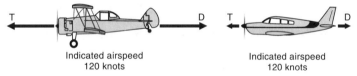

Indicated airspeed
120 knots

Indicated airspeed
120 knots

■ *Figure 4-1* **Low drag requires only low thrust to balance it**

Total Drag

Total drag is the sum of induced drag and parasite drag.

Total drag is the sum of all of the aerodynamic forces which act parallel to, and opposite to, the direction of flight. Total drag is the total resistance to the motion of the aircraft through the air. Note that 'opposite to the direction of flight' is equivalent to 'in the same direction as the relative airflow'.

Total
drag

Total
drag

■ *Figure 4-2* **Total drag is the total resistance to motion**

The total drag is the sum total of the various drag forces acting on the aeroplane. A convenient way of studying these various drags is to separate them into two basic groups:

1. Those drag forces associated with the production of lift, known as **induced drag** (manifested as vortices at the trailing edge of the wing and especially at the wingtips).

2. Those drag forces not directly associated with the development of lift – known as **parasite drag,** which includes form drag, skin friction and interference drag. (Form drag and skin friction are sometimes classified together under the name profile drag.)

Parasite Drag

Parasite drag comprises skin friction, form drag and interference drag.

SKIN FRICTION DRAG. Friction forces between an object and the air through which it is moving produce skin friction drag. The magnitude of the skin friction drag depends on:

- **The surface area of the aircraft.** The whole surface area of the aircraft experiences surface or skin friction drag as it moves through the air.
- **Whether the boundary layer airflow** near the surface is laminar or turbulent. A turbulent boundary layer mixes more with the air around it, causing more drag.
- **Roughness on a surface** (including ice accretion) will increase skin friction drag. The transition from a laminar to a turbulent boundary layer may even occur immediately at the point of roughness. Flush riveting and polishing help to smooth the surface and reduce skin friction drag.
- **Airspeed.** An increase in airspeed increases skin friction drag.
- **Aerofoil thickness.** An increase in aerofoil thickness increases skin friction drag from the wing.
- **Angle of attack.** An increase in angle of attack increases skin friction.

FORM DRAG. When the airflow actually *separates* from the surface, eddies are formed and the streamline flow is disturbed. The turbulent wake so formed increases drag. This is form drag.

Perhaps the easiest way to distinguish form drag from skin friction drag is to consider a flat plate in two different attitudes relative to the airflow. At zero angle of attack the drag is all skin friction. When the flat plate is perpendicular to the airflow, the drag is all form drag.

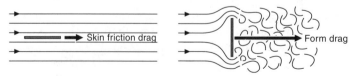

■ Figure 4-3 **Skin friction and form drag**

Eddies are formed in the wake behind the body (which could be an aerofoil or indeed a whole aeroplane), the size of the wake being an indicator of the magnitude of the form drag. This form drag may be a large part of the total drag and good design should reduce it if possible.

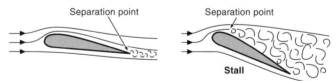

■ *Figure 4-4* **A stalled wing increases form drag substantially**

A spectacular case of airflow separation can be experienced when an aerofoil is at a very high angle of attack. This creates a pressure gradient on the upper surface too severe to allow the boundary layer to adhere to the surface and separation may occur well forward near the leading edge.

The low static pressures ('suction') needed on the upper surface for lift production are lost and stalling occurs. To reduce form drag we need to delay separation of the boundary layer from the surface.

Streamlining of shapes reduces form drag by decreasing the curvature of surfaces, delaying separation of the boundary layer and thereby reducing eddying. The designer may choose an aerofoil of different 'fineness ratio' (thickness/chord) to achieve better streamlining. Streamlining of other parts of the airframe can be achieved by adding fairings.

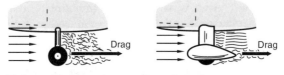

■ *Figure 4-5* **Streamlining reduces form drag**

The streamlining of shapes may be ineffective if ice is allowed to form on them.

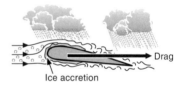

■ *Figure 4-6* **Ice will increase drag**

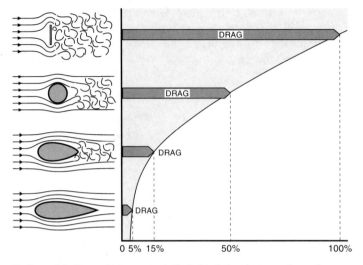

■ *Figure 4-7* **Streamlining, especially behind the shape, reduces form drag substantially**

INTERFERENCE DRAG. If we consider the aircraft as a whole, the total drag is greater than just the sum of the drag on the individual parts of the aircraft. This is due to flow 'interference' at the junction of various surfaces, such as at the wing/fuselage junction, the tail section/fuselage junctions and the wing/engine nacelle junctions.

This flow interference creates an additional drag, which we call interference drag. As it is not directly associated with the production of lift, it is a parasite drag. Airflow from the various surfaces of the aircraft meet and form a wake behind the aircraft. The additional turbulence that occurs in the wake causes a greater pressure difference between the front and rear surfaces of the aircraft and therefore increased drag.

Suitable filleting, fairing and streamlining of shapes to control local pressure gradients can aid in minimising this interference drag. A fairing is part of the skin (external surface) of an aeroplane added to encourage streamline flow, thereby reducing eddying and decreasing drag.

Parasite Drag and Airspeed

At zero airspeed there is no relative motion between the aeroplane and the air. Therefore there is no parasite drag. As the airspeed increases the skin friction, the form drag and the interference drag (which together make up parasite drag) all increase.

> *Parasite drag increases as airspeed increases.*

Airspeed has a powerful effect on parasite drag. Doubling the airspeed gives four times (2-squared, i.e. $2 \times 2 = 4$) the parasite drag. Tripling the airspeed would give $3 \times 3 = 9$ times the parasite drag. Mathematically we call this a square rule, with parasite drag varying as *V-squared*. This 'square rule' often occurs in nature.

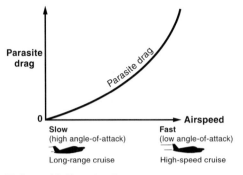

■ *Figure 4-8* **Parasite drag**

Parasite drag is greatest at high speeds and is practically insignificant at low speeds. An aircraft flying at a speed just above the stall may have only 25% of its total drag due to parasite drag (most of the total drag being due to induced drag resulting from the heavy formation of wingtip vortices and the downwash behind the wing).

At a very high speed the total drag may be due almost entirely to parasite drag (with practically no induced drag). The predominance of parasite drag at high flight speeds shows the need for aerodynamic cleanness to obtain high speed performance.

Interestingly, about half of the parasite drag on some aircraft is due to the wings. Any reduction in skin friction, from drag and interference drag from the wings can have a significant effect in reducing the overall parasite drag.

Induced Drag

Induced drag is a by-product of the production of lift and is closely related to the angle of attack.

To produce positive lift, the static pressure on the upper wing surface will be less than that on the lower wing surface. As the air flows rearwards, some airflow will 'leak' or spill around the wingtip from the high static pressure area under the wing to the low static pressure area above the wing. This causes a spanwise flow component of air outwards away from the fuselage on the lower surface and an inwards component towards the fuselage on the upper surface.

At the trailing edge of the wing where these upper and lower flows meet – both moving rearwards but with opposite spanwise (or lateral) components – a sheet of vortices is formed. At the wingtips, where the spanwise flow is greatest, by far the strongest vortices are formed. These are known as **wingtip vortices.**

A **vortex** is a whirling or twisting flow of air or some other fluid. The plural of vortex is *vortices* or *vortexes*. More about wingtip vortices in Chapter 34, *Wake Turbulence*.

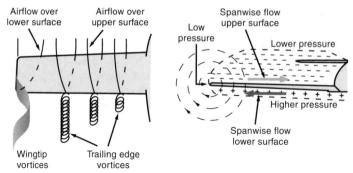

Airflow over lower surface

Airflow over upper surface

Low pressure

Spanwise flow upper surface

Lower pressure

Higher pressure

Spanwise flow lower surface

Wingtip vortices

Trailing edge vortices

■ *Figure 4-9* **Production of lift – induced drag – wingtip vortices**

■ *Figure 4-10* **Wingtip vortex**

When the wings are producing a high value of C_{Lift} (necessary when supporting an aeroplane in manoeuvres, or at low speed and high angles of attack, as in the approach phase), the pressure difference between the lower and upper surfaces of the wing is greatly increased. In these situations very strong wingtip vortices result.

Sometimes, in moist air, the pressure drop in the core of these vortices will cause condensation of the moisture so that the small, twisting vortices are visible as vapour – especially with large passenger aeroplanes on approach and landing in moist conditions.

A similar effect may occasionally be seen near the sharp tips of trailing edge flaps. (These wingtip vortex trails are a different phenomenon to the high altitude vapour trails caused by condensation in the jet engine exhaust, so do not confuse them.)

How Induced Drag is Caused

This explanation is a little beyond what is required in the PPL syllabus but it will assist your understanding of this important phenomenon.

The airflow underneath the wings spills around the wingtips and forms a large twisting vortex at each wingtip. The upward flow in the vortex is outside the span of the wing, but the downward flow is behind the trailing edge of the wing, within the span of the wing. The net effect is a downwash behind the wing.

There is an overall downflow of air behind the trailing edge within the span of the wing.

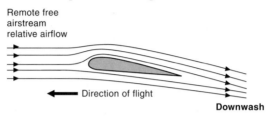

■ *Figure 4-11* **After encountering a wing generating upwards lift, the airflow will be deflected downwards**

Newton's third law of motion (for every action there is an equal and opposite reaction) dictates that, in order for the action of airflow on a wing to generate an upwards lift force, there will be an equal and opposite reaction of the wing on the airflow – (downwards in this case).

The deflection of the airflow downwards causes the wing to experience a local airflow (i.e. an average relative airflow), the direction of which is the average between the remote free airstream well ahead of the wing and the direction of the downwash immediately behind the wing. Since this local or average relative wind experienced by the wing is inclined downwards, the lift force produced by the wing (perpendicular to the local relative airflow) is inclined backwards by the same amount.

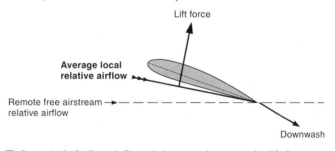

■ *Figure 4-12* **Airflow deflected downwards causes the lift force to be inclined backwards**

When we consider the overall effect of lift and drag on an aeroplane, we need to relate their effects relative to the direction of flight, i.e. relative to the remote free airstream well away from the influence of the local airflows around various parts of the aeroplane.

By convention:

- **the lift** of a wing is referred perpendicular to the remote relative airflow; and
- **the drag** of a wing (or any part of the aeroplane) is referred parallel to the remote relative airflow.

Therefore, the lift force produced by a wing perpendicular to the local airflow will have a component parallel to the remote relative airflow. This component of the lift force that is in the drag direction is the undesirable, but unavoidable, consequence of the production of lift. It is known as **induced drag.**

NOTE The induced drag is separate from the parasite drag (resulting from skin friction, form drag and interference drag). Induced drag is due to the development of lift. A wing will have both induced and parasite drag.

Reducing Induced Drag

High Aspect Ratio Wings

Ludwig Prandtl (1875–1953), a pioneer in the study of aerodynamics, discovered that induced drag could be reduced by having a long, narrow wing (a wing of high aspect ratio).

Compared with a short, stubby wing (low aspect ratio) of the same area, a long narrow wing of high aspect ratio (and therefore smaller wingtips) has weaker wingtip vortices, less induced downwash and therefore less induced drag. Unfortunately, a high aspect ratio wing (long and narrow) is more difficult to build from the structural strength point of view.

$$Aspect\ ratio = \frac{span}{chord}$$

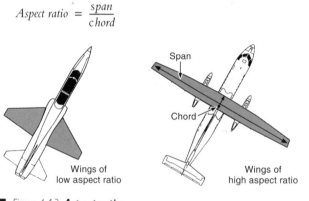

Span

Chord

Wings of
low aspect ratio

Wings of
high aspect ratio

■ *Figure 4-13* **Aspect ratio**

Another way of expressing aspect ratio is:

$$Aspect\ ratio\ =\ \frac{span}{chord}$$

$$=\ \frac{(span \times chord)}{chord\text{-}squared}$$

$$=\ \frac{area}{chord\text{-}squared}$$

Tapered Wings

A tapered wing has weaker wingtip vortices (because there is less wingtip) and so the induced drag is less.

■ *Figure 4-14* **Tapered wings reduce wingtip vortices and induced drag**

Washout

The higher the angle of attack, the greater the pressure differences between the upper and lower wing surfaces. If the wing is built with an inbuilt twist called **washout,** the angle of attack at the wingtip is less than the angle of attack at the wing-root near the fuselage. Therefore most of the lift force is generated on the inner part of the wing, while not so much lift will be generated near the wingtips.

The lower pressure differences between the upper and lower surfaces near the wingtip not only lead to reduced lift production there, but also to less leakage of the airflow around the wingtip, reduced formation of wingtip vortices and a lower induced drag.

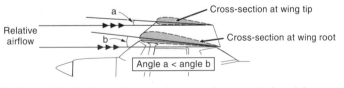

■ *Figure 4-15* **Inbuilt washout on the wings decreases induced drag due to the lower angle of attack towards the wingtips**

Wingtip Modification

Wingtip tanks and modified wingtips can reduce the leakage of the airflow around the wingtip and therefore reduce the formation of induced drag. Also, the installation of wing fences reduces spanwise flow and thus induced drag.

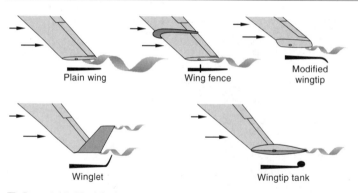

■ *Figure 4-16* **Modified wingtips can reduce formation of vortices**

Flight Conditions that Increase Induced Drag

Low Airspeeds and High Angles of Attack

In straight and level flight at a given weight, the lift must remain constant (to balance the weight) as the speed changes. As the airspeed reduces, the pilot increases the angle of attack (and coefficient of lift) to achieve the same lift – hence high angles of attack are associated with low airspeeds.

The slower passage of air rearwards over the wing allows the spanwise flow of air spilling up over the wingtip to form greater wingtip vortices and greater downwash behind the trailing edge of the wing.

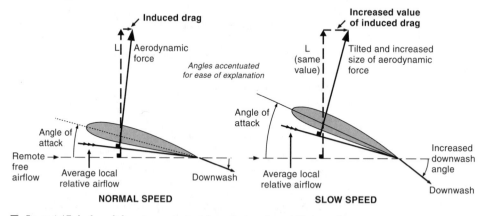

■ *Figure 4-17* **Induced drag is greatest at low airspeeds and high angles of attack**

The greater downwash causes the average local airflow experienced by the wing to be inclined downwards even more, with the lift force produced by the wing being tilted further back, resulting in a stronger component of this lift force in the drag direction – parallel to the remote free airstream.

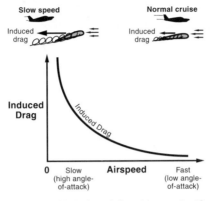

■ *Figure 4-18* **Induced drag is most significant at low speeds and high angles of attack**

Approaching Stalling Angle of Attack

Near the stalling speed in level flight, induced drag could be 75% of the total drag (parasite drag making up the rest), yet at high speed in level flight the induced drag might provide only 1% of the total drag.

Increased Lift Production

A heavy aeroplane requires greater lift to fly straight and level than a light aeroplane. An aeroplane which is manoeuvring requires greater lift than when it is flying straight and level. For example, in a steep turn of 60° bank angle, the wings must generate double the lift force generated in straight and level flight.

Under conditions of high lift, the pressure differential between the lower and upper surfaces increases, resulting in stronger wingtip vortices.

The greater the lift produced, the greater the induced drag.

In level flight at high weights, more lift is required to balance the higher weight, and in manoeuvres, say a steep turn, an excess of lift over weight is required to provide the turning or centripetal force.

Total Drag

Total drag is the sum total of all the drag forces. On some occasions we may talk of the total drag on an aeroplane, while on other occasions we need only refer to the total drag on an aerofoil when only the aerodynamics of that aerofoil in isolation are considered. Be clear in your own mind whether the whole aircraft is under discussion or just the wings.

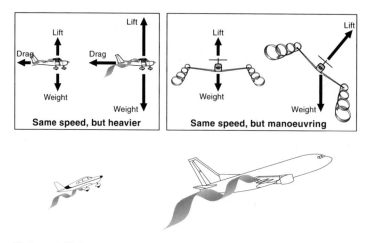

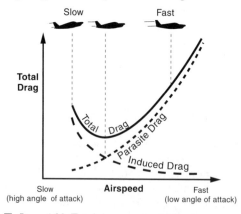

■ *Figure 4-19* **Increased lift means increased induced drag**

As we have seen, the total drag has two components:

☐ **parasite drag;** and
☐ **induced drag.**

If we combine the graphs of each of these drags as they vary with airspeed, we end up with a graph that illustrates the variation of total drag with airspeed for a given aeroplane in level flight at a particular weight, configuration and altitude.

This curve (Figure 4-20) **drag versus airspeed** (angle of attack) is an extremely important relationship. It is a summary of all we need to know about drag. If you understand the message contained in this curve, then you are well on the way to understanding drag and its importance to flight.

■ *Figure 4-20* **Total drag versus airspeed**

The parasite drag increases with speed. The induced drag decreases as the speed increases. The graph shows how induced drag is predominant at low speed, while at high speed the parasite drag predominates. The total drag is least at the point where the parasite drag and the induced drag are equal. Many items of aeroplane performance are related to this **minimum drag speed.**

In straight and level flight, lift equals weight, therefore at the point of minimum drag the wing will be producing that lift required to balance the weight, but with the minimum amount of drag possible.

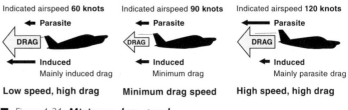

■ *Figure 4-21* **Minimum drag speed**

Thrust is used to balance drag to achieve steady straight and level flight. Figure 4–21 shows that high thrust will be required at both very high and very low airspeeds, and less thrust at intermediate speeds.

The **stall** in level flight under the particular conditions stated on the graph is indicated by a sharp rise in the actual drag, this being contributed by the rapid increase in induced drag as the airspeed drops.

The total drag curve for an aeroplane is a major factor in many items of aeroplane performance, such as landing, take-off, climbing, gliding, manoeuvring, range capability and endurance capability. By combining the induced drag (from wingtip vortices, a by-product of the generation of lift) and the parasite drag (the rest of the drag), we obtain the total drag curve.

Drag from an Aerofoil

At low speeds the total drag from the aerofoil is high (due to induced drag) and at high speeds the total drag is high (due to parasite drag). A formula (similar to that for lift) can be developed for the drag produced by an aerofoil.

$$\textbf{Drag} = \textbf{\textit{C}}_{\textbf{Drag}} \times \textbf{\textit{\tfrac{1}{2}}} \times \textbf{\textit{rho}} \times \textbf{\textit{V-squared}} \times \textbf{\textit{S}}$$

In the drag formula:
- ☐ coefficient of drag (C_{Drag}) represents shape and angle of attack
- ☐ *rho* is air density
- ☐ *V* is velocity (true airspeed) (indicated airspeed = ½ *rho V-squared*)
- ☐ *S* is area.

A **drag curve** for the aerofoil relating C_{Drag} to angle of attack can be developed. This is useful for comparison with the lift curve (C_{Lift} versus angle of attack). Note that at high angles of attack nearing the stalling angle, the coefficient of drag for an aerofoil is high and plays a large role in the formula:

$$Drag = C_{Drag} \times \tfrac{1}{2} \times rho \times \text{V-squared} \times S$$

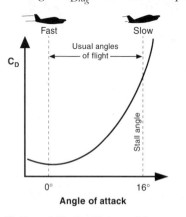

■ *Figure 4-22* **Coefficient of drag versus angle of attack**

At low angles of attack in the cruise, the coefficient of drag for the aerofoil is small, but the airspeed *V* is higher and this has a large effect in the formula. This is why the drag force *D* is high at both extremes of angle of attack (and airspeed). In between these extremes is an angle of attack (and airspeed) where the drag force is a minimum. The minimum C_{Drag} for a typical aerofoil occurs at a small positive angle of attack.

Now complete **Exercises 4 – Drag.**

Lift/Drag Ratio

To determine the performance and efficiency of an aerofoil at a particular angle of attack (and airspeed), both the lift and the drag need to be considered. The relationship of one to the other, called the **lift/drag ratio,** is very important.

We have already discussed the lift curve (C_{Lift} versus angle of attack) and the drag curve (C_{Drag} versus angle of attack).

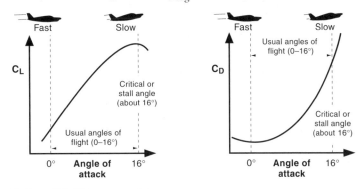

■ *Figure 5-1* **Lift curve and drag curve**

The **lift curve** shows a steady increase in the coefficient of lift as the angle of attack is increased, up to the stalling angle, beyond which C_{Lift} decreases.

The **drag curve** shows that drag increases steadily with change in angle of attack, being least at small positive angles of attack and increasing either side as angle of attack is increased or decreased. As the stalling angle is approached the drag increases at a greater rate. At the stall, the breakdown of streamline flow and the formation of turbulence, or eddies, causes a large increase in drag.

Variation of the L/D Ratio with Angle of Attack

In a sense, lift is the benefit you obtain from an aerofoil and drag is the price you pay for it. For a given amount of lift it is desirable to have the minimum amount of drag, i.e. the best possible L/D ratio.

If you require 120 units of lift and the cost is 10 units of drag from the aerofoil, then L/D = 120 ÷ 10 = 12, i.e. the lift is 12 times greater than the drag from the aerofoil. If the 120 units of lift come with 20 units of drag from the aerofoil, then the lift/drag ratio = 120 ÷ 20 = 6, and the wing is nowhere near as efficient.

An aerofoil has the greatest lifting ability (C_{Lift}) at a high angle of attack, just prior to the stalling angle of attack, in this case approximately 16°. Unfortunately, near the stalling angle, the aerofoil generates a lot of induced drag.

The minimum drag occurs at a fairly low angle of attack, in this case at about 0° angle of attack. Unfortunately, at low angles of attack, the lifting ability (C_{Lift}) of the wing is low.

Neither of these situations (high angle of attack or low angle of attack) is really satisfactory, because the ratio of lift to drag at these extreme angles of attack is low. What is required is the greatest lifting ability compared with the drag at the same angle of attack, i.e. the angle of attack that gives the best lift/drag ratio, and for a normal cambered wing this occurs at about 4° angle of attack.

To find the **lift/drag ratio** we can divide the two equations:

$$\frac{Lift}{Drag} = \frac{C_{Lift} \times \frac{1}{2}\,rho\,V\text{-}squared \times S}{C_{Drag} \times \frac{1}{2}\,rho\,V\text{-}squared \times S} = \frac{C_{Lift}}{C_{Drag}}$$

For each angle of attack we can calculate the L/D ratio by dividing C_{Lift} by C_{Drag} (and these are obtained from the lift and drag curves). We can then develop a curve for L/D versus angle of attack. The resulting L/D versus angle of attack curve shows that L/D increases rapidly up to about 4° angle of attack, where the lift is typically between 10 to 15 times the drag, depending on the aerofoil used.

At angles of attack higher than about 4°, the L/D ratio decreases steadily. Even though the C_{Lift} is still increasing, the C_{Drag} increases at a greater rate. At the stalling angle of attack the L/D ratio for this particular aerofoil is about 5.

The curve in Figure 5-2 shows clearly the specific angle of attack at which the L/D ratio is a maximum, and this angle of attack is where the aerofoil is most efficient – it gives the required lift for the minimum cost in drag.

The angle of attack that gives the **best lift/drag ratio** is the most efficient angle of attack.

In most aircraft you do not have an instrument to indicate angle of attack, but you can read airspeed, which is related to angle of attack. High angles of attack in steady flight are associated with lower airspeeds (and vice versa).

The angle of attack (and airspeed) for the best lift/drag ratio gives the required lift (to balance the weight) for the minimum cost in drag. At any other angle of attack there is a greater cost in terms of increased drag to obtain the same lift (Figure 5-3).

Minimum drag means maximum lift.

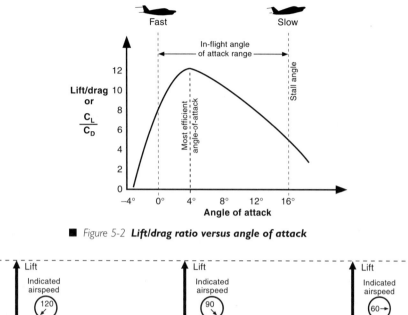

■ *Figure 5-2* **Lift/drag ratio versus angle of attack**

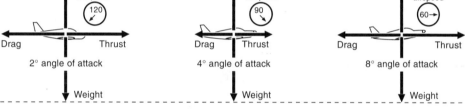

■ *Figure 5-3* **Same lift at a different cost in drag**

In steady flight the drag is balanced by the thrust. If the lift required to balance the weight is obtained at the minimum drag cost, then thrust can be kept to a minimum with the resulting benefits – the engine/propeller can be smaller; better economy through lower fuel and maintenance costs, etc.

Some important in-flight performance characteristics are obtained at the best L/D ratio, such as the maximum cruising range and the maximum power-off gliding range.

Level Flight at a Constant Weight

In straight and level flight:

$$Lift = Weight = C_{Lift} \times \tfrac{1}{2}\ rho\ V\text{-}squared \times S$$

C_{Lift} is a function of angle of attack, and $\tfrac{1}{2}$ *rho V-squared* is related to the indicated airspeed (IAS) that you see on the airspeed indicator. (V is the true airspeed or TAS, which you cannot read directly in the cockpit.)

Lift = Weight = a function of (angle of attack × IAS × S)

☐ **If the angle of attack is increased,** the required lift can be generated at a reduced airspeed.

☐ **If the angle of attack is reduced,** the same required lift will be generated at a higher airspeed.

Therefore, in normal straight and level flight, high angles of attack permit lower airspeeds, and low angles of attack permit higher airspeeds.

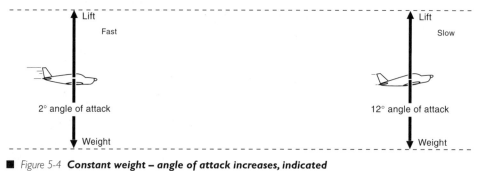

■ *Figure 5-4* **Constant weight – angle of attack increases, indicated airspeed decreases**

Decreased Weight

As a flight proceeds and fuel is burnt off, the overall aircraft weight decreases. A decreased weight requires less lift to balance it. We can reduce the lift produced by flying at a lower angle of attack, which will lead to a gradually increasing speed (unless we reduce power).

Notice that the precise relationship between angle of attack and airspeed changes if the weight changes. At lower weights, the same IAS occurs at a slightly smaller angle of attack.

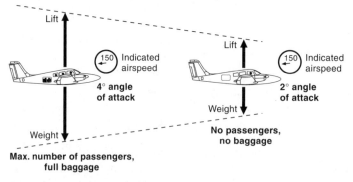

■ *Figure 5-5* **Decreasing weight – same IAS, decreasing angle of attack (decreasing power)**

Suppose you want to fly at the same angle of attack (say the most efficient one for the best L/D ratio at about 4°). As the weight gradually decreases, you should gradually reduce airspeed, so that less lift is generated.

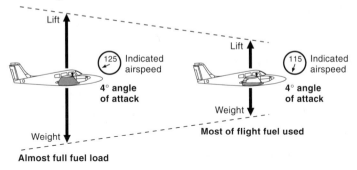

■ Figure 5-6 **Same angle of attack – lower weight has lower IAS and drag**

Changing Cruise Altitudes

Suppose you fly straight and level at a higher altitude, but at the same weight and therefore with the same lift requirement. The relationship between angle of attack and IAS will be the same as before.

At a particular angle of attack, the indicated airspeed (a measure of the magnitude of dynamic pressure ½ *rho V-squared* and displayed in knots) will be the same. Because at higher altitudes the air density *rho* is less, to retain the same value of ½ *rho V-squared,* the value of V (the true airspeed) must be greater.

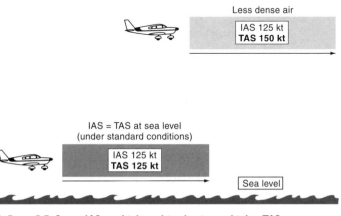

■ Figure 5-7 **Same IAS – a higher altitude gives a higher TAS**

As you fly at higher altitudes, the same indicated airspeed will give you a higher velocity through the air, or higher true airspeed.

Remember that IAS (related to dynamic pressure ½ *rho V-squared*) determines the flying qualities of your aeroplane. It is only necessary to calculate the TAS (V) for navigation purposes.

The relationship between IAS and TAS is considered in more detail under the *The Airspeed Indicator* in Chapter 25. The airspeed indicator displays an IAS that differs from the TAS by a factor that depends on air density.

Changing Wing Area

There is another factor that can be varied and that is the wing area *S*. If we could increase *S*, then we would obtain the same lift at an even lower airspeed. Changing *S* actually changes the shape of the aerofoil and we will consider this in Chapter 9, *Flaps*.

Now complete **Exercises 5 – Lift/Drag Ratio.**

Thrust from the Propeller

A piston engine requires a propeller to convert the power output of the engine into **thrust**. The power is developed by the piston engine, and is transmitted to the propeller, via a shaft, as **engine torque** or **turning effect**. This is used to rotate the propeller, which converts most of this turning effect into a pull or push force, called thrust. The propeller does this by generating forces which result from its motion through the air.

The propeller pulls the aeroplane through the air by generating a basically horizontal 'lift' force which we call thrust.

A cross-section taken through a propeller blade is simply an aerofoil section, and we can study its aerodynamics in the same terms as any other aerofoil, such as a wing.

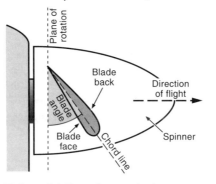

■ *Figure 6-1* **Propeller terminology**

The propeller blade causes the air to flow so that the static pressure ahead of the blade is less than that behind the blade. The result is a forward thrust force on the propeller blade which pulls the aeroplane along.

Consider just one blade section, or blade element as it is sometimes called, at some radial distance from the hub or the centreline of the propeller rotation. The blade section is an aerofoil and it has a leading edge, a trailing edge, a chord line and a camber just like any other aerofoil.

> *The angle which the chord line of a propeller section makes with the plane of rotation is called the* **blade angle.**

The blade angle, as we shall soon see, varies from a large blade angle at the blade root near the hub, gradually becoming less towards the propeller tip. The cambered side of the blade is called the **blade back** and the flatter side is called the **blade face**.

Propeller Motion

Rotational Velocity

If the aircraft is stationary, the motion of the propeller section under consideration is purely rotational. The further out along the blade the section is, the faster its rotational velocity. Also, the higher the rpm (revolutions per minute) of the propeller, the faster the rotational velocity of the section.

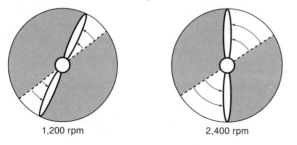

1,200 rpm	2,400 rpm

Figure 6-2 **Speed of blade section depends on radius and rpm**

Forward Velocity

As the aircraft moves forward in flight, the propeller section will have a forward velocity as well as the rotational velocity. This forward motion is superimposed on the rotational motion of the blade section to give it an overall resultant velocity as shown in Figure 6-3. The angle between the resultant velocity of the propeller blade and the plane of rotation is called the **helix angle** or the **pitch angle** or the **angle of advance**.

Helical Motion

Each propeller blade section follows a corkscrew path through the air, called a **helix,** as a result of the combined rotational and forward velocities. The easiest way to picture it is to consider the helix as the path the trailing edge of the propeller section follows.

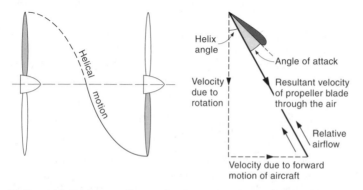

■ *Figure 6-3* **Each propeller section follows its own helical path**

The blade section experiences a relative airflow directly opposite to its own path through the air. The angle between the chord line of the propeller blade section and the relative airflow is its **angle of attack.** Notice that the angle of attack plus the helix angle (pitch angle) make up the blade angle.

When the aeroplane is in flight each propeller blade section will have the same forward velocity component. What will differ, however, is the rotational component of velocity – the further each blade section is from the propeller shaft the faster it is moving. If the blade angle was the same along the whole length of the propeller (which of course it never is), then the angle of attack would be different at all points.

For a propeller with the same blade angle along its length, the angle of attack would vary with distance from the propeller shaft, and the thrust would not be produced in an efficient manner. The propeller blade could even be stalled near the tip.

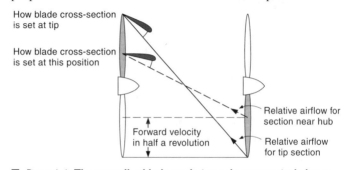

How blade cross-section is set at tip

How blade cross-section is set at this position

Relative airflow for section near hub

Forward velocity in half a revolution

Relative airflow for tip section

■ *Figure 6-4* **The propeller blade angle is made progressively larger from tip to hub to provide efficient angles of attack along its full length**

As with all aerofoils, there is a most efficient angle of attack for a propeller. If the propeller is designed to be most efficient at a certain airspeed of the aeroplane and rpm of the propeller, then the designer will aim to have this most efficient angle of attack along the whole length of the propeller blade when it is operating under the design airspeed and rpm conditions.

To achieve this, the blade angle at the hub needs to be much greater than the blade angle at the tip. This is known as **blade twist** or **helical twist.**

Propeller Sections

There will be aerodynamic losses both near the propeller hub and at the tip. Near the hub the propeller sections must be thick and structurally strong, which may interfere with aerodynamic design. Also, there will be a fair amount of interference to the airflow from the nearby engine and associated structures.

At the propeller tip, there will be tip vortices formed as air spills around from the high-pressure area on the flat blade face to the low-pressure area in front of it, forward of the cambered blade back. (The *back* of the propeller blade is actually to the *front* of the aeroplane.) The formation of vortices at the propeller tip leads to the usual increase in the induced drag (see page 31) and a consequent weakening of the effectiveness of the thrust at the tip.

The propeller tip is the fastest travelling part of the propeller – indeed of the whole aeroplane, as it has its rotational velocity superimposed on the forward speed of the aeroplane as a whole.

Only a small part of the whole propeller blade is effective in producing thrust – that part between about 60% and 90% of the tip radius. The greatest useful thrust is produced at approximately 75% of the tip radius. Thus, when the blade angle of a propeller is quoted, it usually refers to the 75% **station** (position).

Forces on a Blade Section

The airflow around an aerofoil, with the consequent pressure changes, causes a **total reaction** force on the aerofoil. In the case of a wing, we resolve (break up) this total reaction into one component perpendicular to the relative airflow, called **lift,** and another component parallel to the relative airflow, called **drag.** The relative airflow is parallel to the direction of flight, but in the opposite direction.

For propellers, things are slightly different. Because of its rotational velocity, the direction of the relative airflow striking the propeller and the direction of flight of the aeroplane are not parallel. Whereas the relative airflow striking all sections of a main wing comes from a constant direction, the relative airflow striking a propeller blade changes its direction depending on how far that section is from the hub.

Instead of resolving the total reaction on a propeller blade section into a lift component perpendicular to the relative airflow and a drag component parallel to the relative airflow (which would be very complicated when we come to add up the effects along the length of the blade), it is much more convenient to resolve the total reaction into two components:

1. Propeller torque force, in the plane of rotation.

2. Thrust, in the direction perpendicular to the plane of rotation.

For our purposes, we can generally assume the direction perpendicular to the plane of propeller rotation to be the same as the direction of flight, and therefore for the thrust to be considered as acting in the direction of flight.

Propeller torque *is the resistance to motion in the plane of rotation.*

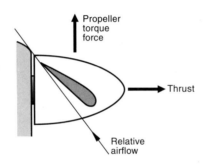

Propeller
torque
force

Thrust

Relative
airflow

■ *Figure 6-5* **Forces on a blade**

For a wing, drag must be overcome to provide lift. For a propeller, the propeller torque must be overcome or balanced by the engine torque for the propeller to provide thrust. Opening the throttle increases the engine power and engine torque, causing the propeller to rotate faster.

NOTE If the aeroplane is put into a dive, the relative airflow is changed because of the higher forward speed and, as a result, the propeller torque force is reduced. The result is an increase in engine speed (i.e. rpm) even though the throttle may not have been moved.

Propeller Efficiency

Variation of Propeller Efficiency

Consider a well-designed fixed-pitch propeller blade. As most of the thrust (and propeller torque) is produced in the blade sections near the 75% station, reference to blade angle, angle of attack, etc. will refer to this most effective part of the propeller blade. (The term *fixed-pitch* means that the blade angle at the section under consideration is fixed and cannot be changed.)

If the propeller rpm is constant, then the direction of the relative airflow and the angle of attack will be determined by the forward speed.

As forward airspeed increases, the angle of attack of a fixed-pitch propeller blade at constant rpm will decrease. At some high forward speed, the angle of attack of the blade will be such that little or no thrust will be produced.

For a given rpm, there will be only one airspeed at which the propeller will operate at its most efficient angle of attack.

A fixed-pitch propeller is most efficient at only one airspeed and rpm.

The designer chooses a fixed-pitch propeller whose best-efficiency airspeed/rpm combination suits the aeroplane's intended purpose.

A preferable situation would be to have a propeller whose blade angle could be varied so that at any airspeed it would operate at an efficient angle of attack, i.e. a variable-pitch propeller. While

this subject will not be examined at PPL level, most of you will
fly an aeroplane with a variable-pitch propeller so we have
included the information below.

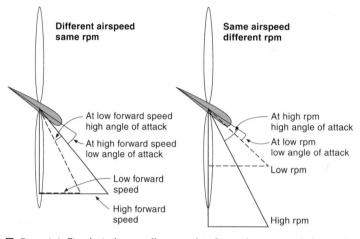

**Different airspeed
same rpm**

At low forward speed
high angle of attack

At high forward speed
low angle of attack

Low forward
speed

High forward
speed

**Same airspeed
different rpm**

At high rpm
high angle of attack

At low rpm
low angle of attack

Low rpm

High rpm

■ *Figure 6-6* **Fixed-pitch propeller – angle of attack varies with forward
speed, and with rpm**

Variable-Pitch Propellers and Constant-Speed Units

An early development in propeller technology was the two-pitch
propeller – a fine pitch for take-off and low-speed operation, and
a coarse pitch for higher airspeeds.

Subsequently the constant-speed propeller was developed,
with a blade angle that could take up any position (i.e. infinitely
variable) between two in-flight limits at the fine and coarse ends
of its range. The pitch-changing mechanisms are usually operated
electrically or hydraulically.

At low airspeeds, the blade angle needs to be small for the angle
of attack to be optimum. This is known as *fine pitch*. As the forward
speed increases, the blade angle needs to increase, or *coarsen,* for
the angle of attack to remain optimum.

The device used to achieve this is the **constant-speed unit**
(CSU), sometimes called the propeller control unit (PCU). It
contains a governor whose function is to regulate the propeller
speed (rpm) to that selected by the pilot. It does that by automatically adjusting the blade angle electrically or hydraulically so that
rpm is maintained irrespective of the airspeed and the power
delivered by the engine.

The aim is to have the propeller working close to the best angle
of attack and maximum efficiency at all times throughout its
working range (Figure 6-7).

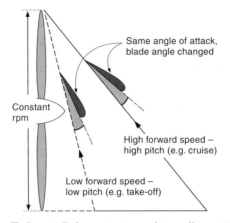

Same angle of attack, blade angle changed

Constant rpm

High forward speed – high pitch (e.g. cruise)

Low forward speed – low pitch (e.g. take-off)

■ *Figure 6-7* **A constant-speed propeller retains an efficient angle of attack over a wide forward speed range by altering blade angle automatically**

In the extreme case of low engine power, the blade angle will fine-off until it reaches the limit, known as the *fine-pitch stop.* From then on, the propeller acts as a fixed-pitch propeller – further power reductions cause a drop in rpm because the pitch cannot fine-off any more due to the fine-pitch stop.

Advantages of Constant-Speed Propellers

A constant-speed propeller is efficient over a range of rpm and airspeed conditions.

A variable-pitch (constant-speed) propeller adjusts to the most efficient angle of attack over a wide range of rpms and airspeeds. A fixed-pitch propeller only operates efficiently under the one set of rpm and airspeed conditions.

Change of Power
The pilot selects the desired rpm using the pitch control. The propeller pitch automatically increases to absorb any extra engine power supplied and yet still retains the same rpm, i.e. constant-speed. The increased thrust gives the aeroplane better performance and it can accelerate or increase its rate of climb.

If the engine power is decreased, the propeller automatically fines-off to balance the power supplied to it by the engine and the rpm will remain constant (unless the blade comes up against the fine-pitch stop). The reduced thrust produced causes a decrease in the aeroplane's performance.

Change of Airspeed
If the aeroplane is put into a climb, without the pilot making any power adjustments, the blade will automatically fine-off just enough to stop the engine/propeller rpm from decreasing and the engine power output will remain unchanged. Similarly, if the

aeroplane is put into a dive without the pilot removing any engine power, the airspeed will increase and the blade will coarsen sufficiently to prevent overspeeding of the propeller and engine.

Two other advantages of some variable-pitch propellers are:

1. The ability to be put into **ground-fine pitch** or **reverse pitch** to provide a braking effect on the ground run.

2. The ability to be **feathered** in flight to reduce drag and further engine damage following an engine failure.

Take-Off Effects of Propellers

Slipstream Effect

A propeller rotating clockwise (as seen from the cockpit) will impart a clockwise rotation to the slipstream as it flows back over the rest of the aeroplane. This causes an asymmetric flow over the fin and rudder, especially in the case of a single-engined aircraft. Under high-power conditions the slipstream would impinge on the left of the fin (an angle of attack would exist between the fin and the slipstream airflow), generating an aerodynamic lift force which pushes the tail to the right and yaws the nose to the left. Some aircraft have an *off-set fin* to help overcome this effect.

Propeller Torque Reaction

If the propeller rotates clockwise (when viewed from behind), the torque reaction will tend to rotate the aircraft anti-clockwise and roll it to the left. This effect is most pronounced under high power conditions and high propeller rpm, such as during take-off, see Figure 6-9.

On the ground this rolling to the left is stopped by the left wheel, which will have to support more load than the right wheel. This will increase the rolling friction force on the left wheel, tending to slow it down, and consequently the aircraft will tend to yaw to the left. Notice that this effect yaws the aeroplane in the same direction as the slipstream effect. (If the propeller rotates the other way, as in some older aircraft, then the yaw will be in the other direction.)

The next two effects will not be examined, but are included for those of you who will be flying tail-wheel aircraft.

Gyroscopic Effect

Early in the take-off run of a tailwheel aircraft such as a *DHC Chipmunk* the tail is lifted off the ground to place the aeroplane into a low drag and flying attitude. As the tail is being raised, a torque force becomes applied to the rotating propeller in a nose-down sense. Because a rotating body tends to resist any attempt to change its plane of rotation, when such a change is forced upon

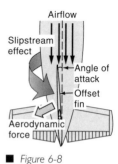

■ *Figure 6-8*

An offset fin helps counteract propeller slipstream effect

Gyroscopic effect is significant on the take-off run in a tailwheel aeroplane as the tail is raised.

it, a *gyroscopic precession* will be superimposed. (More on gyroscopic precession on page 261.)

Gyroscopic precession rotates the applied force 90° in the direction of rotation – a phenomenon called **gyroscopic effect.** When nose-down torque is applied to the aircraft to raise the tail on take-off (which is like a forward force applied to the top of the rotating propeller disc), gyroscopic effect causes a similar force to be applied 90° in the direction of propeller rotation. This will be like a forwards force acting on the right side of the rotating propeller disc, causing the aircraft to yaw. The direction of yaw depends on the direction of propeller rotation.

The amount of gyroscopic effect depends on the mass of the propeller, how the mass is distributed along the blades and how fast the propeller is rotating (all of this being combined into a physical quantity called the *moment of inertia*). It will also depend on how fast you try to change the plane of rotation.

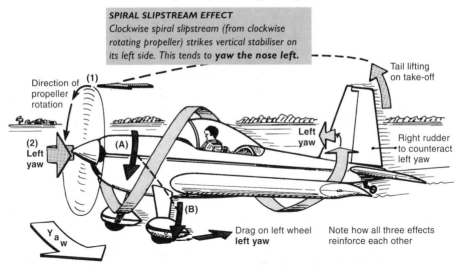

SPIRAL SLIPSTREAM EFFECT
Clockwise spiral slipstream (from clockwise rotating propeller) strikes vertical stabiliser on its left side. This tends to **yaw the nose left.**

Tail lifting on take-off

Direction of propeller rotation (1)

(2) Left yaw

(A)

Left yaw

(B)

Right rudder to counteract left yaw

Yaw

Drag on left wheel **left yaw**

Note how all three effects reinforce each other

SWING DUE TO TORQUE REACTION
Engine rotates propeller clockwise as seen by pilot (on most modern aircraft) – torque. Torque reaction tries to twist engine and airframe the opposite way – anticlockwise. Downward force at (A) presses left wheel hard onto runway at (B). Resultant differential drag on the main wheels **swings nose left**

SWING DUE TO GYROSCOPIC PRECESSION
Tail lifting on take-off causes forces at (1). Fast spinning propeller follows gyro-precession principle. Effect occurs at (2), 90° in direction of rotation. Consequently, **nose yaws left.**

■ *Figure 6-9* **Take-off swing resulting from the combined effects of slipstream effect, torque reaction and gyroscopic precession**

Obviously, raising the tail of a high-powered aeroplane like a *Spitfire* on take-off produces a much greater gyroscopic effect than raising the tail of a *Tiger Moth*.

Asymmetric Propeller Blade Effect

At the start of the take-off run of a tailwheel aircraft when the tail is still on the ground, the propeller shaft is inclined upwards and the plane of rotation of the propeller is not vertical.

Asymmetric propeller blade effect occurs at high angles of attack and high power.

The aeroplane is travelling horizontally and a downgoing propeller blade will therefore have a greater angle of attack than an upcoming blade, causing the downgoing blade to produce more thrust and the aeroplane to yaw accordingly.

The downgoing blade will also travel further than the upcoming blade in the same time (and we have considered half a rotation), causing the velocity between the downgoing blade and the relative airflow to be greater and hence to produce more thrust. Therefore the downgoing half of the propeller 'disc' will produce more thrust than the upgoing half, causing an aircraft with the propeller rotating clockwise (as seen from behind) to yaw to the left while the tailwheel is still on the ground.

■ *Figure 6-10* **Downgoing blade produces more thrust with the tail on the ground**

NOTE The above four effects cause a yaw to the *left* in an aeroplane whose propeller rotates clockwise (as seen from the cockpit), which the pilot will counteract with however much right rudder is required to keep straight. For aeroplanes with anti-clockwise rotating propellers (e.g. *Spitfires, Chipmunks, Tiger Moths*), the yaw on take-off will be to the *right*.

Prevent unwanted yaw with rudder.

Now complete **Exercises 6 – Thrust from the Propeller.**

Stability

Equilibrium in Straight and Level Flight

Four main forces act on an aircraft in flight: lift, weight, thrust and drag.

LIFT acts through the centre of pressure, which moves continually with every change in angle of attack.

WEIGHT acts vertically downwards through the centre of gravity, which moves as fuel is burned off or as cargo or passengers move.

DRAG acts to oppose the motion of the aircraft, therefore is parallel to the relative airflow and in the opposite direction to the flightpath. The point through which the total drag may be considered to act varies with angle of attack, airspeed, operation of flaps, landing gear, etc.

THRUST acts through the propeller shaft, or the centreline of a jet engine. For a single-engined aircraft at least, this is the only constant position that any of the four forces acts through.

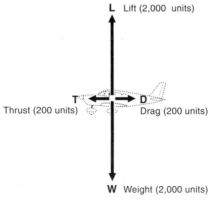

L Lift (2,000 units)

T
Thrust (200 units)   **D**
                             Drag (200 units)

W Weight (2,000 units)

■ *Figure 7-1* **Lift balances weight, thrust balances drag in straight and level flight**

For the aircraft to remain in equilibrium in straight and level flight, the opposing forces must be equal so that they balance out, leaving no resultant force acting on the aeroplane.
- Lift opposes weight, and these two must be equal.
- Thrust opposes drag, and these two must be equal.

The aeroplane is subject to no resultant force and continues in its state of unaccelerated flight – steady motion in a straight and level line.

There is usually a considerable difference between the two pairs of forces, lift and weight being much greater in magnitude than the thrust and drag in normal flight. Lift and weight may be each 2,000 units; thrust and drag each 200 units (recognisable as a lift/drag ratio of $2,000 \div 200 = 10$ to 1).

When in straight and level flight, the lift and weight will only decrease gradually as the weight decreases with fuel burn-off. The thrust and drag will vary considerably depending on angle of attack and therefore airspeed.

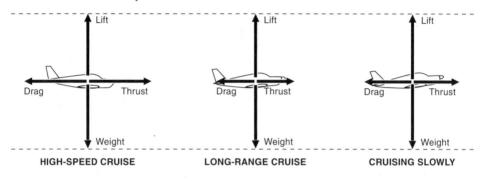

■ *Figure 7-2* **Drag (and thrust requirement) depends on angle of attack and airspeed**

Note the assumption we have made regarding the thrust. While it acts along the propeller shaft or jet engine centreline, and therefore, at the high angles of attack in straight and level flight, would point slightly up, we have assumed that it points in the direction of flight, directly opposing the drag.

Pitching Moments

The positions of the lift force acting through the **centre of pressure (CP)** and weight force acting through the **centre of gravity (CG)** are not constant in flight. Under most conditions of flight the CP and CG are not coincident, i.e. are not at the one point. The CG will move as passengers or crew move around (this is noticeable in airliners as flight attendants walk down the cabin), if freight is shifted and as fuel burns off. The CP changes position according to the angle of attack (and therefore airspeed).

The outcome is that the opposing forces of lift and weight, even though they are equal in magnitude and balance out, will set up a **couple,** causing a nose-down pitching moment if the lift (CP) is behind the weight (CG), or a nose-up pitching moment if the CP is in front of the CG.

*A **couple** is a pair of equal, parallel forces acting in opposite directions which tends to cause rotation because the forces are acting along different axes.*

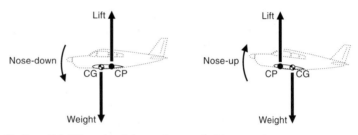

■ *Figure 7-3* **Lift and weight produce a pitching couple**

The different lines of action of the thrust force and the drag force produce another couple, causing a nose-up pitching moment if the drag line is above the thrust line, or a nose-down pitching moment if the drag line is below the thrust line.

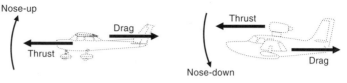

■ *Figure 7-4* ***Thrust and drag form a pitching couple***

Ideally, the pitching moments from the two couples should neutralise each other in level flight so that there is no resultant moment tending to rotate the aircraft.

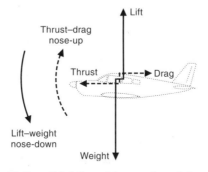

■ *Figure 7-5* **Lift–weight couple and thrust–drag couple in balance**

In many aeroplanes the lines of action are designed to be as shown in Figure 7-5. With this arrangement the thrust–drag couple produces a nose-up pitching moment and the lift–weight couple produces a nose-down pitching moment. The distances between the lines of action are positioned so that the turning effects of the two couples are equal and opposite, thereby cancelling each other out.

The turning moment of a couple depends on the magnitude of the two forces and the distance between their lines of action.

Therefore, for the turning moments of these two couples to balance, the larger forces of lift and weight should have their lines of action (CP and CG) fairly close, and the significantly smaller forces of thrust and drag should have a somewhat greater distance between their lines of action.

There is a practical reason for the lift–weight couple to have a nose-down pitching moment balanced by the thrust–drag nose-up pitching moment. If thrust is lost (e.g. engine-failure), the thrust–drag nose-up couple is weakened and therefore the lift–weight couple will pitch the aircraft nose down (without any action on the part of the pilot) so that it assumes a gliding attitude without a tendency to lose flying speed.

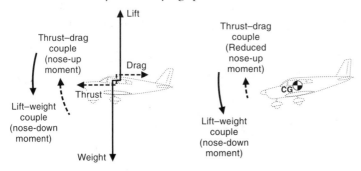

■ *Figure 7-6* **Following a loss of thrust, the lift–weight couple pitches the aeroplane nose down**

Conversely, when power is added, causing thrust to increase, the nose will tend to pitch up. It is rarely possible to have a perfect balance between these four main forces and the two couples formed by them. The tailplane is used to provide the final balancing force.

The Tailplane

The ideal balance of the pitching moments of the lift–weight couple and the thrust–drag couple is difficult to maintain in flight and there is usually a residual pitching moment arising from inequalities in the two main couples.

The function of the tailplane (or horizontal stabiliser) is to counteract these residual pitching moments from the two main couples, i.e. it has a stabilising function.

The tailplane is simply another aerofoil that can generate an aerodynamic force, if required, by being at an angle of attack (positive or negative) relative to the local airflow. This force is usually a downward force, but can be up or down depending on the design of the aeroplane, and so the tailplane usually has a symmetrical aerofoil cross section.

The aerodynamic force produced by the tailplane can be varied by changing its angle of attack relative to the local airflow – either by moving the elevators and holding them there with pilot or trim force, or by moving the entire tailplane (as is possible in some aircraft, e.g. the *Piper Warrior*).

If the residual moment from the four main forces is nose down (usually the case) the tailplane provides a downward aerodynamic force which will produce a nose-up pitching moment to balance the residual nose-down moment from the four main forces.

Because the tailplane is situated some distance from the centre of gravity and its moment arm is therefore quite long, the aerodynamic force provided by the tailplane needs only to be small to have a significant pitching effect. Hence the area of the tailplane (and its aerodynamic capabilities) is small compared with the mainplanes (main wings).

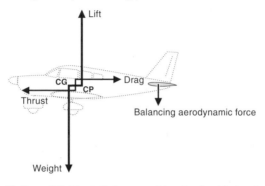

■ *Figure 7-7* **The tailplane provides the final balancing moment**

The turning effect (or turning moment) of a force on the aeroplane depends on its magnitude and distance from the centre of gravity. If the residual moment from the two main couples is nose down, then the tailplane can produce a downward aerodynamic force which will have a nose-up pitching moment to balance out the moment.

Many aircraft are designed to operate most efficiently at cruise speed. The four main forces and the two main couples are designed to be at least in approximate equilibrium when on the cruise, with only small balancing forces required from the tailplane. Generally the centre of pressure (CP) is aft of the centre of gravity (CG) and the tailplane produces a downwards aerodynamic force.

Stability

An aeroplane in flight is continually being disturbed from steady flight by external forces from small (and large) gusts of wind. The stability of the aeroplane is its natural or inbuilt ability to return to its original condition without any action being taken by the pilot.

Stability is concerned with the motion of the body after the disturbing force has been removed. Positive stability indicates a tendency to return to the original equilibrium position or state prior to the disturbance. It is usual to call this stable.

Do not confuse stability with controllability.

Stability is the natural ability of the aeroplane to return to its original condition after being disturbed without any action being taken by the pilot.

Controllability refers to the ease with which the pilot can manoeuvre the aircraft using the control surfaces.

There is a significant trade-off between stability and controllability. A high degree of stability makes the aircraft resistant to change and thereby tends to reduce the controllability, i.e. good stability makes it harder for the pilot to control and manoeuvre the aeroplane.

An aeroplane with some positive stability is a lot easier to fly than an unstable aeroplane that shows a natural tendency to diverge from the trimmed flight attitude. The stability must not be so great, however, as to require high control forces for manoeuvring.

An aeroplane is in a state of equilibrium when the sum of all the forces on it is zero and the sum of all the turning moments on it is zero. The aircraft is *in trim* if all the moments in pitch, roll and yaw are zero. Equilibrium is established in the various phases of flight by use of the surfaces of the aircraft, modified by control surface movement where steady pressures may be held by the effort of the pilot, by trim tabs or by biassing the surface.

The external force most commonly displacing an aircraft in flight is a gust of wind. A stable aeroplane will return to its original condition naturally – an unstable one will not, unless the pilot takes action.

An unstable aircraft is difficult to fly because the pilot must continually interfere by applying control forces. A stable aircraft can almost fly 'hands-off' and requires only guidance rather than second-to-second control inputs.

Our examples so far have been drawn from the pitching plane, but stability in the other planes and about the other axes is just as vital.

The Three Reference Axes

We refer the motion of the aircraft to motion about each of three axes – each passing through the centre of gravity and each mutually perpendicular (at 90° to each other).

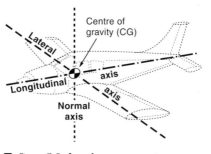

■ *Figure 7-8* **Angular movement can occur about three axes**

The longitudinal axis runs fore and aft through the centre of gravity. Movement around the longitudinal axis is known as rolling. Stability around the longitudinal axis is known as lateral stability, because it is concerned with movement in the lateral or rolling plane.

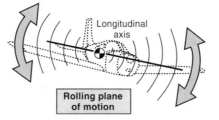

■ *Figure 7-9* **Rolling about the longitudinal axis**

The lateral axis passes through the centre of gravity across the aircraft from one side to the other. Movement around the lateral axis is called pitching (nose up or nose down). Stability around the lateral axis is called longitudinal stability, because it is concerned with stability in the longitudinal or pitching plane.

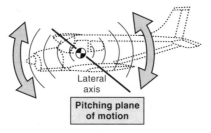

■ *Figure 7-10* **Pitching about the lateral axis**

The normal axis passes through the centre of gravity and is normal (perpendicular) to the other two axes. Movement around the normal axis is called yawing.

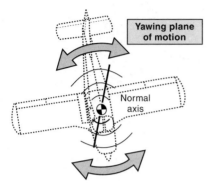

■ *Figure 7-11* **Yawing about the normal axis**

Stability around the normal axis is known as directional stability, because it is concerned with stability in the directional or yawing plane.

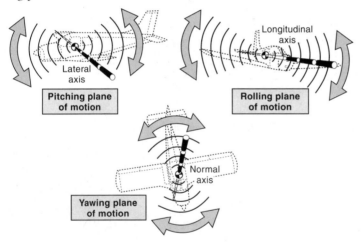

■ *Figure 7-12* **Angular motion can occur in three planes**

Rotation around a point or axis is called **angular motion;** the number of degrees of rotation is called **angular displacement** and the speed with which it occurs, **angular velocity.**

The motion of an aircraft is best considered in each of the planes (or about each of the reference axes) separately, although (except in straight and level flight) the actual motion of the aircraft is a little more complex. For example: rolling into a level turn the aircraft will not only roll but also pitch and yaw. (More of this later).

We will consider longitudinal stability (pitching) first, then directional stability (yawing) and lateral stability (rolling). Roll and yaw are closely connected.

Longitudinal Stability

Longitudinal stability is in the pitching plane and about the lateral axis. To be longitudinally stable, an aircraft must have a natural or inbuilt tendency to return to the same attitude in pitch after any disturbance. If the angle of attack is suddenly increased by a disturbance, then forces will be produced that will lower the nose and decrease the angle of attack.

A longitudinally stable aeroplane tends to maintain the trimmed condition of flight and is therefore easy to fly in pitch.

The Tailplane and Longitudinal Stability

Changes in the tailplane force lead to longitudinal stability.

Consider a situation that is constantly occurring in flight. If a disturbance, such as a gust, changes the attitude of the aircraft by pitching it nose up, the aircraft, due to its inertia, will continue initially on its original flightpath and therefore present itself to the relative airflow at an increased angle of attack.

With the same initial pitch-up caused by the disturbance and the aeroplane at first continuing in the original direction due to its inertia, the tailplane will be presented to the relative airflow at a greater angle of attack. This will cause the tailplane to produce an upwards, or decreased downwards, aerodynamic force, which is different to before the disturbance.

The altered aerodynamic force gives a nose-down pitching moment, tending to return the aeroplane to its original trimmed condition (Figure 7-13).

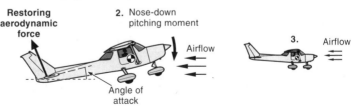

■ *Figure 7-13* **Longitudinal stability following an 'uninvited' nose-up pitch**

Because of the great length of the moment arm between the centre of gravity and the tailplane, the aerodynamic force produced by the tailplane need not be large for its turning effect to be powerful. As the tail is raised and the nose pitches back down, the original angle of attack is restored, the extra upwards, or decreased downwards, aerodynamic force from the tailplane disappears and things are back to where they were prior to the disturbance.

As shown in Figure 7-14, the tailplane has a similar stabilising effect following an uninvited nose-down pitch.

Figure 7-14 **Longitudinal stability following an 'uninvited' nose-down pitch**

A good example of the stabilising effect of a tailplane is the passage of a dart or an arrow through the air, in which the tail-fins act as a tailplane to maintain longitudinal stability.

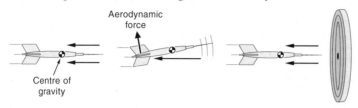

■ *Figure 7-15* **Longitudinal stability is provided by the tail fins of a dart**

The CG and Longitudinal Stability

The further forward the CG of the aircraft, the greater the moment arm for the tailplane, and therefore the greater the turning effect of the tailplane lift force. This has a strong stabilising effect longitudinally.

The position of the CG can be controlled to some extent by the pilot by the disposition of payload and fuel, usually done prior to flight. A forward CG leads to increased longitudinal stability and an aft movement of the CG leads to reduced longitudinal stability.

> *Longitudinal stability is greatest with a forward CG and large tailplane.*

Limits are specified for the range within which the CG must lie for safe flight and prudent pilots always load their aeroplanes and check the trim sheets to ensure that this is so. If the CG is behind the legally allowable aft limit, the restoring moment of the tailplane in pitch may be insufficient for longitudinal stability. The same example of a dart is useful here. A CG further forward leads to more stability.

The more stable the aeroplane, the greater the control force that you must exert to control or move the aeroplane in manoeuvres, which can become tiring. But more importantly, if the CG is too far forward, the elevator will require a high force and may not be sufficiently effective at low speeds to flare the nose-heavy aeroplane for landing.

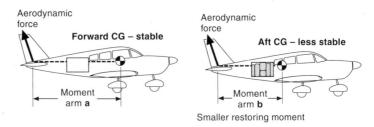

■ *Figure 7-16* **A forward CG – greater longitudinal stability**

Design Considerations

Tailplane design features also contribute greatly to longitudinal stability – tailplane area, distance from the centre of gravity, aspect ratio, angle of incidence and longitudinal dihedral (the difference between the angles of incidence of the wings and tailplane) are considered by the designer. The aim is to generate a restoring force that is effective because of a long moment arm – leading to an aeroplane that is longitudinally stable.

At high angles of attack the mainplane may shield the tailplane or cause the airflow over it to be turbulent. This will decrease longitudinal stability.

Directional Stability

Directional stability of an aeroplane is its natural or inbuilt ability to recover from a disturbance in the yawing plane, i.e. about the normal axis. It refers to an aeroplane's ability to *weathercock* its nose into any crosswind (i.e. a wind with a component from the side).

If the aircraft is disturbed from its straight path by the nose or tail being pushed to one side (i.e. yawed), then, due to its inertia, the aircraft will initially keep moving in the original direction.

The aircraft will now be moving somewhat sideways through the air, with its side or keel-surfaces exposed to the airflow. This is known as a **sideslip.**

The vertical fin (or tail or vertical stabiliser) is simply a symmetrical aerofoil. As it is now experiencing an angle of attack, it will generate a sideways aerodynamic force which tends to take the fin back to its original position. This restores the nose to its original position.

The powerful moment (turning effect) of the vertical fin, due to its large area and the length of its moment arm between it and the centre of gravity, is what restores the nose to its original position.

The greater the fin area and keel surface area behind the CG, and the greater the moment arm, the greater the directional stability of the aeroplane. Thus a forward CG is preferable to an aft CG, as it gives a longer moment arm for the fin.

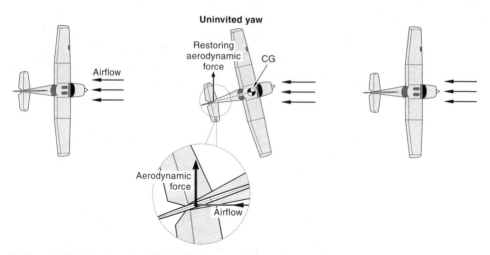

■ Figure 7-17 **Directional stability following an uninvited yaw**

A secondary effect of power or thrust is that caused by the slip-stream. Propeller slipstream can affect the airflow over the fin, and therefore the fin's effectiveness as a vertical stabiliser. Power changes made by the pilot cause changes in the slipstream and can lead to large directional trim changes.

Lateral Stability

Lateral stability is the natural or inbuilt ability of the aeroplane to recover from a disturbance in the lateral plane, i.e. rolling about the longitudinal axis without any control input by the pilot.

A disturbance in roll will cause one wing to drop and the other to rise. When the aeroplane is banked, the lift vector is inclined and produces a sideslip into the turn. As well as the forward motion through the air, the aeroplane slips sideways due to the lift and weight not being directly opposed, causing a resultant side-ways force on the aeroplane. As a result of this sideslip, the aero-plane is subjected to a sideways component of relative airflow. This generates forces that produce a rolling moment to restore the aeroplane to its original wings-level position. See Figure 7-18.

The main contributor to lateral stability is the wing.

Wing Dihedral

Wing dihedral increases lateral stability. Dihedral is found on most low-wing aeroplanes, and is built into the aeroplane during design and construction. Each wing is inclined upwards from the fuselage to the wingtips, and adds to the lateral stability characteristics of the aeroplane. See Figures 7-19 and 7-20.

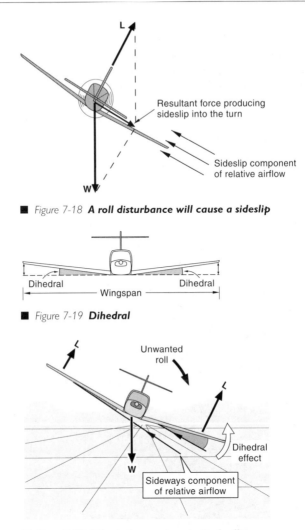

■ *Figure 7-18* **A roll disturbance will cause a sideslip**

■ *Figure 7-19* **Dihedral**

■ *Figure 7-20* **Dihedral corrects uninvited rolling**

As the aircraft sideslips, the lower wing, due to its dihedral, will meet the upcoming relative airflow at a greater angle of attack and will produce increased lift. The upper wing will meet the relative airflow at a lower angle of attack and will therefore produce less lift. It may also be shielded somewhat by the fuselage, causing an even lower lift to be generated. The rolling moment so produced will tend to return the aircraft to its original wings-level position.

Negative dihedral, or **anhedral,** where the wing is inclined downward from the fuselage, has an unstable effect.

Wing Sweepback

The wing can add to lateral stability if it has **sweepback**. As the aircraft sideslips following a disturbance in roll, the lower swept-back wing generates more lift than the upper wing. This is because in the sideslip the lower wing presents more of its span to the air-flow than the upper wing and therefore the lower wing generates more lift and tends to restore the aeroplane to a wings-level position.

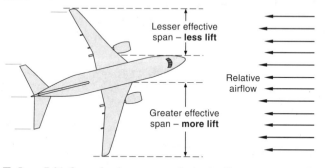

■ Figure 7-21 **Sweepback corrects uninvited roll**

High Keel Surfaces and Low CG

In the sideslip that follows a disturbance in roll, a high sideways drag line caused by high keel surfaces (high fin, a T-tail high on the fin, high wings, etc.), and a low CG will give a restoring moment tending to raise the lower wing and return the aircraft to the original wings-level position.

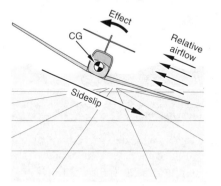

■ Figure 7-22 **High keel surfaces and a low CG correct uninvited roll**

High-Wing Aeroplanes

If a gust causes a wing to drop, the lift force is tilted. The resultant force (i.e. the combined effect of the lift and weight) will cause the aircraft to sideslip. The airflow striking the upper keel surfaces (i.e. above the CG) will tend to return the aircraft to the wings-level condition. The high wings are above the CG and so are part of the keel surfaces tending to level the wings.

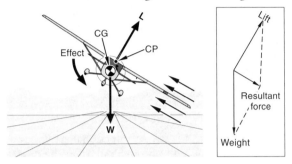

■ Figure 7-23 **Upper keel surfaces tend to level the wings**

Lateral and Directional Stability Together

Roll Followed by Yaw

For lateral stability it is essential to have the **sideslip** which the disturbance in roll causes. This sideslip exerts a force on the side or keel surfaces of the aircraft, which, if the aircraft is directionally stable, will cause it to yaw its nose into the relative airflow. The roll has caused a yaw in the direction of the sideslip and the aeroplane will turn further off its original heading in the direction of the lower wing.

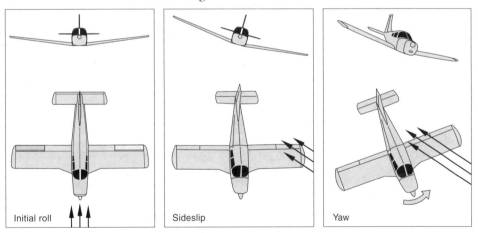

■ Figure 7-24 **Roll causes yaw**

Note the interesting consequence that the greater the directional stability of the aircraft, the greater the tendency to turn away from the original heading in the direction of the lower wing. Also, the nose will tend to drop. This further turn or yaw due to good characteristics of directional stability causes the higher wing on the outside of the turn to move faster and therefore produce more lift.

The lateral stability characteristics of the aeroplane, such as dihedral, cause the lower wing to produce increased lift and to return the aircraft to the wings-level position. There are two effects in conflict here:

- ◼ **the directionally stable** characteristics (large fin) want to steepen the turn and drop the nose further; and
- ◼ **the laterally stable** characteristics (dihedral) want to level the wings.

If the first effect wins out, i.e. strong directional stability and weak lateral stability (large fin and no dihedral), then the aircraft will tend to bank further into the sideslip, towards the lower wing, with the nose continuing to drop, until the aeroplane is in a spiral dive (all without any input from the pilot). This is called **spiral instability.**

Most aircraft are designed with only weak positive lateral stability and have a slight tendency to spiral instability. This is preferable to the reverse situation – an effect called Dutch roll.

If the lateral stability (dihedral) is stronger, the aircraft will right itself to wings-level, and if the directional stability is weak (small fin) the aircraft may have shown no tendency to turn in the direction of sideslip and may have even turned away from the sideslip, causing a wallowing effect known as **Dutch roll,** which is best avoided.

Yaw Followed by Roll

If the aircraft is displaced in yaw, it will initially continue in the original direction of flight due to its inertia, and therefore sideslip. This sideslip will cause the lateral stability characteristics of the aircraft's wing, such as dihedral, sweepback, or high-wing, to increase lift on the forward wing and decrease lift on the trailing wing.

This causes a rolling moment that will tend to raise the forward wing, resulting in the aircraft rolling towards the trailing wing and away from the sideslip.

Another point to note is that, as the aircraft is actually yawing, the outer wing will move faster and produce more lift than the inner wing, giving a tendency to roll towards the inner wing. The aeroplane's inherent directional stability (from the fin) will tend to weathercock or yaw the aircraft in the direction of the sideslip.

Roll causes yaw and *yaw causes roll,* and the two effects need to be studied together.

The sideslip is very important, with lateral stability characteristics (dihedral) tending to raise the forward wing in a sideslip and directional stability characteristics (large fin) tending to weathercock or yaw the aircraft in the direction of sideslip and raise the outer wing in the yawing turn (which is the trailing wing).

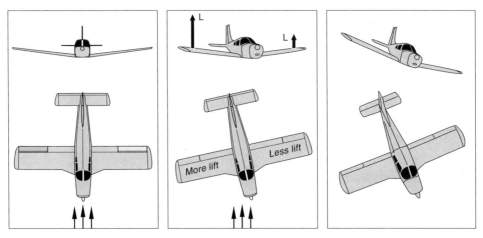

■ Figure 7-25 **Yaw causes roll**

Stability Characteristics and Aeroplane Control

If the directional stability is poor (small fin) and the lateral stability good (dihedral), then a rudder input will cause a significant yaw and sideslip. The dihedral will bank the aeroplane in the direction of yaw (away from the sideslip) and it will enter a banked turn with no aileron input.

If the directional stability is good (large fin) and the lateral stability not so strong, then if the pilot banks the aeroplane with the ailerons, but does not touch the rudder, a sideslip towards the lower wing occurs. The good directional stability characteristics very smartly turn the aeroplane's nose into the sideslip and the turn will be fairly balanced, even without the pilot touching the rudder. There will be at least a little sideslip initially as the turn is entered, but this may be so slight it is unnoticeable.

Stability on the Ground

The centre of gravity (CG) must lie somewhere in the area between the wheels at all times on the ground. The further the CG is away from any one wheel, the less the tendency for the aeroplane to tip over that wheel.

A low CG and widely-spaced wheels reduces the tendency for the aeroplane to tip over on the ground, e.g. when turning, when brakes are applied to stop, or when high power is applied on take-off.

A low thrust-line lowers the tendency for the aeroplane to pitch over on its nose when high power is applied (especially with brakes on). High keel surfaces and dihedral allow crosswinds to have a greater destabilising effect.

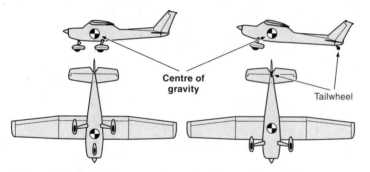

■ *Figure 7-26* **The CG must remain within the area bounded by the wheels**

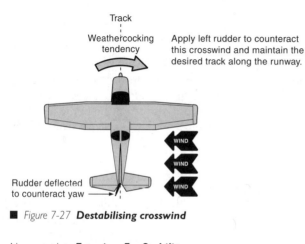

■ *Figure 7-27* **Destabilising crosswind**

Now complete **Exercises 7 – Stability.**

Control

All aeroplanes have a control system to allow the pilot to manoeuvre and trim the aircraft in flight about each of the three axes. The moments (turning forces) required to achieve this are generated by changing the airflow pattern around the aerofoils, by modifying their shape or changing their position.

The control surfaces that the pilot can move are usually hinged surfaces near the extremities of the aerofoils so that they have a long moment arm from the centre of gravity and the greatest leverage effect.

Usually there are three sets of primary control systems and three sets of control surfaces:

■ **the elevator** for longitudinal control in pitch, operated by fore and aft movement of the control wheel or column;

■ **the ailerons** for lateral control in roll, operated by rotation of the control wheel or sideways movement of the control column;

■ **the rudder** for directional control in yaw, operated by movement of the two interconnected rudder pedals.

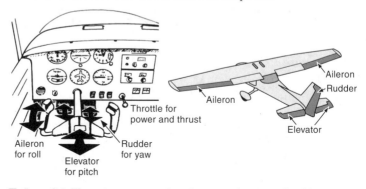

■ *Figure 8-1* **The primary controls – elevator, ailerons and rudder**

Ideally, each set of control surfaces should produce a moment about only one axis, but in practice moments about other axes are often produced as well, e.g. aileron deflection to start a roll also causes adverse yaw (see *Aileron Drag*, page 80).

The control surfaces are connected to controls in the cockpit. The pilot moves the elevators by fore and aft movement of the control column or yoke, the ailerons by rotating the wheel attached to the control column (or by sideways movement of the stick in older aircraft), and the rudder by the rudder pedals.

The deflection of the control surfaces changes the airflow and the pressure distribution over the whole aerofoil and not just over the control surface itself. The effect is to change the lift produced by the total aerofoil–control surface combination. The effectiveness of moving these control surfaces is called the controllability of the aircraft.

As mentioned earlier, an aeroplane with too much stability designed into it (thereby making it very resistant to change) has poor controllability. Stability opposes controllability. The designer must achieve a reasonable balance between stability and controllability, bearing in mind the qualities most desirable for the aeroplane's planned use. For instance, a passenger aircraft would require more stability whereas a fighter would benefit from greater controllability and manoeuvrability. In a sense, controls act as destabilisers.

NOTE Excessive movement of the control surface is prevented by stops at the control surface itself and/or at the controls in the cockpit. When the aeroplane is parked in strong winds or overnight, **control locks** should be fitted to prevent the control surfaces being moved by the wind and suffering damage. The control locks may take the form of a pin that passes through the control column, holding it firmly in place; or blocks that fit into the spaces around the control surface itself. It is vital that the control locks are removed before flight. Usually a flag is attached to make them highly visible.

The Elevator

The pilot controls the elevator by fore and aft movement of the control column – forward movement moves the elevator down, which has the effect of pushing the nose of the aircraft down, and rearward movement of the control column moves the elevator up, which has the effect of pulling the nose of the aircraft up. These movements will become logical and instinctive to you.

> The primary control in the pitching plane is the elevator.

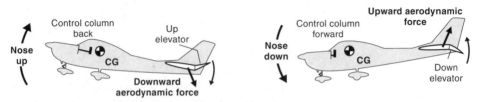

■ *Figure 8-2* ***The elevator is the primary pitching control***

When the control column is moved forward, the elevators move downwards, changing the overall shape of the tailplane-elevator aerofoil section so that it provides an altered aerodynamic force. This supplies a reduced downwards, or even an upwards, aerodynamic force on the tail of the aircraft, depending on the extent of the downwards deflection of the elevator. The effect is to create a pitching moment about the CG of the aircraft that moves the nose down.

Note that, even though the angle of attack of the parent aerofoil may be unaltered, the deflection of the control surface on the trailing edge will alter the aerodynamic force produced. For example, when the control column is pulled back, the elevator moves up and an altered force is produced by the tailplane-elevator aerofoil, causing the nose of the aircraft to pitch up.

The strength of the tail moment depends on the force it produces and the length of the arm between it and the CG. The force generated by the tailplane-elevator combination depends on their relative sizes and shape, the tailplane basically contributing to stability and the elevator to control. The larger the relative size of the elevator, the more the control.

*To retain satisfactory handling characteristics and elevator effectiveness throughout the desired speed range, the position of the CG **must** be kept within the prescribed range.*

If, for instance, the CG is too far forward, the aircraft will be too stable longitudinally because of the long moment arm to the tailplane. Even with the control column pulled fully back there will be insufficient up-elevator to reach the high angles of attack and low speeds sometimes required in manoeuvres such as flying slowly, and take-off and landing. Therefore, the forward allowable limit of the CG is determined by the amount of pitch control available from the elevator. The aft limit of the CG is determined by the requirement for longitudinal stability. (See Chapter 7, *Stability*).

Usually, the most critical situation for a nose-up requirement is in the round-out and landing. A forward CG makes the aeroplane nose-heavy and resistant to changes in pitch. This may make it difficult to raise the nose during a landing, especially since the elevator will be less effective because of the reduced airflow over it at landing speeds.

Sometimes action has to be taken to avoid this situation. For example the *Tiger Moth* is flown solo from the rear seat so that the CG is not too far forward – as could be the case if the solo pilot sat in the front seat. Also, *Concorde* pilots alter the position of the CG by transferring fuel from forward tanks to rear tanks and vice versa, depending on the stability and control qualities desirable in each phase of flight.

With power off and no slipstream effect providing increased air velocities across the tail, the tail is less capable of producing aerodynamic forces. Of course in the final stages of a landing the

power is off and the designer must allow for the elevator to produce a sufficient downwards force to raise the nose in this situation.

To reduce landing speeds, most aircraft have flaps on the trailing edge of the wing that can be lowered or extended. As you will
see in Chapter 9, full extension of flaps usually causes a pitching
moment, which the pilot can counteract with the elevator and
then trim off the control pressure.

■ *Figure 8-3* **Elevator control in the landing flare is critical**

Steady flight at a low speed and a high angle of attack will
require a fairly constant up-deflection of the elevators and backwards pressure on the control column to keep the nose up.

Fast   Slow

■ *Figure 8-4* **Steady elevator deflection at different speeds**

At a high cruise speed there will need to be a steady down-
deflection of the elevators to keep the nose down and maintain a
low angle of attack, hence a steady forward pressure on the control
column.

Because the elevators must provide differing steady forces
when in steady flight at various speeds and angles of attack, trimming devices are provided to carry these steady loads and take the
pressure off the pilot. Trimming devices are covered in more detail
later in this chapter.

The Stabilator or All-Flying Tail

Some designers choose to combine the tailplane and elevator into
the one surface and have the whole tailplane movable – known as
the all-moving tail, the flying tail or the slab tail. As the tailplane
is also known as the horizontal stabiliser you may find the horizontal stabiliser–elevator combination referred to as the stabilator.
When the control column is moved the entire 'slab' moves. Forward movement of the control column will lower the nose (by

raising the leading edge of the stabilator, generating a force that causes the tail to rise).

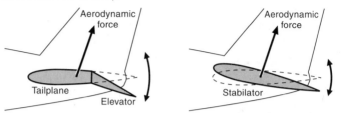

■ *Figure 8-5* **Separate tailplane plus moving elevator (left) and stabilator or all-flying tail (right)**

Some aircraft have a V-tail, combining the functions of the elevator and rudder.

■ *Figure 8-6* **V-tail or butterfly tail (early model Beech Bonanza)**

The Ailerons

The ailerons are usually positioned on the outboard trailing edge of the mainplanes. The ailerons act in opposing senses, one goes up as the other goes down, so that the lift generated by one wing increases and the lift generated by the other wing decreases. The pilot operates the ailerons with rotation of the control wheel or sideways movement of the control column (whichever is fitted).

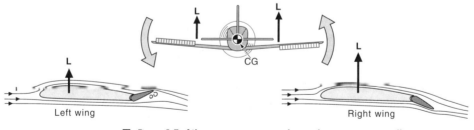

■ *Figure 8-7* **Ailerons – one up and one down causes a rolling moment**

A resultant rolling moment is exerted on the aeroplane. The magnitude of this rolling moment depends on the moment arm (the reason the ailerons are outboard, giving a long moment arm to the CG) and the magnitude of the differing lift forces.

Note that for a wing to rise, its aileron will be deflected downwards. Conversely, for a wing to go down its aileron will be deflected upwards.

- **The downgoing aileron** is on the upgoing wing.
- **The upgoing aileron** is on the downgoing wing.

Adverse Aileron Yaw due to Aileron Drag

Deflecting an aileron down causes an effective increase in camber of that wing and an increase in the effective angle of attack. The lift from that wing increases, but unfortunately so does the drag. As the other aileron rises, the effective camber of that wing is decreased and its angle of attack is less, therefore lift from that wing decreases, as does the drag.

The differing lift forces cause the aircraft to bank one way, but the differential aileron drag causes it to yaw the other way – neither a comfortable nor convenient effect. This is known as aileron drag or adverse aileron yaw and is mainly a low airspeed problem that a pilot would notice with a turn at low speed shortly after take-off.

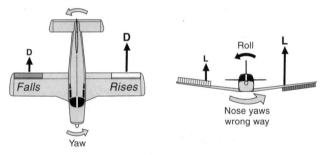

- Figure 8-8 **Rising wing has increased aileron drag – adverse yaw**

Adverse aileron yaw can be reduced by good design incorporating differential ailerons, Frise-type ailerons, or coupling the rudder to the ailerons. To a large extent, aileron drag has been eliminated from modern training aeroplanes.

DIFFERENTIAL AILERONS are designed to minimise adverse aileron yaw by increasing the drag on the downgoing wing on the inside of the turn. This is achieved by deflecting the upward aileron, (on the descending wing) through a greater angle than the downward aileron (on the rising wing).

Differential ailerons overcome adverse aileron yaw.

The greater deflection of the aileron on the descending wing causes it to have increased drag with a tendency to yaw the aeroplane into bank. The adverse yaw is reduced, though not eliminated completely. The remaining unwanted yaw can be removed with rudder.

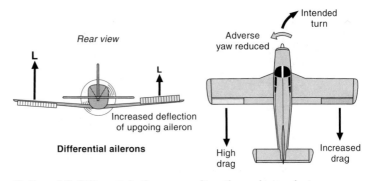

■ *Figure 8-9* **Differential ailerons equalise aileron drag, reducing**
adverse yaw

FRISE-TYPE AILERONS increase the drag of the descending wing on the inside of the turn. As the aileron goes up (to drive the wing down), its nose protrudes into the airstream beneath the wing causing increased drag on the downgoing wing. On the other wing, which is rising, the nose of the downgoing aileron does not protrude into the airstream, so causes no extra drag.

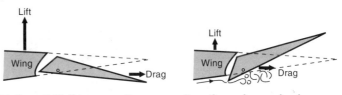

■ *Figure 8-10* **Frise-type ailerons equalise aileron drag and reduce**
adverse yaw

Frise-type ailerons may also be designed to operate differentially, to incorporate the benefit of differential ailerons.

COUPLED AILERONS AND RUDDER cause the rudder to move automatically and yaw the aeroplane into bank, opposing the adverse yaw from the ailerons.

Note the interconnection between roll and yaw throughout this discussion. The primary effect of rudder is to yaw the aeroplane, and the secondary effect is to roll it. The primary effect of ailerons is to roll the aeroplane, and the secondary effect is to yaw it. Using the rudder to neutralise adverse yaw, with the ailerons deflected and the aeroplane rolling, is one of the most important elements of aeroplane control by the pilot.

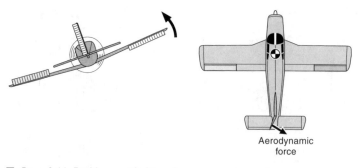

Aerodynamic
force

■ *Figure 8-11* **Rudder coupled to aileron can reduce adverse yaw**

Roll is Followed by Yaw

When the aeroplane is banked using the ailerons, the lift becomes tilted. It now has a horizontal component that is not balanced by any other force and so the aeroplane will slip in that direction. As a result of the slip, an airflow will strike the side of the aeroplane and the large keel surfaces (such as the fin) which are mainly behind the CG, causing the nose of the aeroplane to yaw progressively in the direction of bank. It is in this way that roll is followed by yaw.

The secondary effect of ailerons is to cause yaw.

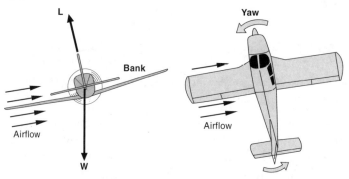

■ *Figure 8-12* **Roll is followed by yaw**

NOTE While the ailerons are deflected, there may be a small amount of adverse aileron yaw opposite to the direction of bank, but, once established in the bank and with the ailerons neutral, the aeroplane will yaw progressively towards the lower wing. It will gradually enter a spiral descent and lose height unless the pilot takes action – levels the wings or exerts back pressure on the control column.

The Rudder

The rudder is hinged to the rear of the fin (or vertical stabiliser). It is controlled from the cockpit by the rudder pedals attached to the rudder bar.

By pushing the left pedal, the rudder will move left. This alters the fin-rudder aerofoil section, and sideways lift is created that sends the tail to the right and yaws the aeroplane to the left about the normal axis. With left rudder applied, the aeroplane yaws left.

Rudder effectiveness increases with speed, so large deflections at low speeds and small deflections at high speeds may be required to give a particular yaw. In propeller-driven aircraft, any slipstream flowing over the rudder will increase its effectiveness.

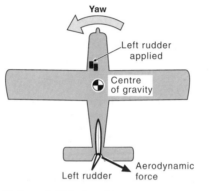

■ *Figure 8-13* **Left rudder pressure – nose yaws left**

Yaw is Followed by Roll

The primary effect of rudder is to yaw the aeroplane. This causes the outer wing to speed up and generate increased lift. Having commenced to yaw, the aeroplane will continue in its original flightpath for a brief period due to inertia – any dihedral on the forward wing causing it to be presented to the airflow at a greater angle of attack, therefore generating more lift. Having yawed the aeroplane, the further effect of rudder is to cause a roll.

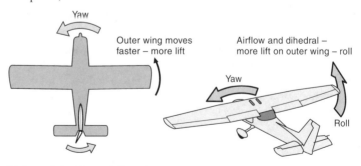

■ *Figure 8-14* **Yaw is followed by roll**

Slipstream Effect

Anything that increases the airflow over the rudder, like a slip-stream, makes it more effective. As the slipstream corkscrews around the fuselage, it strikes one side of the fin/rudder at a different angle to the other. The shape of the fin/rudder aerofoil section is usually symmetrical, however in some propeller-driven aircraft the fin may be constructed a little off-set or structured a little asymmetrically to balance the slipstream effect in the cruise condition.

> Controls are more effective in a strong airflow.

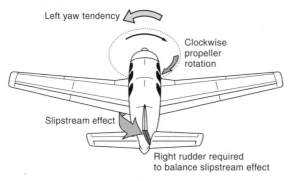

■ *Figure 8-15* **The slipstream strikes one side of the rudder**

If the slipstream over the fin and rudder changes, then the rudder deflection must be changed to balance it. This is especially noticeable at high power and low airspeed, as during take-off.

For example, the propeller in most training aeroplanes, when viewed from the cockpit, rotates clockwise. Its slipstream corkscrews back accordingly, striking the fin on the left side and driving the tail to the right. This causes the nose of the aeroplane to yaw left and so, as you open up power, you must apply right rudder to balance the slipstream effect.

The Rudder in Crosswind Take-Offs and Landings

In ground operations, any crosswind will hit the side of the fin and tend to weathercock the aircraft into wind. The rudder must be used to stop the aircraft yawing into wind and keep it tracking straight along the runway.

On approach to land the most common technique is to crab the aircraft into wind so that it is flying in balance (i.e. directly into the relative wind and with the rudder ball centred) and tracking somewhat 'crab-wise' along the extended centre-line of the runway.

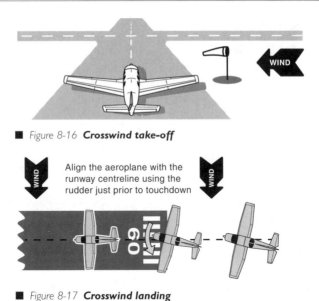

■ *Figure 8-16* **Crosswind take-off**

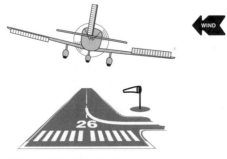

■ *Figure 8-17* **Crosswind landing**

Just prior to touchdown the aircraft is yawed with the rudder so that when the wheels touch they are aligned in the direction of the runway. Another technique in a crosswind landing is the side-slipping approach. On a typical crosswind approach, you would crab the aeroplane into wind so that it is tracking towards the aerodrome along the extended centreline of the runway.

■ *Figure 8-18* **Sideslipping approach**

Near the ground, you would yaw the aeroplane straight (with the rudder) so that it is aligned with the centreline. Unless the wheels touch almost immediately, the wind will cause the aeroplane to drift towards the side of the runway. To avoid this, you would lower (using the ailerons) the into-wind wing sufficiently to stop the aircraft drifting off the centreline prior to touchdown. The aeroplane is now sideslipping and flying a little bit out of balance. Touchdown will be on the upwind wheel.

Not enough wing down, the aeroplane drifts downwind – too much wing down, it sideslips off the centreline into wind. It takes a little bit of juggling, especially as the wind may be gusting and will change in strength and direction as the ground is approached. A demonstration by your flying instructor will make it look easy.

The strongest crosswind that the aircraft can handle is limited by rudder effectiveness, and the maximum crosswind is specified in the Flight Manual and Pilot's Operating Handbook.

NOTE Refer to your flying instructor for the correct crosswind landing technique to use with your particular aeroplane. Cross-wind operations are fully covered in Vol. 1 of this series.

The Power of the Rudder

While the rudder must be sufficiently powerful to handle the above requirements satisfactorily, it must not be too powerful. Given maximum deflection by the pilot it should not cause structural damage.

The maximum allowable speed for maximum control deflection is called the manoeuvring speed (V_A).

Control Effectiveness

The size and shape of the control surface and its moment about the centre of gravity are of great importance in its effectiveness. Since the size and shape are fixed by the designer and the CG only moves small distances, these can be considered constant. The variables in control effectiveness are airspeed and control surface deflection angle.

If an aileron is deflected downwards, the angle of attack and the camber of that wing is increased, thereby increasing the C_{Lift} and the lift produced. The greater the control surface deflection, the greater the change in lift from the aerofoil (provided the stalling angle of attack is not exceeded). The change in turning moment produced is the *change in lift × the moment arm to the CG*.

The other aileron is deflected upwards, reducing the angle of attack and the camber on that wing, thereby reducing the lift produced and reducing the turning moment, hence the aircraft rolls.

As we saw in the chapters on lift and drag, the aerodynamic forces vary with the dynamic pressure (*½ rho V-squared*). If the airspeed *V* is doubled, the effect of this is *V-squared* ($2 \times 2 = 4$). So, doubling the airspeed quadruples the effect of the same control surface deflection.

If the airspeed is halved, the same control surface deflection is only ¼ as effective. Therefore, at low airspeed, achieving a desired change in attitude requires a much greater control surface deflection (commonly known as 'sloppy controls' or less-effective controls). Conversely, at higher airspeeds, controls are more effective.

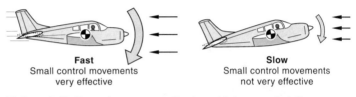

Fast
Small control movements
very effective

Slow
Small control movements
not very effective

■ *Figure 8-19* **Controls are more effective with increased airflow**

Slipstream Increases Rudder and Tailplane Effectiveness

At low airspeeds, but with high power set, the slipstream may flow strongly over the tail section, making the elevator and rudder more effective than at the same speed with no power on. The ailerons are not affected by the slipstream and so will remain relatively ineffective.

Approaching the stall with power on, the elevator and rudder would retain more effectiveness than the ailerons, due to the slipstream flowing over them. Use of the slipstream is made when taxiing tailwheel aircraft on the ground – apply power to give rudder effectiveness to turn.

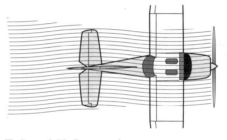

■ *Figure 8-20* **Prop-wash**

Control Pressures on the Pilot

When a control surface is deflected, (for example, a down elevator – by pushing forward on the control column), the aerodynamic force produced by the moving control surface itself opposes its deflection (downwards in this case). This causes a moment to act on the control surface about its hinge line trying to return the elevator to its original faired (i.e. streamlined) position, and the pilot must overcome this to maintain the desired position. The pilot feels this as **stick-force.**

The stick-force depends on the turning moment at the hinge-line of the control surface and the means by which the control column is linked to the control surface.

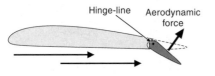

Hinge-line   Aerodynamic force

■ *Figure 8-21* **Hinge moment at the control surface**

If the control surface is hinged at its leading edge and trails from this position in flight, the stick forces required are very high, especially in heavy or fast aircraft, and the pilot needs assistance. This assistance is provided by **aerodynamic balance.**

> *An aerodynamic balance on a control reduces stick load on the pilot.*

The designer provides an **inset hinge,** a **horn balance** or a **balance tab** to use the aerodynamic forces produced by the deflected control surface to partially balance or reduce the moment, i.e. aerodynamic balance of a control surface is designed to reduce the control forces required from the pilot. The designer, however, must be careful not to over-balance the controls, otherwise the pilot will lose all sense of feel.

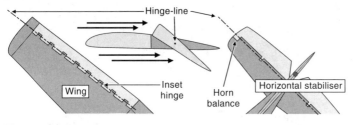

Hinge-line

Wing   Inset hinge   Horn balance   Horizontal stabiliser

■ *Figure 8-22* **Inset hinge balance (left) and horn balance (right)**

Fixed Balance Tab

Some older aircraft have a small flexible metal tab on the rear of the appropriate control surface. If the aeroplane was found to have a flying fault, such as a tendency to fly one wing low due to faulty rigging, this tab could be bent to alter the forces slightly and so correct the flying fault without having to re-rig the aeroplane.

This modification could only be done on the ground and its effectiveness established through test flying.

Balance Tab

On conventional tailplanes it is quite common to have a balance tab incorporated as part of the elevator. It is mechanically linked to the elevator by a linkage that causes it to move in the opposite direction.

If the pilot exerts back pressure on the control column, the elevator is raised and the balance tab goes down. The elevator balance tab unit now generates a small upward aerodynamic force that acts to hold the elevator up, thereby reducing the control load required of the pilot.

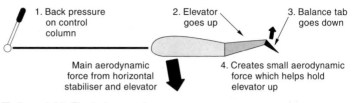

1. Back pressure on control column
2. Elevator goes up
3. Balance tab goes down
Main aerodynamic force from horizontal stabiliser and elevator
4. Creates small aerodynamic force which helps hold elevator up

■ *Figure 8-23* **The balance tab**

The balance tab acts automatically as the elevator moves. This movement should be checked in the pre-flight inspection by moving the elevator one way and noting that the tab moves the other way.

A **servo tab** is a variation of the balance tab where the pilot control (control column or rudder pedals) is connected, not to the main control surface, but to the tab. As the control input moves the servo tab into the airflow, the aerodynamic forces generated drive the main control surface in the opposite direction, causing the desired manoeuvre.

Trim Tabs

Trim tabs are designed to remove the stick load on the pilot.

An aircraft is *in trim* in pitch, roll or yaw, when it maintains a steady state of flight without the pilot having to exert any steady pressure on the particular control surface.

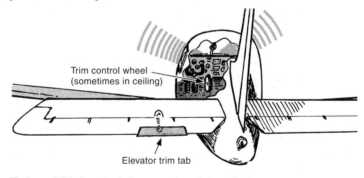

Trim control wheel (sometimes in ceiling)

Elevator trim tab

■ *Figure 8-24* **A typical elevator trim tab installation**

A properly trimmed aircraft is far more pleasant to fly than an untrimmed aircraft. It requires control inputs only to manoeuvre and not to maintain an attitude or a heading. The function of the trim tab is to reduce the moment at the hinge line of the control surface to approximately zero for that condition of flight, so that the aeroplane will maintain it 'hands-off'.

Almost all aircraft have an elevator trim; many light singles and all multi-engined aircraft have a rudder trim, and the more sophisticated aeroplanes have an aileron trim.

Trim tabs can differ in sophistication – from simple metal strips that can be set on the ground, or springs that can apply a load to the control column, to trim tabs that the pilot can operate from the cockpit, usually by a trim-wheel or trim-handle, and which may be mechanical or electrical. Metal strips can be found on an aileron of some aircraft types and may be altered after a test flight to make wings-level flight more easily achievable without steady pressure being required on the control column.

In most light aircraft, trim systems are mechanically operated by a trim wheel that acts in a natural sense. For example, if the pilot is pressing forward on the control column to maintain a desired attitude, then, by moving the top of the elevator trim-wheel forward, the stick force can gradually be released until the aircraft maintains the desired attitude without any steady pressure being required.

If the trim is electrical, then the switch will be spring-loaded to the central OFF position. To remove a steady load that he is holding on a control surface, the pilot will move the switch in the natural and instinctive sense and then release it, when it will return to the OFF position.

The method of trimming is to hold the aircraft exactly how you want it with control pressures and then trim these pressures out to zero. As you trim the relevant control, pressure is gradually relaxed until it is zero.

Do not use the trim to change the attitude of the aeroplane. Change attitude with the elevators – and then trim-off steady control pressures once stable flight has been achieved.

> *Use trim to remove control pressures, **not** to change attitude.*

Although the control surface may be moved by the pilot to manoeuvre the aircraft, the trim tab itself will remain in the same fixed position relative to the control surface until the pilot decides to re-trim. There is a small proviso to this – some tabs perform a dual function, both as a trim tab and as an aerodynamic balance as the control surface moves. Its average position will be trimmed in by the pilot and it will vary about this mean position automatically to serve its other function of balancing control surface movements. This is typical with a balance tab.

The aircraft will stay in trim until the power changes, or the airspeed changes, or the position of the centre of gravity moves. The pilot should then re-trim. Aircraft with all-flying tailplanes (i.e. stabilators) usually have the elevator trim incorporated so that trimming moves the entire slab.

Mass Balancing

At high speeds some control surfaces have a tendency to 'flutter'. This is a vibration that results from the changes in pressure distribution over the surface as its angle of attack is altered.

> *A mass balance prevents flutter.*

If part of the structure starts to vibrate (and control surfaces are particularly susceptible to this) then these oscillations can quickly reach dangerous proportions. To avoid this tendency to flutter, the designer needs to alter the mass distribution of the surface.

The aim of mass-balancing is not for the control to be balanced in the sense of remaining level, but to alter the mass-distribution of the control to avoid any flutter or vibration.

The **mass balance** is placed forward of the hinge-line to bring the CG of the control surface up to the hinge-line or even slightly ahead of it. On the *inset hinge* or *horn balance* this mass can easily be incorporated in that part ahead of the hinge line, but on others the mass must be placed on an arm that extends forward of the hinge-line. The distribution of mass on control surfaces is very important.

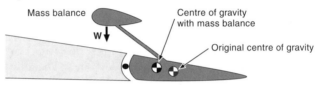

■ *Figure 8-25* **Mass-balance to avoid control flutter**

Anti-Balance Tab

An anti-balance tab increases stick load on the pilot to prevent overcontrolling.

Because of their combined function, stabilators have a much larger area than elevators and so produce a more 'powerful' response to control input, i.e. small movements can produce large aerodynamic forces. To prevent pilots from moving the stabilator too far and over-controlling (especially at high airspeeds), a stabilator often incorporates an anti-balance tab.

An anti-balance tab moves in the *same* direction as the stabilator's trailing edge and generates an aerodynamic force which makes it harder to move the stabilator further, as well as providing 'feel' for the pilot.

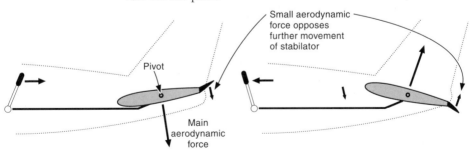

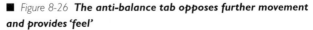

■ *Figure 8-26* **The anti-balance tab opposes further movement and provides 'feel'**

Correct movement of the anti-balance tab can be checked in the pre-flight inspection by moving the trailing edge of the stabilator and noting that the anti-balance tab moves in the same direction.

Summary of Controls

The **primary controls** are the elevator, ailerons and rudder.

Plane	Axis	CONTROL	Initial Effect	Further Effect
pitch	*lateral*	*Elevator*	*pitch*	*airspeed change*
roll	*longitudinal*	*Ailerons*	*roll*	*yaw*
yaw	*normal*	*Rudder*	*yaw*	*roll*

Other controls include the throttle, pitch lever (for variable pitch propellers), mixture control, carburettor heat, flaps, and undercarriage lever (for aircraft with retractable landing gear). These are covered later in this volume.

Although the **throttle** is an ancillary control, it does affect the aeroplane in flight sufficiently for us to consider it here. The initial effect of applying throttle is to increase the power and thus the thrust – this increases the thrust–drag nose-up turning moment and pitches the nose up. It will also increase the slipstream effect, causing the aeroplane to yaw unless counteracted by rudder.

With a propeller rotating clockwise as seen from the cockpit, applying power will raise the nose and yaw the aeroplane to the left (counteracted by applying forward pressure on the control column and right rudder).

When the power is removed, the nose will tend to drop and yaw to the right (counteracted by holding the attitude with a back pressure and applying left rudder).

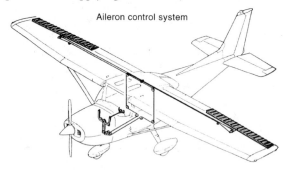
Aileron control system

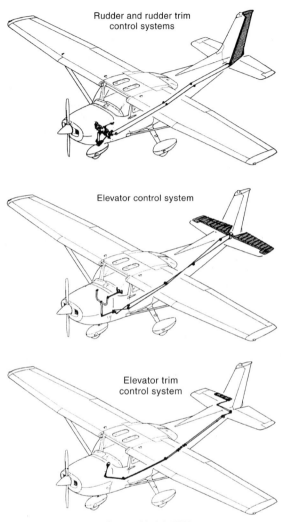

Rudder and rudder trim
control systems

Elevator control system

Elevator trim
control system

Cessna Model 172N

■ *Figure 8-27* **Typical light aircraft flight control systems**

Control on the Ground

DIRECTIONAL CONTROL is by use of the rudder, nosewheel steering (which may be connected to the rudder pedals), power and brakes. Airflow over the rudder increases its effectiveness. Do not turn too sharply, especially when taxiing fast – a high CG, a narrow wheelbase, or an unfavourable wind-effect may all combine to roll you onto the outer wingtip. Any wind will tend to weathercock the aeroplane into wind – so take care when taxiing in crosswinds and tailwinds.

SPEED is controlled by power and brakes. Applying power with the throttle is generally used to accelerate the aeroplane and, once moving, the power can usually be reduced. Air resistance, ground friction and wheel brakes will slow the aeroplane. It is good airmanship not to use power against brakes. Hard braking, especially in a tailwheel aircraft, may cause it to nose-over. Braking a tailwheeler may destabilise it directionally – the CG (due to inertia) will try to move ahead of the main wheels on which the brakes are being applied. In a nosewheel (tricycle undercarriage), braking will not cause the aircraft to yaw.

> Do not use excessive power against brakes.

CROSSWIND EFFECT. A side-wind will tend to lift the up-wind wing, especially if it has dihedral. The wings can be kept level with aileron. There will also be a weathercock tendency to turn the nose into wind.

TAILWIND EFFECT. A tailwind will assist fast taxiing, which is not good. It will also decrease directional stability by trying to blow the large tail surfaces forward and a turn, once commenced, may be difficult to control. In a strong tailwind, your flying instructor may advise you to hold the control column forward – this deflects the elevator down and avoids the tailwind creating a lifting force on the tailplane.

Now complete **Exercises 8 – Control.**

Flaps

In phases of flight such as take-off and landing it is desirable to have a wing that has an increased lifting capability (increased coefficient of lift), so that slower speeds are possible.

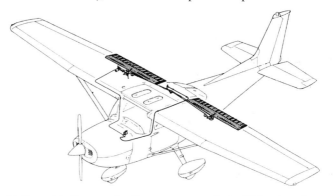

■ *Figure 9-1* ***Cessna wing flap system – typical of light aircraft***

The primary purpose of flaps is to give the required lift at a lower airspeed. At other times it is convenient to have increased drag to slow the aeroplane down or increase its rate of descent. Devices that do this are categorised as **lift augmentation** and **drag augmentation**.

Producing more lift from a wing has obvious benefits. In straight and level flight the weight is balanced by the lift:

Lift = Weight = $C_{Lift} \times \tfrac{1}{2}$ *rho V-squared* $\times$ *S*

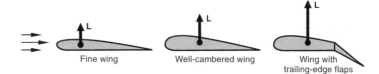

Fine wing   Well-cambered wing   Wing with trailing-edge flaps

■ *Figure 9-2* ***Same airspeed: camber and/or flaps give higher lift***

If some means of changing the basic aerofoil into a shape that has an increased $C_{Lift\ maximum,}$ and possibly an increased wing area *S,* is used, then the required lift can be generated at much lower speeds.

At the $C_{Lift\ max}$, reached near the stalling angle of attack, the required lift will be generated at a much lower airspeed. When the stalling angle is finally reached, the airspeed is much lower than for the 'clean' wing. This means that all the other speeds which are factored on the stall speed, such as take-off speed, approach speed, landing speed, etc., will be lower – a safer situation allowing the use of shorter take-off and landing distances.

50 KIAS
Stall speed clean

40 KIAS
Stall speed with full flaps

■ *Figure 9-3* **Flaps lower the stalling speed**

Increasing $C_{Lift\ maximum}$ with High-Lift Devices

There are two main types of high-lift devices that are capable of augmenting (increasing) $C_{Lift\ max}$:

☐ **Slats and slots** – either automatic or pilot-controlled, such as those on the *Tiger Moth* and *Boeing 727*.

☐ **Flaps** (pilot-controlled), which may be trailing edge or leading edge – most aircraft have trailing edge flaps.

Cockpit Flap Controls

The wing flaps are controlled from the cockpit usually by either:

☐ **an electrical switch** spring-loaded to OFF, which allows any degree of flap between full-up and full-down to be selected, with the precise degree displayed on a cockpit indicator; or

☐ **a mechanical lever** or handle, which usually allows the flap to be selected in set stages, with the stage displayed on an indicator at the base of the handle.

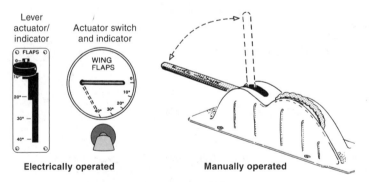

Lever actuator/ indicator

Actuator switch and indicator

Electrically operated

Manually operated

■ *Figure 9-4* **The flap control and indicator**

As the flap lever is operated, the flaps on both wings move identically. It is usual to check the flaps carefully during the pre-flight external inspection to ensure that they are securely attached, that they both extend to the same degree and that the flap (and wing) surfaces are free from damage.

Trailing Edge Flaps

Flaps alter the camber of the aerofoil section. An aerofoil designed to give high lift has a curved mean camber line (the line equidistant between the upper and the lower surfaces) – and the greater the mean camber line, the greater the lift capability (the *maximum* C_{Lift} possible) of the wing. By a *high-lift* wing we mean one that can produce the required lift at a lower airspeed.

Most high-speed aerofoils, however, have a mean camber line that is fairly straight and hardly curved at all. If the trailing edge or the leading edge can be hinged downwards, then a more highly cambered aerofoil section results – which means it can produce the required lift at a lower airspeed, i.e. it has become more of a high-lift wing.

Virtually all aircraft have trailing edge flaps. Larger aircraft, especially those with swept-back wings, often have leading edge flaps as well. These have a similar function to trailing edge flaps in that they increase the camber of the wing and thus increase its effectiveness in producing lift.

Effects of Flaps

Increased Lift

Flap extension increases lift.

The increased camber will give increased lift (more lift at the same airspeed or the same lift at a lower airspeed).

The initial effect of lowering the flaps is to give increased lift (C_{Lift} increases and at the same speed (V) this gives a greater lift force). Unless the pilot lowers the nose to decrease angle of attack (and C_{Lift}), the aeroplane will experience a short-lived and unpleasant climb – a 'balloon'. It is only short-lived because the increased drag soon slows the aeroplane down, reducing airspeed, and consequently the lift force is reduced.

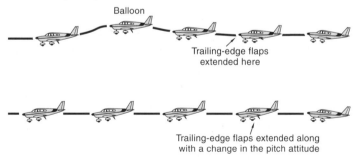

Balloon

Trailing-edge flaps
extended here

Trailing-edge flaps extended along
with a change in the pitch attitude

■ *Figure 9-5* **Lowering flap can cause a 'balloon' unless the pilot adjusts the pitch attitude**

Pitch Attitude

Because the increased camber due to extending trailing edge flaps occurs at the rear of the wing, the centre of pressure moves aft as the flaps are lowered, thereby altering the lift–weight couple. The thrust–drag couple may also be altered due to the change in drag. The resultant pitching effect will vary between aircraft types depending on whether the nose-down lift–weight couple or nose-up thrust–drag couple predominates.

Flap extension usually causes the nose to pitch.

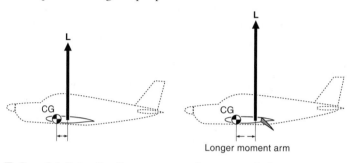

Longer moment arm

■ *Figure 9-6* **Extending flap may cause the nose to pitch**

Decreased Lift/Drag Ratio

When the flaps are lowered the lift increases, but so too does the drag. When we consider the angles of attack giving the best lift/drag ratio, the drag increase is proportionately much greater than the lift increase, i.e. the L/D ratio is less with flap extended.

Flap extension decreases the L/D ratio.

As a result of a lower L/D ratio, the aeroplane will not glide as far with flap as it would when clean, nor will it climb as steeply. Also, it will require more fuel to travel the same distance – if you cruise with flaps down.

Increased Drag

As flap is extended, the drag, as well as the lift, increases. In the early stages of the extension the lift increases quite markedly (sometimes causing the aircraft to 'balloon'), with some increase in drag. In the later stages of flap extension, the increase in drag is much greater.

Flap extension increases drag.

Think of the trailing edge flaps at their early extension as *lift flaps* (when the lifting capability of the wing is increased significantly for little cost in drag), and when fully extended as *drag flaps*. The latter stages of trailing edge flap extension give only a small increase in lifting capability for a large increase in drag.

When the flaps are extended, because the drag increases, the speed will commence to decrease unless power is added or the rate of descent increased – or both.

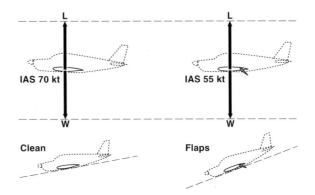

■ *Figure 9-7* **Extending flap – either more thrust or a steeper descent is required to balance the increased drag**

Lower Stalling Angle of Attack

The angle of attack is measured against the chord line of the original 'unflapped' wing. This means that there is a constant reference line against which to measure angle of attack in all stages of flight.

The trailing edge flaps do not extend along the whole of the trailing edge, but usually only along the inner sections. The flaps are lowered simultaneously and symmetrically on each side of the aircraft.

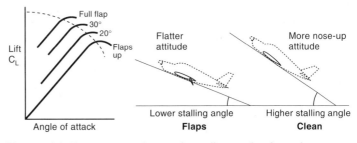

■ *Figure 9-8* **Flap extension lowers the stalling angle of attack**

Flap extension lowers the stalling angle of attack.

With the flaps down, the stalling angle of attack (referred to the chord of the 'unflapped' wing) is less than the stalling angle of attack when the wing is 'clean'. You will see this as a lower nose attitude when stalling with flaps down compared to flaps up.

Do not confuse angle of attack with attitude as they are two different things. The attitude has no fixed relationship to the angle of attack while the aircraft is manoeuvring. The attitude is the angle of the aircraft with respect to the horizontal and the angle of attack is the angle with respect to the relative airflow.

Angle of attack

■ Figure 9-9 *Same aircraft pitch attitudes but different angles of attack*

Flaps in the Take-Off

By partially lowering the flaps to the recommended take-off position (specified in the aircraft Flight Manual), you can obtain a lift
advantage for a small drag penalty. The increased lift coefficient
(C_{Lift}) means that the required amount of lift can be obtained at a
lower airspeed and that the stalling speed is lowered. This allows
the aircraft to fly at a lower speed and the take-off run to be shortened, even though the drag may be slightly increased.

The variation between the climb-out gradients with and without flaps will vary from aircraft to aircraft, and for the one aeroplane will vary according to the amount of flap selected.

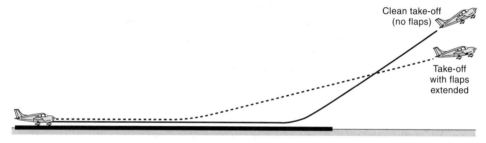

Clean take-off
(no flaps)

Take-off
with flaps
extended

■ Figure 9-10 *Flaps allow a shorter take-off ground run*

If you set the flaps at an angle greater than that recommended
for take-off, then you are taking on increased drag with very little
improvement in lift. This greatly increased drag at the larger flap
extensions will decrease your rate of acceleration on the ground
take-off run and diminish your climb-out performance.

Flap Management on Take-Off

Choose an appropriate flap setting for take-off, bearing in mind
take-off run available (TORA) and obstacle clearance in the take-
off path.

In flight, prior to retracting the flaps, ensure that you have sufficient flying speed for the new configuration. If the flaps are
retracted at too low a speed, the clean wing (or the less-flapped
wing if you are retracting in stages) produces less lift and, if insufficient to support the aeroplane, causes it to sink or stall.

As you raise the flaps the aeroplane will tend to sink because of the reduction in lift that the wing is producing. To counteract this sinking, you need to raise the nose and increase the angle of attack (and the C_{Lift}). If you do not raise the nose to make up the loss of lift as the flaps come in, the aircraft will sink until it has gained sufficient airspeed to make up the reduced lift.

When you retract the flaps, the reduction in camber at the rear of the wing moves the centre of pressure forwards and there is also a change in drag. There is usually a tendency for the nose to pitch, in which case re-trimming would be necessary. If you are accelerating towards a higher climb speed or cruise speed, further re-trimming will be necessary as speed increases.

To achieve the same lift at the same speed clean (as compared to flapped), your nose attitude must be higher. By raising the nose slightly as the flaps are retracted the C_{Lift} generated remains about the same, and so the aircraft does not sink. Even though the C_{Lift} is the same, the C_{Drag} will be reduced with the flaps retracted, and this drag reduction allows the aircraft to accelerate faster.

Flaps on Approach and Landing

Lowering the flaps for landing allows the wing, because of the increased C_{Lift}, to generate the required lift at a lower speed and therefore makes a lower approach speed possible. The stall speed is lowered significantly by the increased C_{Lift} and hence the landing speed, which must be at least $1.3 V_{Stall}$ in the approach configuration (30% buffer above the stall speed), is lowered. There are a number of things to consider before lowering the flaps:

- **Speed** – ensure you do not lower flaps at too high a speed – the aircraft's Flight Manual and Pilot's Operating Handbook specify the maximum flap extension speed (V_{FE}).
- **Ballooning** – as the trailing edge flaps are extended, the C_{Lift} will increase and the aircraft will tend to 'balloon' unless counteracted with a lower attitude.
- **Pitch attitude** – when lowering the flaps there is usually a tendency for the nose to pitch. You should set and hold the desired attitude, then trim off any pressure held on the control column in steady flight.

Note also that the increase in drag (with lowered flaps) will require higher power settings to maintain airspeed and altitude or to maintain a steady rate of descent. If you want a steeper angle of descent, then lowering the flaps (and not applying any power) will achieve that.

Flaps Increase the Pilot's Visibility

With trailing edge flaps extended, the aeroplane's required nose attitude is lower. This improves visibility for the pilot – especially important during approach and landing.

Sometimes a *precautionary cruise* is required. This is a low-speed cruise used, for example, when you want to inspect the ground, or when finding your way in poor visibility (which should have been avoided). Partially lowering the flaps allows a slower cruise, the adequate margin above the stall, and increased visibility from the cockpit.

■ *Figure 9-11* **Extended flaps improve the pilot's forward field of vision**

Trailing Edge Flap Types

There are various flap types that may be found on light aircraft. They include:

☐ **Simple flaps.**
☐ **Split flaps.**
☐ **Slotted flaps,** which allow high energy air from beneath the wing to flow through the slot and over the upper surface of the flap, thereby delaying the stall.
☐ **Fowler flaps,** which move both backwards and down, thus increasing wing area as well as camber.

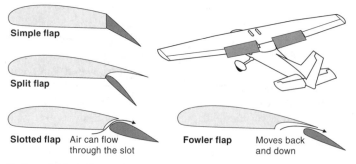

■ *Figure 9-12* **Different types of trailing edge flaps**

Leading Edge Devices

At high angles of attack the airflow breaks away (or separates) from the upper surface of the wings and becomes turbulent. This leads to a stalled condition which destroys much of the lifting ability of the wing.

Some aircraft have leading edge devices that cause some of the high-energy air from beneath the wing to flow through a **slot** and over the upper surface of the wing, thereby delaying separation and the stall, allowing the aeroplane to fly at a higher angle of attack and a lower airspeed. This can be achieved with **slats** which form part of the upper leading edge of the wing in normal flight, but which can be extended forward and/or down to form a slot.

Some wings have fixed-slots actually built-in to the wing leading edge but this is less common because they generate high drag at cruising speeds. On a high-performance aircraft this would be unacceptable and so the more complicated **extendable slat** would be fitted.

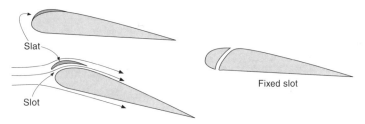

Slat

Slot

Fixed slot

■ *Figure 9-13* **Slots delay the stall**

Spoilers

Most advanced jet transports and gliders have spoilers on the upper surfaces of their wings. These are hinged control panels which, when extended, disturb the airflow over the upper lift-producing part of the wing, thereby decreasing (or 'spoiling') lift and increasing drag.

Pilots use spoilers to reduce airspeed and/or steepen the descent path without increasing airspeed.

On large jet aircraft, pilots deploy the spoilers after touchdown to dump the lift and get all of the weight onto the wheels, thus making the wheel brakes more effective.

Now complete **Exercises 9 – Flaps.**

Straight and Level

In steady straight and level flight the aeroplane is in equilibrium. This means that all the forces acting on it are in balance and there is no resultant force to accelerate or decelerate it. Acceleration is a change in velocity, which means a change in speed or a change in direction, or both. In straight and level flight, the aeroplane is not forced to change either speed or direction.

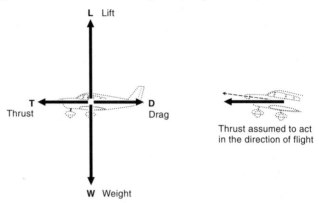

■ *Figure 10-1* **The four main forces**

The **four main forces** acting on the aeroplane are **lift, weight, thrust** and **drag.** We assume that thrust acts in the direction of flight, as shown in Figure 10-1. Each of the four main forces has its own point of action:

- ▢ the **lift** through the **centre of pressure;**
- ▢ the **weight** through the **centre of gravity;**
- ▢ the **thrust** and the **drag** in opposite senses, parallel to the direction of flight, through points that vary with aircraft attitude and design.

We assume that the thrust force from the engine–propeller is acting in the direction of flight, even though this is not always the case. For instance, at a high angle of attack and slow speed the aircraft has a nose-high attitude with the propeller shaft inclined upwards to the horizontal direction of flight. This assumption that thrust acts in the direction of flight simplifies our discussion considerably.

In straight and level flight:

Lift = Weight   *and*   **Thrust = Drag**

The lift–weight forces are much larger that the thrust–drag forces. For more about each of these forces refer back to their individual chapters.

Pitching Moments

The centre of pressure (CP) and the centre of gravity (CG) vary in position – the CP changes with angle of attack, and the CG with fuel burn-off and passenger or cargo movement. The result is that the lift–weight combination sets up a **couple** which will cause a nose-down or nose-up pitching moment, depending on whether the lift acts behind or in front of the CG.

> A **couple** is a pair of equal, parallel forces acting in opposite directions which tends to cause rotation because the forces are acting along different axes.

Similarly the effect of the thrust–drag couple depends on whether the thrust line is below the drag line (as is usually the case) or vice versa.

The usual design is to have the CP behind the CG, so that the lift–weight couple is nose down, and the thrust line lower than the drag line so that the thrust–drag couple is nose up. Any loss of power will weaken the nose-up couple, and consequently the nose-down lift–weight couple will pitch the aeroplane into a descent, thereby maintaining flying speed – a fairly safe arrangement.

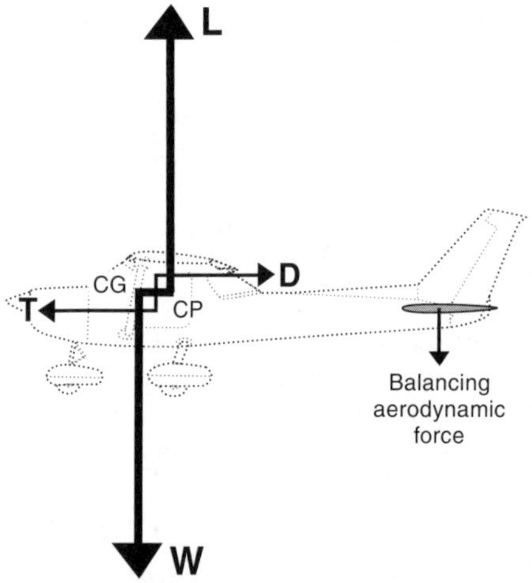

■ Figure 10-2 **The tailplane provides the final balancing moment**

The lift–weight couple and the thrust–drag couple should counteract each other in straight and level flight so that there is no residual moment acting to pitch the aeroplane either nose up or nose down. This ideal situation between the four main forces rarely exists, and so the tailplane/elevator is designed into the aeroplane to produce a balancing force. This force may be up or down, depending on the relationship that exists at the time between the lift–weight nose-down couple and the thrust–drag nose-up couple.

If you have to exert a steady pressure on the control column, so that the elevator produces the required balancing force, then you can trim this pressure off with the elevator trim-wheel. Hold the desired attitude, and then trim to relieve the load.

Variation of Speed in Level Flight

For level flight, lift = weight. From our now (hopefully) familiar lift formula:

$$L = C_{Lift} \times \tfrac{1}{2}\ rho\ V\text{-}squared \times S$$

– we can see that if the speed factor V (the true airspeed, TAS) is reduced, then the lift coefficient C_{Lift} (angle of attack) must be increased to maintain the balance of lift = weight.

V is the true airspeed – the speed of the aeroplane relative to the air mass that it is passing through. TAS is not shown on a cockpit instrument. What can be read in the cockpit, however, is indicated airspeed – and this depends on the dynamic pressure $\tfrac{1}{2}\ rho$ $V\text{-}squared$.

We need to be careful in our discussion not to become confused between TAS and IAS. Where you see V, think of true airspeed (TAS), and where you see the formula $\tfrac{1}{2}\ rho\ V\text{-}squared,$ think of dynamic pressure and indicated airspeed (IAS).

▢ **TAS determines** the distance travelled through the air.

▢ **IAS determines** the aerodynamic effects – the lift and the drag.

Attitude in Level Flight

To obtain the required lift, at low speed a high angle of attack (high C_{Lift}) is required, while at high speed only a small angle of attack (low C_{Lift}) is needed.

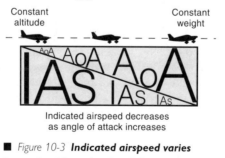

Indicated airspeed decreases
as angle of attack increases

■ *Figure 10-3* **Indicated airspeed varies inversely with angle of attack**

Since we are considering level flight, the pilot 'sees' these angles as an aeroplane pitch attitude relative to the horizon – nose-up at low speeds and fairly nose-level at high speeds.

The Effect of Weight on Level Flight

In a normal flight the weight gradually reduces as fuel is burned-off. If the aeroplane is to fly level, the lift produced must gradually decrease as the weight decreases.

If there is a sudden decrease in weight, say by half a dozen parachutists leaping out, then to maintain straight and level flight the lift must reduce by a corresponding amount. The C_{Lift} (angle of attack) or the airspeed must be reduced so that lift generated is less.

Suppose that the aeroplane is flying at a particular angle of attack, say at that for the best L/D ratio (about 4°). To maintain this most efficient angle of attack (C_{Lift} for best L/D ratio) as the weight reduces, the velocity factor V must be reduced to lower the lift produced so that is still balances the weight.

So, if the height and the angle of attack are kept constant, then the airspeed will have to be reduced. The power (thrust) will be adjusted to balance the drag. For most efficient flying (best L/D ratio), the cruising speed will decrease with decreasing weight.

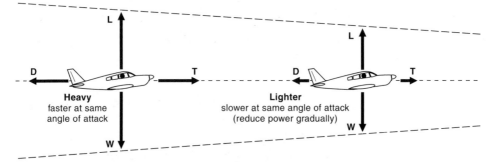

■ *Figure 10-4* **Same angle of attack – lighter aeroplane must fly slower**

If the power is kept constant and you want to maintain height as the weight decreases, the lift must be decreased by lowering the angle of attack (decreasing the C_{Lift}). Therefore the speed will increase until the power produced by the engine–propeller is equalled by the power required to overcome the drag.

If you want to keep the speed constant and maintain height, then as the weight reduces you must reduce the lift produced, and you do this by decreasing C_{Lift} (angle of attack). In cruising flight this will mean less drag, and therefore the power required from the engine–propeller is less. If the power is not reduced as the weight decreases, the airspeed will tend to increase.

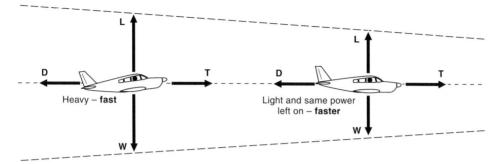

■ *Figure 10-5* **Same power – lighter aeroplane has lower angle of attack and flies faster**

If your aim is to maintain a constant airspeed, then you would raise the nose a little to avoid the airspeed increasing. Without any reduction in power, the aeroplane would commence a climb and gradually a new set of equilibrium conditions (balance of forces) would establish themselves for a steady climb – no longer level flight. (This is covered in Chapter 11, *Climbing*.)

A practical relationship to remember is that:

> **Power + Attitude = Performance** *(airspeed or rate of climb)*

If you have excess power, then you can adjust the attitude so that the height remains the same and the airspeed increases; or you can hold the attitude for the same airspeed and accept an increase in the rate of climb.

Sometimes the weight increases in flight, for instance by the formation of ice on the structure. An increased weight will mean that increased lift is required to maintain level flight – and once again the above discussion applies, but in reverse.

Frost on a wing disturbs the airflow, reduces its lifting ability, and can prevent an aeroplane from becoming airborne.

ICE ACCRETION means more than just a weight addition. If ice forms on the wings, especially on the upper surface near the leading edge, it will cause a drastic decrease in the lift-producing qualities (C_{Lift} for a particular angle of attack) of the wing. There will also be a significant increase in drag. The aeroplane must be flown at a greater angle of attack to return C_{Lift} to its original value, and so the speed will decrease unless power is added.

If ice forms on the propeller blades, it diminishes their thrust-producing qualities. Icing means reduced performance all round, so avoid it if possible.

> The remainder of this chapter goes a little beyond what is required for *The Aeroplane – Technical exam* but is useful reference material.

Performance in Level Flight

The thrust required for steady (unaccelerated) straight and level flight is equal to the drag (T = D) and so the thrust-required curve is identical to the familiar drag curve.

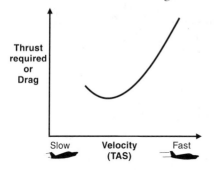

■ *Figure 10-6* **The thrust-required curve (or the drag curve)**

Note the following points from the thrust-required or drag curve (Figure 10-6):

☐ **High thrust** is required at high speeds and low angles of attack to overcome what is mainly parasite drag.

☐ **Minimum thrust** is required at the minimum drag speed (which is also the best L/D ratio speed, since L = W in straight and level flight and D is at its minimum value).

☐ **High thrust** is required at low speeds and high angles of attack to overcome what is mainly induced drag (caused in the production of lift).

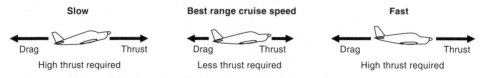

■ *Figure 10-7* **Both low speed and high speed require high thrust**

The engine–propeller combination is a power-producer (rather than a thrust-producer like a jet engine). The fuel flow (in litres per hour or gallons per hour) of an engine–propeller combination is a function of power produced (rather than thrust).

Power is defined as the *rate* of doing work, or the speed at which an applied force moves a body. Therefore the power required for flight depends on the product of:

☐ **thrust required;** and

☐ **flight velocity** (true airspeed).

We can develop a power-required curve from the thrust-required curve (Figure 10-6) by multiplying the *thrust required at a point on the curve* by the *TAS at that point*. This will give us the power required to maintain level flight at that speed, see Figure 10-8.

These graphs are easy to understand if you take it slowly. If you want to fly at a particular velocity (TAS), then by reading up from that TAS on the airspeed axis, the power curve will tell you the power that the engine–propeller must deliver. This power will supply sufficient thrust to balance the drag and maintain speed straight and level.

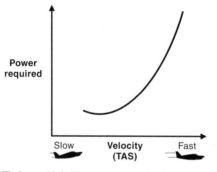

■ *Figure 10-8* **The power required curve**

In straight and level flight you would set the attitude for the desired airspeed (different airspeeds require different angles of attack) and adjust the power to maintain this speed.

Maximum Level Flight Speed

Maximum level flight speed for the aeroplane occurs when the power available from the engine–propeller matches the power required to produce enough thrust to balance the drag at the high speed. At higher speeds, there is insufficient power available.

Minimum Level Flight Speed

At low speeds (slower than the minimum drag speed), higher power from the engine–propeller is required to provide thrust to balance the higher drag (mainly induced drag).

The minimum level flight speed is usually not determined by the power capabilities of the powerplant, but by the aerodynamic capabilities of the aeroplane. As airspeed reduces, the stalling angle is reached, or some condition of instability or control difficulty usually occurs, prior to any power limitation of the powerplant.

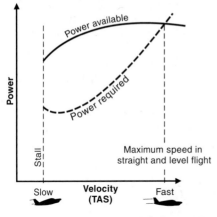

■ *Figure 10-9* **Maximum level flight speed**

Maximum Range Speed

For propeller-driven aeroplanes maximum range in still air is achieved at the TAS which allows:

- ■ **maximum air distance** for a given fuel burn-off; or conversely
- ■ **minimum fuel burn-off** for a given air distance (i.e. the lowest *fuel burn-off/air distance* ratio).

> Maximum range speed occurs at the TAS where drag is least and the L/D ratio greatest.

By converting burn-off and air distance to rates, this ratio becomes *fuel burn-off per unit time/air distance per unit time*, i.e. *fuel flow/TAS*. Since fuel flow depends on power, the ratio becomes *power/TAS*, and maximum range will be achieved at the TAS for which this ratio is least. This occurs at the point on the power vs TAS curve where the tangent from the origin meets the curve. At all other points, the ratio *power/TAS* is greater.

Power is defined as *force × velocity*, so:

$$Power\ required\ =\ thrust\ required \times TAS$$
$$=\ drag \times TAS\ (since\ thrust = drag)$$

therefore:

$$Power/TAS\ ratio\ =\ \frac{drag \times TAS}{TAS}$$
$$=\ drag$$

The power/TAS ratio will have a minimum value when actual drag is a minimum, i.e. maximum range TAS is the TAS for minimum total drag.

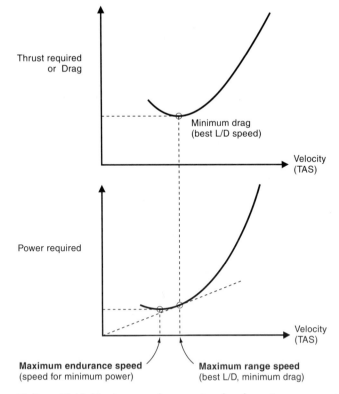

■ *Figure 10-10* **Maximum endurance speed and maximum range speed**

Performance Equals Power Plus Attitude

While in flight you of course do not refer to these graphs. Instead you adjust both the power from the engine–propeller and the pitch attitude of the aeroplane to achieve the desired performance.

> **Power + Attitude = Performance**

To sum up, the maximum range speed shows up on the drag curve at the minimum drag point (which, as explained earlier, is also the point of maximum L/D ratio).

Maximum Endurance Speed

Maximum endurance speed occurs at the TAS where power is minimum.

Maximum endurance means either:

☐ **the maximum time in flight** for a given amount of fuel; or
☐ **a given time in flight** for the minimum amount of fuel.

It is appropriate to fly at maximum endurance speed when the speed over the ground is not significant, for instance when:

☐ **holding overhead** or near an aerodrome waiting to land; or
☐ **conducting a search** in a specific area.

Since fuel flow for an engine–propeller combination depends on power set, minimum fuel flow (and therefore maximum endurance) will occur when minimum power is required.

Speed Stability

HIGHER SPEED RANGE. In the higher speed range above minimum drag speed, any minor speed fluctuation (due to say a gust or wind variation) is corrected without any pilot action. This is called **speed stable.**

An increase in airspeed will increase the total drag, as can be seen from the drag curve, mainly due to an increase in parasite drag. This drag increase is not balanced by the thrust from the powerplant and so the aeroplane slows down.

A decrease in airspeed due to a gust will decrease the total drag (due mainly to a decrease in parasite drag) and the thrust, which now exceeds the drag, will cause the aeroplane to accelerate back to its original speed.

In the normal flight range (above the minimum drag speed) the pilot does not have to be too active on the throttle since the aeroplane is speed stable and, following any disturbance, will tend to return to its original equilibrium airspeed without pilot action.

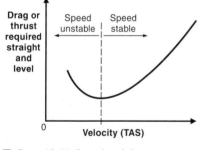

■ *Figure 10-11* **Speed stability**

LOWER SPEED RANGE. At low airspeeds towards the stalling angle it is a different matter, however. If a gust causes airspeed to decrease, the total drag increases (due to an increase in induced drag) and D now exceeds T, causing the aeroplane to slow down even further unless the pilot responds with more power.

If a gust causes airspeed to increase, the total drag decreases (due to a decrease in induced drag) and D is now less than T, causing the aeroplane to accelerate further away from the original speed unless the pilot reacts by reducing power.

In low-speed flight (near the stalling angle), the pilot needs to be fairly active on the power lever(s) to maintain the desired speed (e.g. in a precautionary approach to land in a short field).

The thrust required for steady straight and level flight is equal to the drag, and so the curve is identical to the familiar drag curve – which is a graph of drag versus speed.

Straight and Level Flight at Altitude

At any altitude, if the aeroplane is in steady straight and level flight the lift must balance the weight.

$$Lift = C_{Lift} \times \tfrac{1}{2}\, rho\ V\text{-squared} \times S$$

As altitude is increased, air density (*rho*) decreases. One way to generate the required lift and compensate for the decreased density (*rho*) is for the pilot to increase the true airspeed V so that the value of ½ *rho V-squared* remains the same as before, i.e. the decrease in *rho* with altitude can be compensated for with an increase in V (the TAS) so that ½ *rho V-squared* remains the same.

The term ½ *rho V-squared* (dynamic pressure) is related to the indicated airspeed and the pilot can read it in the cockpit on the airspeed indicator. If ½ *rho V-squared* remains the same, the indicated airspeed (IAS) remains the same. (More about the difference between IAS and TAS in Chapter 25, *Pressure Instruments*.)

> To produce the same lift at a different altitude, you still fly at the same indicated airspeed (true airspeed will increase).

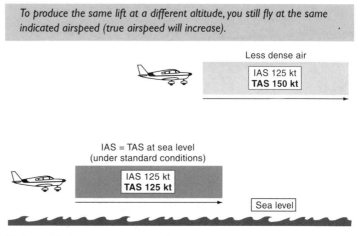

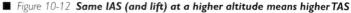

■ *Figure 10-12* **Same IAS (and lift) at a higher altitude means higher TAS**

At higher altitudes the maximum power available from the engine–propeller will be less than at sea level.

Now complete **Exercises 10 – Straight and Level.**

Climbing

As an aeroplane climbs, it is gaining potential energy (the energy of position, in this case due to altitude). An aeroplane can do this by making either:

- ☐ a zoom climb; or
- ☐ a steady climb.

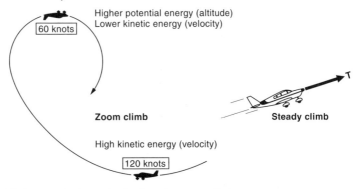

Higher potential energy (altitude)
Lower kinetic energy (velocity)

60 knots

Zoom climb

Steady climb

High kinetic energy (velocity)

120 knots

■ *Figure 11-1* **A steady climb and a zoom climb**

Climbing can be a temporary gain in height for a loss in airspeed, or it can be a long-term steady climb.

ZOOM CLIMB. A zoom climb is climbing by exchanging the kinetic energy of motion ($\frac{1}{2}mV^2$) for potential energy (mgh), i.e. by converting a high velocity V to an increase in height h by zooming the aeroplane. Zooming is only a transient (temporary) process, as the velocity cannot be decreased below flying speed.

Of course, the greater the speed range of the aeroplane and the greater the need for a rapid increase in attitude, the greater the value and capability of zooming. For example, a jet fighter being pursued at high speed can gain altitude rapidly with a zoom, or an aerobatic glider can convert the kinetic energy of a dive into potential energy at the top of a loop.

STEADY CLIMB. A steady climb is climbing by converting propulsive energy in excess of that needed for straight and level flight to potential energy. The propulsive energy comes from fuel energy which is converted to propulsive energy via the engine and propeller. In this way a steady climb can be maintained. It is the steady climb that is of importance to us.

Forces in the Climb

We assume that, for the normal steady en route climb, the thrust force acts in the direction of flight, directly opposite the drag force. The lift force acts perpendicular to the direction of flight. The weight force acts vertically, but note how, in the climb, it has a component that acts in the direction opposing flight.

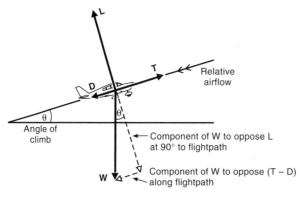

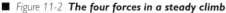

■ *Figure 11-2* **The four forces in a steady climb**

If you maintain a **steady climb** at a constant indicated airspeed, the engine–propeller must supply sufficient thrust to:
- [ ] **overcome the drag** force;
- [ ] **help lift the weight** of the aeroplane at a vertical speed, known as **rate of climb.**

In steady climb there is no acceleration. The system of forces is in equilibrium and consequently the resultant force acting on the aeroplane is zero.

An interesting point is that, when climbing, the lift force (developed aerodynamically by the wing at 90° to the direction of flight) is marginally less than the weight. The equilibrium is possible because the excess force of *thrust minus drag* has a vertical component to help balance the weight force.

> *In a climb: thrust is greater than drag; lift is less than weight.*

Angle of Climb (Climb Gradient)

The angle of climb depends directly on the **excess thrust** (the thrust force in excess of the drag force) and the weight. A heavy aeroplane will not climb as well as when it is lighter. The higher the weight, the poorer the climb performance.

The lower the weight (W), the greater the angle of climb. A light aeroplane can climb more steeply than a heavy one. Thrust is used to overcome drag. If the engine–propeller can provide thrust in excess of that needed to balance the drag, then the aeroplane is capable of climbing.

The greater the thrust (T), the greater the angle of climb. The lower the drag (D), the greater the angle of climb. For good climb-gradient capability, the aeroplane should generally be kept in a low-drag configuration, e.g. flaps up. This is a very important consideration for take-off. Flap for take-off decreases the take-off run prior to lift-off, but once in flight the angle of climb may be less due to the higher drag with flaps down.

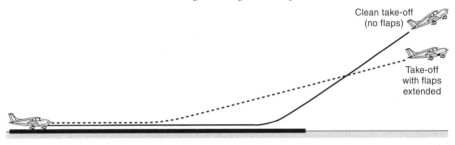

Clean take-off
(no flaps)

Take-off
with flaps
extended

■ *Figure 11-3* **Climb gradient may be less with flaps extended**

Since the pilot normally cannot vary the weight significantly in flight, the only way to improve the angle of climb is to make sure the aeroplane is 'clean' (low drag), and to fly at the speed which gives the maximum **excess thrust** force.

Rate of Climb

Vertical velocity is called **rate of climb** and is usually expressed in feet per minute (fpm or ft/min). A rate of climb (RoC) of 500 fpm means that the aeroplane will gain 500 ft of altitude in one minute. Rate of climb is shown in the cockpit on the vertical speed indicator (VSI).

The greater the excess power, the greater the rate of climb. The lower the weight, the greater the rate of climb. The maximum rate of climb usually occurs at a speed somewhere near that for the best lift/drag ratio, and is faster than the speed for maximum angle of climb (gradient).

The best rate of climb speed will gain altitude in the shortest time.

Various Climb Speeds

When considering climb performance, you must think of both angle (gradient) and rate, and then choose the climb speed which best suits the situation.

MAXIMUM GRADIENT (ANGLE) CLIMB is used to clear obstacles, as it gains the greatest height in the shortest *horizontal distance*. **Maximum gradient speed** (V_X) is the lowest of the three climb speeds.

It is usually carried out at high power and for only sufficient time to clear obstacles. The low speed leads to less cooling and consequently higher engine temperatures, so should only be used for short periods while clearing obstacles.

MAXIMUM RATE CLIMB is used to reach cruise altitude as quickly as possible, as it gains the most height in the shortest time. **Maximum rate climb speed** (V_Y) is usually near the speed for the best lift/drag ratio.

CRUISE CLIMB is a compromise climb that allows for a high speed (to hasten your arrival at the destination) as well as allowing the aeroplane to gain height and reach the cruise altitude without too much delay. It also allows for better engine cooling due to the higher speed, and better forward visibility because of the lower pitch attitude. The cruise climb will be a shallower climb at a higher airspeed.

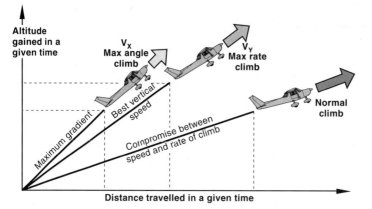

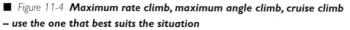

■ Figure 11-4 **Maximum rate climb, maximum angle climb, cruise climb – use the one that best suits the situation**

Refer to your Pilot's Operating Handbook or Flight Manual for the various climb speeds for your particular aeroplane. Typically, maximum gradient climb speed (V_X) is about 10 kt less than maximum rate climb (V_Y).

Factors Affecting Climb Performance

Performance in the climb, either angle or rate of climb, will reduce when:
- ▢ power is reduced;
- ▢ aeroplane weight is increased;
- ▢ temperature increases because of lower air density;
- ▢ altitude increases because of lower air density; and
- ▢ the incorrect airspeed is flown (either too fast or too slow).

Temperature

High ambient temperatures decrease climb performance. If the temperature is high, then the air density (*rho*) is less. The engine–propeller and the airframe will both be less efficient, so the performance capability of the aeroplane is less on a hot day than on a cold day.

Altitude

Increasing altitude decreases climb performance. Power available from the engine–propeller decreases with altitude. Even though sea-level performance can be maintained to high altitudes with supercharging, sooner or later power available starts to fall off. The climb performance, the rate of climb, and the angle of climb capability, will therefore all decrease with altitude.

The altitude at which the climb performance falls close to zero and a steady climb can no longer be maintained is known as the **ceiling**. The **service ceiling** is the altitude at which the steady rate of climb has fallen to just 100 ft/min. The **absolute ceiling** is the slightly higher altitude at which the steady rate of climb achievable at climbing speed is zero (and therefore almost impossible to climb to).

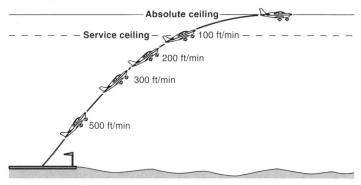

■ *Figure 11-5* **Climb performance decreases with altitude**

The aircraft Flight Manual and Pilot's Operating Handbook normally contain a table or graph with climb performance details. See Figure 11-6 for an example.

Flying Too Fast

If you fly faster that the recommended speeds, say at the speed where the *thrust = drag,* and the *power available = power required,* then there is no excess thrust to give you an angle of climb, and no excess power to give you a rate of climb. The aeroplane can only maintain level flight. At higher speeds, there would be a thrust deficiency and a power deficiency, causing the aeroplane to have an angle of descent and a rate of descent, rather than a climb.

MAXIMUM RATE OF CLIMB

CONDITIONS:
Flaps Up
Full Throttle

NOTE:
Mixture leaned above 3,000 feet for maximum rpm.

WEIGHT LBS	PRESS ALT FT	CLIMB SPEED KIAS	RATE OF CLIMB – FPM			
			−20°C	0°C	20°C	40°C
1,670	S.L.	67	835	765	700	630
	2,000	66	735	670	600	535
	4,000	65	635	570	505	445
	6,000	63	535	475	415	355
	8,000	62	440	380	320	265
	10,000	61	340	285	230	175
	12,000	60	245	190	135	85

Climbing IAS for best rate of climb decreases with altitude.

Rate of climb decreases with altitude increase.

Rate of climb decreases with temperature increase.

> **Climb performance** decreases as air density decreases (at high altitudes and high air temperatures).
> **Climbing IAS** for best performance decreases as altitude is gained.

■ *Figure 11-6* **A typical climb performance table**

Flying Too Slowly

Flying slower than the recommended speeds will cause the excess thrust and excess power to be less than optimum (due to the high drag and high angles of attack that they must overcome) and so climb performance will be decreased. At low speed the engine–propeller loses efficiency and produces less thrust. The aeroplane at low speed has a high drag (mainly induced drag). Eventually the aeroplane will come up against the stall if flown too slowly.

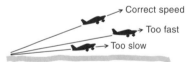

→ Correct speed
→ Too fast
→ Too slow

■ *Figure 11-7* **The correct climb speed for the best performance**

Climbing flight is possible in the speed range where the engine–propeller can produce sufficient power to provide excess thrust (i.e. thrust in excess of drag). On the low speed side you may be limited by the stalling angle.

The Effect of a Steady Wind on Climb Performance

The aeroplane flies in the medium of air and it 'sees' only the air. Rate of climb will not be affected by a steady wind. Similarly, the angle of climb through the air will not be affected by a steady wind.

> A headwind increases climb performance. A tailwind reduces it.

However, if we consider the angle of climb (or the gradient of climb) over the ground (the flightpath), a headwind increases the effective climb gradient over the ground and a tailwind decreases the effective climb gradient over the ground.

Taking off into wind has obvious advantages for obstacle clearance – it improves your clearance of obstacles on the ground.

> Wind does not affect rate of climb, but does affect angle of climb over the ground.

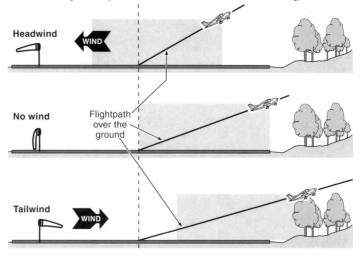

■ *Figure 11-8* **Wind affects the flightpath achieved over the ground**

The Effect of Windshear

A **windshear** is defined as a change in wind direction and/or speed in space. A windshear is a changing wind. This can mean a wind whose speed alters as you climb or descend to a different altitude. It can mean a wind whose direction changes from place to place or it can mean an updraft or a downdraft that an aircraft has to fly through. Windshear is generally understood to mean a wind change within a short distance or a short space of time.

OVERSHOOT EFFECT. Flying into an **updraft** will increase the rate of climb and will increase the angle of climb relative to the ground. Flying into a **downdraft** will have the opposite effect.

Due to its own inertia (or resistance to change), an aeroplane flying into an increasing headwind will want to maintain its original speed relative to the ground. Thus the effect of flying into an increasing headwind will be to increase the airspeed temporarily.

Attempting to maintain the correct climbing speed by raising the nose will lead to increased climb performance (only transient as the shear is flown through).

In this way, the climb performance will increase when flying into an increasing headwind, a decreasing tailwind or into an updraft. The aeroplane has a tendency to overshoot, or go above, the original flightpath, or to gain airspeed temporarily – hence the term **overshoot effect**.

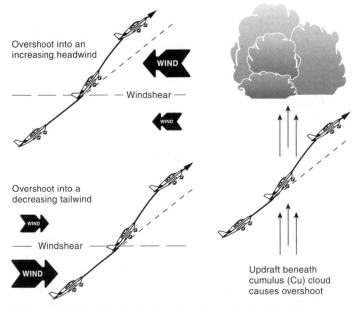

Overshoot into an
increasing headwind

WIND

— — — —Windshear—

WIND

Overshoot into a
decreasing tailwind

WIND

— Windshear —

WIND

Updraft beneath
cumulus (Cu) cloud
causes overshoot

■ *Figure 11-9* **Overshoot effect is a (temporary) gain in performance**

Again, the advantages of taking off into wind are obvious. Wind strength usually increases as you climb away from the ground, so you would normally expect an aircraft taking off into the wind to climb into an increasing headwind. This leads to increased climb performance over the ground, i.e. a steeper climb-out gradient over ground obstacles.

UNDERSHOOT EFFECT. Taking off downwind, the aeroplane would normally climb into an area of increasing tailwind. Due to its inertia, the aeroplane would temporarily tend to maintain its original speed over the ground, leading to a decreased airspeed. To maintain the target climb speed, the pilot would have to lower the nose. Climb performance, both rate and gradient, would fall off.

Exactly the same effect of decreased climb performance will occur flying into an increasing tailwind, a decreasing headwind, or a downdraft. The aeroplane will tend to fall below the original flightpath, or to lose speed, hence the term **undershoot effect.**

An initial overshoot effect (for example, when flying into an increasing headwind coming out of the base of a cumulonimbus storm cloud) may be followed by a severe undershoot effect as you fly into the downdraft and then the rapidly increasing tailwind. Treat cumulonimbus clouds with great caution.

Avoid flying near cumulo-nimbus (Cb) clouds.

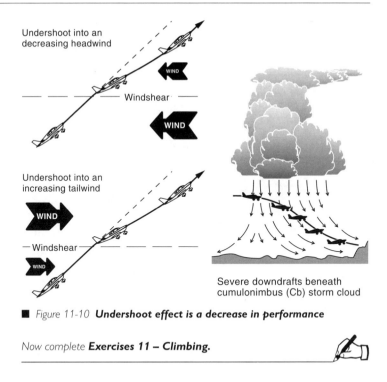

Undershoot into an
decreasing headwind

Windshear

Undershoot into an
increasing tailwind

Windshear

Severe downdrafts beneath
cumulonimbus (Cb) storm cloud

■ *Figure 11-10* **Undershoot effect is a decrease in performance**

Now complete **Exercises 11 – Climbing.**

Descending

In a steady glide lift, weight and drag are in equilibrium.

If an aeroplane is descending, with no thrust being produced by the engine–propeller, only *three* of the four main forces will be acting on the aeroplane – **weight, lift and drag.** In a *steady* glide these three forces will be in equilibrium as the resultant force acting on the aeroplane is zero.

Suppose that the aeroplane is in steady straight and level flight and the thrust is reduced to zero. The drag force is now unbalanced and will act to decelerate the aeroplane – unless a descent is commenced where the component of the weight force acting in the direction of the flightpath is sufficient to balance the drag. This effect allows the aeroplane to maintain airspeed by descending and converting potential energy due to its altitude into kinetic energy (motion).

Resolving the forces in the flightpath direction shows that a component of the weight force acts along the flightpath in a descent, balancing drag and contributing to the aeroplane's speed.

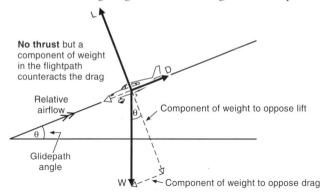

■ *Figure 12-1* **In a glide, a component of weight balances the drag**

Resolving the forces vertically, the weight is now balanced by the total reaction (the resultant of the lift and drag).

Maximum glide range is obtained if the aeroplane is at the best L/D ratio (minimum drag).

Notice that the greater the drag force, the steeper the glide. The shallowest glide is obtained when, for the required lift, the drag is least, i.e. at the best lift/drag ratio.

☐ **If the L/D is high,** the angle of descent is shallow, i.e. a flat gliding angle, and the aeroplane will glide a long way.

☐ **If the L/D is low** (a poor situation), with a lot of drag being produced for the required lift, then the aeroplane will have a large angle of descent, i.e. a steep glide angle, and will therefore not glide very far.

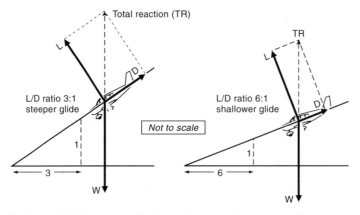

■ *Figure 12-2* **Lift and drag balance the weight in a steady glide**

Two points can be made here:

1. An aerodynamically efficient aeroplane is one which can be flown at a high lift/drag ratio. It has the capability of gliding further for the same loss of height than an aeroplane that is flown with a lower L/D ratio.

2. The same aeroplane will glide furthest through still air when it is flown at the angle of attack (and airspeed) that gives its best L/D ratio. This angle of attack is usually about 4°.

Because you cannot read angle of attack in the cockpit, flying at the recommended gliding or descent speed (in the Pilot's Operating Handbook) will ensure that the aeroplane is somewhere near this most efficient angle of attack.

Factors Affecting Glide Angle

Airspeed

If the aeroplane is flown at a smaller angle of attack (and therefore faster), the L/D ratio will be less and the aeroplane will not glide as far – it will 'dive' towards the ground faster and at a steeper angle.

> *The wrong airspeed (too fast or too slow) steepens the glide.*

If the aeroplane is flown at a greater angle of attack (lower airspeed) than that for the best L/D ratio, the L/D ratio will be less and therefore the optimum glide angle will not be achieved. This may be deceptive for the pilot – the nose attitude may be quite high, yet the aeroplane is descending steeply. The wrong airspeed (too fast or too slow) steepens the glide.

> To glide the furthest in still air, fly at the recommended airspeed (and therefore angle of attack) that gives the best lift/drag ratio.

If you are gliding at the recommended airspeed and it looks as if you will not reach the desired point, do not raise the nose to increase the glide distance. It will not work! The higher nose attitude may give the appearance of stretching the glide, but in fact it will decrease your gliding distance.

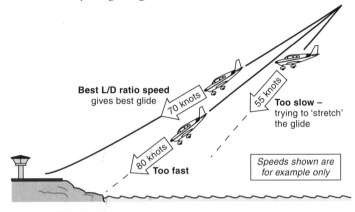

Best L/D ratio speed
gives best glide

70 knots

55 knots

Too slow –
trying to 'stretch'
the glide

80 knots

Too fast

Speeds shown are
for example only

■ *Figure 12-3* **The flattest glide is achieved at best L/D airspeed**

Flap Setting

Flaps reduce the L/D ratio and steepen the glide.

Any flap settings will increase the drag more than the lift and consequently the L/D ratio is lower. This gives a steeper glide (increases the glide angle).

The smaller flap settings increase lift significantly, with only a small increase in drag – hence the name **lift flaps** sometimes given to low flap settings.

The larger flap settings give large increases in drag with only a small increase in the lift – hence the name **drag flaps** for the larger flap settings. Large flap settings will give a much steeper glide. And the lower nose attitude required with flap extended gives the pilot much better visibility.

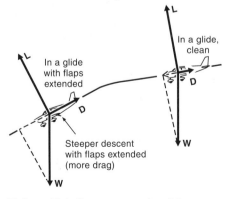

L

In a glide,
clean

L

D

In a glide
with flaps
extended

D

W

Steeper descent
with flaps extended
(more drag)

W

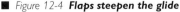

■ *Figure 12-4* **Flaps steepen the glide**

Weight

If the weight is less, the aircraft will have a lower airspeed at any particular angle of attack compared to when it is heavy.

At the angle of attack for the best L/D ratio (and therefore for the best glide), the airspeed will be lower but the glide angle the same. This also means that the rate of descent for the aeroplane when it is lighter will be less.

The recommended gliding speed (stated in the Flight Manual and Pilot's Operating Handbook) is based on maximum all-up-weight. The variation in weight for most training aircraft is not large enough to significantly affect the glide if the recommended glide speed is used at all times – even though, theoretically, a slightly lower glide speed could be used when lightly-loaded.

> *Reduced weight does not change the glide angle, but reduces the best gliding speed.*

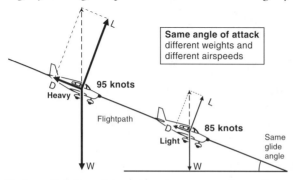

■ *Figure 12-5* **Best glide angle is the same at all weights (best L/D) but airspeed must be lower at lower weights**

The recommended descent speed in your Pilot's Operating Handbook will be suitable for all normal weights of your light training aircraft.

Gliding Distance over the Ground

A headwind reduces the gliding distance over the ground, even though it does not affect the gliding distance through the air, nor does it affect the rate of descent.

> *A headwind reduces glide distance over the ground. A tailwind increases it.*

■ **Glide angle** means relative to the *air mass* and is not affected by wind.

■ **Flightpath** means relative to the *ground* and is affected by wind.

The aeroplane 'sees' only the air in which it is flying. Figure 12-6 shows three identical glides through an air mass – same airspeed, same nose attitude, same angle of attack, same rate of descent (therefore same time taken to reach the ground) in all three cases. The only difference is that the air mass is moving over the ground in three different ways and carrying the aeroplane with it. The ground distance covered differs.

> *Wind does not affect rate of descent.*

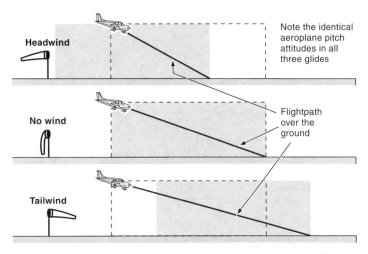

■ Figure 12-6 **More ground is covered gliding with a tailwind and less with a headwind**

A tailwind increases the gliding distance over the ground (even though is does not affect the gliding distance relative to the air mass nor the rate of descent).

Still Air Gliding Distance

If you refer to Figures 12-2 and 12-3 of the forces acting in a glide you will see that, for the best L/D ratio, the gliding distance is furthest.

If the L/D ratio is 5:1, the aeroplane will glide five times as far as it will descend. If you are 1 nautical mile high (about 6,000 ft), you will glide for about 5 nautical miles. If you are at about 12,000 ft (2 nm), you will glide approximately 10 nm.

An aeroplane with a L/D ratio of 12:1 will glide 12 times further horizontally in still air than the height it descends. See Figure 12-7.

Controlling the Powered Descent

Power Flattens the Descent

Flatten the descent by increasing power.

If the engine–propeller is producing power, then the thrust force will help overcome part of the drag force. The result is that the aeroplane will have a shallower descent angle and a lower rate of descent than in the power-off glide. Of course, with sufficient power, the descent angle may be zero, i.e. the aeroplane will fly level. With even more power, the aeroplane may climb. See Figure 12-8.

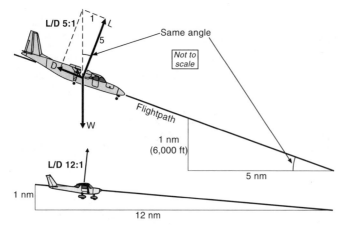

■ Figure 12-7 **'Air distance/altitude' is the same ratio as 'lift/drag'**

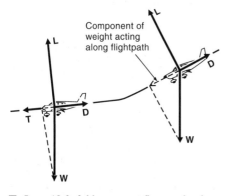

■ Figure 12-8 **Add power to flatten the descent**

Flaps Steepen the Descent

If you are sinking *beneath* your desired flightpath, the correct procedure is to apply some power and raise the nose (raising the nose
alone simply worsens the situation by steepening the glide). Any
change in power will require some small adjustments to the nose
attitude for the desired airspeed to be maintained.

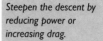

Steepen the descent by
reducing power or
increasing drag.

If you are descending *above* your desired descent path, there are
two things that you can do:

☐ **reduce the thrust,** and/or

☐ **increase the drag** by extending the flaps, or lowering the landing gear. Usually when you extend the flaps, a lower nose attitude is required.

Now complete **Exercises 12 – Descending.**

Turning

Forces in a Turn

A moving body tends to continue moving in a straight line at a constant speed (from Newton's first law of motion). To change this state – either to change the speed or to change the direction, i.e. to accelerate the body – a force must be exerted on the body (Newton's second law of motion).

A body constrained to travel in a curved path has a natural tendency to travel in a straight line, and therefore to fly off at a tangent. To keep it on its curved path, a force must continually act on the body forcing it towards the centre of the turn. This is called the **centripetal force.**

Holding a stone tied to a string, your hand supplies a 'lift' force equal and opposite to the weight of the stone. If you swing the stone in a circle, your hand supplies not only a vertical force to balance the weight but also a centripetal force to keep the stone turning. The total force exerted through the string is greater and you will feel the increase.

The horizontal component of the lift force provides the centripetal force that pulls the aircraft into a turn.

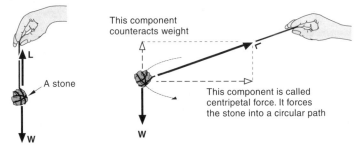

■ *Figure 13-1* **Centripetal force pulls a body into a turn**

To turn an aeroplane, some sort of force towards the centre of the turn needs to be generated. This can be done by banking the aeroplane and tilting the lift force so that it has a sideways component.

Flying straight and level, the lift force from the wings balances the weight of the aeroplane. If you turn the aeroplane, the wings still need to supply a vertical force to balance the weight (unless you want to descend) plus a centripetal force towards the centre of the turn to keep the turn going.

The lift force in a level turn will be greater than the lift force when flying straight and level. To develop this increased lift force at the same airspeed, the angle of attack of the aerofoil must be increased by backward pressure on the control column.

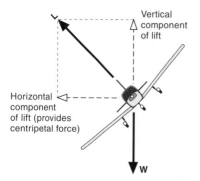

■ *Figure 13-2* **By banking, lift from the wings provides a centripetal component**

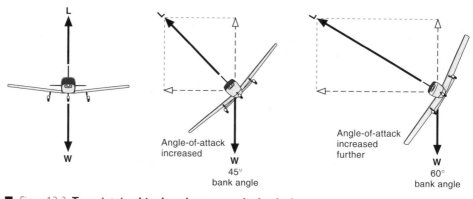

■ *Figure 13-3* **To maintain altitude – the steeper the bank, the greater the lift force required from the wings**

The steeper the level turn, the greater the lift force required. You turn the aeroplane using **ailerons** (to select the bank angle) and **elevator** (to increase the angle of attack and increase the lift generated). You use the ailerons to maintain the desired bank angle and the elevator to maintain the desired altitude. The rudder (as yet) has not been necessary.

The stability designed into the aeroplane may make it resist turning, and the application of a little rudder (left rudder for a left turn and vice versa) helps bring the tail around and turn the nose into the turn, i.e. the rudder is used to *balance* the turn.

You are forced into the turn along with the aeroplane and feel this as an increase in the force exerted on you by the seat; it feels like an apparent increase in your weight.

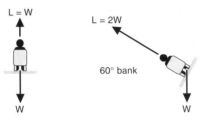

■ *Figure 13-4* **The steeper the bank, the greater the g-forces**

Load Factor in a Turn

Load factor increases as bank angle increases.

In straight and level flight, the wing produces a lift force *equal* to the weight, i.e. L = W. The load factor is said to be 1. You experience a force from the seat equal to your normal weight, and feel it as 1g.

In a banked turn of 60°, the wings produce a lift force equal to *double* the weight, i.e. L = 2W. This means the loading on the wings is doubled when compared to straight and level flight, i.e. each square metre of wing has to produce twice as much lift in a 60° banked turn as it does in straight and level flight. You experience a force from the seat equal to twice your weight. This is 2g and the load factor is 2.

The load factor is the ratio of the lift force produced by the wings compared to the weight force of the aeroplane.

$$\text{Load factor} = \frac{\text{lift}}{\text{weight}} = \frac{\text{wing loading in manoeuvre}}{\text{wing loading straight and level}}$$

At angles of bank beyond 60°, the lift force generated by the wings must increase greatly so that its vertical component can balance the weight – otherwise height will be lost.

Increased lift from the wings means increased wing loading and an increased **load factor**. We can show this in a curve of load factor versus bank angle (Figure 13-5).

NOTES:

☐ **In a 30° banked turn** you will experience 1.15g load factor. The wings will produce 15% more lift than when straight and level, and you will feel 15% heavier.

☐ **At 60° bank angle,** the load factor is 2. The wings have to produce a lift force equal to double the weight to maintain height. The g-force is 2g, and you will feel twice as heavy.

☐ **At 70° bank angle,** the load factor is 3.

☐ **At 80° bank angle,** the load factor is 6. The wing is required to produce 6 times the lift as in straight and level flight for the aeroplane to be capable of an 80° banked turn without losing height – this requires a very-high-performance aeroplane.

■ **In a 90° banked turn,** the lift force is horizontal, and, even if of infinite size, would have no vertical component to balance weight. Therefore height cannot be maintained.

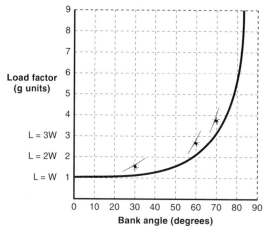

■ *Figure 13-5* **Load factor versus bank angle**

Thrust in a Turn

In a turn, increased lift from the wings is required to maintain height. This is achieved by applying back-pressure on the control column to increase the angle of attack.

In a turn, extra thrust is required to maintain height and airspeed.

The steeper the bank angle, the greater the angle of attack and back-pressure required. As we saw in our discussion on drag, an increase in the angle of attack will lead to an increase in induced drag. If a constant airspeed is to be maintained in a level turn, an increase in thrust is required to balance the increased drag in a turn.

If extra thrust is not added the airspeed will reduce in a level turn. Airspeed could be maintained by allowing the aeroplane to lose height, i.e. to trade potential energy for kinetic energy.

The Stall in a Turn

In a turn, the angle of attack has to be greater than at the same speed in straight and level flight. This means that the stalling angle of attack will be reached at a higher speed in a turn – the steeper the angle of bank, the higher the airspeed at which the stalling angle of attack is reached.

The stalling angle of attack occurs at higher airspeeds in a level turn.

■ **At 30° bank angle,** the stall speed is increased by 7% over the straight and level stall speed.
■ **At 45° bank angle,** the stall speed is increased by 19%.
■ **At 60° bank angle,** the stall speed is increased by 41%.
■ **At 75° bank angle,** the stall speed is increased by 100%.

If your aeroplane stalls at 50 kt straight and level, then in a 60° banked turn it will stall at (141% of 50 kt) = 71 kt – a significant increase. In steep turns, you will feel the onset of the stall buffet at these higher speeds.

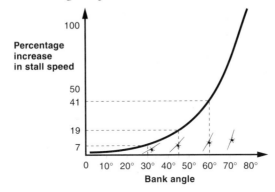

■ *Figure 13-6* **Percentage increase in stall speed versus bank angle**

Overbank in Level and Climbing Turns

To commence a level turn, you apply bank with the ailerons. Once the aircraft starts turning, the outer wing travels faster than the inner wing and so generates more lift. The tendency is for the bank angle to increase.

To overcome the tendency to overbank in a level turn, once in the turn you may have to hold-off bank.

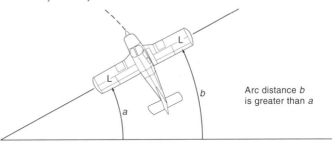

Arc distance *b* is greater than *a*

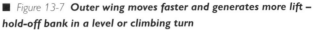

■ *Figure 13-7* **Outer wing moves faster and generates more lift – hold-off bank in a level or climbing turn**

In a climbing turn, the outer wing travels faster and produces more lift than the inner wing.

There is a second effect to consider also: that as the inner and outer wings climb through the same height, the outer wing travels a greater horizontal distance as it is on the outside of the turn.

The angle of attack of the outer wing is greater than that for the inner wing and so the lift produced by the outer wing in a climbing turn will be even greater. Once in a climbing turn, you may have to hold-off bank to avoid the turn becoming too steep – there is no need to plan this, just watch what is happening and hold the desired bank angle with the ailerons.

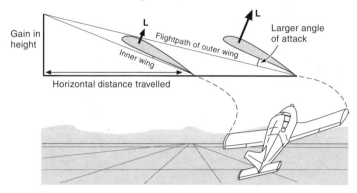

■ *Figure 13-8* **Tendency to overbank in a climbing turn**

Underbank/Overbank in Descending Turns

In a descending turn, the outer wing travels faster and wants to produce more lift than the inner wing, but, due to the descent, the inner wing travels a smaller horizontal distance for the same height loss when compared to the outer wing and so has a larger angle of attack. Therefore, the inner wing tends to produce more lift – and the two effects may cancel out.

In a descending turn, you may have to hold bank on (or off), depending on the aircraft. Again, there is no need to plan this, just hold the desired bank angle with the ailerons.

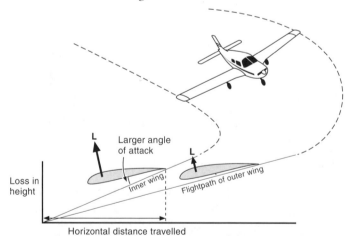

■ *Figure 13-9* **Underbanking tendency – due to larger angle of attack on inner wing in a descending turn (higher speed of outer wing may compensate)**

Balancing the Turn

The pilot banks the aeroplane using the ailerons, and exerts back pressure on the control column, using the elevator to increase the angle of attack and the lift produced. The natural stability of the aeroplane will cause it to turn its nose into the turn, due to the sideslip effect on keel surfaces behind the centre of gravity.

There is an effect that tends to turn the nose away from the turn – known as **aileron drag.** As the outer aileron goes down into the high pressure area under the wing, it not only causes increased lift (to bank the aeroplane by increasing the angle of attack of the up-going wing), but also suffers increased induced drag.

This increase in drag on the up-coming wing causes the nose to yaw in the direction opposite to the turn – and this is neither comfortable nor efficient. The aircraft is said to be *slipping* into the turn. The rudder ball will be on the down-side of the turn. You will feel as though you are slipping down to the low side of the aircraft (see Figure 13-10).

SLIPPING TURN

Pilot slips
into turn

■ *Figure 13-10* **Slipping turn: more right rudder required**

By pressuring the rudder ball back into the centre with the appropriate foot, the nose of the aircraft (and the tail) is yawed so that the longitudinal axis of the aeroplane is tangential to the turn. The rudder ball will be in the centre and the turn will be balanced. You will feel comfortable in the seat and not as though you are slipping down into the turn.

BALANCED TURN

■ *Figure 13-11* **A comfortable and balanced turn**

If the tail tends to skid onto the outside of the turn, the rudder ball (and you) will also be thrown to the outside. If the ball is out to the left, use left rudder pressure to move it back into the centre.

SKIDDING TURN

Pilot thrown
to outside of turn

■ *Figure 13-12* **Too much right rudder in this case – a skidding turn**

Constant Angle Turn

An aeroplane in a 30° banked turn will travel around different circular paths depending on its airspeed. At low speed the turn is tighter (the radius of turn is smaller) than at high speed.

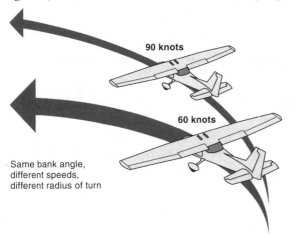

90 knots

60 knots

Same bank angle,
different speeds,
different radius of turn

■ *Figure 13-13* **Turning performance is increased at low airspeeds**

Constant Radius Turn

To fly a turn of the same radius at a higher speed a greater bank angle is required.

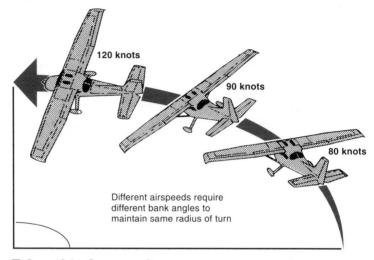

Different airspeeds require different bank angles to maintain same radius of turn

■ *Figure 13-14* **Constant radius turn**

Constant Speed Turn

At a constant airspeed, the greater the bank angle, the tighter the turn (the smaller the radius of turn) and the greater the rate of turning (in degrees per second).

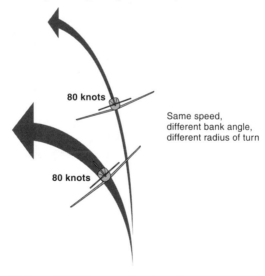

Same speed, different bank angle, different radius of turn

■ *Figure 13-15* **A steeper bank angle at constant speed increases turn performance**

Constant Rate Turn

The **rate of turn** of an aircraft in degrees per second is important. Instrument flying usually requires **rate-1** (or standard-rate) turns of 3° per second. This means that the aeroplane will turn through:

☐ **180° in 1 minute;**
☐ **360° in 2 minutes.**

A rate-1 turn at a higher airspeed requires a steeper angle of bank.

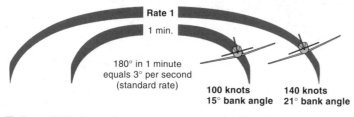

■ *Figure 13-16* ***A rate-1 turn requires steeper bank at higher speed***

An easy way to estimate the bank angle (in degrees) required for a rate-1 turn is: ¹⁄₁₀ of the airspeed in knots, plus ½ of this.

For example, the required bank angle for a rate-1 turn at 120 kt is 120 ÷ 10 = 12, plus ½ of this (12 ÷ 2) = + 6 =18°.

A rate-2 turn is 6° per second.

Now complete ***Exercises 13 – Turning.***

Stalling

The airflow around an aerofoil varies as the angle of attack is increased. For most conditions of flight this flow is streamline flow and Bernoulli's theorem applies – increased velocity goes hand in hand with decreased static pressure. The increased flow velocity (especially over the upper surface of the wings) leads to decreased static pressure – so a lift force is generated. Drag is also present.

The lifting ability, or coefficient of lift, of the aerofoil increases as the angle of attack increases – but only up to a **critical angle.**

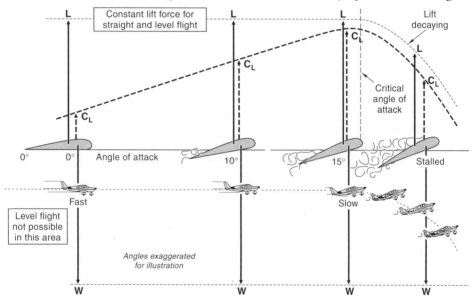

■ *Figure 14-1* **An aerofoil reaches C$_{Lift\ max}$ at the critical angle**

Ideally the airflow around an aerofoil is streamline. In real life the streamline flow breaks away (or separates) at some point from the aerofoil surface and becomes turbulent. At low angles of attack this separation point is towards the rear of the wing and the turbulence is not significant.

At higher angles of attack the separation point moves forwards. As the angle of attack is increased, a critical angle is reached beyond which the separation point will suddenly move well forward, causing a large increase in the turbulence over the wing.

The formation of low static pressures on the upper surface of a wing (the main contributor to the generation of the lift force) is reduced by the breakdown of streamline flow. Turbulent flow does not encourage the formation of low static pressure areas.

The lifting ability of a wing (coefficient of lift, C_L) decreases markedly beyond this critical angle of attack as a result of the breakdown of streamline flow.

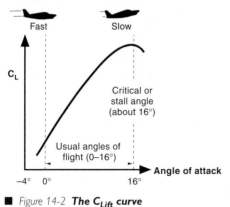

■ *Figure 14-2* ***The C_{Lift} curve***

A stall occurs at the critical angle of attack.

The significant breakdown of streamline flow into turbulence over a wing is called **stalling** of the aerofoil. The **critical angle** or **stalling angle** of attack is where C_L reaches its maximum value and beyond which C_L decreases markedly.

Beyond the stalling angle, the centre of pressure (which has been gradually moving forward as angle of attack increases) suddenly moves rearwards and there is also a rapid increase in drag.

Recognition of the Stall

There are natural and artificial warnings of an impending stall.

Approaching the stalling angle of attack, the streamline flow breaks down over parts of the wing and turbulent air flows back over the tailplane. The airframe may shake or *buffet* as a result – known as **pre-stall buffet** or **control buffet.**

At the stall, the decrease in lift will cause the aeroplane to sink. The rearwards movement of the centre of pressure will cause the nose to drop.

■ *Figure 14-3* ***Turbulent flow over the tailplane***

Stalling is associated with a particular angle of attack.

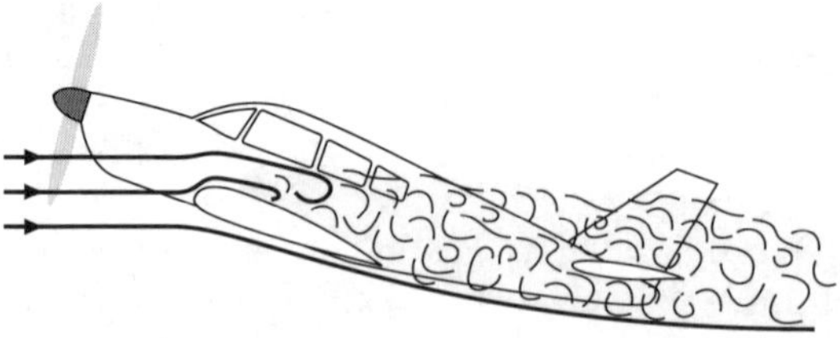

For most training aircraft, the stalling angle of attack is about 15° to 16°. $C_{Lift\ maximum}$ occurs at the stalling angle of attack, but beyond it C_{Lift} decreases.

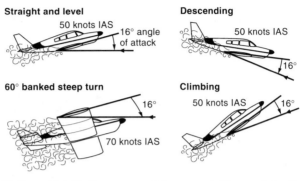

■ Figure 14-4 **Stalling occurs at the same stalling angle in all phases of flight**

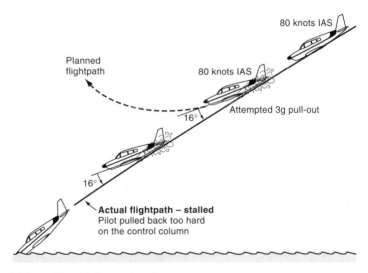

■ Figure 14-5 **High speed stall**

Recovery from the Stall

To recover from a stall, the angle of attack must be reduced. This is achieved by moving the control column forward to lower the nose. If airspeed is low, which is often the case, full power should also be applied to increase the airspeed as quickly as possible. Stall recovery should be initiated at the first indication of an impending stall.

Stalling Angle and Stalling Speed

The lift formula is:

$$Lift = C_{Lift} \times \tfrac{1}{2}\ rho\ V\text{-}squared \times S$$

Of the factors that determine the value of the lift force, the pilot can only readily change angle of attack (C_{Lift}) and indicated airspeed ($\tfrac{1}{2}\ rho\ V^2$). You can change these by altering the attitude and/or power. For a given aerofoil:

Stalling *occurs at a particular angle of attack.*
*When the aerofoil reaches this critical angle of attack – **it will stall.***

It does not matter what the airspeed is; if the stalling angle for a particular aerofoil is 16°, it will stall at 16° – irrespective of the airspeed.

A specific aerofoil will stall at a particular angle of attack, however the stall may occur, for example, at:

☐ **50 knots** straight and level for an aeroplane at maximum weight;
☐ **45 knots** straight and level when it is light;
☐ **54 knots** in a 30° banked turn;
☐ **70 knots** in a 60° banked turn; and
☐ **80 knots** if you experience 3g pulling out of a dive. (Do not bother memorising these figures.)

Also, the indicated airspeed (IAS) at which the aircraft stalls in straight and level flight is approximately the same at all altitudes.

Stalling depends directly on angle of attack and not on airspeed.

There is, however, some connection between *angle of attack* and *indicated airspeed*. Their precise relationship depends on:

☐ **lift** produced by the aerofoil;
☐ **weight**;
☐ **load factor**;
☐ **bank angle**;
☐ **power**; and
☐ **flap setting** (which changes aerofoil shape and therefore C_{Lift}).

Factors Affecting Stalling Speed

Square-Root of Lift

We have mentioned that *square laws* are common in nature. The principles involved in the production of lift are no exception:

$$Lift = C_{Lift} \times \tfrac{1}{2}\ rho\ V\text{-}squared \times S$$

Indicated airspeed (IAS) is directly proportional to true airspeed (TAS or V) and can be written as $IAS = k \times TAS$ or $IAS = k \times V$, where k is a constant at a particular altitude and whose value depends on the ratio of air density (*rho*) at sea level to the ambient air density at the aircraft's altitude. (Again, there is no need to remember this – it is discussed in more detail in Chapter 25, under *The Airspeed Indicator.*) We can now write the lift equation as:

Lift is a function of $C_L \times (IAS)^2$

At the stalling angle, the coefficient of lift reaches its maximum value, written as C_{Lmax}, and so the relationship at the stall becomes:

Lift *at the stall* is a function of $C_{Lmax} \times (IAS\ stall)^2$

Since C_{Lmax} will be constant for the particular aerofoil, the relationship can be simplified even further to:

Lift *at the stall* is a function of $(IAS\ stall)^2$

In other words, the square of the indicated stalling speed depends on the lift that the wing has to generate. Then, taking the square root of each side of this relationship, we can say:

Indicated airspeed *at the stall* depends on the square root of the lift. This means that:

> Anything that requires the generation of extra lift (such as extra weight or pulling g in a manoeuvre like turning) will cause an increase in the indicated stalling speed.

Mathematically these two statements may be written:

$$(IAS_{Stall})^2 \propto L$$

$\propto$ means *is proportional to,* or *varies directly with.*

$$\therefore\ IAS_{Stall} \propto \sqrt{L}$$

The airspeed that the performance of the aeroplane depends on, and the airspeed that the pilot can read in the cockpit, is the indicated airspeed (IAS). At the stall:

> Stalling speed depends on the square root of the lift required and the lift required depends on the weight and the load factor.

If the lift required is increased by 44% to 1.44 times the original lift, then the stalling speed will increase by the square root of 1.44, i.e. 1.2 times the original straight and level stalling speed – an increase of 20%. A straight and level stall speed of 50 kt would become 60 kt (a 20% increase) if, for some reason, a 44% increase in lift were required.

An increased lift (over and above that needed for straight and level flight, where L = W) is required for a steep level turn, or for pulling out of a dive or, indeed, whenever there is an increased load factor (L/W) and g-forces are experienced. Another name for load factor or g-forces is **dynamic loading.**

The stalling angle of attack remains the same (as always for a particular aerofoil), but the stalling speed increases whenever the dynamic loading or load factor increases.

Now, of course, you cannot sit in the cockpit and calculate the square root of this and that – but you do need to know that:

Stalling speed increases when load factor increases.
If you feel g-forces, then stalling speed is increased.

Estimating the Stalling Speed when Pulling g

If the load factor is greater than 1 (g is being pulled), then the stalling speed will be increased. When performing manoeuvres in flight you do not have time to do precise calculations, but you must be aware that stall speed will be increased quite significantly on occasions.

Pulling 4g (outside the limit of most training aeroplanes), the stalling speed is doubled, i.e. it increases by a factor equal to the square root of 4, which is 2.

Pulling 2g (say in a 60° banked turn), the stalling speed is increased by a factor equal to the square root of 2, i.e. 1.41, which is an increase of 41%. This is illustrated on the graph below.

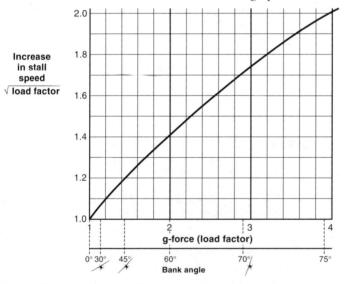

Examples

1. At 2g (load factor 2) the stall speed increases by 1.41, and at 3g by 1.73 times the level stall speed for the aeroplane.

2. In a 60° bank turn the load factor is 2 and the stall speed increase is by 1.41.

■ *Figure 14-6* **Increase in stall speed is a function of g; stalling speed increases in a turn (at which time load factor increases)**

As increased lift is required in a turn (because the lift force is tilted and yet a vertical component equal to weight must still be produced), the lift in a turn must exceed the weight, and therefore the load factor exceeds 1.

The steeper the turn, the greater the load factor (g-forces) and the higher the stalling speed. It is useful and practical to know the percentage increase in straight and level stalling speed at a few bank angles.

- **In a 30° banked turn, stalling speed increases by 7%.** In a 30° bank, lift must be increased from 100% to 115% of the straight and level value, i.e. to 1.15 times the original value. Therefore the stall speed will increase to (the square root of 1.15) = 1.07 times its original straight and level value, i.e. a 7% increase. A 50 kt stalling speed straight and level becomes 54 kt in a 30° banked turn.

- **In a 45° banked level turn, stalling speed increases by 19%.** In a 45° banked turn, lift is 1.41 times greater than the lift when straight and level. The load factor is 1.41. Therefore the stalling speed will increase to (the square root of 1.41) = 1.19 times its original value. A 50 kt stall speed straight and level becomes 60 kt in a 45° banked level turn.

- **In a 60° banked turn, stalling speed increases by 41%.** In a 60° banked turn, lift must be doubled to retain altitude, i.e. L is increased to 2 times its original value. The load factor is 2. Therefore the stalling speed will increase to (the square root of 2) = 1.41 times its original value. A 50 kt straight and level stalling speed becomes 71 kt in a 60° banked turn.

Load Factor

Stall speed increases with load factor, for a given weight.

Any time the lift force from the wings is increased, the load factor increases and the stalling speed increases. This will occur in turns, when pulling out of dives, in gusts and turbulence.

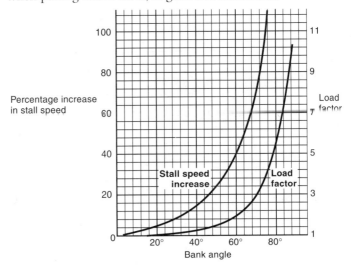

■ *Figure 14-7* **Stall speed increases with load factor**

What happens to stall speed can be represented graphically as in Figure 14-7. (There is no need to remember these graphs, but you should be able to interpret them. You may be presented with them in exams.) Just enter the graph with the information you have, and read off what you want to find.

Weight

In straight and level flight, sufficient lift must be generated to balance the weight. A heavier aeroplane means an increased lift force is required.

Stalling speed increases with weight (stall angle of attack stays the same).

We saw earlier that stalling speed varies with the square root of lift. If the weight decreases 20% to only 0.8 of its original value, then the stall speed will decrease to (the square root of 0.8) = 0.9 times its original value (9 × 9 = 81, so the square root of 80 is close to 9, and the square root of 0.8 is close to 0.9).

If the stalling speed at maximum all-up weight (say 2,000 kg) was stated in the Flight Manual to be 50 kt, then at 1,600 kg (20% less, and only 80% of the maximum weight), the stalling speed is only 90% of the original stalling speed (a drop of 10%), i.e. 45 kt.

Similarly, an increase in weight will give an increase in stalling speed.

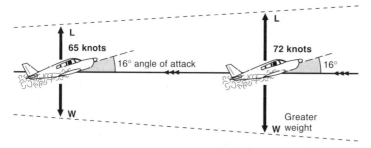

■ *Figure 14-8* **Stall speed is a function of weight**

The Flight Manual states the stalling speed for straight and level flight, with power off, at maximum allowable all-up weight.

Altitude

Stalling speed is a function of $C_{Lift\ max}$ (which occurs at the stalling angle) and indicated airspeed (which is related to ½ $rho\,V^2$).

Stalling indicated airspeed does not vary with altitude.

A variation in altitude will not affect $C_{Lift\ max}$ and so the stalling angle will be reached (straight and level) at the same stalling indicated airspeed.

Power

With power on, the slipstream adds kinetic energy (of motion) to the airflow. The separation of the airflow from the upper surface of the wing is delayed, and so the stall occurs at a lower indicated airspeed.

As the stalling angle is approached with power on, the high nose attitude allows the thrust to have a vertical component which will partially support the weight. Therefore, the wings are off-loaded a little and less lift is required from them. Less lift means a lowered stalling speed.

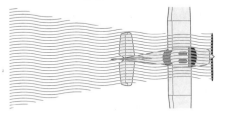

■ *Figure 14-9* **Slipstream can lower stalling speed**

As the power-on stall is approached, the slipstream will provide a fast airflow over the tailplane. The rudder and elevator will remain effective, but the ailerons, not being affected by the slipstream, will become 'sloppy' or less-effective.

If the slipstream encourages the generation of lift from the inner parts of the wing, then the outer sections of the wing may stall first. Any uneven production of lift from the outer sections of the two wings will lead to a rapid roll.

WASHOUT. If there is an uneven loss of lift from the outer sections of the wings near the tips by one of them stalling first, then a strong rolling moment is set up due to the long moment arm from the outer sections of the wing to the centre of gravity. Also, the effectiveness of the ailerons is affected.

Stalling at the wing-roots is preferable – it allows the control buffet over the tailplane (due to the turbulent air from the inner sections of the wing) to be felt, while the outer sections of the wings are still producing lift and the ailerons may still be effective. An uneven loss of lift on the inner sections, if one wing stalls ahead of the other, does not have as great a rolling moment.

The wing can have **washout** – a lower angle of incidence (and therefore a lower angle of attack) at the wing-tip compared with the wing-root. This means that the wing-root will reach the stalling angle prior to the wing-tip. (Washout also helps to reduce the induced drag from wing-tip vortices.)

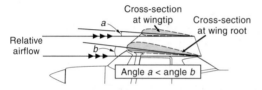

■ *Figure 14-10* **In-built washout causes the wing-tip to stall later than the root**

Stalling at the wing-root first can be achieved in a number of ways by the designer. For instance, small metal plates can be placed at the inboard leading edges to encourage the early onset of the stall at the wing-root.

Ice, Frost and other Wing Contamination

Ice accretion has two effects:

1. **Ice-accretion on the wings** (particularly the front half of the upper surface where most of the lift is generated) will cause a breakdown or streamline flow at angles of attack well below the normal stalling angle. Therefore stalling will occur at higher speeds.

Ice, frost or other wing contamination increases stalling speed.

2. **Ice increases weight,** and so the stall speed will be increased.

Any ice at all, even if only the texture of very fine sandpaper, should be removed from the wing prior to flight. It pays to remove any accumulation of such things as insects and salt from the wing leading edges for the same reason.

Flaps

Extending flaps gives a new aerofoil shape with an increased $C_{Lift\ max}$, i.e. the 'new' aerofoil has a greater lifting ability and can support the same load at a lower speed. The airspeed can decrease to a lower value before $C_{Lift\ max}$ is reached and the wing stalls.

Flap extension decreases the stalling speed.

The lowering of stalling speeds is the main advantage of flaps. It makes for safe flight at lower speeds – very useful for take-offs, landings (shorter fields) and low-speed searches. Extending trailing edge flaps allows lower nose-attitudes. Not only is visibility increased, but the stalling angle will be reached at a lower nose-attitude also.

The stall with flaps extended may be accompanied by a wing-drop. Use rudder to pick it up, not aileron. Because of the increased drag with flaps extended, any speed loss, especially with power-off, could be quite rapid, with little advance warning to the pilot of an impending stall.

Use rudder to correct a wing drop.

In the stall with flaps down, turbulence over the tailplane may cause very poor control from the elevator – known as *blanketing* of the elevator. Some training aircraft have a T-tail with the tailplane high on the fin to avoid blanketing of the elevator in the stall.

Stall Warning Devices

Most aircraft are fitted with a device such as a horn, flashing red light or a whistle to warn of an impending stall. Such a device is only secondary to the aerodynamic stall warnings that you must learn to recognise, such as stall buffet, decreasing speed, g-forces or load factor, and less-effective controls.

The Spin

To spin, an aeroplane must first be stalled.

The spin is a condition of stalled flight in which the aeroplane follows a spiral descent path, following a yaw with a wing drop on the point of stall. In a spin the aeroplane is:

☐ stalled;
☐ rolling;
☐ yawing;
☐ pitching;
☐ sideslipping; and
☐ rapidly losing height.

How a Spin Develops

A spin is a condition of stalled flight, so the first prerequisite is that the wings be at a high angle of attack. This is achieved by moving the control column progressively back, as in a normal stall entry.

A wing-drop is essential to enter a spin and this may occur by itself or (more likely) be induced by the pilot yawing the aeroplane with rudder or 'misusing' the ailerons just prior to the aeroplane stalling. During a premeditated spin entry, as the pilot yaws the aeroplane near the point of stall:

☐ **the outer wing speeds up** and generates more lift, causing it to rise; its angle of attack decreases, taking it further from the stalling angle; and
☐ **the inner wing slows down** and generates less lift, causing it to drop; its angle of attack increases and the dropping wing stalls (or, if already stalled, goes further beyond the stalling angle).

Autorotation will commence through the dropping wing becoming further stalled, with a consequent decrease in lift and increase in drag. The aeroplane will roll, a sideslip will develop and the nose will drop. If no corrective action is taken, the rate of rotation will increase and a spin will develop. It will be an unsteady manoeuvre with the aeroplane appearing to be very nose-down. The rate of rotation may increase quite quickly and the pilot will experience a change of g-loading.

An aeroplane will not usually go straight from the stall into a spin. There is usually a transition period which may vary from aeroplane to aeroplane, typically taking two or three turns in the unsteady and steep autorotation mode, before settling into a fully-developed and stable spin.

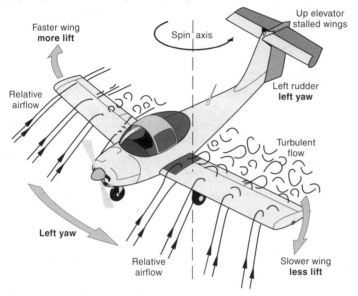

■ Figure 14-11 **The aeroplane in a spin**

Misuse of Ailerons

Trying to raise a dropped wing with opposite aileron may have the reverse effect when the aeroplane is near the stall. If, as the aileron goes down, the stalling angle of attack is exceeded, instead of the wing rising it may drop quickly, resulting in a spin. This is the spin entry technique on some aircraft types.

On some aeroplanes, misuse of ailerons can cause a spin.

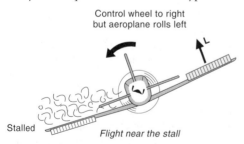

■ Figure 14-12 **Inducing a spin with opposite aileron**

It is not a requirement that full spins be carried out in PPL training, although they will be practised to the incipient spin stage before the wings pass through 90°. Pilots training in approved aeroplanes may have the opportunity to practise fully developed spins.

Instrument Indications

The best instrument to use in identifying the direction of spin is the turn coordinator or turn indicator. The attitude indicator may have toppled and be useless. The coordination ball will be unreliable, but usually settles in the bottom left hand corner of the instrument *irrespective* of spin direction.

NOTE If the spin is *inverted*, the turn coordinator will also be unreliable. Aerobatic pilots be warned!

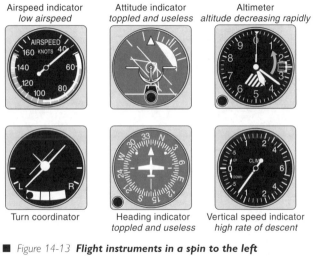

Airspeed indicator
low airspeed

Attitude indicator
toppled and useless

Altimeter
altitude decreasing rapidly

Turn coordinator

Heading indicator
toppled and useless

Vertical speed indicator
high rate of descent

■ *Figure 14-13* **Flight instruments in a spin to the left**

Now complete **Exercises 14 – Stalling.**

Section **Two**

Airframe, Engines
and **Systems**

The Airframe

Aeroplane Components

The major components of an aeroplane are:
- the fuselage;
- the wings;
- the tail assembly;
- the flight controls;
- the landing gear (or undercarriage);
- the engine and propeller.

Fuselage

The fuselage forms the body of the aeroplane to which the wings, tail, engine and landing gear are attached. It contains a cabin with seats for the pilot and passengers, plus the cockpit controls and instruments, and may also contain baggage lockers.

The fuselage of many modern training aircraft is of semi-monocoque construction, a light framework covered by a skin (usually aluminium) that carries much of the stress. It is a combination of the best features of a strut-type structure, in which the internal framework carries almost all of the stress, and a monocoque structure which, like an egg-shell, has no internal structure, the stress being carried by the 'skin'.

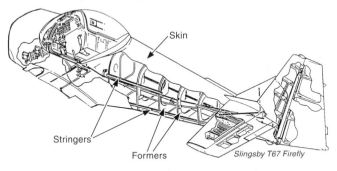

Skin

Stringers

Formers

Slingsby T67 Firefly

■ *Figure 15-1* **Typical semi-monocoque construction**

Wings

The wings are designed to generate lift and are exposed to heavy loads, well in excess of the total weight of the aeroplane in manoeuvres. Wings generally have one or more internal **spars** attached to the fuselage and extending to the wingtips. The spars carry the major loads, which are upward bending where the lift is generated and downward bending where they support the fuselage and the wing fuel tanks.

In addition to the spar(s), some wings also have external **struts** to provide extra strength by transmitting some of the wing loads to the fuselage.

Ribs, roughly perpendicular to the spar(s), assisted by stringers running parallel to the spars, provide the aerofoil shape and stiffen the skin which is attached to them. The ribs transmit loads between the skin and the spar(s).

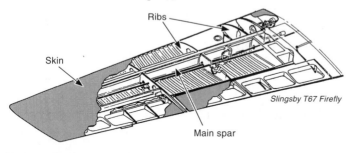

■ Figure 15-2 **Spars, ribs and formers in the wing**

Monoplanes are designed with a single set of wings placed such that the aeroplane is known as either a high-wing, low-wing, or mid-wing monoplane. The *Cessna 172* is a high-wing monoplane; the *Piper Warrior* is a low-wing monoplane. Biplanes, such as the *Tiger Moth* or *Pitts Special,* are designed with a double set of wings.

■ Figure 15-3 **Monoplanes, and a biplane**

Ailerons are fitted at the outer trailing edge of each wing, and move in opposite directions to allow the pilot to control roll. **Wing flaps** are fitted on the inner trailing edges and are lowered in unison to increase the lifting ability of the wing, or to increase its drag. The wings in most aeroplanes also contain **fuel tanks.**

Tail
The **tail** unit is generally built similarly to the wings and consists of a vertical and horizontal stabiliser to which the **rudder** and **elevator** are attached. There are variations in design: some aeroplanes have a stabilator (all-flying tailplane), others have a ruddervator (combined rudder and elevator) in the form of a butterfly tail, and

yet others have a high T-tail. The elevator (and, on some aircraft, the rudder) will have a **trim tab.** This enables the pilot to remove prolonged loads on the controls aerodynamically.

Flight Controls

The main flight controls (elevator, ailerons and rudder) are operated from the cockpit, usually via an internal system of cables and pulleys. Turnbuckles may be inserted in the cables to allow adjustment of their tension. This should only be done by qualified personnel.

To protect the control surfaces from excessive movement in flight and on the ground, there are usually *stops* fitted to the structure as well as stops in the flight control system itself, (e.g. to physically limit the control column movement).

Landing Gear

The landing gear (or undercarriage) supports the weight of the aeroplane when it is on the ground and may be of either the tricycle type with a nosewheel or the tailwheel type. Most tricycle landing gear aeroplanes are fitted with nosewheel steering through the rudder pedals, and almost all aeroplanes have main wheel brakes. Advanced aeroplanes have retractable landing gear; most training aeroplanes have fixed landing gear. Landing gear and brakes are covered in detail in Chapter 24.

Engine–Propeller

The engine is usually mounted on the front of the aeroplane, and separated from the cockpit by a **firewall.** In most training aeroplanes, the engine drives a fixed-pitch propeller. More on engines in Chapters 16 to 21.

Tie-Down

At the end of a flight, consideration should be given to the safety of the aeroplane if it is to be left outside overnight or if strong winds or a weather change for the worse is forecast. A normal procedure is to chock the wheels and to tie the aeroplane down.

Ensure that a **tie-down kit** is carried on overnight flights or whenever you think a tie-down might be necessary. A typical tie-down kit will contain at least:

- [ ] **3 tie-down ropes** of adequate length;
- [ ] **3 pegs;**
- [ ] a hammer or mallet;
- [ ] a minimum of two **wheel chocks.**

PARK THE AEROPLANE INTO WIND or facing into any expected wind, set the brakes to PARK (refer to the Flight Manual to check if this is recommended for your aeroplane) and chock the wheels.

Chock both in front of and behind the wheels to prevent movement in any direction.

On some aeroplanes the nosewheel or the tailwheel can be locked straight, (e.g. the *Dakota (DC-3)* and *Thrush Commander*). As well as assisting in directional control on the ground during take-off and landing, having the wheel locked straight helps prevent the tail from swinging around when parked in a wind – so lock the tailwheel when parking, if your aeroplane has this facility.

LOCK THE CONTROL SURFACES. Some aircraft have a control column lock (e.g. *Cessna 172*), which, by locking the control column, holds the control surfaces firm. Other aircraft have external locks that can be fitted to prevent control surface movement, (e.g. aileron locks for a *Fokker Friendship*). Care must be taken pre-flight to ensure the removal of any control surface locks – locked control surfaces are potentially disastrous!

TIE THE AEROPLANE DOWN. There are tie-down rings designed into the modern aeroplane somewhere along the wings, at the tail and possibly at the nose. In a field you may have to drive pegs into the ground and attach the tie-down ropes to them. The ropes attached to the wing should be angled forward and out, and the pegs driven in, in such a manner as to provide the best anchor. Some operators prefer two ropes from each wing point, one angled forward and out at 45° and the other angled rearward and out at 45°.

At permanent tie-down points on aerodromes, there are often tie-down anchors – large concrete blocks with metal rings or, better still, tie-down points already installed in the tarmac itself.

Nylon rope is better than manila rope, as it is more elastic and will not shrink when wet. Tie the aircraft down 'loosely, but not too loosely', using a non-slip knot. With manila tie-down ropes, leave a bit of slack. If the ropes are too tight, especially if it rains and the ropes shrink, stresses are placed on the airframe.

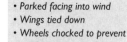

- Parked facing into wind
- Wings tied down
- Wheels chocked to prevent wind moving aircraft backward
- Tail rope stops aircraft moving backward.

■ *Figure 15-4* **How to tie-down the aircraft**

If the ropes are too loose, a wind could lift the aeroplane over the wheel-chocks, or cause it to jerk against the rope, placing stress on the airframe or pulling the peg out of the ground. Ensure that the tie-down ropes are of adequate strength.

COVER THE PITOT HEAD. Any contamination, (e.g. wasps) in the pitot tube or static vent can cause erroneous readings of the pressure instruments (airspeed indicator, altimeter). Once again, a pre-flight inspection should ensure their removal prior to flight.

COVER THE ENGINE OR THE ENGINE-OPENINGS to prevent birds or insects making a nest around the oil cooler and so on. Birds can build a complete nest within a matter of hours. Over-heating, possibly even an in-flight fire, can result.

LOCK THE DOORS AND WINDOWS after securing any loose equipment in the cockpit or in the cabin.

NOTE For full instructions on tie-down, etc., of your particular aeroplane, refer to the Pilot's Operating Handbook.

Cabin Fire

Although a rare event, cabin fire is a possibility, especially if passengers are careless with cigarettes. As well as causing distress to the pilot and passengers, fire can damage the aeroplane structure. A cabin fire should be quickly extinguished with the fire extinguisher and the cabin window or air vents opened to ensure that there is adequate ventilation and to remove the fumes from the fire and the extinguisher.

Cabin Ventilation, Heating and Demisting

Pilot comfort is important for safe and efficient flight and most aeroplanes have built-in ventilation and heating systems. Clear forward vision is important, so provision is usually made for hot air to be directed onto the windscreen when necessary to demist or defrost it.

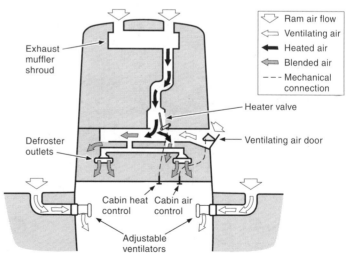

■ *Figure 15-5* **A typical cabin ventilation, heating and demisting system**

VENTILATION. Good ventilation is essential to ensure that the occupants have an adequate supply of fresh air. Directing flow from the cabin air vents over passengers is also useful in preventing and combating motion sickness.

CABIN HEAT. Cabin heat should be used to keep the cockpit environment comfortable enough to be able to fly in shirt sleeves. Many cabin heating systems use warm air from around the engine and exhaust manifold (where the air is heated) and allow the pilot to direct it to various points in the cabin. Temperature control can be achieved by mixing the heated air with the cooler ventilating air. Cabin heating is necessary in cold climates, but it may also be necessary in warm climates when flying at high altitudes (since, on average, temperature decreases by about 2°C per 1,000 ft gain in altitude).

CARBON MONOXIDE POISONING. There is a risk in using cabin heating that you should be aware of. Any leaks in the heat exchanger/exhaust manifold area could allow carbon monoxide from the engine to enter the cabin in the heating air. Carbon monoxide is produced during combustion and is a colourless, odourless, but very dangerous gas. It displaces oxygen from the blood and may cause:

- ☐ headache;
- ☐ dizziness;
- ☐ nausea;
- ☐ deterioration in vision;
- ☐ a slower breathing rate;
- ☐ unconsciousness; and
- ☐ death.

Engine smells from other exhaust gases associated with the carbon monoxide are a warning, and if carbon monoxide is suspected in the cabin, shut off all cabin heat, stop all smoking and increase the supply of fresh air through vents and windows. If oxygen masks are operational, then don them. Under normal conditions, you should always ensure some fresh and cool ventilating air is mixed with the heated air.

DEMISTING. Demisting and/or defrosting of the windscreen may be necessary from time to time when the aeroplane has been flying in cool and moist conditions. Hot air directed onto the inside of the windscreen should clear at least some of it from mist or, in icing conditions, frost or ice.

*Now complete **Exercises 15 – The Airframe.***

The Aeroplane Engine

Aeroplanes can be powered by a variety of engines, and the two fundamental types are **piston** or **reciprocating engines** and **gas turbines** (jets). The jet engine will not be considered in this manual.

The piston engine can be designed in various ways, many of which are suitable for aircraft. Older engine types often had the cylinders arranged **radially** around the crankshaft, for example the Pratt and Whitney radial engine in the *Dakota (DC-3), DHC Beaver* and *Harvard (T-6),* and the Bristol Centaurus engine in the *Tempest Mk II* fighter.

The *DHC Beaver* and the *Grumman Ag-Cat* are two types with radial engines which are still in widespread commercial use. Radial engines have an excellent power/weight ratio in the high power range required for operations such as agricultural spraying.

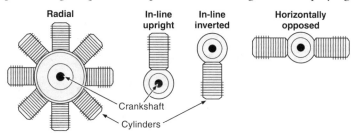

■ *Figure 16-1* **Common cylinder layouts in aircraft engines**

Some aircraft have **in-line engines,** where the cylinders are arranged in one line – the same basic design as in many cars. Some of the earliest aeroplanes had upright, in-line engines, with the cylinder head at the top of the engine and the crankshaft/propeller shaft at the bottom, e.g. the *de Havilland Cirrus Moth.*

Raising the thrust line to a suitable position, due to design requirements, put the cylinders and the main body of the engine in a very high position. This obscured the pilot's vision and prevented effective streamlining.

Another problem with a low crankshaft/propeller shaft is the ground clearance of the propeller, requiring long struts for the main wheels. The easiest way to solve this problem is to invert the engine and have the crankshaft/propeller shaft at the tip of the engine, quite different to automotive engine design where the crankshaft is always at the bottom. Many aircraft have inverted in-line engines, e.g. *Tiger Moth, Chipmunk.*

There are other possibilities as well, such as the V-engines and the H-engines (V and H describes the layout of the cylinders) used in military aircraft such as *Spitfires,* which required high horsepower (2,000–3,000 horsepower) from a compact engine.

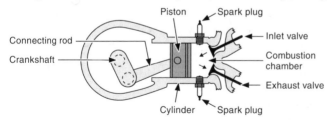

The **piston,** moving within the cylinder, forms one of the walls of the combustion chamber. The piston has rings which seal the piston in the cylinder, preventing any loss of power around the sides of the piston and passage of oil into the combustion chamber.

The **crankshaft** and **connecting rod** change the straight-line motion of the piston to a rotary, turning motion. The crankshaft also absorbs the power from all the cylinders and transfers it to the propeller.

The **connecting rod** forms a link between the piston and the crankshaft.

An **inlet valve** lets the fuel/air mixture into the cylinder.

The **cylinder** forms part of the chamber in which the fuel/air mixture is compressed and burned.

An **exhaust valve** lets exhaust gases out of the cylinder after the combustion process.

Spark plugs ignite the compressed fuel/air mixture.

■ *Figure 16-2* **Basic parts of a reciprocating engine**

The usual engine found in modern light aircraft is the reciprocating piston engine, with four, six, or eight cylinders in a **horizontally opposed configuration.**

The most common light aircraft powerplant is the horizontally opposed reciprocating engine.

Basic Principles of the Piston Engine

The reciprocating engine has a number of cylinders in which pistons move back and forth (hence the name *reciprocating engine*). In each cylinder a fuel/air mixture is burned, the heat energy causing the gases to expand and drive the piston down the cylinder. This is a conversion of chemical energy (in the fuel) to heat energy to mechanical energy.

The piston is connected by a rod to a shaft, which it turns. This *connecting rod,* or *conrod,* converts the back–forth motion of the piston into a rotary motion of the crankshaft, which transmits the power generated by the engine to the propeller. Light aircraft with fixed-pitch propellers (and most with constant-speed propellers) have the propeller directly coupled to the crankshaft, i.e. the crankshaft is also the propeller shaft. The propeller produces the thrust force necessary for powered flight.

Four-Stroke Engine Cycle

A complete cycle of this type of piston engine is comprised of four strokes of the piston travelling within the cylinder, hence the name *four-stroke engine*. Nikolaus Otto developed this engine in 1876, so the four-stroke cycle is also known as the *Otto cycle*. The four strokes are: **(1) intake** (or induction); **(2) compression; (3) power** (or expansion); **(4) exhaust.**

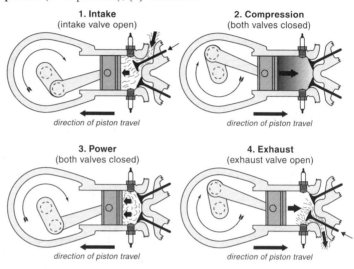

■ *Figure 16-3* **The four strokes of a reciprocating engine**

In the **intake** (or induction) **stroke,** the fuel/air mixture is 'sucked' or induced to flow into the cylinder. The piston moves from the top to the bottom of the cylinder, decreasing the pressure in the cylinder. This causes air to flow into the induction system, through the carburettor (where fuel is metered into the airflow to give a combustible fuel/air mixture) and on into each cylinder via the inlet manifold and (open) inlet valve.

Early in the **compression stroke,** the inlet valve closes and the piston moves back towards the tip (or head) of the cylinder. This progressively increases the pressure of the fuel/air mixture and, because of the compression, the temperature of the fuel/air mixture rises.

As the piston is completing the compression stroke, the fuel/air mixture is ignited by an electrical discharge between the spark plug electrodes and a progressive burning (or combustion) commences in the chamber. This causes the gases to expand and exert a strong pressure on the piston which, as it has now passed the tip of its stroke, is driven back down the cylinder in the **power stroke.**

Just prior to the completion of the power stroke, the exhaust valve opens and then, as the piston returns to the top of the cylinder in the **exhaust stroke,** the burned gases are forced out of the cylinder into the atmosphere via the exhaust manifold.

As the piston is approaching the cylinder head again, while the last of the burned gases is being exhausted, the inlet valve opens in preparation for the next induction stroke. And so the cycle continues ...

Notice that, in this one complete Otto cycle of the engine, of the four strokes of the piston only one stroke provided power, but the crankshaft (which carries this power to the propeller) has rotated twice.

To increase the power developed by the engine, and to provide smoother running, the engine has a number of cylinders whose power strokes occur at different positions during the revolution of the crankshaft. The spacing of these power strokes is equal so that evenly spaced power impulses are imparted to the crankshaft. Thus, in a full Otto cycle of a four-cylinder engine (common in light aircraft) the crankshaft would, in its two revolutions, receive power from four different power strokes – one per cylinder. In an engine with six cylinders, in two revolutions the crankshaft would receive six impulses of power – a smoother engine.

Engine Compression

Engines are designed so that the amount of compression pressure produced by the piston suits the type of fuel to be used. Higher compression gives more power (for a given engine cubic capacity) but requires a higher-quality fuel able to withstand high pressure and temperatures, and not explode or 'detonate' (see Chapter 18, *The Fuel System*). The penalty of the higher performance is more cylinder wear, however, in such engines.

The **compression ratio** of an engine is the ratio of the *total cylinder volume* with the piston at the bottom of its stroke (bottom-dead-centre) compared to the *clearance volume* above the piston when it is at the top of its stroke (top-dead-centre). The cylinder volume swept by the piston in the course of a stroke is known as the *swept volume*.

$$\text{So, } compression\ ratio = \frac{total\ volume}{clearance\ volume}$$

Valves and Valve Timing

The inlet valve, through which the fuel/air mixture is taken in, and the exhaust valve, through which the burned gases are exhausted, must open and close at the correct times with respect to the movement of the individual piston. To achieve this there is a **camshaft** which is gear-driven by the crankshaft.

The camshaft rotates at half crankshaft speed and in most engines operates rocker arms and push rods which push the appropriate valve open (against spring pressure) at what has been determined by the designer to be the most suitable time in the cycle.

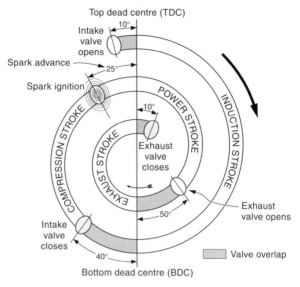

■ *Figure 16-4* **Typical valve timing in the four-stroke cycle**

A typical engine speed while cruising is 2,400 revolutions per minute – abbreviated to rpm (or rev/min). Each inlet valve opens once in the four strokes of the piston, i.e. once in every two revolutions of the crankshaft. The same applies to the exhaust valve.

The inlet and exhaust valves each open and close once in every two revolutions of the crankshaft. Therefore the camshaft rotates at half engine speed. At 2,400 rpm, each valve will open and close 1,200 times – 1,200 times in 60 seconds means 20 times a second – quite amazing.

The power that the engine can develop depends on how much fuel/air mixture can be induced through the inlet valve during the intake stroke- and the time involved is extremely short.

The inlet valve opening just prior to the piston reaching **top-dead-centre (TDC),** and not closing until the piston has passed **bottom-dead-centre (BDC),** following the induction stroke, allows maximum time for the intake of the fuel/air mixture to occur. This is called **valve lead** and **valve lag.** Similarly the exhaust valve opens just prior to the piston reaching BDC on the power stroke and remains open until a little after the piston passes TDC for the exhaust stroke and commences the induction stroke.

Power is increased by increasing the amount of fuel/air mixture entering the cylinder by extending the time of the intake stroke using valve lead and valve lag.

Note that, for a brief period at the start of the induction stroke, the burned gases are still being exhausted through the still-open exhaust valve while a fresh slug of fuel/air mixture is commencing induction through the just-opened inlet valve. This brief period when both the inlet and exhaust valves are open together is known as **valve overlap.**

Ignition

A high voltage (or high tension) spark occurs in the cylinder just prior to the piston reaching top-dead-centre shortly before it commences the power stroke. This slightly advanced spark enables a controlled flame-front to start moving through the fuel/air mixture that has been compressed in the cylinder. The burning gases then expand and exert a very high pressure on the piston during its downwards power stroke. The purpose of the ignition system is to provide this correctly timed spark to each cylinder.

Most aircraft engines have **dual** (and independent) **ignition** systems running in parallel with one another, with each system supplying one of the **two spark plugs per cylinder.** A dual ignition system is safer in the event of failure of one ignition system; and results in more even and more efficient fuel combustion.

Dual ignition is safer and results in improved fuel combustion.

The necessary high tension electrical current for the spark plugs comes from self-contained components called **magnetos,** with one magneto for each of the two ignition systems. Each magneto is mechanically driven by the engine and self-generates electrical power which is distributed to the spark plugs at the correct times.

The magneto consists of a magnet that is rotated (within the magneto housing) near a conductor which has a coil of wire wound around it. The rotation of the magnet induces an electrical current to flow in the coil. Around this (primary) coil is wound a secondary coil of many more turns of wire – a transformer – which transforms the primary voltage into a much higher voltage. The higher voltage is fed to each spark plug at the appropriate time, causing a spark to jump between the two electrodes and ignite the compressed fuel/air mixture in the combustion chamber.

The timing of the spark is critical. Each magneto has a set of **breaker points** which are forced open and shut by a small cam that is part of the rotating magnet shaft of the magneto. The breaker points are in the circuit of the primary coil and, when they open, the electrical current in the primary coil is interrupted. This sudden collapse of the primary current (aided by a condenser or capacitor placed across the points) induces the required high voltage in the secondary coil.

The **spark plug** is in the circuit of the secondary coil and the large voltage, something like 20,000 volts, across its electrodes causes a spark to jump between them.

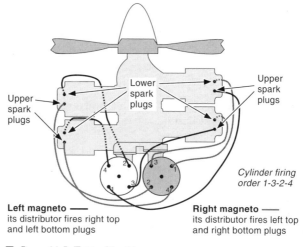

Cylinder firing order 1-3-2-4

Left magneto ——
its distributor fires right top and left bottom plugs

Right magneto ——
its distributor fires left top and right bottom plugs

■ Figure 16-5 **Typical ignition system**

As each cylinder is operating out of phase with the others, the current must be distributed to each spark plug at the correct moment (just prior to commencement of the power stroke). The **distributor**, which is part of the magneto, does this.

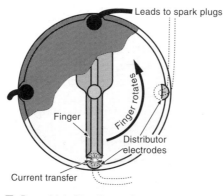

■ Figure 16-6 **Distributor finger**

Each cylinder fires once in every two revolutions of the crankshaft and the distributor has a rotor which is geared to the crankshaft in such a way that it turns once only for every two turns of the crankshaft. In other words, the distributor finger (rotor) turns once in every complete four-stroke cycle. Once during each turn the distributor rotor transfers the high tension secondary current to each cylinder, in the correct firing order.

Separate leads to each of the spark plugs belonging to that ignition system (one per cylinder) emanate from different terminals of the distributor case. These leads are often bound together, forming an **ignition harness.** Leakage of current from the ignition harness will lead to rough running. (This may occur at high altitudes, even if there is no leakage at sea-level.) One item of the pre-flight inspection is a visual check for chafing and heat cracking of those parts of the ignition harness easily seen.

The Starter

Most modern training aircraft have an **electric starter motor** that is powered by the battery and activated by turning the ignition key to the START position in the cockpit.

Starting the engine causes a very high current to flow between the battery and the starter motor, and this requires heavy duty wiring. If the ignition switch in the cockpit in its START position were directly connected into the starter circuit, heavy duty cabling to the cockpit switch would be required. This would have a number of disadvantages, including the additional weight of the heavy cable, a significant loss of electrical energy over the additional length, and high electrical currents through the cockpit environment (which would introduce an unnecessary fire risk). To avoid these disadvantages, the starter circuit connecting the battery to the starter motor is remotely controlled from the cockpit using a solenoid-activated switch.

By moving the ignition key to START, you cause a small current to flow through the starter key circuit and energise a **solenoid** (an electromagnet with a movable core). The energised solenoid operates a heavy duty switch that closes the heavy duty circuit between the battery and the starter motor. High current flows through this circuit, activating the starter motor which then turns the engine over.

Electric starters often have an associated **starter warning light** in the cockpit that glows while the starter is engaged. It should extinguish immediately you release the starter. If by any chance the starter relay sticks (so that electrical power is still supplied to the starter motor even though the starter switch has been released from the START position) the warning light will remain on. The engine should be stopped (mixture control to IDLE CUT-OFF) to avoid damage to the engine and/or starter motor.

NOTE On start-up of a cold engine, an oil pressure rise should be indicated on the oil pressure gauge within 30 seconds to ensure adequate lubrication (sooner if the engine, and its oil, is warm) – if an oil pressure rise is not indicated within this approximate time, shut the engine down to avoid possible damage.

Only one spark per cylinder is necessary for start-up, so the left magneto only is provided with a device called an impulse coupling (see page 174). When the ignition key is in the START position, the right magneto system is automatically de-energised and only the left magneto system provides a high tension supply to the spark plugs. After the start-up, the ignition key being returned to BOTH activates the right magneto system as well.

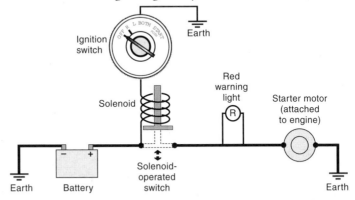

■ *Figure 16-7* **The electrical starter system**

Older aircraft which have the starter switch separate from the magneto switches, should only have the left magneto switch on for start-up. Once the engine is started, you should ensure that the engine is running on both magnetos.

There are two design limitations with magnetos that significantly affect starting an engine:

1. When you turn the engine over (either by hand-swinging the propeller or by an electric starter motor powered by the aircraft's battery), the engine rotates comparatively slowly (approximately 120 rpm, as against about 800 rpm at idle speed). Because the magneto rotates at half crankshaft speed (to supply one spark per cylinder every two revolutions of the crankshaft) magneto speed at start-up is therefore about 60 rpm or less. To generate a sufficiently high voltage to produce a spark to ignite the fuel/air mixture requires a magneto speed of about 100–200 rpm. Thus some device must be incorporated in the system to overcome this.

2. When the engine is running (800–2,400 rpm is typical operating range) the spark occurs at a fixed number of degrees *prior* to the piston reaching top-dead-centre at the commencement of the power stroke. This is known as **spark advance**. On start-up, with only very low revs occurring, unless the spark is **retarded** (delayed) until the piston is at or past top-dead-centre,

ignition of the gases could drive the piston down the cylinder prematurely, causing the crankshaft to turn in the wrong direction. This is called engine **kick–back.**

To overcome these two limitations, some devices have been developed for incorporation in the magneto; the most common in small aero engines is the **impulse coupling.** (In other engines a component called the induction vibrator is used, but this is not covered until CPL level.)

Impulse Coupling

The impulse coupling has two functions:

1. To accelerate the rotating magnet momentarily to generate a high voltage.

2. To effectively retard the ignition-timing at low cranking rpm until just after top-dead-centre, and then, immediately after start-up, allow the timing of the spark to return to its normal position just before top-dead-centre.

Impulse coupling generates a high voltage and retards the ignition timing to start the engine.

To accelerate the magnet, the impulse coupling initially prevents the magnet from rotating as the engine is turned over, the energy from the initial rotation being stored by winding up a coiled spring. When a set amount of energy is stored, the coupling releases and the spring accelerates the magnet rapidly. This generates a current of sufficient strength to create a spark across the electrodes of the spark plug. It also retards the spark sufficiently to allow the burning fuel/air mixture to drive the crankshaft in the correct direction.

Once the engine is started and is running at its usual rpm, the magnet accelerates away from the coiled spring, which has no further effect. The spark is then produced normally (by the engine rotating the magnet), and the timing is no longer retarded but operates normally, with the spark occurring just prior to commencement of the power stroke.

Notice that, as the impulse coupling does not depend on any electrical power source, the engine can be started by swinging the propeller. (This should only be done by trained and qualified personnel.) However, if you use an electric starter powered by the aircraft battery then, once the engine is running, disconnecting the battery will have no effect (except that the battery will not be re-charged).

Use of the Ignition Switch

There are two separate ignition systems for safety in the event of failure of one of them, as well as for more efficient burning of the fuel/air mixture with two sparks in the cylinder instead of one. Older aircraft often have separate switches for each magneto, while most modern aircraft have rotary switches operated by the ignition key. With these, you can select the left system *L*, the right system *R*, or BOTH. BOTH is selected for normal engine operation.

The aircraft will run on just one magneto, but not as smoothly as on two, and with a slight drop in rpm. With one spark instead of two, there will be only one flame front advancing through the fuel/air mixture in the cylinder instead of two. This increases the time for full combustion to occur and decreases the efficiency of the burning.

If L is selected, only the left magneto system supplies a spark. The *R* magneto is earthed, i.e. its current runs to earth and no spark is generated. Therefore, going from BOTH to *L* should cause a drop in rpm and possibly slightly rougher running. If a slight drop in rpm does not occur, then either the *R* system is still supplying a spark or else the *R* magneto was not working previously when BOTH was selected.

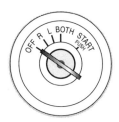

Just prior to take-off, you will normally check both left and right magneto systems in this way as part of a power check. Switching from BOTH to *L*, note the rpm drop and return to BOTH, when the rpm originally set should be regained. Then switch from BOTH to *R*, note the rpm drop, and back to BOTH.

Comparisons are made between the two rpm drops, which should be within certain limits (see your Pilot's Operating Handbook). Some typical figures are: check at 1,600 rpm on BOTH, magneto drop 125 rpm maximum on either *L* or *R*, with a difference between these two drops not to exceed 50 rpm.

Always treat a propeller as 'live'.

REMEMBER that turning the ignition switch to OFF earths the primary winding of the magneto system so that it no longer supplies electrical power, i.e. with a particular magneto's ignition switch OFF, that system is supposed to be earthed and unable to supply a spark. With a loose or broken wire, or some other fault, switching the ignition off may not earth both of the magnetos. Therefore, any person swinging the propeller may inadvertently start the engine, even though the ignition is switched off. It has happened – often with fatal results – and is still happening.

If you want to reposition the propeller when the engine is stopped, rotate it in the direction opposite to its normal motion so that you are protected against an inadvertent start.

If the ignition is switched off and the engine continues to run, this indicates that the system is not grounded, which is a dangerous situation.

You have no visual method of checking that the magneto systems, although switched off, are deactivated. Just before shutting an engine down, some pilots do a system function test at idle rpm, checking BOTH, *L*, *R* followed by a 'dead cut', i.e. to OFF, when a sudden loss of power should be apparent, and rapidly back to BOTH to allow the engine to run normally, prior to being shut down normally using the idle cut-off function of the mixture control.

Some instructors advise against a dead-cut check as it may damage the engine. Refer to your Pilot's Operating Handbook.

The Exhaust System

The burned gases leave the engine and are carried out to the atmosphere via the exhaust system. It is important that there is no leakage of exhaust fumes into the cabin because they contain carbon monoxide, a colourless and odourless gas that is difficult to detect but can cause unconsciousness and death.

Engine Failure in Flight

Due to improved manufacturing and operating procedures, mechanical engine failure is becoming a rare event, but fuel starvation as a cause of engine stoppage is not as uncommon as it should be.

Fuel starvation can be caused by:

☐ **insufficient fuel;**
☐ **mishandling** of the fuel tank selection;
☐ **incorrect use** of the mixture control;
☐ **ice forming** in the carburettor; or
☐ **contaminated fuel** (e.g. water in the fuel).

If the **mixture control** is left in LEAN for descent (instead of being moved to RICH), the fuel/air mixture will gradually become more and more lean as the aeroplane descends into denser air, possibly resulting in the engine stopping. **Carburettor ice** can also be a problem on descent when the engine is idling and not producing much heat.

Electrical failure in both magneto systems will also cause the engine to stop.

In all these cases, the airflow past the aeroplane may cause the propeller to windmill and turn the engine over, even though it is not producing power.

Mechanical failure, such as the break-up of pistons or valves, will probably be accompanied by mechanical noise and the engine and propeller may be unable to rotate. In such cases any attempt to restart the engine is not advisable.

Irrespective of whether you decide to glide down for a landing or attempt to restart the engine, you must ensure that flying speed is maintained.

Some obvious items to be considered in an attempted engine restart are:

☐ **a fuel problem:**
    – change fuel tanks;
    – fuel pump on (if fitted);
    – mixture RICH;
    – primer locked;

◻ **an ignition problem:**
  – check magneto switches individually (BOTH – LEFT – RIGHT). If the engine operates on one magneto as a result of a fault in the other magneto system, then leave it there, otherwise return to BOTH;

◻ **an icing problem:**
  – carburettor heat FULL HOT.

Engine Fire in Flight

Engine fire is also a rare event, but you should be prepared to cope with it. The firewall is designed to protect the structural parts of the airframe from damage and the cockpit occupants from injury if a fire breaks out in the engine bay, provided the fire is extinguished without delay.

The initial reaction to an engine fire in flight should be to turn off the fuel (fuel selector OFF or mixture control to IDLE CUT-OFF) and allow the engine to run itself dry of fuel and stop. The engine and induction system will then be purged of fuel and the fire should extinguish. At this point, the ignition should be switched off and a forced landing carried out.

Now complete **Exercises 16 – The Aeroplane Engine.**

The Carburettor

Gasoline (petrol) needs to be mixed with oxygen in the correct ratio to burn properly. The oxygen is provided by mixing the fuel with air, and the correct fuel/air ratio is about 1 part of fuel to 12 parts of air by weight. The device normally used to mix fuel with air in an engine is called the **carburettor.**

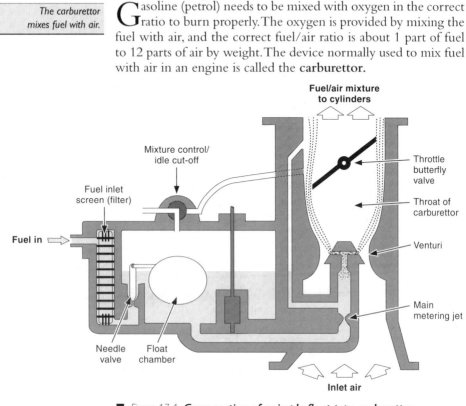

■ *Figure 17-1* **Cross-section of a simple float-type carburettor**

Combustion can occur in the cylinders when the fuel/air ratio is between approximately 1:8 (**rich mixture**) and 1:20 (**lean mixture**). The ideal or **chemically correct mixture** of fuel/air is one in which the fuel and the oxygen are perfectly matched so that, after burning, all of the fuel and all of the oxygen has been used. The chemically correct mixture may be referred to as the *ccm* or *stoichiometric* mixture.

If the mixture is *rich,* there is excess fuel. After burning, some unburned fuel will remain, i.e. rich = excess fuel. If the mixture is *lean,* there is a shortage of fuel in the sense that, after all of the fuel has burned, there is still some oxygen remaining, i.e. lean = excess oxygen.

A simple carburettor has a venturi through which the amount of airflow is controlled by a **throttle valve** (or **butterfly**).

The venturi has fuel jets positioned in it so that the correct amount of fuel by weight is metered into the airflow, i.e. sucked in by low air pressure in the venturi. The butterfly valve in the carburettor is controlled by moving the throttle in the cockpit.

It is important that the throttle is moved slowly so that unnecessary stress is not placed on the many moving parts in the engine. To open or close the throttle fully should take about the same time as a '1-2-3' count.

A simple float-type carburettor has a small chamber that requires a certain level of fuel. If the level is too low, the float-valve opens and allows more fuel from the fuel tanks to enter. This is happening continuously as fuel is drawn from the float chamber into the venturi of the carburettor. The air pressure in the float chamber is atmospheric.

The acceleration of the airflow through the carburettor venturi causes a decreased static pressure (Bernoulli's principle – increased velocity; decreased static pressure). The higher atmospheric pressure in the float chamber forces fuel through the main metering jet into the venturi airflow. The faster the airflow, the greater the differential pressure and the greater the quantity of fuel discharged to the airflow, i.e. the mass of fuel that flows through the carburettor is controlled by the airflow through the carburettor venturi.

As the level of fuel in the chamber decreases, the float falls, causing the needle valve operated by the float to open and allow more fuel to enter. The required level of fuel in the float chamber is continuously maintained.

Many carburettors have a **diffuser** fitted that premixes the fuel with air and prevents the main jet providing excessive fuel as engine speed is increased. The diffuser also helps in vaporising the fuel at low engine speeds.

Accelerator Pump

When you open the throttle to maximum power, the butterfly valve is fully opened and does not restrict the airflow through the venturi. The airflow therefore increases significantly.

If the throttle is opened quickly, the airflow initially increases at a rate greater than the fuel flow, which results in an insufficiently rich mixture. This would cause a lag in the power-increase if it were not for the **accelerator pump.** In other words, the accelerator pump prevents a *weak-cut* when the throttle is advanced rapidly.

The accelerator pump consists of a small plunger within the float chamber, that is connected to the throttle linkage so that it gives an extra spurt of fuel as the throttle is opened.

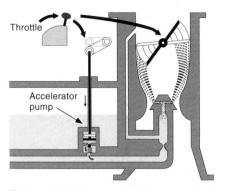

■ *Figure 17-2* **The accelerator pump discharges extra fuel as the throttle is opened**

Idling System

When the engine is idling with the butterfly valve almost closed, the pressure differential between the venturi and the float chamber is not great enough to force fuel through the main jet.

To allow for this, there is a small **idling jet** with an inlet near the butterfly valve, where a small venturi effect is caused when the valve is almost closed. This provides sufficient fuel to mix with the air to keep the engine idling at low rpm.

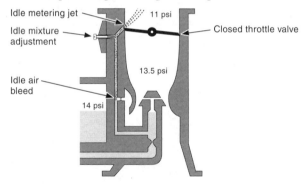

■ *Figure 17-3* **The idling system**

Fuel/Air Mixture Control

The carburettor is designed to operate under mean sea level conditions in the International Standard Atmosphere (ISA). This is at a pressure altitude of zero (mean sea level, QNH 1013 mb/hPa) and +15°C.

The size of the main metering jet which controls the fuel flow from the carburettor is designed for these ISA MSL conditions. The aeroplane will not operate under these conditions at all times (in fact, most in-flight conditions will differ markedly from ISA

MSL), and any significant deviation from these conditions will require a change of fuel flow.

(The terms *pressure altitude,* QNH, and ISA MSL are explained in Chapter 25, *Pressure Instruments.*)

Use of the Mixture Control

At a given throttle setting and rpm, the carburettor will process the same volume of air per second, irrespective of the density or weight of the air.

At higher altitudes and/or higher temperatures, the density of the air is less, i.e. there are fewer air molecules per unit volume. Therefore, the volume of air passing through the carburettor will contain fewer molecules and weigh less. However, the density of the liquid fuel will not change. The same volume and weight of fuel will be drawn into the carburettor venturi.

The same number of fuel molecules, but fewer air molecules, means too much fuel by weight for the amount of air – the mixture is too rich, leading to rough running and excessive fuel consumption.

To maintain a correct mixture, i.e. the correct fuel/air ratio, the pilot must reduce the amount of fuel entering the carburettor venturi and mixing with the less-dense air as the altitude increases – called *leaning* the mixture. This is done using the **mixture control** – usually a red knob somewhere near the throttle. The mixture control moves a small needle to restrict the fuel flow through the main jet, thereby restoring the correct fuel/air mixture.

> *Vary the fuel/air mixture with the mixture control.*

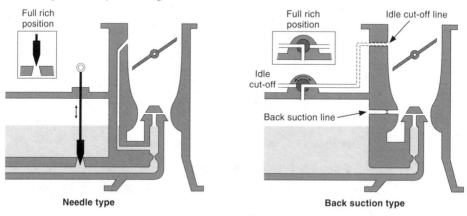

Needle type   **Back suction type**

 *Figure 17-4* **Mixture control systems**

For normal operations in the United Kingdom where most aerodromes are within 2,000 feet of sea level, the temperature moderate and the air fairly dense, the mixture control is in FULL RICH for the take-off.

Using the Mixture Control for Climbing

Usually the mixture is kept in FULL RICH for the climb, unless the climb is an extended one to a cruising altitude in excess of 5,000 ft, where the cruise power will most likely be less than 75% maximum continuous power in standard conditions. The excess fuel is used as a cooling agent for the cylinder walls and piston tops to assist in the prevention of detonation. Some of the more sophisticated engines require leaning during the climb, but for training aeroplanes this is not usually the case.

As the aircraft climbs, the fuel/air mixture becomes over-rich, causing a loss of power, which is indicated by a drop in rpm for a fixed-pitch propeller, and by rougher running.

Using the Mixture Control at Cruise Altitude

On the cruise and with cruise power set, you should consider leaning the mixture to regain a more chemically correct fuel/air ratio, which gives more efficient burning of the gases in the cylinders, more efficient operation of the engine (slightly higher rpm for a fixed-pitch propeller) and better fuel economy. In some light aircraft, correct leaning can reduce the fuel consumption by over 25% compared to FULL RICH – allowing greatly improved range and endurance.

The mixture should be slightly on the rich side of the chemically correct mixture, provided the cruise power setting is less than 75% – (normal cruise for most aircraft is about 55–65% for normal cruise, when leaning the mixture is advisable).

NOTE Above 5,000 feet density height, an unsupercharged engine can not achieve more than 75% maximum continuous power (even at full throttle).

At high power settings (in excess of 75%) rich mixture is necessary to provide excess fuel as a coolant. The Pilot's Operating Handbook for the specific aircraft type contains information on how to achieve the *best power* mixture and *best economy* mixture.

TO LEAN THE MIXTURE, slowly move the mixture control towards the lean position. As a chemically correct fuel/air ratio is regained, the rpm will increase. Eventually, with further leaning, the rpm will decrease slightly and the engine will show signs of running a little roughly. The mixture control is gently pushed back in a little to regain the best rpm, indicating a chemically correct mixture, and smoother running. The mixture control is then moved to a slightly richer position to:

Ensure that the engine is operating on the rich side of the chemically correct mixture.

This procedure must be repeated when either your cruising altitude or power-setting is changed significantly. Some aeroplanes are fitted with an exhaust gas temperature (EGT) gauge which indicates peak EGT when there is a chemically correct mixture and can help in leaning the mixture correctly.

For a constant-speed propeller, the leaning is done with reference to a fuel flow gauge, to obtain minimum fuel flow for smooth running. Refer to your aircraft handbook.

Using the Mixture Control for Take-Off and Landing

During take-off (and landing, when high power in case of a go-around should be anticipated), the mixture control should be in FULL RICH. The mixture is rich to protect against detonation, pre-ignition and overheating in the cylinders. These are more likely to occur at power settings above 75% METO (maximum except for take-off, or maximum continuous power) than at the normal cruise power settings (55–65%), when leaning is advisable. More on detonation and pre-ignition on pages 185 and 186.

Rich and Lean Mixtures

AN OVER-RICH MIXTURE will cause a loss of power, high fuel consumption, fouling of the spark plugs and formation of carbon (from unburnt fuel) on the piston heads and valves. The extra fuel in a rich mixture causes cooling within the cylinders by its evaporation – this absorbs some of the heat produced in the combustion chamber. A lean mixture will therefore have higher cylinder head temperatures.

A mixture that is too rich is preferable to a mixture that is too lean.

AN EXCESSIVELY LEAN MIXTURE will cause excessively high cylinder head temperatures, leading to detonation. Severe detonation can damage an engine very quickly. The pilot is then faced with a loss of power and quite possibly complete engine failure. Having adjusted the mixture, check that the cylinder head temperature and the oil temperature are still within the operating limits. It may take about five minutes for these temperature readings to stabilise.

High Density Altitudes

Operations at very high density altitudes, where the air density (*rho*) is low (i.e. hot, high, or both), may require leaning prior to take-off. Aerodromes at high elevation, aerodromes at sea level with temperatures approaching 40°C, and aerodromes that are both hot and high, such as at Nairobi, Kenya, require some thought about the mixture control setting for take-off.

EXAMPLE 1 Aerodrome elevation 3,000 ft, QNH 1013 mb(hPa), air temperature 34°C.

The density altitude can be worked out and is in fact 6,000 ft, i.e. the engine/propeller and the airframe will perform as if the aeroplane is at 6,000 feet in the International Standard Atmosphere.

Refer to your Pilot's Operating Handbook and seek the advice of your flying instructor before operating at high density altitudes.

Idle Cut-Out or Idle Cut-Off

The idle cut-off is the normal means of shutting the engine down. In a typical system, when the mixture control is moved right out to the IDLE CUT-OFF position by the pilot, a small needle moves to cut off the fuel flow between the float chamber and the venturi. The fuel supply to all the fuel jets is cut off.

The engine will continue running until all the fuel/air mixture in the inlet manifold and the cylinders is burned. This leaves no combustible fuel/air mixture anywhere in the system, which would not be the case if the engine was stopped by turning the ignition off.

Abnormal Combustion

Detonation

Detonation *is the instantaneous, explosive combustion of the unburned fuel/air charge in the cylinder.*

Correct progressive burning of the fuel/air mixture should occur as the flame-front advances through the combustion chamber. This causes an increase in pressure which smoothly forces the piston down the cylinder in the power stroke.

When a gas is compressed, it experiences a rise in temperature. (You can feel this if you hold your hand over the outlet of a bicycle pump during the 'compression stroke'.) If the pressure and the temperature rise is too great for the fuel/air mixture in the engine cylinders, the burning will not be progressive, but *explosive,* spontaneous combustion.

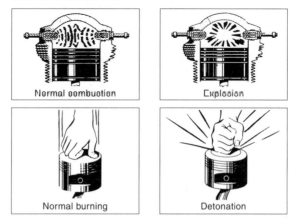

■ *Figure 17-5* **A comparison between normal combustion and detonation**

This explosive increase in pressure is called **detonation** and can cause severe damage to the pistons, the valves and the spark plugs, and a decrease in power and quite possibly **complete engine failure.**

Severe detonation can damage an engine very quickly.

Using a lower fuel grade than recommended, a time-expired fuel, an over-lean mixture, too high a manifold pressure, or an over-heated engine can cause detonation.

Aircraft engines are normally designed to operate a little on the rich side, the extra fuel acting as a coolant to prevent the mixture becoming too hot and to cool the cylinder walls by evaporation.

If detonation is suspected (i.e. rough running and high cylinder head temperatures):

- **richen the mixture;**
- **reduce pressure** in the cylinders (throttle back);
- **increase airspeed** to assist in reducing cylinder head temperatures.

Pre-Ignition

Pre-ignition is a progressive burning of the fuel/air mixture but is a burning that commences before the spark from the plug. This early or pre-ignition can be caused by a hot-spot in the cylinder (e.g. a carbon deposit) becoming red-hot and igniting the mixture. The result is rough running, possibly back-firing, and a sudden rise in the cylinder head temperature.

Pre-ignition is the uncontrolled firing of the fuel/air charge before the spark ignition.

Pre-ignition can be caused by a 'carboned-up' engine, or use of high power when the mixture is too lean (hence no extra fuel for cooling). It may occur in one cylinder only, where a hot-spot exists, whereas detonation will normally appear in all cylinders.

Pre-ignition is a function of the condition of a particular cylinder or cylinders – detonation is a function of the fuel/air mixture/temperature being supplied to all cylinders.

Both detonation and pre-ignition can be prevented – provided the correct fuel and operating limitations of the engine are observed. This information is available in the Pilot's Operating Handbook.

Carburettor Icing

The expansion of the air as it accelerates through the carburettor venturi causes it to drop in temperature. Quite warm air can cool to below zero and, if there is moisture in the air, ice can form. This will seriously degrade the functioning of the carburettor, even to the point of stopping the engine!

Impact Ice

Impact ice will occur when super-cooled (below freezing point) water droplets in the intake air impact on the metal surfaces of the inlet air scoop and ducting to the carburettor – immediately forming into ice. (This can happen in fuel-injection systems as well as normal float-type carburettors.)

Impact ice can occur when the outside air temperature is near or below zero and the aeroplane is in cloud, rain or sleet – i.e. visible moisture – and the water droplets are at or below zero, or if the inlet surfaces themselves are below zero, e.g. an aircraft descending from levels above the freezing level into visible moisture in warmer temperatures.

Fuel Ice

Fuel ice can form downstream of the jet where the fuel is introduced into the carburettor airstream, where it vaporises, causing a substantial reduction of the temperature due to latent heat absorption on vaporisation.

If the temperature of the fuel/air mixture drops to between 0°C and −8°C, water will precipitate from the incoming air if it is moist and will freeze onto any surface it encounters, e.g. the inlet manifold walls and the throttle valve (butterfly). This will seriously restrict the airflow and thus reduce the engine's power output.

Fuel ice can occur even in ambient air temperatures well above freezing (+20° to +30°C) when the *relative humidity* is above 50% or so.

In some reference texts, fuel icing may be called **refrigeration icing,** as it is caused by the vaporising of a liquid – the same process as that used in most refrigerators.

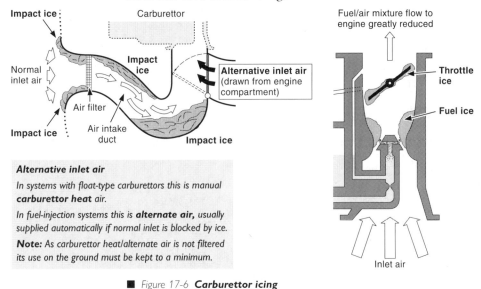

Impact ice   Carburettor   Fuel/air mixture flow to engine greatly reduced

Normal inlet air

Impact ice

Air filter

Air intake duct

Impact ice

Impact ice

Impact ice

Impact ice

Alternative inlet air (drawn from engine compartment)

Throttle ice

Fuel ice

Inlet air

Alternative inlet air

In systems with float-type carburettors this is manual **carburettor heat** air.

In fuel-injection systems this is **alternate air,** usually supplied automatically if normal inlet is blocked by ice.

Note: As carburettor heat/alternate air is not filtered its use on the ground must be kept to a minimum.

■ Figure 17-6 **Carburettor icing**

Throttle Ice

As the fuel/air mixture of gases accelerates past the throttle valve, there is a decrease in static pressure and a consequent drop in temperature. This process can cause icing on the throttle valve. The acceleration and resulting temperature drop is greatest at small throttle openings because the throttle butterfly restricts the airflow most at these power settings, creating a substantial pressure drop. Therefore, there is a greater likelihood of carburettor icing at low throttle settings, for instance, on descent when reduced power is usually set.

NOTE Visible moisture is not necessary for the formation of throttle ice.

Formation of Carburettor Ice

Both fuel ice and throttle ice can occur when the outside air temperature (OAT) is high. It is expansion that causes the cooling to freezing point – and just because it is 35°C in Casablanca does not mean that you will not get carburettor icing. If the humidity is high, it can form easily.

> Carburettor ice is most likely to form when the temperatures is between −10°C and +20°C and the relative humidity is high.

All of this carburettor icing can have a very serious effect on the running of the engine. The size and shape of the carburettor passages are altered, the airflow is disturbed, the fuel/air mixture ratio is affected – leading to rough running, a loss of power and possibly a total engine cut, unless prompt corrective action is taken.

Typical symptoms of carburettor ice formation are:
- **A power loss** (drop in rpm for a fixed-pitch propeller; drop in manifold pressure for a constant-speed propeller), resulting in poorer performance – loss of airspeed or poorer rate of climb.
- **Rough running.**

Carburettor Heat

Most modern light aircraft have a carburettor heat system to counteract icing. This usually involves passing the induction air past the hot engine exhaust manifold. When heated, its density is less, and so the initial effect of applying carburettor heat is a decrease in engine power (seen as a decrease in rpm for a fixed-pitch propeller) – possibly by 10–20%.

> If you suspect carburettor icing, apply **full** carburettor heat.

The **carburettor heat control** is usually located near the throttle in the cockpit. By pulling it out fully, heated air is passed into the carburettor. It is usual, if carburettor ice is suspected, to apply full carburettor heat. As the hot air passes through the carburettor venturi, it will melt the ice. There may be some rough running if there has been some ice build-up and a lot of the melted ice (now water) is fed through the cylinders, but this will quickly disappear.

Clearing ice from the carburettor will allow better running of the engine and the power to increase (and the rpm of a fixed-pitch propeller to rise) as the ice is cleared. A fixed-pitch propeller will show an initial drop in rpm (power) − due to the lower density hot air which richens the fuel/air mixture − followed quickly (hopefully) by an increase in rpm as the ice is cleared. Following this, carburettor heat may be removed and normal (cold) air used again.

If carburettor ice re-forms, this operation will have to be repeated. After this, partial carburettor heat may be necessary to prevent further ice formation, and if carburettor ice forms yet again, apply full heat again and then use an even higher setting of partial carburettor heat to prevent its return. Under some conditions, continuous full carburettor heat may be required.

NOTE Partial use of carburettor heat may raise the temperature of the induction air into the temperature range that is most conducive to the formation of carburettor icing.

Carburettor Heat on Descent and Approach

On descent with low power and shortly before landing, particularly in conditions of high humidity (e.g. in coastal areas), it is usual to apply full carburettor heat to ensure that no carburettor icing forms or is present. The small throttle butterfly openings at low power increase the chance of carburettor ice formation. Then, on final approach to land, the carburettor heat control is normally returned to FULL COLD, in case full power is needed for a go-around. Some aircraft are fitted with a carburettor air temperature gauge, which can be used to keep the carburettor air temperatures out of the icing range.

Carburettor Heat on the Ground

Avoid using carburettor heat on the ground (except during the vital pre-take-off check) because the hot air is usually taken from around the exhaust manifold and is unfiltered. This will avoid introducing dust and grit into the carburettor and engine, with obvious benefits to both engine performance and wear. For this reason, the pre-take-off check of carburettor heat should be carried out on a hard surface. The check involves:

- **applying full carburettor heat** and observing the rpm drop; then
- **returning the control to** FULL COLD or OFF and noting that the rpm returns to the original value (indicating that no ice was present).

If the rpm returns to a significantly higher figure, then ice was present and has been at least partially melted; repeat the procedure until all ice is melted, taking care that no carburettor ice re-forms prior to take-off.

Fuel-Injection Systems

More sophisticated engines have fuel directly metered into the induction manifold and then into cylinders without using a carburettor. This is known as **fuel injection.**

A venturi system is still used to sense the pressure differential. This is coupled to a **fuel control unit (FCU),** from which metered fuel is piped to the **fuel manifold unit** (fuel distributor). From here a separate fuel line carries fuel to the **discharge nozzle** in each cylinder head, or into the cylinder inlet port just prior to the inlet valve. The mixture control in this system also controls the idle cut-off.

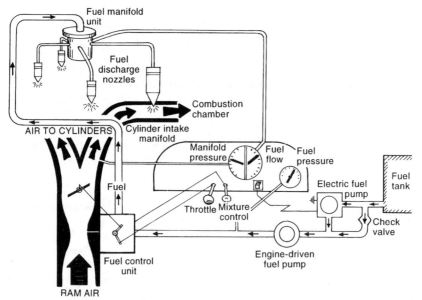

■ *Figure 17-7* **A fuel-injection system**

With fuel injection, each cylinder can be provided with a correct mixture by its own separate fuel line. (This is unlike the system where a carburettor supplies the same fuel/air mixture to all cylinders – a slightly richer-than-ideal mixture has to be supplied to most of the cylinders by the carburettor to ensure that the leanest-running cylinder does not run too lean.)

Advantages of Fuel-Injection Systems

☐ **Freedom from vaporisaton ice** (fuel ice), thus making it unnecessary to use carburettor heat except in the most severe atmospheric conditions.

☐ **More uniform delivery** of the fuel/air mixture to each cylinder.

☐ **Improved control** of fuel/air ratio.

☐ **Fewer maintenance problems.**

☐ **Instant acceleration** of the engine after idling with no tendency for it to stall, i.e. instant response.

☐ **Increased engine efficiency.**

Disadvantages of Fuel-Injection Systems

☐ **Starting an already hot engine** that has a fuel-injection system may be difficult due to vapour locking in the fuel lines. Electric boost pumps that pressurise the fuel lines can help alleviate this problem.

☐ **Having very fine fuel lines,** fuel-injection engines are more susceptible to any contamination in the fuel, such as dirt or water.

Correct fuel management is imperative! Know the fuel system of your aeroplane!

☐ **Surplus fuel** provided by a fuel-injection system will pass through a **return line** which may be routed to only one of the fuel tanks. If the pilot does not retain an awareness of where the surplus fuel is being returned to, it may result in fuel being vented overboard (thus reducing flight fuel available). A secondary effect could be asymmetric (uneven) fuel loading in some early model single-engined aeroplanes.

Engine Fire on Start-Up

If a fire starts in the engine air intake during start-up, a generally accepted procedure to minimise the problem is:

☐ **Continue cranking** the engine with the starter (to keep air moving through).

☐ **Move the mixture control** to IDLE CUT-OFF (to remove the source of fuel).

☐ **Open the throttle** (to maximise the airflow through the carburettor and induction system and purge the system of fuel).

The fire will probably go out, but if it does not, then further action would be taken:

☐ **Fuel** – OFF.

☐ **Switches** – OFF.

☐ **Brakes** – ON.

☐ **Evacuate** the aircraft, taking the fire extinguisher.

Now complete **Exercises 17 – The Carburettor.**

The Fuel System

The function of a fuel system is to store fuel and deliver it to the carburettor (or fuel injection system) in adequate quantities at the proper pressures. It should provide a continuous flow of fuel under positive pressure under all normal flight conditions:

☐ change of altitude;

☐ change of attitude;

☐ sudden acceleration; or

☐ deceleration of the engine.

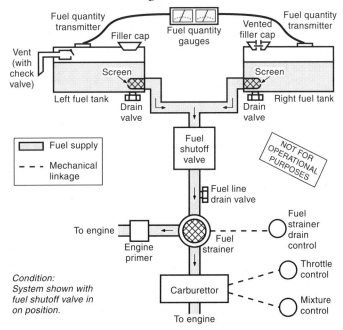

■ Figure 18-1 **A simple fuel system**

Fuel is stored in **fuel tanks,** which are usually installed in the wings. A sump and drain point at the lowest point of each tank allows heavy impurities (such as water) to gather, be inspected and drained off. The tanks often contain **baffles** to prevent the fuel surging about in flight – especially with large attitude changes or in turbulence.

The fuel supply line commences higher than the sump to avoid any impurities (water or sludge) entering the fuel lines to the carburettor, even though there is a **fuel filter** in the line to catch any small quantity of impurities. Because the fuel supply line to the engine is not right at the bottom of the fuel tank, there will always be some unusable fuel in the tanks.

The top of the fuel tank is vented to the atmosphere to allow atmospheric pressure to be retained in the tank as altitude is changed and as fuel is used up. Any reduced pressure (due to ineffective venting) in the tank could reduce the rate of fuel flow to the engine and also cause the fuel tanks to collapse inwards. The **fuel vents** should be checked in the pre-flight external inspection to ensure that they are not blocked or damaged. A blocked fuel tank vent in flight will prevent air flowing in and out of the tank above the fuel, and this could restrict fuel from being drawn from the tank to the carburettor and engine.

As well as allowing for reduced pressure, there must be some allowance for an increased pressure. An **overflow drain** prevents excessive pressure building up if fuel volume increases because full tanks have been warmed in the sun.

A high-wing aircraft with the tanks in the wings will generally allow the fuel to be **gravity-fed** to the carburettor, with no need for a **fuel pump**. If there is no carburettor, but a fuel-injection system, then electric **boost-pumps** are necessary.

In a low-wing aircraft, the tanks, being lower than the engine, need a fuel pump to lift the fuel to the carburettor. Prior to engine start, an electric auxiliary (boost) pump is used to prime the fuel lines and purge any vapour from them. Once the engine is started, the engine-driven mechanical **fuel pump** takes over. Correct functioning of the pump can be monitored with a fuel pressure gauge.

It is usual to have the electric fuel pump switched on for critical manoeuvres such as take-off, landing, and low-level flying in case the mechanical fuel pump fails and the engine is starved of fuel.

It is important, especially on low-wing aircraft with fuel carried in tanks below the level of the engine, that the **fuel strainer drain valve** is checked *closed* during the pre-flight external inspection. If it is not closed, the engine-driven fuel pump may not be able to draw sufficient fuel into the engine (sucking air instead), and the engine may be starved of fuel.

The Priming Pump

The fuel primer is a hand-operated pump in the cockpit which is used to pump fuel into the engine induction system in preparation for starting. This fuel does not pass through the carburettor.

> *A priming pump sends fuel directly into the engine prior to start-up.*

The primer must be locked during flight to avoid excessive fuel being drawn into the cylinders, especially at low power settings, which could stop the engine due to the fuel/air mixture being too rich.

Fuel Selection

A fuel line will run from each tank to a selector valve in the cockpit, which the pilot uses to select the tank from which fuel will be taken or to shut the fuel off. Incorrect selection by the pilot has led to numerous incidents and accidents, so read this section of the Pilot's Operating Handbook for your aircraft carefully. The sounds of silence while you still have fuel in a tank somewhere can be very loud indeed!

It is advisable when changing tanks to switch on the electric auxiliary or booster fuel pump (if fitted) to guarantee fuel pressure to the carburettor and to positively monitor the fuel pressure as the tanks are changed.

Any sudden and unexpected loss of power should bring two possible causes immediately to mind:
- lack of fuel to the engine; or
- carburettor icing.

If the cause is incorrect fuel selection your actions should include:
- **closing the throttle** (to avoid a sudden surge of power as the engine re-starts);
- **setting** the mixture control to FULL RICH;
- **switching** the electric fuel pump on; and
- **checking** fuel tank selection/content.

If the cause of the engine problem is carburettor ice, then apply full carburettor heat.

Fuel Boost Pumps (Auxiliary Pumps)

The reasons for installing electric fuel boost pumps are to:
- **provide** fuel at the required pressure to the carburettor or to the fuel metering unit of a fuel injection system;
- **purge** the fuel lines of any vapour;
- **prime** the cylinders for start-up;
- **supply** fuel if the engine-driven pump fails.

If an electric fuel pump is fitted, it is usual to also have a fuel pressure gauge to monitor its operation.

Fuel Gauges

Most light aircraft have fuel gauges in the cockpit which may be electrical (in which case the master switch will have to be ON for them to register) or direct-reading. It is good airmanship not to rely on them, since they can read quite inaccurately, especially when the aeroplane is not straight and level.

Always carry-out a visual check of the contents in the fuel tanks during the pre-flight external inspection by removing the fuel caps, looking into the tanks and then securely replacing the caps.

The fuel consumption rate specified in the Pilot's Operating Handbook assumes correct leaning of the mixture which, if not done, could lead to a fuel burn 20% in excess of the 'book-figures' and the fuel gauges reading much less than expected.

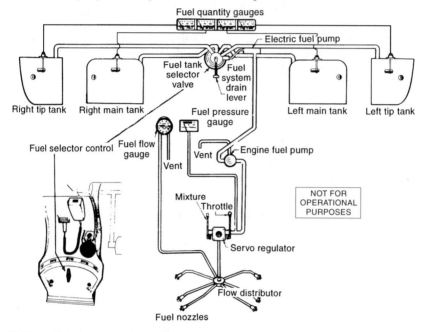

■ *Figure 18-2* **A more sophisticated fuel system**

Refuelling

For safety during refuelling, the aeroplane should be parked well away from other aircraft and buildings, the engine should not be running, and the ignition switches should be off. The location of firefighting equipment should be noted in case it is needed. A no-smoking rule should be enforced and passengers should be kept well clear.

To prevent the possibility of a spark of static electricity igniting fuel vapour you should connect earth wires between the aero-plane, the refuelling equipment and the ground to ensure that they are all at the same electrical potential. This should be done before you even remove the fuel caps, when fuel vapour could be released into the air. See also guidelines at the end of this chapter.

Fuel Grades

The most important thing is to ensure that you are loading the correct fuel type. Petrol (Avgas) is required for piston engines, and kerosene (Avtur) for gas turbine engines (jets). Kerosene is straw-coloured and has a distinctive smell.

Do not use Avtur
(kerosene) in piston
engines.

There are moves afoot to ensure that Avtur refuelling nozzles will not fit into tank openings of Avgas aeroplanes, and for all Avgas fittings to be painted red and Avtur fittings to be painted black. See end of this chapter for more on colour coding.

AVGAS (aviation **gas**oline) comes in various grades to cater for the requirements of different types of piston engines – some high-performance and some low-performance. These various grades of Avgas are colour coded to assist you in checking that the correct fuel is on board. Normal fuel for light aircraft is 100LL (low lead), which is coloured blue.

Fuel should possess **anti-detonation** or 'anti-knock' qualities which are described by the octane rating or performance numbers. The higher the rating or grade, the greater the compression that the fuel/air mixture can take without detonating. Lead is added to higher octane fuels to improve their anti-detonation qualities.

The higher performance number indicates the power possible (compared to the standard reference fuel) before a rich mixture would detonate, and the lower number indicates the power possible before the same fuel leaned-out would detonate. Certain engines require certain fuel – make sure you know which one and use it. Also, make sure that the fuel already in the tanks is the same as the fuel being loaded.

If you use fuel of a *lower grade* than specified, or fuel that is *date expired,* detonation is likely to occur, especially at high power settings, with a consequent loss of power and possible engine damage.

If you use fuel of a *higher grade* than specified, the spark plugs could be fouled by lead, and also the exhaust valves and their sealing faces could be eroded by the higher performance fuel that is exhausting.

Mogas and Motor Gasoline

Mogas is motor fuel produced in batches to certain specifications and quality; however, be wary of Mogas and do not use motor gasoline.

Aviation gasoline (Avgas) comes in batches with tight quality control. Ordinary motor fuel from service stations does *not* have such tight quality control, does not come in batches, and there is no verification of its purity. Also, it has different burning characteristics to Avgas.

In an aircraft engine, motor fuel would cause a lower power output, lead-fouling of the spark plugs and a strong possibility of detonation. Also, motor fuel is more volatile than Avgas and vaporises more readily; thus motor fuel can cause vapour locks in the fuel system of an aircraft engine and possibly starve it of fuel.

Use of Mogas is the subject of Leaflet No. 4A in the CAA General Aviation Safety Sense series. See also CAA Airworthiness Notice No. 98.

Fuel Checks

Fuel which is about to be loaded should be checked first for contamination. The most common contaminant is water. It can leak into ground fuel storage tanks and from there be loaded into the fuel truck and into the tanks of an aircraft quite easily.

Fuel must be checked for water and other contaminants.

Fuel naturally contains a small amount of water and this can condense out, say with a drop in temperature, contaminating the fuel system and possibly resulting in a loss of engine power. What is necessary to check for, however, is a large quantity of water which, if introduced into an engine cylinder, would interrupt the combustion process and cause the engine to stop.

Water can also block the fuel passages within the carburettor through the formation of water globules, thereby interrupting the power.

There are fuel-testing pastes and papers available which react when water is present; the fuelling agent will use these on a regular basis to guarantee the purity of the fuel in his storage tanks.

CONDENSATION AND IMPURITIES. There is usually a drop in air temperature overnight and, if the airspace above the fuel in the aircraft's fuel tanks is large (i.e. the tanks are close to empty), the fuel tank walls will become cold and there will be much more condensation than if the tanks were full of fuel. If the tanks are kept full when the aircraft is not being used for some days, or overnight if low temperatures are expected, this will help minimise condensation. The disadvantages of refuelling overnight include:

Full fuel tanks minimise condensation in low temperatures.

- **If the aircraft** has a take-off weight restriction the following day, it will have to be partially defuelled to reduce the weight or adjust the balance.
- **If the tanks** are full and the temperature rises, the fuel will expand and possibly overflow the tank a little. This could be a fire hazard.

There can be other impurities besides water. Rust, sand, dust and micro-organisms can cause similar problems. Filtering or straining the fuel should indicate the presence of these and hopefully remove them prior to refuelling.

Be especially careful when refuelling from drums which may have been standing for some time. Always check drum fuel with water-detection paste, for date of expiry and for correct grade of fuel. Filter the fuel through a chamois prior to loading.

Water, being more dense than fuel, will tend to gather at the low points in the fuel system. Once in the aeroplane tanks, a small quantity of fuel should be drained regularly from the bottom of each tank and from the fuel strainer drain valve to check for impurities, especially water which will sink to the bottom of the glass. Fuel drains are usually spring-loaded valves at the bottom of each fuel tank and the fuel strainer drain is usually found at the lowest point in the whole fuel system.

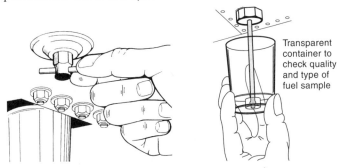

Transparent container to check quality and type of fuel sample

■ *Figure 18-3* **Fuel drains are located at the lowest point of the fuel tanks**

WATER IN FUEL TANKS. What do you do if you find water in the fuel tanks? This is an operational matter and guidance will be given by your flying instructor. In general terms, if a large quantity of water was found in the tanks, your actions should include the following:
- **inform the ground engineer;**
- **drain the tanks** until all the water has been removed;
- **positively rock the wing** to allow any other water to gravitate to the water trap;
- **drain off more fuel** and check for water at *all* drain points.

Fuel Management
- **Ensure that the aircraft** has the correct grade of fuel on board and that it is free of impurities.
- **Ensure that sufficient fuel** for the flight plus adequate reserves are on board. Do not rely only on the fuel gauges as they are often inaccurate. Calculate the fuel required, inspect visually and measure the fuel on board prior to flight. Remember that some of the fuel in the tanks will be unusable fuel.
- **Carry out a fuel drain** if required or if you think it is advisable.
- **Ensure there are no leaks,** that fuel caps are replaced and that tank vents are clear and unobstructed.

Always check that fuel tank caps are secure.

Fuel tank caps are usually on the upper surface of the wing, which is a low-pressure area in normal flight. Fuel will be siphoned out very quickly in flight if the tank caps are not secured. With high-wing aircraft especially, where the tank caps are not visible from the ground or when in flight, extra care should be taken. The minor inconvenience of finding a ladder to check the fuel caps pre-flight is far preferable to finding that you have almost empty tanks in the air.

Be familiar with, and follow, the procedures recommended in the Pilot's Operating Handbook. Understand the fuel system, especially the functioning of the fuel selector valves. When selecting a new tank, ensure the selector valve is moved firmly and positively into the correct detent.

Do not change tanks unnecessarily immediately prior to take-off or landing. If possible, verify prior to take-off that fuel is being drawn from the appropriate tanks. If operation is possible from more than one tank at the one time, this is usually preferred for operations near the ground. If boost pumps are fitted, their use for take-off is generally advised. (Refer to your Pilot's Operating Handbook for correct procedures.)

When changing tanks, check that there is indeed fuel in the tank about to be selected, if an electric fuel pump is fitted, switch it on and, if a fuel pressure gauge is fitted, monitor during and after the transfer.

Now complete **Exercises 18 – The Fuel System.**

from CAP 434 – *AVIATION FUEL AT AERODROMES*

4 LABELLING AND COLOUR CODING

4.1

All tanks should be labelled and colour coded to identify the grade of fuel they contain. Pipelines should also be similarly labelled and colour coded. The form and dimensions of labelling and colour coding are illustrated in Fig. 1. The overall dimensions of the grade labels should not be less than illustrated, but the dimensions of the coloured segments on both labels and pipelines may be varied provided that the primary indicator colours for the grades (Red for AVGAS, and Black for Jet A-1) predominate. The grade wording as illustrated should always be used.

4.2

As an additional measure to avoid refuelling errors it is recommended that the appropriate grade markings or a band of the appropriate primary grade indicator colour referred to in 4.1 should be painted on delivery hoses or pipes as close as practicable to the delivery nozzle, but not on the nozzle itself. Any colour coding on the delivery nozzle should be provided by a material which will not flake or separate from the nozzle in general use, for example a securely attached plastic sleeve or ring.

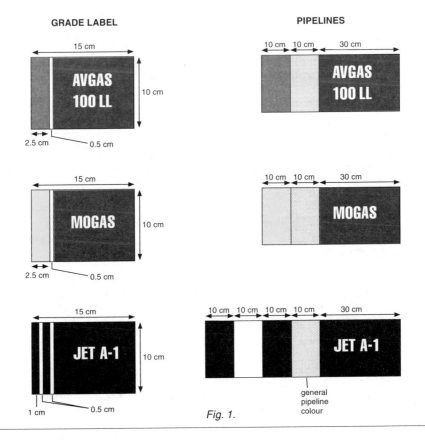

Fig. 1.

FUELLING OF AIRCRAFT

6.1 Introduction

In spite of well known and well publicised procedures to avoid loading of incorrect fuel, cases continue to occur from time to time mainly with general aviation aircraft. The most critical case is the piston-engined aircraft refuelled with turbine fuel, since piston engines will invariably stop as soon as pure turbo fuel reaches the engine; alternatively a mixture of the two fuels reaching the engine can lead to detonation and the consequent risk of destruction of the engine. Either circumstance can easily coincide with a critical stage of flight and in recent years there have been a number of serious accidents resulting from this error.

6.2 Refuelling Procedures

6.2.1

It is the aircraft commander's responsibility to ensure that the aircraft is refuelled with the correct type and quantity of fuel and refuelling crews should not commence to refuel an aircraft until they have established the precise requirements from the aircraft commander or his authorised representative.

6.2.2

The following minimum precautions should always be observed:

6.2.2.1

The aircraft commander or his authorised representative should ensure that the refuelling crew is in no doubt as to the type and quantity of fuel required.

6.2.2.2

The commander should satisfy himself that steps have been taken to check that the correct type of fuel is being supplied and correct delivery should be verified from the supplier's delivery note.

6.3 Marking of Aircraft Refuelling Points

6.3.1

Most regulatory authorities require that aircraft filler points be marked with the word 'FUEL' and the appropriate type. In addition to these markings it is strongly recommended that all 'over-wing' type filler points are further identified by means of a coloured circle or square either around or immediately adjacent to the filler point using the following colours:

Gasoline filler points — RED
Turbine fuel filler points — BLACK

Ideally these markings should also incorporate the words 'AVGAS' for gasoline points and 'AVTUR' or 'JET A-1' for turbine fuel points.
NB: Red and black are respectively the primary colours used for gasoline and turbine fuel in the internationally accepted colour coding scheme for aviation fuel ground installations and piping.

6.3.2

If it is necessary to achieve adequate differentiation between the identification colour and the aircraft colour scheme, the above markings should be outlined in white. The precise size of such markings may be varied as required, but it is important that they do provide prominent identification of the filler points. All such markings should be maintained in a legible condition.

6.3.3

Where the actual filler cap is beneath a hinged cover panel, the above markings may, if desired, be applied to the undersurface of the cover panel provided always that they become and remain prominently visible with the panel in its normal 'open' position for refuelling.

The Oil System

Functions of Engine Oil

If a small film of oil separates two metal surfaces it will prevent them from rubbing together. Without oil there would be high friction forces, causing very high temperatures to develop quickly in the metal, with extreme wearing of the metal surfaces, and, probably, mechanical failure.

Sufficient oil of the correct type in an engine is essential.

Oil reduces friction.

The oil film will allow the two metal surfaces to slide one over the other without actually touching each other. There will be only low friction forces and, consequently, high temperatures in the metal are avoided. The metallic friction is replaced by internal friction in the lubricating oil.

A thin layer of oil will adhere to each metal surface and, as the metal surfaces move relative to each other, there will be shearing of the layers of oil between the two surfaces (i.e. sliding of one layer over the other). Heat generated in the oil film due to this shearing is removed by the oil continually being circulated – the hot oil is carried away and cooled in a component known as the **oil cooler,** which is exposed to the airflow,

Engine components subjected to high loads, such as the bearings at either end of the connecting rods, especially the crankshaft (or 'big end') bearings, are cushioned by a layer of oil and the mechanical shock on them is reduced.

Oil cools the hot sections of the engine.

The pistons absorb a lot of heat from the combustion chamber and are cooled by oil splashed or sprayed onto them from below, (i.e. from the connecting rod area). Lubrication and cooling of the bearings and pistons is essential – and this is the main function of the oil.

Oil carries away contaminants.

Oil circulating through an engine can carry away dirt and other foreign material, thereby reducing abrasive wear on the moving parts of the engine. This contamination is removed by the **oil filter.** If the filter is not kept clean (by correct maintenance or replacement at the recommended service intervals) it may block, causing dirty oil to bypass the filter and circulate within the engine's lubrication system. Dirty oil has poorer cooling and lubricating qualities and so the engine will suffer – there will be an increased wear rate which will shorten the life of the engine.

Oil provides a seal.

Oil also provides a seal, e.g. between the cylinder wall and the piston as it moves up and down. This prevents the compressed gases (fuel/air) escaping past the piston rings into the crankcase.

Oil Properties

1. Oil must be sufficiently *viscous* over the operating temperature range of the engine – it must flow freely, but not be too thin. An oil of high viscosity (stickiness) flows slowly; an oil of low viscosity flows more easily. High temperatures make oil less viscous and cause it to flow more freely.

> *Oil does not lubricate properly if it is too hot, so watch your oil temperature.*

Excessively high temperatures affect the lubricating qualities of oil, impairing its effectiveness, so keep an eye on the oil temperature gauge.

The oil must remain sufficiently viscous under the wide range of operating temperatures and bearing pressures found in aviation engines.

The owner or operator of the aeroplane may decide to use an oil of lower viscosity than normal in a severely cold climate. Likewise an oil of higher viscosity could be used if the aeroplane is to be operated in a continually hot climate. As the pilot, be aware of the oil grade being used and do not mix oil grades.

> *Do not mix oil grades.*

2. The oil must have a sufficiently high flash point and fire point to ensure that it will not vaporise excessively or catch fire easily.

3. The oil must be chemically stable and not change its state or characteristics.

A Typical Oil System

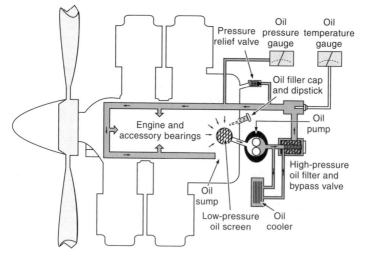

■ *Figure 19-1* **A typical oil system**

After doing its work in the engine, the oil gathers in the **sump,** which is a reservoir attached to the lower part of the engine casing.

A **wet sump** engine has a sump in which the oil is stored. Most light aircraft engines are wet sump engines.

A **dry sump** engine has scavenge pumps that scavenge oil from the sump attached to the lower part of the engine casing and pump it back into the oil tank, which is separate from the engine. It is usual to have a dry sump oil system on aerobatic aircraft that commonly find themselves in unusual attitudes. The *Tiger Moth* and *Chipmunk* have dry sump systems. Radial engines such as in the *Harvard, Dakota (DC-3)* and *DHC Beaver* also have dry sump oil systems.

There is usually an **engine-driven oil supply pump** that supplies oil from the sump or the tank through oil lines, passages and galleries to the moving parts of the engine. Within the oil pump is a spring-loaded **oil pressure relief valve.** If the pressure set on the pressure relief valve is exceeded, it will open and relieve the pressure by allowing oil to be returned to the pump inlet.

An **oil pressure gauge** in the cockpit indicates the oil pressure provided by the oil pump, i.e. the oil pressure sensor is situated after the oil pump and before the oil does its work in the engine.

Oil filters and screens are placed in the system to remove any foreign matter such as dirt or carbon particles from the circulating oil. The oil filters should be replaced at regular intervals, as required in the Maintenance Schedule, and inspected, as the foreign matter collected may give an indication of the condition of the engine, e.g. small metal particles might indicate an impending mechanical failure.

Within the oil filter housing is an **oil filter bypass valve.** This valve permits the oil to bypass the filter in the event of the filter becoming clogged. Dirty and contaminated oil is preferable to no oil.

The oil circulates around the moving parts and through the engine – lubricating and cooling as it goes – and is then returned to the wet sump by gravity, or to a separate oil tank by scavenge pumps (in a dry sump system). The scavenge pumps have a greater pumping capacity than the oil supply pressure pump in order to ensure that all the oil is scavenged from the engine.

The engine oil absorbs a large amount of heat during its passage through the engine, and the cooling that occurs in the sump is usually insufficient, so most engines have an **oil cooler** which operates on a heat-exchange process with the slipstream. The oil reaches the oil cooler after it has been pumped from the sump through the oil filter.

If the oil is already cool, a thermally operated valve routes the oil past the cooler, as further cooling is unnecessary. Once the oil is hot (when the engine has warmed up), it is directed through the cooler. Should the cooler become blocked, a **pressure bypass valve** allows the oil to bypass the cooler.

The oil cooler is usually situated in the oil system so that the oil cools a little in the sump, then passes through the oil cooler for further cooling, before entering the main parts of the engine.

As part of your **daily/pre-flight inspection (Check A)** you should check the condition of the oil cooler for:

☐ **freedom from insects, bird nests** and other contamination – in other words, for free air passages; and

☐ **any oil leakage or fatigue cracks.**

An **oil temperature gauge** is fitted in the cockpit. It is connected to a temperature probe that senses the temperature of the oil after it has passed through the oil cooler and before its use within the hot sections of the engine.

Some aeroplanes have a **cylinder head temperature (CHT) gauge** to provide another indication of engine temperature, this time in the area surrounding the cylinder heads.

Oil Changes

Oil changes are necessary periodically. As the same oil is continually used, over a period of time it will become increasingly dirty because the filters cannot clean it perfectly. Chemical changes will also occur in the oil in the form of:

☐ **oxidation** caused by contamination from some of the by-products of the fuel combustion in the engine; and

☐ **absorption of water** that condenses in the engine when it cools after being shut down.

Therefore the oil must be changed at regular intervals, as required by the Maintenance Schedule.

Use only the recommended type and grade of oil and **do not mix oil grades.**

NOTE The Pilot's Operating Handbook will usually show the oil grade as an SAE rating (Society of Automotive Engineers). However, commercial aviation oil has a *commercial aviation number* which is double the SAE rating: 80 grade oil = SAE 40; 100 grade oil = SAE 50.

There are different types of oils designed for different operating conditions. Use only the correct type of oil as directed in the Pilot's Operating Handbook, and do not use turbine (jet) oil in piston engines.

'Running In' New or Overhauled Engines

If the engine is brand new or has had a recent top-end overhaul, 'running in' procedures must be strictly followed. It is normal practice to operate the engine for the first 25 to 50 hours using 'straight' oil (oil which does *not* contain additives such as ashless dispersants). If in doubt seek engineer's advice, as incorrect running in procedures or using the wrong oil may cause significant damage.

Malfunctions in the Oil/Lubrication System
Oil Type
The incorrect type of oil will possibly cause poor lubrication, poor cooling and engine damage. Oil temperature and pressure indications may be abnormal.

Oil Quantity
The oil level should be checked prior to flight, as it gradually decreases due to:
- **burning** with the fuel/air mixture in the cylinders;
- **loss** as a mist or spray through the oil breather; and
- **leaks.**

There will be an **oil dip-stick** in the tank. The dip-stick is calibrated to show maximum and minimum oil quantities. If the oil quantity is *below* the minimum, you will find that the oil overheats and/or the oil pressure is too low or fluctuates. If the oil quantity is *too great,* then the excess oil may be forced out through various parts of the engine, such as the front-shaft seal.

Low Oil Pressure
At normal power, a low oil pressure may indicate a lack of oil and an impending engine failure. Low oil pressure could mean:
- **a lack of oil** due to a failure in the oil system;
- **insufficient oil;**
- **a leak** in the oil tank or oil lines;
- **a failure** of the oil pump;
- **a problem** in the engine, such as failing bearings;
- **the oil pressure relief valve** (PRV) is stuck open.

On start-up, the oil pressure gauge should indicate a rise within approximately 30 seconds.

High Oil Temperature
Too little oil being circulated will also be indicated by a high oil temperature, i.e. a rising oil temperature may indicate a decreasing oil quantity. Prolonged operation at excessive cylinder head temperatures will also give rise to a high oil temperature indication. This would be most likely to occur in situations of high power and low airspeed (climbing), especially in high ambient air temperatures.

Faulty Oil Pressure Gauge

Occasionally oil pressure gauges or sensors develop faults and give incorrect readings. A low oil pressure indication may be recognised as a faulty indication – and not a genuine low pressure – by noting that the oil temperature remains normal over a period of time. Keep your eye on both gauges.

High Oil Pressure

A pressure relief valve in the system should ensure that the oil does not reach an unacceptably high oil pressure. A high oil pressure may cause some part of the system to fail, rendering the whole oil system inoperative.

Low or Fluctuating Oil Pressure

Where an indication of low or fluctuating oil pressure occurs and is associated with a rise in oil temperature while in flight – play it safe and land as soon as possible, as it could indicate a serious problem in the lubrication system.

> No oil → engine seizure → immediate loss of power.

Gradual Loss of Oil

If an engine was slowly losing oil, then its oil temperature would gradually rise because less oil had to do the same amount of work – cooling and lubricating the engine. In this situation the oil pressure would probably be maintained, but with the oil temperature rising, until the oil quantity reached a critically low level when a sudden drop in oil pressure (and consequent engine problems) could occur.

> If you suspect a problem concerning oil, you should plan a landing before the time you estimate the oil problem will become serious. This is a matter of judgement, especially if the choice of nearby landing areas is limited.

Now complete **Exercises 19 – The Oil System.**

The Cooling System

The piston engine converts the chemical energy of the fuel into heat and pressure energy by combustion with air, and this is further converted into mechanical energy to drive the propeller. The transfer to mechanical energy is not complete and perfect. Energy losses such as heat and noise may total more than half the original energy of the fuel. The burning of the fuel/air mixture in the engine's cylinders, and friction of its moving parts, results in the engine heating up. Excessively high engine temperatures should be avoided as they will:

- **reduce the efficiency** of the lubrication system;
- **adversely affect combustion** of the fuel/air mixture;
- **cause detonation** in the cylinders;
- **weaken engine components** and shorten the engine's life.

Most modern light aircraft engines are **air-cooled** by exposing the cylinders and their cooling fins to an airflow. The fins increase the exposed surface area to allow better cooling.

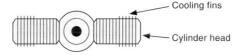

■ *Figure 20-1* **Cooling fins on a horizontally opposed engine**

As the airflow passes around a cylinder it may become turbulent and break away in such a manner that uneven cooling occurs, forming local, poorly cooled hot-spots. To avoid this uneven cooling, cowling ducts at the front of the engine capture air from the high-pressure area behind the propeller and baffles distribute it as evenly as possible around the cylinders. After cooling the engine, the air flows out of holes at the bottom rear of the engine compartment.

Air cooling is least effective at high power and low airspeed, e.g. on take-off or go-around. The high power produces a lot of heat and the low airspeed provides only a reduced cooling airflow. At high airspeed and low power, e.g. on descent, the cooling might be too effective.

Some aircraft have moveable cooling **cowl flaps** that can be operated (electrically or manually) from the cockpit, giving the pilot more control over the cooling of the engine. Open cowl flaps permit more air to escape from the engine compartment. This causes increased airflow over and around the engine. The open cowl flaps cause the parasite drag to increase (sometimes referred to as 'cooling drag'). Closed or 'faired' cowl flaps will reduce the airflow compared to when they are open, thereby reducing the cooling.

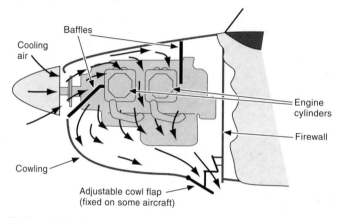

■ *Figure 20-2* **Cowl flaps and cooling of the engine**

Cowl flaps are normally open for take-off, partially open or closed on climb and cruise, and closed during a power-off descent. They will be open on final approach in readiness for a go-around, when high power at a low airspeed will be required. Cowl flaps should be open when taxiing, to help dissipate the engine heat.

The deciding factor in where to position the cowl flaps is the cylinder head temperature, or the anticipated cylinder head temperature, and this may be indicated in the cockpit by a cylinder heat temperature (CHT) gauge.

You should monitor the cylinder head temperature gauge throughout the flight and also on the ground, when cooling will be poor. The Pilot's Operating Handbook will give advice on satisfactory temperatures.

Monitor CHT and adjust engine cooling accordingly.

If excessive cylinder head temperatures are noted in flight, the cooling of the engine can be improved by:

☐ **opening the cowl flaps** fully (to allow greater airflow around the engine);
☐ **making the mixture richer** (extra fuel has a cooling effect in the cylinders due to the greater amount evaporated, so a rich mixture cools better than a lean mixture);
☐ **reducing engine power** (so that less heat is produced);
☐ **increasing airspeed** (for greater air cooling).

Just how you achieve the latter two is a matter of pilot judgement. On a climb you could reduce power, increase speed and climb with a reduced rate of climb. On a cruise (straight and level) at normal cruise speeds, you could not reduce the power and increase the airspeed except by commencing a descent; however, terrain clearance may prevent this.

Other factors influencing engine cooling which the pilot has little control over during flight include:

☐ **Condition of the oil cooler.** A dirty and inefficient oil cooler will not allow the best cooling of the circulating oil. The oil, being warmer than desired, will be unable to carry as much heat away from the engine, as well as having its viscosity and lubricating qualities reduced, which may lead to the creation of higher temperatures in the engine.

☐ **Outside air temperature.** Obviously, warm air will not cool the engine as well as cool air.

NOTE On some aircraft the propeller **spinner** is part of the 'airflow director' for the cooling air, so these aircraft should *not* be flown without the spinner fitted. If you find yourself in such a situation, reference to the operator or the CAA will establish what is allowable for your aeroplane.

Now complete **Exercises 20 – The Cooling System.**

Engine Handling

Extreme care must be taken when operating an aeroplane. As pilot you will have many things on your mind, especially in the early stages of learning to fly, and it is not unusual to feel unable to cope with all aspects of flying. Your instructor will lead you through each procedure several times and then monitor your actions the next few times. Build up, by repetition, good safe procedures so that they become second nature.

Good airmanship is perhaps the most important pilot quality and its most important component is common sense. It involves careful pre-flight inspection of the aircraft, verifying that any required maintenance has been completed, ensuring the brakes are on and the area near the propeller is clear prior to starting the engine, correct procedures and checks, and well-placed confidence in yourself and your ability – confidence that you can complete the required flight without undue worries.

'Confidence' is not 'over-confidence', which has given many pilots (and their passengers) grey hairs. Having the confidence in yourself to make correct decisions firmly, as is necessary throughout the course of every flight, is a skill you should develop.

Understanding this theory side of aviation is a necessary preparation – and look at professional pilots – they never stop studying and reading.

'Flying the aeroplane' should always be your primary concern. Navigation calculations, radio work, operating the engine within the defined limitations, handling engine problems – all these are secondary to maintaining the aeroplane on a safe flightpath.

Keep your priorities right – flying the aeroplane takes precedence over everything else.

A controlled descent, while you sort out an engine problem, shows far better airmanship than a quick solution of the engine problem, with no attention being given to the flightpath and airspeed, allowing a spiral dive to develop.

Some incredible accidents have occurred – a trivial problem, a faulty bulb in the landing gear indicator, once diverted the attention of a three-man crew long enough for a large aeroplane to descend several thousand feet into the ground. Never divert your attention from the flightpath of the aeroplane for more than a few seconds.

A mistake in loading 20,000 *pounds* of fuel instead of the required 20,000 *kilograms* caused a modern wide-body airliner to actually run out of fuel in flight. So, keep a fuel awareness. Occasional reference to the source of your engine power shows good airmanship. Ensure that the fuel selection is correct and that sufficient fuel remains for completion of your flight, plus reserves.

Engine Handling

At all times, follow recommended procedures found in the manufacturer's handbook. This will ensure correct operation of the engine, thereby avoiding spark plug fouling, avoiding over-stressing the engine components, achieving best fuel economy and so on. Know the manufacturer's engine limitations and do not exceed them – for reasons of safety.

MONITOR THE OIL TEMPERATURE GAUGE (and the cylinder head temperature gauge if fitted) to help guard against high temperatures which are damaging to the engine. Avoid running the engine on the ground for prolonged periods if possible, but if unavoidable, face the aircraft into wind for better cooling and, if they are fitted, open the cowl flaps. If the limiting red-line temperatures are approached during ground operations, consider taxiing clear of the runway and shutting the engine down to allow cooling.

PREVENT SPARK PLUG FOULING by avoiding operating the engine at very low rpm for long periods. At low idling rpm, deposits can form on the spark plugs which will increase their electrical conductivity and may lead to misfiring.

DO NOT TAXI OVER ROUGH GROUND that could cause the propeller to hit long grass or other obstructions or even the ground itself. A sudden burst of high power on the ground, say when taxiing on rough ground or to clear a small ditch or gutter, can compress the nosewheel oleo and lower the propeller. If the propeller blades strike the ground (or even long grass), there may be propeller damage and possibly a bent engine crankshaft – a costly lack of common sense.

AVOID ENGINE RUN-UPS ON STONY SURFACES. The strong airflow and vortices around a propeller can easily pick up stones or gravel. Damage such as nicks to the blades degrade the propeller's performance considerably. Nicks are liable to cause cracks in the blade as it flexes and can ultimately lead to blade failure in flight, with disastrous results. Propeller nicks and other damage should be brought to the attention of a ground engineer immediately.

The normal remedy is to 'dress the nick out' with a file, or blend it into the blade shape. This will reduce the propeller's life, so avoid taxiing over surfaces which are likely to cause nicks in the blades.

Stones thrown back by the propeller or the airflow around it can also damage other parts of the aircraft. If you want to remain friends with other users of the airfield, avoid taxiing near open hangar doors and blowing stones, dirt and dust into the workshop area. Good airmanship includes thinking of others.

Cross-Checking Engine Instruments

If one engine instrument indicates a problem, verify this, if possible, by checking against another instrument, e.g. an oil pressure gauge that suddenly shows zero could indicate that all the oil has been lost out of the system or it could be simply a faulty gauge.

Cross-reference to the oil temperature gauge should establish the fault – a continuing normal oil temperature would indicate sufficient oil is still circulating, a rapidly increasing oil temperature approaching the maximum limit would indicate that a loss of oil has occurred and that the oil remaining cannot cope. In this case remedial action would have to be initiated quickly.

If you are in flight, a serious loss of oil will mean an engine shut-down, so in a single-engine aeroplane prepare to land as soon as possible. With a faulty gauge, the engine will continue to operate normally.

An aeroplane with a constant speed (rpm) propeller will have a **manifold pressure gauge** to indicate the air-pressure in the manifold between the carburettor and the cylinders. At a constant rpm, the manifold pressure will decrease as the aircraft climbs into air of lower density. Another cause of a decrease in manifold pressure is carburettor icing. Reference to the **carburettor air temperature gauge** can assist you in determining if the decrease in manifold pressure is due to an increase in altitude and/or carburettor ice.

Using the Engine Controls

Advance and retard the throttle smoothly.

Misuse of controls can lead to engine damage. Advance and retard the throttle smoothly. Opening the throttle by ramming it forward can induce an incorrect fuel/air mixture and cause the engine to cut-out or it can encourage detonation. Opening the throttle from idle to full in about three seconds is usually about as fast as you should go.

When reducing power, especially from high settings such as after take-off, do it slowly. Rapid changes of engine loading are best avoided – engine failures often occur at changes of power setting, both decreasing as well as increasing the power.

On a prolonged descent at low power, to avoid the engine becoming too cool, it is good airmanship to slowly open the throttle for brief periods. Closing cowl flaps, if fitted, also helps. This will avoid a sudden temperature shock to the engine when it is returned to high power.

Use the mixture control correctly. A too-lean mixture at high power and low altitudes can cause detonation. It is usual to lean the mixture when cruising at altitude, depending on the manufacturer's recommendations. On a very hot day, even at 1,000 ft above mean sea level the density altitude may be several thousand feet, and leaning may be required for efficient operation.

Rough Running

The Engine

Engine rough running can be continuous or intermittent. If the engine starts running roughly, refer immediately to the engine instruments to see if they indicate the cause. In all cases, refer to the procedures in the Pilot's Operating Handbook. A thorough knowledge of these is essential. Some causes of engine rough running follow.

INADEQUATE FUEL SUPPLY. A fuel quantity gauge showing empty and a fuel selector positioned to that tank would require immediate selection of a new fuel source if the rough running is not to result in a total loss of power. With any change of tanks or any suspected problem with the supply of fuel to the engine, you should switch on the fuel boost pumps (if fitted) to ensure a steady fuel pressure.

CARBURETTOR ICE. The presence of moisture, even as high humidity, could indicate the formation of ice in the carburettor. This causes a loss of power and possibly rough running. A carburettor air temperature gauge can assist you in determining this as the cause.

CARBURETTOR HEAT. Application of full carburettor heat will cause an initial decrease in performance (a drop in rpm for a fixed-pitch propeller), followed by an increase in power and smoother running as the ice is removed. The initial decrease in power is caused by the hot air entering the carburettor being less dense, mixing with the same weight of fuel as before application of 'carb heat' and therefore richening the mixture. As the ice melts and the airflow improves, the power increases and the rough running disappears (hopefully).

If there is no carburettor ice present to begin with, then application of carburettor heat will still cause a decrease in rpm for a fixed-pitch propeller – but there will be no consequent rise in rpm as there is no carburettor ice to be melted.

Unless the aircraft is fitted with a carburettor air temperature gauge, carb heat should be either full hot or full cold. Intermediate settings could worsen the situation by only changing the temperature marginally and allowing the formation of even more ice. Read again the section on carburettor icing in Chapter 17.

Because the hot air provided when carburettor heat is applied is usually unfiltered (unlike the normal air induced into the carburettor), it is advisable to avoid use of carb heat during ground operations since it may introduce dust and grit into the carburation system and engine.

INCORRECT MIXTURE. A prolonged climb will gradually lead to a richening of the mixture as the air density falls, with consequent rough running – unless the mixture is leaned correctly. A prolonged descent will require you to move the mixture control towards the RICH position.

FAULTY MAGNETO/IGNITION SYSTEM. Select a low cruise power and select each magneto individually. If the engine runs smoothly on one particular magneto, but roughly on BOTH or on the other magneto, then select the single magneto system that gives smoother running. Consider landing at the nearest suitable aerodrome – the aeroplane engine will still operate satisfactorily, but you now have all your eggs in one basket, and a failure of the second magneto system may leave you with none.

☐ **Spark plug fouling** can cause faulty ignition. Sometimes this can be cured by leaning the mixture to raise the temperature and perhaps burn the residue off the plug, or by changing the power setting.

☐ **Leakage of the ignition current,** which can sometimes occur around the ignition harness (the ignition leads that carry the 'spark' to the cylinders), could be the cause; however, this cannot be remedied in flight. This leakage from the ignition harness may be worse at high altitude/high power settings and in wet weather.

EXCESSIVE FUEL AND OIL CONSUMPTION. While this may not cause rough running or a noticeable decrease in short-term performance, it certainly indicates a decrease in the performance of the engine that should be investigated. Inspect for leaks and check fuel and oil caps. Bring excessive consumption to the attention of a ground engineer.

The Propeller

An out-of-balance propeller can cause vibration.

Vibration or rough running usually indicates a problem or impending problem. An out-of-balance propeller can cause vibration. If the vibration is due to a damaged propeller, possibly an out-of-balance propeller due to nicks, etc., then a change of rpm or airspeed might reduce the vibration. This is only a temporary remedy until the aeroplane has landed.

If the vibration does not diminish, but worsens, it could indicate a loosening of the bolts attaching the propeller to the shaft. In this case, a shutting down of the engine is advisable. If you suspect this defect in a single-engine aeroplane, a landing as soon as possible (a forced landing, if necessary) should be contemplated.

If the out-of-balance condition is caused by ice on the propeller blades, then removal of the ice will remedy the vibration.

Starting the Engine

Ensure that adequate safety precautions are always taken. Position the aircraft prior to start so that it is clear of obstructions, other aircraft, open hangar/workshop doors, refuelling installations and so that a clear taxi path is available.

Set the park brakes on or have the aircraft chocked, to avoid the embarrassing and dangerous situation of the aeroplane commencing its own taxiing. Chocking the nosewheel is not advisable due to its proximity to the propeller. Chocking the main wheels is safer for a single-engine aeroplane.

Be aware of the availability of fire-fighting equipment – just in case. Ensure there are no naked flames, cigarettes or fuel spillages in the vicinity.

Be prepared to discontinue the start immediately if a problem develops or if someone approaches the danger area near the propeller.

Starting the Engine in Cold Temperatures

Starting an engine in cold conditions usually requires some priming (providing an initial charge of fuel to the cylinder). Many aircraft have a priming pump (electrical or manual) in the cockpit for this purpose.

In extremely cold conditions (approaching zero or below, or with frost or ice), it is good airmanship to turn the engine through two or three revolutions (magneto switches checked OFF of course, and possibly rotation in the reverse direction should be considered). This will break the oil seal on moving parts, thereby reducing the frictional drag within the engine. The electrical load on the starter motor and battery is therefore reduced – this might mean the difference between starting or not, and not draining the battery.

Starting a Hot or Over-Primed Engine

Start the engine with the mixture control in IDLE CUT-OFF so that no more fuel enters the cylinders. As the mixture in the cylinders reaches the right balance the engine should fire, at which stage the mixture control should be moved to the RICH position to provide a continuing fuel supply.

If the engine does not fire, then when you feel the cylinders have been cleared after several rotations, move the mixture control to RICH to allow fuel to be drawn into the cylinders.

Know the procedures recommended in your Pilot's Operating Handbook. These differ from aeroplane to aeroplane and engine to engine. You should understand the reasons why a certain procedure is recommended and when it is appropriate to vary them slightly – an over-primed (flooded) engine or re-starting a hot engine may require a different technique to starting a cold engine in a cold climate.

Starting a Fuel-Injected Engine

This may require a slightly different technique, especially when the engine is hot. Hot air and vapour in the fine fuel lines of a fuel-injected engine may disturb the fuel supply when starting.

One technique is to switch on the fuel boost pumps. This will pressurise the fuel lines up to the fuel control unit, removing any vapour in that part of the system. Leave the mixture control in IDLE CUT-OFF so that fuel does not reach the cylinders but is re-cycled back into the tank.

Some engines require the throttle to be opened for the boost pumps to work in HIGH. After 15 to 20 seconds, the narrow fuel lines to the fuel injectors should have been purged of vapour and now be full of fuel. A little fuel will probably have found its way into the fuel nozzles near the cylinders and so a start, with the throttle in idle, can be made without priming.

Hand-Swinging a Propeller

Do not attempt to hand-swing a propeller without adequate instruction.

Brakes and chocks should be checked. Follow the normal starting procedures to the point of actually engaging the starter. Verify that the throttle is in idle or close to it. Do not touch the propeller until you ensure the ignition switches are OFF. Position the propeller into a suitable position for swinging – the aim is to swing it, (firmly pull it) through the compression stroke.

Immediately prior to attempting a start, check that you have no loose clothing that could become caught in a spinning propeller, that you have a firm footing such that, after the swing and follow through, your body will have a natural tendency to move out of the plane of rotation of the propeller.

Always treat a propeller as live!

The propeller should be held near the tip, the ignition switched ON, and pulled in such a manner with a follow through that, if the engine fires, your body has a natural swing away from the arc of propeller rotation. At all times, treat the propeller as live!

Stopping the Engine

A brief cooling period at idle rpm is usually recommended before shutting down the engine; this allows gradual cooling and gives you time to consider the condition of the engine, any abnormal indications, and to perform a systems check of the ignition system for OFF, if so desired. See Chapter 16.

Most engines are shut down from a low power position by moving the mixture control to IDLE CUT-OFF, thus allowing the cylinders to be purged of fuel. All switches are usually moved to OFF. After the engine has been shut down, it is good practice to:

☐ **leave the mixture control** in the IDLE CUT-OFF position; and

☐ **leave the throttle** in the closed position in case someone turns the propeller and firing occurs due to a 'live' magneto system.

Constant-Speed Propeller Operations

While almost all training aeroplanes are fitted with a fixed-pitch propeller whose rpm is controlled with the throttle, more advanced aeroplanes that you may soon fly will have a variable-pitch propeller controlled by a constant-speed unit (CSU).

A variable-pitch propeller enables better take-off, climb and cruise performance because the blade pitch can be set to provide optimum thrust for the particular stage of flight. On the cruise (the majority of flight operations) the powerplant (engine–propeller) can be operated at optimum settings, giving the best fuel consumption and airspeed. Refer back to pages 52–53 in Chapter 6 covering CSUs.

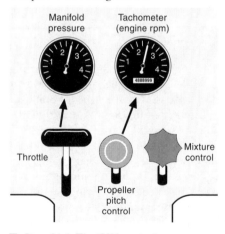

■ *Figure 21-1* **The CSU control**

Change rpm with the pitch control. Change MP with throttle.

The engine controls for a CSU are:
☐ **the pitch control,** to set propeller rpm; and
☐ **the throttle,** which controls the fuel flow, determining the manifold pressure (abbreviated MP or MAP).

Power produced is a product of *rpm × manifold pressure (MP)*.
☐ **High power** can be produced by *high rpm × high MP.*
☐ **Medium power** can be produced by *high rpm × lower MP,* or by *medium rpm × medium MP,* or by *lower rpm × higher MP.*

Never exceed recommended manifold pressures.

For a given rpm, excessive manifold pressure causes:
☐ **high cylinder pressures** and cylinder head temperatures; and
☐ **possible detonation,** and mechanical failure if prolonged.

The manufacturer recommends certain power settings (rpm/MP combinations) to achieve a desired power, all of which have been tested as satisfactory for the engine. The most efficient (best specific fuel consumption) rpm/MP combination usually uses the lowest rpm and highest MP for the desired power. This combination has a lower friction penalty due to the lower rpm.

High rpm settings can increase oil consumption and limit the engine's 'volumetric efficiency' due to the friction of the air flowing through the intake manifold.

A typical power setting table is shown in Figure 21-2. Interpolation is required to obtain intermediate values. Note that the table cautions operators to "observe maximum allowable manifold pressure limitations".

POWER SETTING TABLE - LYCOMING MODEL TIO-540-S1AD 300 HP ENGINE

Press. Alt. Feet	Std Alt Temp °C	165 HP - 55% Rated Approx Fuel 13.8 GPH* RPM AND MAN. PRESS.				195 HP - 65% Rated Approx Fuel 15.7 GPH* RPM AND MAN. PRESS.			225 HP - 75% Rated Approx Fuel 21.9 GPH** RPM AND MAN. PRESS.			243 HP - 81% Rated Approx Fuel 24 GPH** RPM AND MAN. PRESS.		Press. Alt. Feet
		2200	2300	2400	2575	2300	2400	2575	2300	2400	2575	2400	2575	
SL	15	23.5	22.7	22.0	20.7	25.9	25.0	23.5	29.2	28.0	26.0	30.2	28.0	SL
2,000	11	23.3	22.5	21.8	20.5	25.6	24.7	23.1	29.0	27.8	25.7	30.0	27.7	2,000
4,000	7	22.9	22.2	21.5	20.3	25.3	24.4	22.9	28.9	27.8	25.7	29.9	27.5	4,000
6,000	3	22.6	21.8	21.0	19.7	25.1	24.1	22.5	28.8	27.5	25.3	29.8	27.4	6,000

To maintain constant power, correct manifold pressure approximately 1% MAP for each 6° C variation in induction air temperature from standard altitude temperature. Add manifold pressure for air temperatures above standard; subtract for temperatures below standard. Observe maximum allowable manifold pressure limitations.

*Best Economy
**Best Power

■ *Figure 21-2* **Excerpt from a typical power setting table for a high-performance engine**

Changing Power with a Constant-Speed Unit

To avoid overboosting the engine (i.e. for a given rpm, to avoid exceeding the maximum manifold pressure) follow these guidelines.

INCREASING POWER. When increasing power significantly (say from cruise power to go-around power):

1. **Set the higher rpm** (MP will automatically drop a little due to less time per cycle to induce the fuel/air mixture into the cylinder, hence a smaller charge for combustion and more exhaust strokes per second, leading to a reduction of pressures in the cylinder); and then

2. **Increase the MP.**

REDUCING POWER. When reducing power significantly (say from take-off power to climb power):

1. **Reduce the MP** (about 1″Hg lower than desired); and then

2. **Set the lower rpm** (as rpm reduces, MP increases about 1″Hg). With the rpm reduction, there is more time per cycle to induce the fuel/air mixture into the cylinder, hence a larger charge for combustion and fewer exhaust strokes per second, leading to a build-up of pressure in the cylinder. After the power reduction, some minor readjustment of MP (throttle) will be necessary.

For detailed information on CSU operation of a particular aeroplane type, refer to its Pilot's Operating Handbook.

Now complete **Exercises 21 – Engine Handling.**

The Electrical System

Most aeroplanes require an electrical system to operate such things as cabin lights, landing lights, instrument lights, starter motors, electric flaps, radios, radar, pitot heaters, fuel gauges, fuel boost pumps, electrically retractable undercarriage, and so on.

The Pilot's Operating Handbook will contain information on the electrical system of your aircraft. A typical modern light aircraft has a **direct current (DC)** electrical system. The current is produced by an **alternator** when the engine is running, or from a battery or external power source when the engine is not running.

The current runs through the wires and the **bus bar** to the electrical component requiring power, does its work there and then runs to ground through an **earthing wire** attached to the airframe structure (the return path of the electrical current).

The Bus Bar

The bus bar is the distribution centre of the electrical system. It is a metal bar that allows electrical current to be supplied to various electrical circuits or units.

Electrical power is usually supplied to the bus bar by an alternator (or a generator) and a battery, and is distributed, via the bus bar, to the circuits and electrical components that require power.

The Battery

The battery provides initial electrical power to start the engine and a back-up source of electrical power for emergency use.

> The battery provides emergency electrical power, and electrical power for engine start.

Most light aircraft have a **lead-acid battery** that creates an electrical current (amperes, or *amps*) by a chemical reaction between lead plates immersed in weak sulphuric acid which acts as an electrolyte. To prevent corrosion from any spillage of the acid, the battery is usually housed in its own compartment. The battery needs to be vented to exhaust the hydrogen and oxygen formed when it is being charged.

Batteries are classified according to the voltage across the terminals – usually 12 or 24 volts – and their capacity to provide a current for a certain time (amp-hours).

> The battery should recharge after engine start.

A 30 amp-hour battery is capable of steadily supplying a current of 1 amp for 30 hours (or 6 amps for 5 hours). If its electrical energy is depleted, e.g. by an engine start, the battery needs to be recharged. This normally occurs after the engine is running, when it absorbs power produced by the alternator. The largest current draw on the battery is during start-up, when it supplies electrical power to the starter motor to turn the engine over – so the greatest rate of battery recharging will normally occur immediately after engine start.

Connecting two 12-volt 40 amp-hour batteries in parallel is equivalent to a single 12-volt battery capable of supplying (2 × 40) = 80 amp-hours.

Connecting two 12-volt 40 amp-hour batteries in series is equivalent to a single 24-volt battery capable of supplying 40 amp-hours.

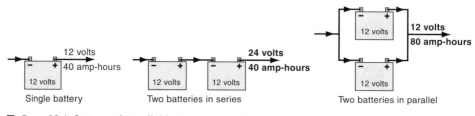

■ *Figure 22-1* **Series and parallel battery connection**

The serviceability of the battery can be checked by:
- ☐ **Testing** the acidity of the electrolyte liquid using a hydrometer.
- ☐ **Checking** that it retains its voltage under load.
- ☐ **Checking** that the fluid covers the plates. If the fluid level is well below the top of the plates, the battery will not retain its full charge for very long, and the ammeter will indicate a high charging rate in flight.

Leaks, connections and the security of the battery should also be checked. This is carried out in the regular maintenance schedule by engineers.

Do not commence a flight with a flat battery – it could result in having no electrical power in flight. If the battery is flat, replace it or have it recharged before flight.

Do not fly with a flat battery.

Do not start the engine with radios and other unnecessary electrical equipment switched on. Large voltage fluctuations when the starter is engaged may severely damage sensitive electronic circuits. Turn on this ancillary electrical equipment after the engine is started, and after you have checked that the alternator is charging the battery. For the same reasons, turn off the ancillary electrical equipment before shutting down the engine.

Turn off ancillary electrical equipment before starting and stopping the engine.

The Alternator and Generator

The electrical power in most modern light aircraft is usually supplied by an **alternator,** which is belt-driven by the engine. On older aircraft, the electrical power may be produced by a **generator,** which is electrically self-sufficient because it has its own permanent magnetic field. Once the rotor is mechanically turned, the generator will produce electrical current. Alternators, on the other hand, require battery power to *excite* a magnetic field in order for them to provide a current.

Both alternators and generators initially produce alternating current (AC) – an electric current that flows in alternate directions. Since most aircraft require direct current (DC) – electric current that flows in only one direction – the AC has to be *rectified,* or converted to DC. The AC within the alternator is rectified into DC electronically with diodes, whereas within the generator an electromechanical device known as the commutator performs this function. Also, the diodes in the alternator prevent any reverse current flow out of the battery, whereas a generator requires a reverse current relay.

In addition to providing power for the electrical equipment, an important function of the alternator or generator is to recharge the battery, ensuring that it is ready for further use. Most aircraft electrical systems are direct current of 14 or 28 volts. Note that these voltages are marginally higher than the battery voltages, to allow the battery to be fully recharged.

The Advantages of an Alternator

Alternators:

- **are lighter than generators** because alternators do not contain as heavy electro-magnets and casings, and have a simpler and lighter brush assembly compared to generators;
- **produce a relatively constant voltage,** even at low rpm;
- **are easier to maintain** (because of their simpler brush assembly and the absence of a commutator).

The Disadvantage of an Alternator

An aircraft with an alternator must have a serviceable battery.

Unlike a generator, an alternator requires an initial current from the battery to create a magnetic field, which is necessary to 'excite' the alternator before it can produce an electrical current. Therefore an aircraft with an alternator must have a serviceable battery, and a flat battery must be replaced. Even if you hand-swing the propeller to start the engine, the alternator will not come on-line unless the battery has at least some residual voltage. An alternator's advantages outweigh this disadvantage, however.

Voltage Regulator

The correct output voltage from the generator/alternator is maintained by a voltage regulator, over which the pilot has no direct control.

Overvoltage Protector

Some aircraft have overvoltage protectors. Refer to your Pilot's Operating Handbook for information.

The Ammeter

An ammeter measures the current (amps) flowing into or out of the battery. (In some aircraft a voltmeter is provided to measure the electromotive force available to deliver the current.)

There are two quite distinct types of ammeter presentations, and you should understand what the instrument is telling you.

Left-Zero Ammeter

A left-zero ammeter measures only the output of the alternator or generator. It is graduated from zero amps on the left end of the scale, increasing in amps to the right end of the scale – or it may be shown as a percentage of the alternator's rated load. As the left-zero ammeter indicates the electrical load on the alternator, this type of ammeter can be referred to as a *loadmeter*.

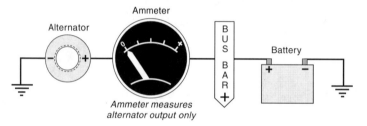
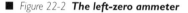

■ *Figure 22-2* **The left-zero ammeter**

With the battery switch ON and the engine not running, or, with the engine running and the alternator switch OFF, the ammeter will show zero. If the engine is started and the alternator turned ON, the alternator will then show the alternator output.

During start-up, the battery discharges electrical power, so immediately after engine start the ammeter indication will be quite high during the initial battery recharging.

When the battery is fully charged, and the alternator is operating, the ammeter should show a reading slightly above the zero graduation if all the other electrical circuits are switched off. As these extra circuits are switched on (lights, radios, etc.), the ammeter reading will increase.

If the ammeter reading drops to zero in flight, it probably means an alternator failure. Some electrical systems have a red warning light that illuminates when the alternator fails to supply electrical power. You should be familiar with the procedures for electrical failure in your Pilot's Operating Handbook; they may allow you to restore electrical power.

Generally it is advisable to reduce the electrical load to a minimum, as only the battery will be supplying electrical power. Land as soon as possible and have the problem corrected.

Centre-Zero Ammeter

The centre-zero ammeter measures the flow of current (amperage) into and out of the battery.

☐ **Current into** the battery is *charge,* with the ammeter needle deflected right of centre.

☐ **Current out** of the battery is *discharge,* with the ammeter needle deflected left of centre.

☐ **Zero current flow** either into or out of the battery is shown by the needle being located in the centre-zero position.

☐ **With the battery switch** ON and no alternator output, the ammeter will indicate a discharge from the battery, i.e. the battery is providing current for the electrical circuits that are switched on. The ammeter needle is to the left (discharge) side of centre-zero.

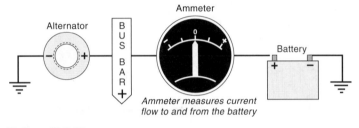

Ammeter measures current flow to and from the battery

■ *Figure 22-3* **The centre-zero ammeter**

☐ **With the alternator** ON and supplying electrical power, if the electrical load required to power the circuits switched on is less than the capability of the alternator, the ammeter will show a charge, i.e. there will be a flow of current to the battery.

☐ **If the alternator is** ON, but incapable of supplying sufficient power to the electrical circuits, the battery must make up the balance and there will be some flow of current from the battery. The ammeter will show a discharge. If this continues, the battery could be completely drained (flattened). Off-load the electrical system by switching off unnecessary services until the ammeter indicates a charge, i.e. a flow of current from the alternator into the battery.

The Master Switch

The master switch (or battery switch/alternator switch) controls all of the aeroplane's electrical systems, with one important exception – the ignition system, which receives electrical power directly from the engine-driven magneto. (This is not completely true if the aircraft has an electric clock, which will draw a very small amount of power at all times.)

The master switch needs to be ON for any other electrical system to receive power, or for the battery to be recharged when the engine is running. It should be turned OFF after stopping the engine, to avoid the battery discharging via services that are connected to it.

In aircraft fitted with an alternator, the master switch is split (with two halves that can be switched ON and OFF separately).

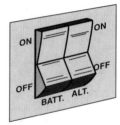

- **One half** operates the **battery switch** (or master relay for the electrical systems), which connects battery power to the bus bar (electrical load distribution point or bar).

■ *Figure 22-4*

The master switch

- **The other half** operates the **alternator switch,** for energising the alternator. It connects the alternator field to the bus bar, thus providing the alternator with battery power for field excitation.

Both switches must be ON for normal operation of the electrical system. If either switch has to be turned OFF in flight, then you should consider terminating the flight as soon as possible.

They can be switched on separately, but only the alternator can be switched off separately – switching the battery OFF will automatically switch the alternator off as well.

Fuses, Circuit Breakers and Overload Switches

Fuses, circuit breakers and overload switches are provided to protect the equipment from any electrical current overload. If there is an electrical overload or short-circuit, a fuse-wire will melt or a circuit breaker (CB) will pop, i.e. pop out, and break the circuit so that no current can flow through it. It may prevent the circuit from overheating, smoking or catching fire.

It is normal procedure (provided there is no smell or other sign of burning or overheating) to reset a circuit breaker once only, by pushing it back in or resetting it. If a circuit breaker pops again, you can be fairly sure there is an electrical problem and so it should not be reset a second time. Similarly a fuse-wire should not be replaced more than once (with the correct amperage first checked on the replacement fuse-wire). Spare fuses of the correct type and rating should be available in the cockpit.

Do not reset a circuit breaker or replace a fuse more than once.

Do not replace a blown fuse with one of a higher rating (e.g. 15 amp is a higher rating than 5 amp) as this may allow excessive current to flow through the electrical circuit that it is supposed to protect. An electrical fire could result.

Do not replace a fuse with one of a higher rating.

Overload switches are combined ON-OFF switches and overload protectors. Overload switches will switch themselves off with an electrical overload. You can switch them back on like a resettable circuit breaker.

Some aircraft handbooks recommended a delay of a minute or two prior to resetting, to allow for cooling of the possibly over-loaded circuit. If you detect fire, smoke or a burning smell, then caution is advised. Resetting the CB or replacing the fuse in such cases is not advisable.

Relays

A relay is a device in one electrical circuit that can be activated by a current or a voltage to produce a change in the electrical condition of another electrical circuit.

Instead of having high currents and heavy wiring running to where the switches are in the cockpit (with consequent current losses, fire danger from arcing, etc.), a low-amperage current operated by a switch can be used to close a remote relay and complete the circuit for a much-higher-amperage circuit, such as for the starter motor.

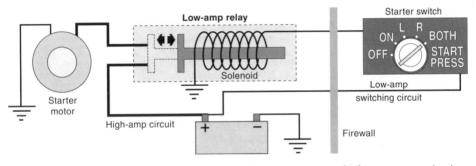

■ *Figure 22-5* **Low-amp relay circuit activates high-amp starter circuit**

A relay is usually operated on the **solenoid** principle. A sole-noid is a metal bar or rod with a coil of wire wound around it. If a current passes through the coil, it establishes a magnetic field that can move the metal rod, which can then perform some mechanical task, such as making or breaking a contact in another electrical circuit.

A typical relay consists of a contact held open by a spring, thereby interrupting an electrical circuit. Around the stem of the relay is wound a coil of wire. If a current is made to pass through this coil, a magnetic field is created that will move the relay to the closed position, thereby completing the circuit and allowing current to flow in it.

The current that activates the relay is in a completely different circuit to the relay.

Occasionally a relay will stick even though its activating current has been removed, and an unwanted current will flow through the circuit. Many electric starters have an associated red warning light that will stay illuminated to warn the pilot of the starter relay sticking and the starter motor still operating even though the starter has been switched to OFF. (In this situation, the engine would be stopped by starving it of fuel – mixture control to IDLE CUT-OFF.)

External Power Socket or Ground Servicing Receptacle

The more sophisticated light aircraft and most large aircraft have provision for a suitable external power source to be plugged into the aeroplane's electrical system – either to provide ground power over an extended period when the engine or engines are not running or to conserve the aircraft battery during an engine start.

On some aircraft types, with an unserviceable battery, external power can be plugged in but will not connect into the aircraft electrical system – a small current from the battery is needed to operate the relay that connects the plugged-in external power to the aircraft circuit. There are other systems that operate differently to this, so refer to your Pilot's Operating Handbook. Ensure a ground power unit (GPU) of the correct voltage is used. (Putting a 28V GPU on a 12 volt aircraft will damage the radios and electrics.)

Electrical Malfunctions

An electrical overload will normally cause a fuse-wire to melt or a circuit breaker to pop. This protects the affected circuit. Allow two minutes to cool and, if no indication of smoke, fire or burning smell, replace the fuse or reset the circuit breaker – but reset once only. If the CB pops or the fuse melts again – do not reset or replace a second time.

The ammeter should be checked when the engine is running to ensure that the alternator is supplying sufficient current (amps) for the electrical services and to recharge the battery. The ammeter usually indicates the rate at which current is flowing into the battery and recharging it. With the engine running, the ammeter can indicate two faults:

1. Insufficient current to charge the battery.

2. Too much current.

With insufficient current from the alternator, or none at all, electrical services activated should be reduced to a minimum to conserve the battery, and thought should be given to making an early landing. Most batteries cannot supply all electrical services for a long period.

With too much current and an excessive charge rate, the battery could overheat and the electrolyte (which may be sulphuric acid) begin to evaporate, possibly damaging the battery. If the cause of the excessive current is a faulty voltage regulator, equipment such as the radio could be adversely affected. Many aircraft have an overvoltage sensor that would, in these circumstances, automatically shut-down the alternator and illuminate a red warning light in the cockpit to alert the pilot.

NOTE Operations of an alternator-powered electrical system with a partially charged battery (e.g. unable to turn the engine over) are not recommended for the above reasons.

If the alternator fails (indicated in most aircraft by either the ammeter indication dropping to zero or by a red warning light), the battery will act as an emergency source of electrical power. To extend the period for which the battery can supply power following failure of the alternator the electrical load should be reduced. This can be done by switching off non-essential services such as lighting and radios. Consideration should be given to terminating the flight at a nearby suitable aerodrome while electrical power is still available.

Typical Electrical Systems

The Pilot's Operating Handbook for each aeroplane will contain a diagram of its electrical system and the services to which electrical power is supplied. It is good airmanship to be aware of what powers vital services and instruments in your aeroplane. The arrangement varies greatly between aeroplanes, but certain important services that could be powered by the electrical system include:

☐ **Some or all gyroscopic flight instruments** (turn coordinator, attitude indicator and heading indicator). A common arrangement is electrically powered turn coordinator with vacuum-driven AI and HI to reduce the possibility of all gyroscopic instruments failing simultaneously. Note that the pitot-static instruments (ASI, altimeter, VSI) are not electrically powered.

☐ **Fuel quantity indicators,** and perhaps an oil temperature gauge, or carburettor air temperature gauge (if fitted).

☐ **Starting system.**

☐ **Landing lights,** beacon, strobe, cabin lights, instrument lights.

☐ **Radios.**

Check the electrical system diagram for your particular aeroplane. Figure 22-6 shows a schematic diagram of a typical light aircraft electrical system.

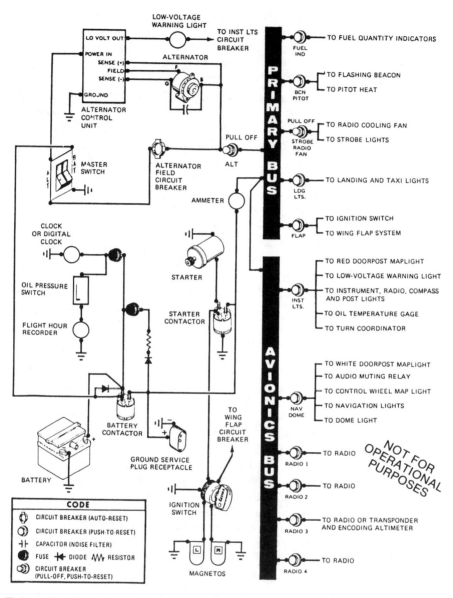

■ *Figure 22-6* **A typical light aircraft electrical system**

Now complete **Exercises 22 – The Electrical System.**

The Vacuum System

The gyroscopes in the flight instruments may be spun electrically or by a stream of high-speed air directed at buckets cut into the perimeter of the rotor. The vacuum system (which draws, or induces, this high-speed air into the gyro instrument cases and onto the gyro rotors, causing them to spin very fast) needs a little explaining. (Chapter 26 explains the instruments themselves.)

Engine-Driven Vacuum Pump

Most modern vacuum systems use an engine-driven suction pump. This evacuates the cases of the gyroscopic-driven instruments, creating a 'vacuum' (low pressure).

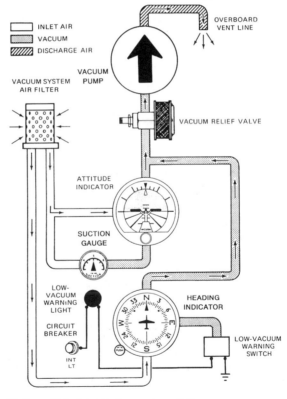

■ *Figure 23-1* **A typical vacuum system**

The required suction is 3 to 5 inches of mercury (i.e. a pressure 3 to 5 inches of mercury less than atmospheric), indicated in the cockpit on a suction gauge. Filtered air is continuously drawn in at high speed through a nozzle directed at the gyro buckets, causing the gyro to spin at high rpm, often in excess of 20,000 rpm. This air is continuously being sucked out by the suction pump and exhausted into the atmosphere.

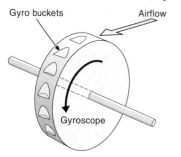

■ *Figure 23-2* **Gyroscope buckets**

'CAGING' GYROSCOPES. When the gyros are not being used, they should normally be caged (if provision is made for this), i.e. locked in a fixed position. This is also recommended in the Pilot's Operating Handbook of some aircraft when performing aerobatic manoeuvres.

Vacuum System Malfunctions

The effects of various malfunctions of the vacuum system are summarised below.

BLOCKED AIR FILTER. If the air filter blocks, or the vacuum system fails, the reduced airflow may allow the gyroscopes to gradually run down, and the air-operated instruments will eventually indicate erratically or incorrectly, or respond slowly. A lower suction will be indicated on the gauge.

VACUUM PUMP FAILURE. Failure of the vacuum pump will be indicated by a zero reading on the suction gauge. With luck, the gyroscopes may have sufficient speed to allow the instruments to read correctly for a minute or two before the gyros run down following failure of the vacuum pump. A zero reading on the suction gauge could also mean a failure of the gauge (rather than the vacuum pump), in which case the instruments should operate normally.

EXCESSIVE VACUUM PRESSURE. If the vacuum pressure is too high, the gyro rotors may spin too fast and suffer mechanical damage. To prevent this, a vacuum relief valve (or vacuum regulator) in the system will admit air from the atmosphere to reduce the excessive suction.

Vacuum Provided by a Venturi Tube

Some aircraft (especially older ones) have their vacuum system operated by a **venturi-shaped tube** on the outside of the airframe. When air flows through the tube and speeds up due to its shape, the static pressure decreases (Bernoulli's principle). This low-pressure area, if connected to the gyro instrument cases, will cause air to be drawn through each instrument via an internal filter and spin the gyroscopes, as in the engine-driven system.

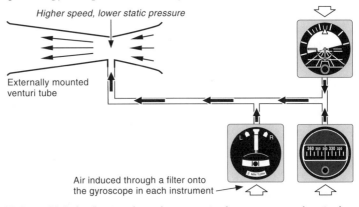

■ *Figure 23-3* **Air flowing through a venturi tube can create a 'suction', and power a vacuum system**

Before the venturi-powered vacuum system can work there must be an adequate airflow through the venturi tube. This is normally created by the forward motion of the aeroplane through the air – sufficient airflow being provided at flying speeds. It may be several minutes after take-off before the gyroscopes are spinning fast enough for the instrument indications to be reliable. This is a significant disadvantage compared to the engine-driven system.

Other disadvantages are the increased drag caused by the externally mounted venturi-tube, and the possibility of ice affecting it (like a carburettor).

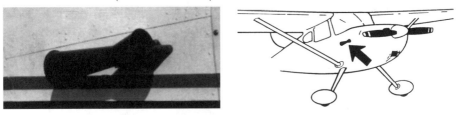

■ *Figure 23-4* **A typical venturi tube**

Now complete **Exercises 23 – The Vacuum System.**

Landing Gear, Tyres and Brakes

The typical training aeroplane has a fixed tricycle landing gear consisting of two main wheels which incorporate brakes, and a nosewheel which can be steered by moving the rudder pedals. A typical pre-flight check will include:

- ☐ **check landing gear** and its support points for damage, such as cracks, corrosion or distortion;
- ☐ **check oleo struts** for cleanliness, leaks and correct extension;
- ☐ **check tyres** for inflation, damage and creep;
- ☐ **inspect brake installation** for external evidence of leaks, and for damage and security.

Landing Gear

The **main wheels** carry most of the load when the aeroplane is on the ground, especially during the take-off and landing, and so are more robust than the nosewheel. They are usually attached to the main aircraft structure with legs in the form of:

- ☐ **a very strong spring leaf** of steel or fibre-glass;
- ☐ **struts and braces;** or
- ☐ **an oleo-pneumatic unit.**

The **nosewheel** is of lighter construction that the main wheels and is usually attached to the main structure of the aircraft (often near the engine firewall) with an oleo-pneumatic unit.

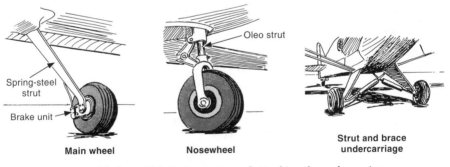

Spring-steel strut

Brake unit

Oleo strut

Main wheel

Nosewheel

Strut and brace undercarriage

■ *Figure 24-1* **Various means of attaching the undercarriage**

The landing gear legs or struts and their attachment points must carry heavy stresses, especially during landings and take-offs, or when taxiing over rough surfaces, hence the need to inspect them carefully prior to flight. Obvious damage should be inspected by a qualified engineer before the aeroplane flies again.

The **oleo-pneumatic unit** is of telescopic construction, with a piston that can move within a cylinder against an opposing pressure of compressed air. The piston is attached to the wheel by an oleo-strut and the cylinder is attached to the airframe. The nosewheel attachment is often near the firewall directly behind the engine.

The greater the load on the strut, the more the air is compressed by the piston. While the aeroplane is running along the ground, the load will be varying and so the strut will move up and down as the compressed air absorbs the loads and shocks, preventing jarring of the main aeroplane structure.

Special oil is used as a **damping agent** to prevent excessive in and out telescoping movements of the oleo-pneumatic unit and damp its rebound action.

When the aircraft is stationary, a certain length of polished oleo strut should be visible (depending of course to some extent on how the aeroplane is loaded) and this should be checked in the pre-flight external inspection. Items to check are:

- [ ] **correct extension** when supporting its share of the aeroplane's weight;
- [ ] **the polished section** of the oleo strut is clean of mud or dirt (to avoid rapid wearing of the seals during the telescoping motion of the strut); and
- [ ] **there are no fluid leaks.**

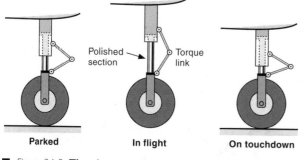

Polished section Torque link

Parked   **In flight**   **On touchdown**

■ *Figure 24-2* **The oleo-pneumatic unit**

A **torque-link** is used on nosewheel assemblies to correctly align the nosewheel with the airframe. It links the cylinder assembly that is attached to the aeroplane structure with the nosewheel assembly, and is hinged to allow for the telescopic extension and compression of the oleo.

Some aircraft have **nosewheel steering,** achieved by moving the rudder pedals which are attached by control rods or cables to the nosewheel assembly, thereby allowing greater directional control when taxiing.

Other aircraft have **castoring nosewheels** which are free to turn, but are not connected by controls to the cockpit. The pilot can turn the aeroplane by using the rudder when it has sufficient airflow over it (due to either slipstream or airspeed) or with differential braking of the main wheels. Most tailwheels castor, allowing the pilot to steer by differential braking, or by using the rudder if it has sufficient airflow over it.

Nosewheel oleo-pneumatic units are prone to **nosewheel shimmy,** an unpleasant and possibly damaging vibration caused by the nosewheel oscillating a few degrees either side of centre as the aeroplane runs along the ground. To prevent this, most nosewheel assemblies are fitted with a **shimmy-damper,** a small piston-cylinder unit that dampens out the oscillations and prevents the vibration. If nosewheel-shimmy does occur, it could be because the shimmy-damper is insufficiently pressurised or the torque link has failed.

■ *Figure 24-3* **The shimmy-damper**

Tyres

Aeroplane tyres are pneumatic and must be operated at approximately the correct pressure for them to function as designed. Vibration during taxiing, uneven wear and burst tyres may result from a pressure that is too high. Damage to the tyre structure and a tendency for the tyre to *creep* with respect to the rim will occur if the pressure is too low. Correct inflation is important in achieving a good service life from a tyre.

Creep will occur in normal operations because of the stresses during landing, when a stationary tyre is forced to rotate on touching the ground and has to 'drag' the wheel around with it, and when the aeroplane is braking or turning. If the tyre creeps too far, the inner tube may suffer and the valve may become unusable or even break.

To monitor creep, there are usually paint marks on the wheel flange and on the tyre which should remain aligned. If any part of the two creep marks is still in contact, that amount of creep is acceptable; but if the marks are separated, then the inner tube may suffer damage and the tyre should be inspected and serviced. This may require removal and re-fitting, or replacement.

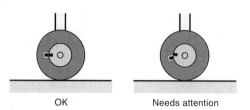

OK   Needs attention

■ *Figure 24-4* **'Creep' marks on the tyre and wheel flange enable visual checks for creep**

The strength of a tyre comes from its carcass, which is built up from casing cords and then covered with rubber. The *ply rating* is a measure of its supposed strength. Neither the rubber sidewalls nor the tread provide the main strength of the tyre; the sidewalls protect the sides of the tyre carcass, and the rubber tread provides a wearing surface at the contact points between the tyre and the runway.

Shallow cuts or scores in the sidewalls or on the tread, or small stones embedded in the tread, will not be detrimental to tyre strength. However, any large cuts (especially if they expose the casing cords) or bulges (that may be external indications of an internal casing failure) should cause you to reject the tyre prior to flight.

The condition of the tyres should be noted during the pre-flight external inspection, especially with respect to:
- **inflation;**
- **creep;**
- **wear,** especially flat spots caused by skidding;
- **cuts, bulges** (especially deep cuts that expose the casing cords);
- **damage** to the structure of the sidewall.

Wheel Brakes

Most training aeroplanes are fitted with **disc brakes** on the main wheels. These are hydraulically operated by the *toe brakes* which are situated on top of the rudder pedals. Pressing the left toe brake will slow the left main wheel down and pressing the right toe brake will slow the right main wheel down. Used separately, they provide **differential braking,** which is useful for manoeuvring on the ground; used together, they provide normal braking.

A typical system involves a separate master cylinder for each brake containing hydraulic fluid. As an individual toe brake is pressed, this toe pressure is transmitted by the hydraulic fluid to a slave cylinder which closes the brake friction pads (like calipers) onto the brake disc. The brake disc, which is part of the wheel assembly, has its rotation slowed down.

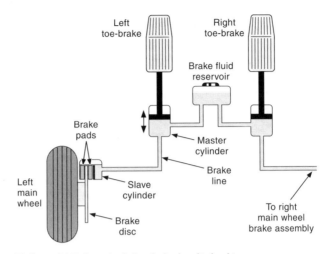

■ *Figure 24-5* **A typical simple hydraulic braking system**

Most aircraft have a **parking brake** (usually hand-operated, sometimes in conjunction with the toe-brakes) that will hold the pressure on the wheel brakes and can be used when the aeroplane is parked.

During the pre-flight external inspection, you should check the brakes to ensure that they will function when you need them, noting especially that:

☐ **there are no leaks** of hydraulic brake fluid from the brake lines;

☐ **the brake discs** are not corroded or pitted;

☐ **the brake pads** are not worn-out;

☐ **the brake assembly** is firmly attached.

A severely corroded or pitted disc will cause rapid wear of the brake pads, as well as reducing their effectiveness, and, in an extreme case, the disc may even fail structurally. Fluid leaks from the brake lines or cylinders indicate a faulty system that may in fact provide no braking at all when it is needed. Any brake problems should be rectified prior to flight.

Following a satisfactory external inspection, you should still test the brakes immediately after the aeroplane first moves, by closing the throttle and gently applying toe brake pressure. **Brake wear** can be minimised by judicious use of the brakes during ground operations.

Now complete **Exercises 24 – Landing Gear, Tyres and Brakes.**

Section **Three**

Flight Instruments

Pressure Instruments

The first impression most people have of an aeroplane cockpit or flight deck is of the number of instruments. When you analyse the instrument panels of even the largest jet transport aeroplanes, you will find that the instrumentation is not all that complicated. In fact, the basic instruments will be very similar to those found in the smallest training aeroplane. Aircraft flight instruments fall into three basic categories:

- **pressure instruments** – which use variations in air pressure;
- **gyroscopic instruments** – which use the properties of gyroscopic inertia;
- **magnetic instruments** – which use the earth's magnetic field.

The basic flight instruments that inform the pilot of airspeed (airspeed indicator), altitude (altimeter) and rate of change of altitude (vertical speed indicator) are pressure instruments.

As we saw in the *Principles of Flight* section there are two aspects of air pressure that need to be considered – static pressure and dynamic pressure.

Static Pressure

At any point in the atmosphere, **static pressure** is exerted equally in all directions. It is the result of the weight of all of the molecules composing the air above that point pressing down. Static pressure of the atmosphere is being exerted at all points on the skin of your hand right now. As its name implies, static pressure does not involve relative movement of the air. Static pressure is measured on the surface of an aeroplane by a **static vent**.

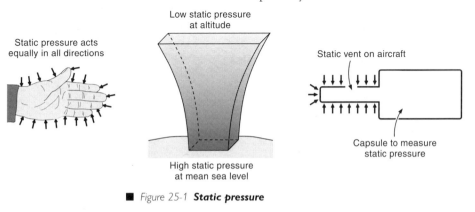

Static pressure acts equally in all directions

Low static pressure at altitude

High static pressure at mean sea level

Static vent on aircraft

Capsule to measure static pressure

■ *Figure 25-1* **Static pressure**

Dynamic Pressure

If you hold your hand up in a strong wind or out of the window of a moving car, then an extra wind pressure is felt due to the air striking your hand. This extra pressure, over and above the static pressure which is always present, is called **dynamic pressure** or pressure due to relative movement. It is felt by a body which is moving relative to the air, i.e. it could be moving through the air or the air could be flowing past it.

Just how strong this dynamic pressure is depends on two factors:

1. THE SPEED OF THE BODY RELATIVE TO THE AIR. The faster the car drives or the stronger the wind blows, then the stronger the extra dynamic pressure that you feel on your hand. This is because more molecules of air strike it per second.

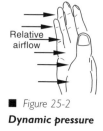

■ *Figure 25-2*
Dynamic pressure

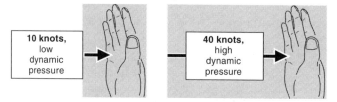

■ *Figure 25-3* **Dynamic pressure increases with airspeed**

2. THE DENSITY OF THE AIR. In outer space no matter how fast you travelled you would not feel this dynamic pressure because there are practically no molecules to strike you.

At sea level, where the atmosphere is densest, your hand would be struck by many molecules per second, certainly many more than in the upper reaches of the atmosphere. So, even though you might be travelling at the same speed, you will feel a much lower dynamic pressure in the higher and less dense regions of the atmosphere.

Outer space:
no molecules of air strike
a moving body

High altitude:
many molecules of air
per second strike
a moving body

Low altitude:
many, many molecules
of air per second strike
a moving body

Earth

■ *Figure 25-4* **Dynamic pressure depends on air density**

At higher altitudes, you would feel less dynamic pressure than at lower altitudes where the atmosphere is denser, even though you were moving through the air at the same speed. The measure of this dynamic pressure is written:

Dynamic pressure = ½ rho V-squared

- where *rho* is air density, decreasing with altitude, and *V* is the speed of the body relative to the air (i.e. it does not matter whether the body is moving through the air, or the air blowing past the body, or a combination of both — as long as they are moving relative to one another there will be a dynamic pressure).

Dynamic pressure varies directly with *V-squared*. It is one of the square laws common in nature.

Total Pressure

In the atmosphere, some static pressure is always exerted, but, for dynamic pressure to be exerted, there must be motion of the body relative to the air. Total pressure consists of static pressure plus dynamic pressure.

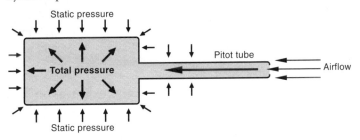

■ *Figure 25-5* **Total pressure is measured by a pitot tube**

NOTE Total pressure is also called as **pitot pressure, ram pressure** or **impact pressure.**

Much airflow theory was developed by Daniel Bernoulli and is expressed as:

Static pressure	**+**	**dynamic pressure**	**=**	**total pressure**
measured by static line (barometer/altimeter)		*½ rho V-squared*		*measured by pitot tube*

Subtracting static pressure from both sides:

Dynamic pressure = total pressure − static pressure

NOTE The airspeed indicator (ASI), which we will discuss shortly, indicates dynamic pressure (i.e. the difference between total pressure and static pressure). The ASI scale is calibrated to read in units of speed (knots) rather than units of pressure.

The Pitot-Static System

Three flight instruments make use of pressure readings.

☐ **The altimeter** relates static pressure to height.

☐ **The vertical speed indicator** relates the rate of change of static pressure to a rate of climb or descent.

☐ **The airspeed indicator** relates the difference between total (or pitot) pressure and static pressure to the speed through the air.

A pitot tube provides the measurement of total pressure and a static vent provides the measurement of static pressure. There are two common arrangements of the pitot-static system:

☐ **a combined pitot-static head;** or

☐ **a pitot tube** (possibly on the wing) and a static vent (or two) on the side of the fuselage.

The pitot tube must be mounted on the aeroplane in a position where the airflow is not greatly disturbed; often forward of or beneath the outer section of one wing. Otherwise the airspeed indication system will suffer from significant errors.

Pitot heaters are sometimes provided as a precaution against ice blocking the pitot tube. These are electrical elements built into the pitot tube, operated by a switch from the cockpit. It is important that a pitot heater is switched OFF when the aeroplane is not in flight or overheating damage could result.

Some aircraft have two static vents, one on each side of the fuselage, so that the reading for static pressure, when evened out, is more accurate, especially if the aeroplane is slipping or skidding (i.e. is being flown out-of-balance).

There is often an **alternate static source** fitted in the cabin in case of ice or other matter obstructing the external vents. Cabin pressure is often slightly less than the external atmospheric pressure and will cause the instrument readings to be slightly in error when the alternate static source is being used.

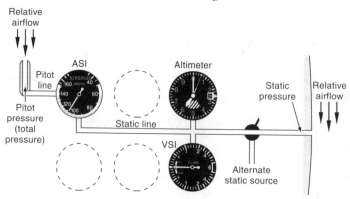

■ *Figure 25-6* **The pitot-static system**

It is vital that the pitot tube and static vent(s) are not damaged or obstructed, otherwise false readings from the relevant flight instruments could degrade the safety of the flight. They should be carefully checked in the pre-flight external inspection. The pitot cover, used to prevent water or insects accumulating in the tube, should be removed. They should not be tested by blowing in them, since very sensitive instruments are involved.

The Airspeed Indicator

The airspeed indicator displays indicated airspeed (IAS). It is related to dynamic pressure.

We can find dynamic pressure by subtracting the static line measurement from the pitot tube measurement. This is easily done by having a diaphragm with total pressure from the pitot tube being fed onto one side of it and static pressure from the static line being fed onto the other side of it.

The diaphragm will position itself and a pointer connected to it, according to the difference between the total pressure and the static pressure – which is dynamic pressure, *½ rho V-squared*.

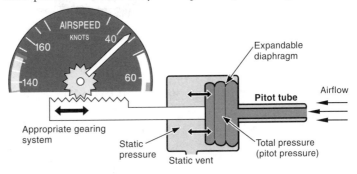

■ *Figure 25-7* **The airspeed indicator measures dynamic pressure**

In practice we assume that the density of air remains constant at its mean sea level value, which of course it does not, but this allows us to graduate the scale around which the pointer moves in units of speed (usually knots). This does, however, give us an airspeed indicator that reads accurately the airspeed on an ISA standard day at mean sea level (MSL in the International Standard Atmosphere is 15° Celsius, pressure altitude 0 ft).

As airspeed increases, the dynamic pressure increases, but the static pressure remains the same. The difference between the total pressure (measured by the pitot tube) and the static pressure (measured by the static vent or static line) gives us a measure of the dynamic pressure (which is related to indicated airspeed). This difference between total and static pressure causes the diaphragm to reposition itself, and the pointer to indicate a higher airspeed.

Colour Coding on the Airspeed Indicator

To assist the pilot, ASIs in modern aircraft have certain speed ranges and certain specific speeds marked according to a conventional colour code.

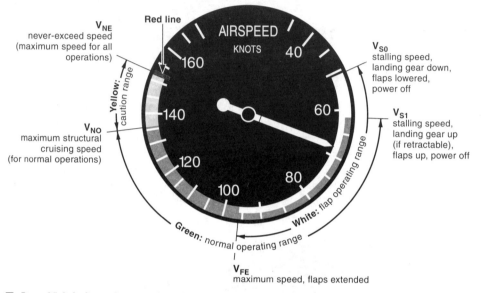

■ *Figure 25-8* **Indicated airspeed is what we read on the ASI**

GREEN ARC. Denotes the **normal operating speed range,** from stall speed at maximum all-up weight (flaps up, wings level) up to V_{NO} (normal operating limit speed or maximum structural cruising speed) which should not be exceeded except in smooth air. Operations at indicated airspeeds in the green arc should be safe in all conditions, including turbulence.

YELLOW ARC. Denotes the **caution range,** which extends from V_{NO} (normal operating limit speed) up to V_{NE} (the never exceed speed). The aircraft should only be operated at indicated airspeeds in the caution range in smooth air.

WHITE ARC. Denotes the **flap operating range,** from stall speed at maximum all-up weight in the landing configuration (full flap, landing-gear down, wings level, power-off) up to V_{FE} (maximum flaps extended speed).

RED RADIAL LINE. Denotes V_{NE}, the **never exceed speed.**

NOTE 1 Some ASIs have blue radial lines to denote certain important speeds, (e.g. best single-engine speed for a light twin-engined aeroplane).

NOTE 2 All ASI markings refer to indicated airspeed (IAS) and *not* true airspeed (TAS). Where weight is a factor in determining the limit speed (e.g. stall speeds) the value marked is for the maximum all-up weight (max AUW) situation in all cases.

Indicated Airspeed (IAS) and True Airspeed (TAS)

The fact that indicated airspeed (IAS) and true airspeed (TAS or V) are usually different seems to worry many inexperienced pilots, but it need not. IAS is an aerodynamic airspeed which is closely related to dynamic pressure – *½ rho V-squared*.

The dynamic pressure (*½ rho V-squared*) is a vital aerodynamic quantity because the amount of lift produced is a function of dynamic pressure:

$$Lift = C_{Lift} \times \text{½ } rho \text{ } V\text{-}squared \times S$$

– the amount of drag created is also a function of dynamic pressure:

$$Drag = C_{Drag} \times \text{½ } rho \text{ } V\text{-}squared \times S$$

When we discuss the flight performance of the aeroplane – lift, drag, stalling speed, take-off speed, maximum speeds, climbing speed, long-range cruise speed, etc. – we talk in terms of indicated airspeed (IAS). The IAS is vital performance information for the pilot, as the aerodynamic qualities of the aeroplane depend on it.

The true airspeed (TAS) is the actual speed of the aeroplane relative to the air. TAS (or *V*) is important for navigation purposes, such as describing speed through the air (TAS). From TAS we can find speed over the ground – groundspeed or GS.

Indicated airspeed (IAS) is important aerodynamically.

True airspeed (TAS) is important for navigation.

True Airspeed Usually Exceeds Indicated Airspeed

We will consider the situation in a climb: it is usual to maintain the same climbing indicated airspeed throughout the climb, i.e. a constant reading on the ASI. As the aeroplane gains height it climbs into less dense air because air density (*rho*) decreases with increasing altitude.

For IAS to remain the same, then the value of the dynamic pressure (which is *½ rho V-squared*) must remain the same. Therefore, because air density (*rho*) is decreasing with altitude, to retain a constant *½ rho V-squared* (and consequently a constant indicated airspeed) the value of *V* (the true airspeed) must be greater. So if you are climbing to a higher altitude with the airspeed indicator showing a constant IAS, the TAS will be increasing gradually.

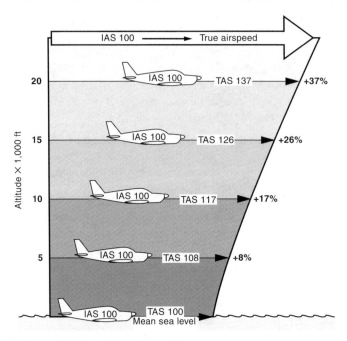

■ *Figure 25-9* **With IAS constant, TAS increases with increase in altitude**

On hot days and at high-elevation aerodromes, to generate sufficient lift for take-off the aeroplane must be accelerated to a higher V (i.e. TAS) to compensate for the decreased air density. (IAS shown on the ASI will remain the same.) This, coupled with possibly poorer performance from the engine–propeller, will mean a longer take-off distance.

> At 5,000 ft your TAS exceeds the IAS by about 8%.
> At 10,000 ft your TAS exceeds the IAS by about 17%.

These are handy figures to remember for mental calculations and for when experienced pilots are talking about the speeds that their aeroplanes 'true-out' at. If you are cruising at 5,000 ft with IAS 180 kt showing on the airspeed indicator, then your true airspeed will be approximately 8% greater. (8% of 180 = 14), i.e. 194 kt TAS.

Some Airspeed Indicators can Display TAS

Some airspeed indicators have a manually rotatable scale attached to them (known as the *temperature/altitude correction* scale), which allows you to read TAS as well as IAS and which is valid up to speeds of approximately 220 knots TAS. (Above this speed the compressibility of the atmosphere needs to be allowed for – this is considered in the professional pilot licences.)

Setting the temperature/altitude scale on the airspeed indicator performs exactly the same function as setting the same scale on a navigation computer.

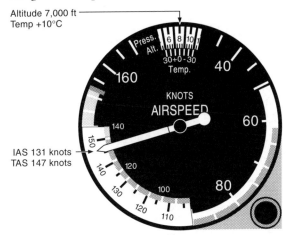

■ *Figure 25-10* **IAS (and TAS) indicator**

It allows the indicated airspeed read on the ASI to be matched with the true airspeed, which is of navigational value when cruising. For performance purposes (take-off, landing and stalling speeds), it is IAS that is important, and not TAS. For this reason, some TAS scales do not extend into the low speed area.

ASI Problems with a Blocked Static Vent or Pitot Tube

A blockage or icing over will cause the pressure to be trapped in that particular line to the pressure instruments.

CLIMB. If you are climbing and the static vent ices over, then the static pressure trapped in the line will be higher than the actual static pressure where the aeroplane has climbed to. The measured difference between pitot (total) pressure and static pressure will be less than actual – therefore the ASI will under-read, i.e. show a lower IAS than actual.

If the static vent becomes blocked the ASI will read low in a climb, and high in a descent.

DESCENT. On a descent, the reverse would be the case – a blocked static vent would cause the ASI to over-read, i.e. show an IAS higher than actual. This is a dangerous situation if the pilot does not recognise it and reduces the speed, because the aeroplane will be flying at a speed less than that indicated.

TAKE-OFF. If you commence a take-off with a completely blocked pitot tube, only the static pressure trapped in the pitot tube will be fed to the ASI to be compared to the static pressure from the static vent. The ASI will indicate zero.

A blocked pitot tube will cause the ASI to read high in a climb, and low in a descent.

The Altimeter

You need to know how high you are for three basic reasons:

1. **For terrain clearance,** to ensure that the aircraft will not collide with terrain or fixed obstacles.

2. **For traffic separation,** to allow pilots to cruise at different altitudes and ensure safe vertical separation.

3. **For performance calculations,** to calculate the performance capabilities of the aircraft, and to operate it safely and efficiently.

The pressure altimeter is a *barometer* (instrument that measures atmospheric pressure). It works on the principle that in the atmosphere:

> **Air pressure decreases with altitude,** i.e. the higher you are in the earth's atmosphere, the lower is the static air pressure.

There are various types of pressure altimeters. The most compact and robust type for installation in an aircraft is the *aneroid* barometer, similar to those seen hanging on living-room walls.

As an aircraft climbs, the pressure in its immediate vicinity drops (usually about 1 millibar for every 30 ft gain in altitude). The aneroid, which is an expandable and compressible metal capsule containing a fixed amount of air, is able to expand. This movement is transmitted via a linkage system to a pointer which moves around the altimeter scale.

> Atmospheric pressure reduces by 1 millibar for every 30 ft increase in altitude.

The altimeter scale is graduated, not in units of pressure (millibars, hectopascals, or inches of mercury), but in **feet (ft)**.

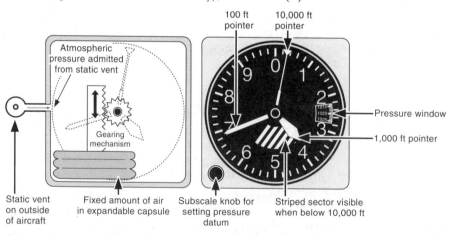

■ *Figure 25-11* **The altimeter converts variations in static pressure into indications of height (this altimeter is reading 3,690 ft)**

As the aircraft descends, the aneroid compresses due to the increasing pressure, and drives the pointer to indicate a lower altitude.

Errors in the Altimeter

A number of errors are evident in altimeters:

- ▢ **Instrument errors** – imperfections in the design, manufacture, installation and maintenance of the individual altimeter.
- ▢ **Instrument lag** – the altimeter takes a second or two to respond to rapid pressure changes.
- ▢ **Position error** – poor design may place the static vent in a position where the static pressure is not representative of the free atmosphere in that vicinity.
- ▢ **Blockages of the static vent** – if ice or wasps (or anything else) blocks the static vent completely, then that static pressure will remain fixed in the line to the altimeter. A constant altitude will be indicated, even though the aircraft may be changing altitude.

If ice forms over the static vent on a climb-out, the altimeter will continue to read the altitude at which the static vent blocked, and not indicate the higher altitude that the aeroplane is actually at, i.e. it will under-read the actual altitude.

Similarly, on a descent, a blocked static vent will cause the altimeter to indicate a constant altitude, i.e. show an altitude higher than the actual altitude the aeroplane has descended to, i.e. it will over-read (dangerous, if terrain clearance is a problem).

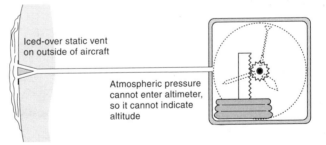

Iced-over static vent on outside of aircraft

Atmospheric pressure cannot enter altimeter, so it cannot indicate altitude

■ *Figure 25-12* **A blocked static vent – altimeter reads constant irrespective of aircraft altitude**

The Unit of Pressure

The unit of pressure used in aviation in the United Kingdom is the *millibar* (mb); however, a new term – the *hectopascal* (hPa) – has been adopted in many countries. At the time of writing, the millibar is the unit to be used for the immediate future in the United Kingdom, but you will come across hectopascals internationally.

The two units, millibars (mb) and hectopascals (hPa), are equivalent so the change of unit has no operational significance other than the name change itself. In *The Air Pilot's Manual* the unit of pressure will be shown as mb(hPa); however, for the UK, using mb will be sufficient for examination and other purposes.

In the United States of America yet another unit of pressure is standard in aviation – the inch of mercury (abbreviated "Hg). Altimeter subscales are graduated in this unit, commonly called inches. It refers to the amount of pressure required to support a specific column of the element mercury (Hg).

The International Standard Atmosphere (ISA)

Conditions in the actual atmosphere change from place to place and time to time. To have some sort of 'measuring stick' an International Standard Atmosphere (ISA) has been defined as having:

The main use of the International Standard Atmosphere is to calibrate altimeters.

☐ **A mean sea level pressure** of 1013.2 millibars (hectopascals), which, in the lower levels of the atmosphere, decreases by 1 mb (hPa) for every 30 ft gained (approximately). For practical purposes, 1013 mb for ISA MSL pressure is sufficiently accurate. (If you fly in the USA, standard pressure is 29.92 inches, which is the same as 1013.2 millibars.)

☐ **A mean sea level temperature** of 15° Celsius, that decreases by 2°C (approximately) for every 1,000 ft gained. For example, at 3,000 ft altitude in the ISA, the temperature should have fallen by 6° to be 9° Celsius.

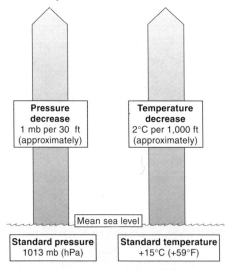

■ *Figure 25-13* **The International Standard Atmosphere**

Pressure Altitude

> **Pressure altitude** is the height in the International Standard Atmosphere above the 1013.2 mb(hPa) pressure level at which the pressure equals that of the aircraft or point under consideration.

With 1013.2 mb on the subscale the altimeter reads pressure altitude.

If the pressure in the vicinity of the aeroplane is the same as that at 6,800 ft in the ISA, then its *pressure altitude* is 6,800 ft. If the altimeter in the aircraft has its subscale set to 1013.2 millibars, it will read height above the 1013 mb(hPa) pressure level.

Altimeter Subscale Settings

If the mean sea level pressure differs from the ISA MSL pressure of 1013 mb(hPa), there is a small subscale on the altimeter that allows us to set this actual MSL pressure, known as **QNH.**

QNH is usually within 20 mb(hPa) either side of 1013. As the altimeter will read the altitude above whatever pressure level is set in the subscale – with QNH set in the subscale, the altimeter will read altitude (i.e. height above mean sea level). This is handy for checking the amount of vertical clearance above terrain, radio masts, etc., which are shown on maps and charts in height amsl.

In the UK, the term **regional QNH** (or regional pressure setting) applies to the lowest QNH in a defined region. Its use is described in Vol. 2 of *The Air Pilot's Manual*, under *Altimeter Setting Procedures.*

> The altimeter reads height above whatever pressure level is set in the subscale.

If 1013 mb(hPa) is set in the altimeter subscale, the altimeter will indicate pressure altitude, i.e. the equivalent height in the ISA above the 1013 mb(hPa) pressure level. If the **aerodrome surface pressure (QFE)** is set in the altimeter subscale (i.e. on the ground, the altimeter will indicate 0), then in-flight the altimeter will indicate height above the aerodrome (only useful if you are not flying away from that aerodrome). QFE will be different for each aerodrome.

Ambient pressure on the airport is the QFE pressure setting, and with QFE set on the ground the altimeter will read zero.

Wind on millibars, wind on height.

Notice that, if your aircraft stays at the same level, winding on millibars in the altimeter subscale will wind on more height, and vice versa.

With QFE 990 mb set in the subscale (Figure 25-14), the altimeter reads 3,860 ft above the aerodrome level (and 0 ft when the aeroplane is on the aerodrome).

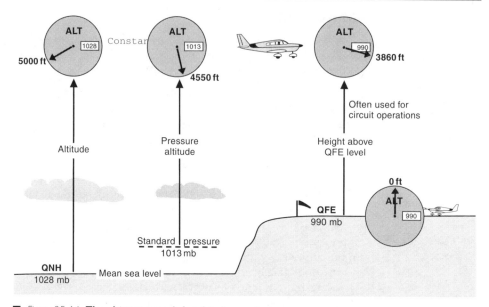

If you wind on millibars (with the setting knob) until 1013 is set in the subscale, you also wind on height to 4,550 ft – an increase of 23 mb and 690 ft (30 ft for each millibar) – yet the aircraft has not changed its level. If you further rotate the subscale until the current QNH of 1028 mb is set, you also wind on height to 5,000 ft – yet still the aircraft has not changed level.

When the aircraft in Figure 25-14 lands on the runway, its altimeter should read:

☐ **zero** if aerodrome QFE is set; and
☐ **aerodrome elevation** if the aerodrome QNH is set.

The Vertical Speed Indicator (VSI)

While you could form some idea of how fast you are changing altitude by comparing the altimeter against a stopwatch (a somewhat tedious process), the vertical speed indicator can provide a direct read-out of the rate of change of altitude.

The VSI is a pressure instrument based, like the altimeter, on the fact that air pressure decreases with altitude. The VSI converts a rate of change of static pressure to a rate of change of altitude, which is expressed in hundreds (or thousands) of feet per minute (fpm or ft/min). The VSI is also called the rate of climb indicator.

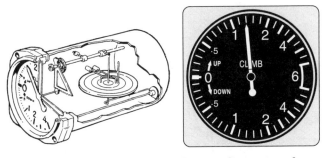

■ *Figure 25-15* **The vertical speed indicator indicates rate of change of altitude in feet per minute**

If the aeroplane commences a descent, the new and higher pressure is conducted straight into the capsule. Because there is some delay in the new pressure being conducted through the capillary or 'choke' to the surrounding area, the capsule will expand. This drives the pointer around the scale (graduated in fpm) to indicate a rate of descent, e.g. 500 fpm.

If the static vent becomes iced over or blocked, then the two pressure areas (inside the capsule and surrounding it) will equalise and the VSI will read zero, even though the aeroplane's height might be changing.

The Alternate Static Source

The static pressure is vital to the functioning of the airspeed indicator, the altimeter and the vertical speed indicator. Many aircraft have an alternate source of static pressure that can be fed to the instruments in the event of the primary source not providing correct static pressure for some reason.

The alternate static source (in unpressurised aircraft) often taps static pressure from within the cockpit, which is slightly less than the outside pressure. The instruments will then indicate slightly in error:

- **The altimeter** will indicate an altitude higher than actual.
- **The airspeed indicator** will show an IAS greater than the actual IAS, because the difference between total pressure and static pressure will be greater than actual (and the ASI measures this difference).
- **The VSI** will initially indicate a climb when first connected to the alternate static source, but will then settle down and read correctly – the VSI reads the rate of change of static pressure.

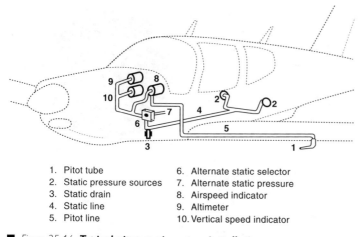

1. Pitot tube
2. Static pressure sources
3. Static drain
4. Static line
5. Pitot line
6. Alternate static selector
7. Alternate static pressure
8. Airspeed indicator
9. Altimeter
10. Vertical speed indicator

■ *Figure 25-16* **Typical pitot-static system installation**

Now complete **Exercises 25 – Pressure Instruments.**

Gyroscopic Instruments

Gyroscopes

A gyroscope is a rotating wheel (or rotor) mounted so that its axis can turn freely in one or more directions. A rotating mass is capable of maintaining the same absolute direction in space despite what goes on around it – this property is called *rigidity in space*. Therefore the gyroscope is useful as an indicator of direction and attitude. Due to the property of rigidity in space, the gyro is able to remain stable in space while the aeroplane moves around it.

The degree of rigidity of a gyroscope depends on the mass of the rotor, the speed at which it is rotating, and the radius at which the mass is concentrated. A large mass concentrated near the rim and rotating at high speed provides the greatest directional rigidity.

A gyroscope has a second property called *precession*. If a force is applied to the gyroscope, the change in direction brought about by the force is not in line with the force, but is displaced 90° further on in the direction of rotation.

If a gyroscope rotates slower than it should, then its rigidity in space will be less and the precession force less, causing it to under-read – i.e. under-rpm ⇒ under-read.

■ *Figure 26-1*

Gyroscopes are rotating masses

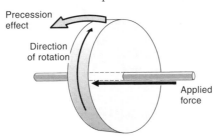

Precession effect

Direction of rotation

Applied force

■ *Figure 26-2* **Gyroscopic precession**

Gyroscopic Effect

Gyroscopic effect is common in everyday objects (you use it every time you lean your bicycle over to turn a corner), but difficult to understand. To demonstrate the effect yourself, take a 'barrel-type' vacuum cleaner with the hose removed. Balance it by the handle so that its 'nose' is free to move vertically. Then apply a force to move the nose of the cleaner horizontally, and watch the effect in the vertical plane.

1. With the motor not running, sharp movements of the nose left or right have no vertical effect.

2. With the motor running the rotating mass acts as a gyro rotor:
   – a sharp movement of the nose horizontally to the right causes the nose to drop vertically;
   – a sharp movement of the nose horizontally to the left causes the nose to rise vertically.

The same effect is apparent if you hold a spinning bicycle wheel by the axle – hold it so the spinning wheel is vertical and try to rotate the axle horizontally.

In aircraft, gyroscopes are used in the turn coordinator/turn indicator, attitude indicator and heading indicator. There are various ways of mounting a gyroscope on one or more axes of rotation (gimbals), depending on the information required from that gyroscopic instrument.

Vacuum-Driven Gyroscopes

Many gyroscopes are operated by a vacuum system which draws high-speed air through a nozzle and directs it at the gyro rotor blades. A vacuum pump that draws air through is generally preferable to a pressure pump that blows air through, since the air may pick up contaminants such as oil from the pump which could affect the delicate rotor.

The suction is shown on a gauge in the cockpit and, typically, is of the order of 3″ to 5″Hg (5 inches of mercury below atmospheric pressure). If the vacuum reading is too low, the air flow will be low, the rotor(s) will not be up to speed and the gyros will be unstable or only respond slowly; if it is too high, the gyro rotors may spin too fast and be damaged.

The vacuum in most aeroplanes is provided by the engine-driven vacuum pump, but some older aeroplanes may have the vacuum provided by an externally mounted venturi tube (making the gyroscopic instruments unusable until after several minutes at flying speed following take-off).

Electrically Driven Gyroscopes

When the electrical master switch first goes on, you will probably hear the gyroscopes start to spin up. The gyroscopic instruments should self-erect and red power-failure warning flags (if fitted) should disappear.

If the engine is shut down on the ground and the master switch is left on, these instruments will be drawing power from the battery and the battery may become flat. Not a desirable situation, so ensure that there is no power to the electrically driven gyroscopes when leaving the aeroplane for any length of time.

Turn Coordinator/Turn Indicator

The turn coordinator and turn indicator both use *rate gyros*. The rotating mass has freedom to move about two of its three axes and is designed to show the rate of movement of the aircraft about the third axis (in this case the turning or normal axis). This rate of movement is indicated in the cockpit in one of two presentations – either a **turn indicator** (which has a vertical needle or 'bat') or a **turn coordinator** (which has a symbolic aeroplane).

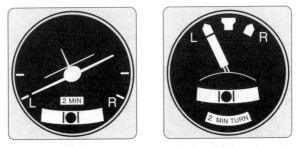

■ *Figure 26-3* **The turn coordinator (left) and the turn indicator**

Both these instruments indicate the aircraft's **rate of turn** but *not* bank angle. However, because the gyro in the turn coordinator is mounted slightly differently to that in the turn indicator, the turn coordinator will also show **rate of bank** or **roll rate**. It will respond when an aeroplane banks, even before the turn actually commences. Also note that the symbolic aeroplane on the turn coordinator (even though it resembles that on an attitude indicator) does not give pitch information.

If the aeroplane is turning to the left, this turning force is passed to the gyroscope as shown in Figure 26-3, the spin axis of the turn indicator being horizontal. The applied force causes the gyro to change its direction a further 90° in the direction of rotation, i.e. it will cause the gyro to tilt (or precess). The greater the turning force, the greater the tendency to tilt. That is, the turn indicator derives its turning information from the precession of a gyro which has its spin axis horizontal, see Figure 26-4. The gimbal axis of a turn coordinator, however, is tilted slightly from the horizontal (approximately 30°), which provides a reaction not only to turning but also to rate-of-roll.

This tilting of the gyroscope stretches a spring, which makes the gyro precess with the aircraft turn until the rates match, when further tilt ceases. A pointer moved by the gimbal tilting indicates the rate of turn against a scale – a turn indicator.

The scale is graduated to show a **rate 1** turn (3° a second, therefore 180° in one minute, 360° in 2 minutes), a **rate 2** turn (6° a second) and so on. This is a means of checking the accuracy of the turn indicator – time yourself through a steady turn to say 90 or 180° and see if the number of degrees per second matches up with the turn indicator.

The gyroscope may be rotated electrically or spun by a small jet of air directed at small 'buckets' cut into the edge of the gyro wheel.

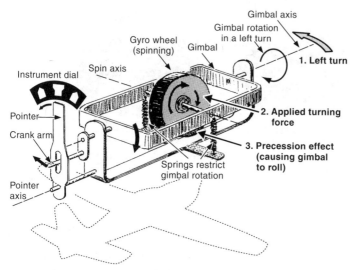

■ *Figure 26-4* **Turn indicator mechanism**

In the latter case, you should check that the vacuum system is providing sufficient air (a 'suction' of 2.5 inches of mercury is usually adequate), otherwise the gyro rpm will be low, its rigidity in space less than desired, causing less pointer movement for a particular rate of turn to occur. That is, with a low vacuum – the turn indicator under-reads (i.e. the rate of turn will be greater than the rate indicated).

The Balance Indicator

A small curved glass cylinder containing a ball can be used to indicate the balance of the aeroplane. If no yawing forces are present, the ball will be at the bottom centre position. If there is yawing force, the ball will be driven to one side – the greater the yaw, the greater its movement up the curved glass cylinder.

In a balanced turn, the ball will still be in the central position and you will not feel thrown to one side.

If the aircraft is *slipping* into the turn, the ball will be on the low side and you will feel as though you are falling down in the direction of turn. A bit of rudder on the low side will put the ball back into the centre and you will feel comfortable in your seat, "Ball to the left, use left rudder."

If the aircraft is *skidding* out of the turn, the ball and you will be thrown to the outside of the turn. A bit of rudder on the high side will balance the turn.

In balance   Out of balance

■ *Figure 26-5* **The balance indicator, usually positioned at base of turn coordinator and turn indicator)**

While the balance indicator is not a gyroscopic instrument, but purely a mechanical indicator of balance, we present it here because it is found in a combined turn and balance indicator in most aeroplanes.

Turn and Balance Indicator

The correct use of the combined instrument is to bank the aeroplane to get the desired angle of bank and rate of turn, and then to balance the turn with the rudder so that the ball is central.

If the ball is to the left, use left rudder – if the ball is to the right, use right rudder. In the days gone by, instructors said, "Kick the ball back into the centre." "Pressure the ball back into the centre" is preferable.

Pilot checks for the serviceability of this instrument should include:

- **checking gyro rotation speed** (whirring sound and no failure flags if electrically driven, correct vacuum if pressure-driven);
- **correct indications** in a turn while taxiing ("turning left, skidding right – turning right, skidding left"), and if in any doubt, a timed turn in flight (clock versus a turn through a known number of degrees).

The Attitude Indicator (AI)

As the aircraft changes its attitude, the *earth gyro* that is the basis of the attitude indicator retains its rigidity relative to the earth's vertical. This means that the aeroplane moves around the gyro rotor of the attitude indicator which, as Figure 26-6 shows, has a vertical spin axis.

Attached to the gyroscope is a picture of the horizon, around which the aeroplane (and the instrument panel) moves. The attitude of the aeroplane to the real horizon is symbolised by the artificial horizon line attached to the gyro and a small symbolic aeroplane attached to the instrument dial.

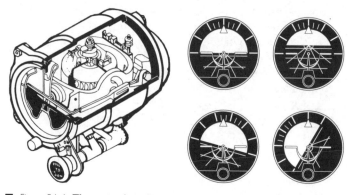

■ Figure 26-6 **The attitude indicator**

The attitude indicator shows **pitch attitude** and **bank angle** (roll). It shows a picture of the aircraft's attitude, but tells you nothing about the performance of the aeroplane. The same nose-high attitude could occur in a steep climb or in a stalled descent – to know the performance of the aeroplane, you need to refer to other instruments (airspeed indicator, altimeter, vertical speed indicator).

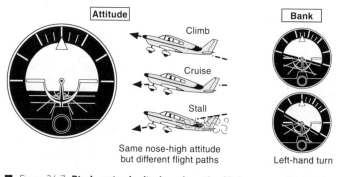

■ Figure 26-7 **Pitch attitude displayed on the AI does not reflect climb/descent performance**

You should check the power source of the attitude gyro (whether it is electrical, or vacuum – about 4.5″Hg). Some indicators, especially the vacuum-driven ones, have limits of pitch and bank which, if exceeded, may cause the gyro to topple and give erroneous readings (your Pilot's Operating Handbook may contain this information, otherwise refer to your instructor).

Some gyros are caged when not being used. If caged, it should be uncaged when the aeroplane is straight and level and the gyro is up to speed. This should be done shortly before take-off or in straight and level unaccelerated cruising flight. Also, the small model or index aeroplane should be aligned with the artificial horizon on the instrument when the gyro is up to speed and the aeroplane is straight and level (in flight or on the ground).

The attitude indicator is subject to small errors when the aircraft accelerates or decelerates. This affects the pendulous gravity unit used to keep the axis of rotation vertical. Acceleration, as on take-off, may cause a small transient error in pitch and roll, but this is hardly visible in training aircraft with low acceleration.

The attitude indicator is also known as the **artificial horizon** and **gyro horizon.**

The Heading Indicator (HI)

The magnetic compass is the primary indicator of direction in most aircraft. It is, however, difficult to read in turbulence and subject to acceleration and turning errors. It is a difficult instrument to fly accurately on.

The heading indicator (HI) is a gyroscope that is aligned with the magnetic compass periodically in flight. It takes its direction from the compass, but is not subject to acceleration and turning errors (making accurate turns and heading-keeping possible) and is easy to read in turbulence. The heading indicator is also known as the **direction indicator (DI)** or **directional gyro (DG).**

■ *Figure 26-8* **The heading indicator**

There are mechanical errors in the HI (friction) that will cause it to drift off accurate alignment with magnetic north. This is called *mechanical drift.*

The 'perfect' HI rotor will maintain its alignment precisely in space. However, due to the movement of the aeroplane through space, the line in space from the aeroplane to north will steadily change. This gives rise to *apparent drift* – a natural phenomenon caused, not by changes in the gyro's plane of rotation due to mechanical imperfections, but by motion of the earth through space and motion of the aircraft relative to the earth.

(This topic is pursued further at CPL level. At PPL level, all you need to remember is to re-align the HI with the magnetic compass every 10 or 15 minutes, following the procedure described below.)

Checks on the Heading Indicator

You should check the power source (the electrical system or the vacuum system, depending on type), and when taxiing, the correct turn indications on the HI ("turning right, heading increases – turning left, heading decreases").

The HI has a *slaving knob* that enables you to re-align the HI with the magnetic compass – correcting for both mechanical drift and apparent drift. This should be done every 10 to 15 minutes – about a 3° drift is acceptable in this time.

Some older heading indicators have to be uncaged after re-aligning with the magnetic compass.

Re-Aligning the HI with the Magnetic Compass

1. **Choose a reference point** directly ahead of the aircraft, aim for it and fly steadily straight and level.

2. **Keep the nose precisely** on the reference point, and read the magnetic compass heading (when the compass is steady).

3. **Maintain the aeroplane's heading** towards the reference point. Then refer to the HI, and adjust its reading (if necessary) to that taken from the magnetic compass.

4. **Check that the aircraft** has remained heading steadily towards the reference point during the operation – (if not, repeat the procedure).

Errors in Gyroscopic Instruments

If the gyroscope is not up-to-speed, the instrument may indicate erratically, respond only slowly to changes in attitude and/or heading, or indicate incorrectly.

- ☐ **Check for** a red power-failure warning flag on electrically driven instruments, and check for correct suction on vacuum-driven instruments.
- ☐ **Check that** the heading indicator is aligned with the magnetic compass during steady straight and level flight. Check that the attitude indicator, if it has a caging device, has been uncaged, also in steady straight and level flight or in a level attitude on the ground.

Now complete **Exercises 26 – Gyroscopic Instruments.**

The Magnetic Compass

Heading 090°M

■ *Figure 27-1*

Magnetic compass

The 'simple' magnetic compass is one of the most poorly understood instruments in the cockpit. Since it is found in almost all aircraft – from *Tiger Moths* to *Boeing 747s* – we have decided to give it the full treatment.

In most light aircraft, the magnetic compass is the primary source of direction information, to which other heading indicators are aligned. In steady flight, the **lubber line** of the magnetic compass indicates the **magnetic heading** of the aeroplane.

If you handle the compass incorrectly, then accurate directional information may not be available to you.

Direction

There are two common ways to describe direction – using the cardinal points (the four chief directions) of north, south, east and west, or by using a circle of 360° going clockwise from north (true or magnetic as the case may be).

Direction is almost always expressed as a three-figure group (251, 340, 020, etc.). The only exception is runway direction where the numbers are rounded-off to the nearest 10°. A runway bearing 247°M would be referred to as Runway 25.

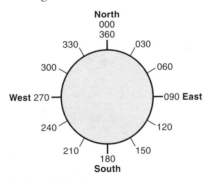

■ *Figure 27-2* **Direction**

This text goes a little beyond what is required for the examination, but it will help to save you flight time as you learn about turning onto compass headings.

A bar magnet that is freely suspended horizontally will swing so that its axis points roughly north-south. The end of the magnet that points towards the earth's north magnetic pole is called the *north-seeking pole* of the magnet.

The magnet is an ancient means of determining direction and it is still used in almost every aeroplane flying.

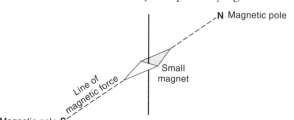

■ *Figure 27-3* ***A simple bar magnet***

The Earth's Magnetic Field (Terrestrial Magnetism)

The earth acts like a large and weak magnet. The surface of the earth is covered by a weak magnetic field – lines of magnetic force that begin deep within the earth near Hudson Bay in Canada and flow towards a point deep within the earth near south Victoria Land in Antarctica.

Because of their proximity to the north and south geographical poles (which are known as true north and true south on the earth's axis of rotation), the magnetic poles are referred to as the north magnetic pole and south magnetic pole.

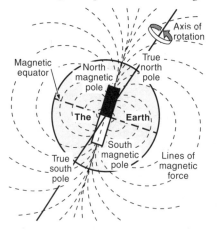

■ *Figure 27-4* ***The earth has a magnetic field***

Magnetic Variation

The latitude-longitude grid shown on maps is based on the geographical poles – true north and true south. Our small compass magnet, however, does not point exactly at true north and true south. The perfect compass magnet points at the north magnetic pole.

The angular difference between true north and magnetic north at any particular point on the earth is called **variation** − if the magnet points slightly east of true north, then the variation is said to be east. If the compass points to the west of true north, then the variation is west.

Isogonals

On maps, as well as the lines forming the latitude-longitude grid, are dashed-lines joining places that have the same magnetic variation, known as **isogonals.**

For example, the 4° west isogonal is drawn through all the places with a variation of 4°W. If you are anywhere on this line, then you can relate the message your compass is giving you about magnetic north to true north − your compass will point at magnetic north, which will be 4° west of true north.

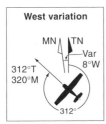
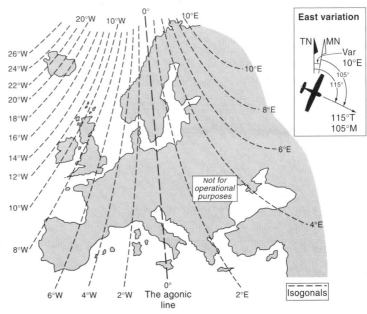

■ *Figure 27-5* **Variation is the angle between true and magnetic; isogonals join places of equal magnetic variation**

An easy way to remember the relationship between true and magnetic is:
Variation west, magnetic best,
Variation east, magnetic least.

EXAMPLE 1 If your compass indicates due east, i.e. 090° magnetic, and magnetic variation where you are is 4° west, then your heading related to true north is 090 − 4 = 086° true.

EXAMPLE 2 If the magnetic variation in your area is 10° east and your aeroplane is heading 295 on the magnetic compass, what is your true heading?

Variation east, magnetic least,
so 295°M is 295 + 10 = 305°T.

Deviation

Unfortunately, the magnet in the compass is affected not only by the magnetic field of the earth, but by any magnetic field. The aeroplane is made up of metal, rotating parts of an engine, radios, etc., all of which can generate their own magnetic field.

The effect that these fields in a particular aeroplane have on its magnetic compass is called **deviation,** and they cause the compass to deviate or deflect from precisely indicating magnetic north.

In each aeroplane is a small placard, known as the **deviation card,** which shows the pilot the corrections to make to the compass reading to obtain the magnetic direction. This correction usually involves only a few degrees and is an easy mental calculation to do in flight.

DEVIATION CARD

FOR					
N	30	60	E	120	150
STEER					
001	031	060	089	118	149

FOR					
S	210	240	W	300	330
STEER					
181	213	242	089	271	330

ON ⊠ RADIOS ☐ NO

■ Figure 27-6 **Deviation card**

Construction of the Aircraft Compass

The modern aeroplane has a direct-reading compass, usually filled with a liquid in which a float supporting a bar magnet is pivoted. The liquid supports some of the weight, decreases the friction on the pivot and, most importantly, dampens (decreases) the oscillations of the magnet and float during flight. This allows the compass to give a steadier indication and makes it easier to read.

Attached to the pivot assembly and the float is a compass card graduated in degrees. This can be read by the pilot against a reference marker attached to the bowl of the compass, and therefore attached to the rest of the aeroplane. Remember that it is the aeroplane that turns around the magnet inside the compass.

Ideally, the compass magnet points due (magnetic) north and south at all times. As the aeroplane changes direction, the compass magnet should not.

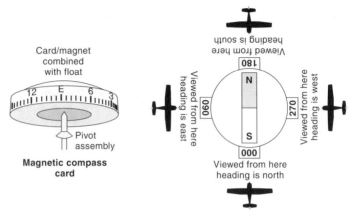

■ *Figure 27-7* **The magnetic compass**

Pilot Serviceability Checks

☐ **Pre-flight, check** that the compass is securely installed and can be easily read.

☐ **The liquid** in which the magnet is suspended should be free of bubbles and should not be discoloured.

☐ **The glass** should not be broken, cracked or discoloured, and it should be secure.

☐ **Check the position** of the compass deviation card in the cockpit.

☐ **Check that** the compass indication is at least approximately correct.

■ *Figure 27-8* **Always cross-check compass direction**

Runways are named according to their magnetic direction, e.g. a runway pointing 243° magnetic is called Runway 24, so when pointing in the same direction as this runway, your compass should indicate approximately the same.

When you are taxiing out prior to take-off, turn the aircraft left and right and check that the response of the magnet is correct. Remember that the magnet should remain in the same direction and the aeroplane turn around it.

Precautions when Carrying Magnetic or Metal Goods

The compass deviation card is written out by an engineer who has actually checked the compass in that particular aeroplane. This deviation correction card allows only for the magnetic influences in the aeroplane that were present when he tested the compass.

Any other magnetic influences introduced into the aeroplane will not be allowed for, even though they can significantly affect the compass. Therefore, ensure that no metal or magnetic materials, such as metal pens, clipboards, books with metal binders, key rings, headphones, electronic calculators, transistor radios, etc. are placed anywhere near the compass.

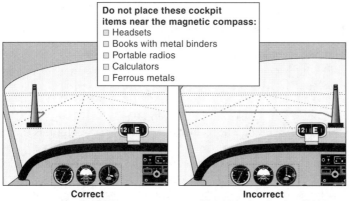

Do not place these cockpit items near the magnetic compass:
□ Headsets
□ Books with metal binders
□ Portable radios
□ Calculators
□ Ferrous metals

Correct	Incorrect
Heading 095	Pilot thinks heading is still 095 but in reality it is now 040

■ *Figure 27-9* **Keep foreign objects away from the magnetic compass**

Magnetic or metal materials placed near the compass may introduce large and unpredictable errors. Many pilots have been lost – or 'temporarily uncertain of their position' – as a result of random deviations in the compass readings caused by these extraneous magnetic fields.

Swinging the Compass

'Swinging the compass' is the engineering procedure to check and adjust the aeroplane compass. The aeroplane is taken to a special area on the aerodrome and aligned precisely with known directions. The compass is adjusted as accurately as possible and any remaining errors entered on the deviation card.

Pilots do not usually perform this function – but can advise when they think that it should be done.

The compass should be 'swung' when it is new, when any electrical circuit or magnetic influence in its vicinity has been altered, after a considerable change in magnetic latitude (i.e. if you have flown several thousand miles north or south), after passing through a severe magnetic storm, after major and minor inspections, and whenever the pilot suspects the accuracy of the compass.

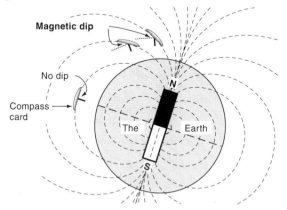

■ *Figure 27-10* **Magnetic dip is strongest nearest the poles**

Magnetic Dip and Compass Errors

Near the magnetic equator, the lines of magnetic force are parallel to the surface of the earth. As the magnetic poles are approached, the lines of magnetic force dip towards them and any magnet bar will also try to dip down and align itself with them.

In the northern areas of the United Kingdom, for example, a freely suspended magnet would dip down towards the north at about 65 to 70° to the horizontal. In the south of Australia, the angle of dip is approximately 60° down towards the south. This is known as the angle of **magnetic dip.**

Magnetic dip is zero at the magnetic equator and increases to 90° at the magnetic poles – (i.e. a magnet would point straight down).

The strength of the magnetic field is fairly constant over the whole surface of the earth. Its strength can be resolved into two components – a horizontal one parallel to the surface of the earth, which is used to align the compass with magnetic north, and a vertical component, which causes the magnetic needle to dip down.

At the magnetic equator, the horizontal component of the earth's magnetic field is at its strongest and so the magnetic compass is very stable and accurate.

At the higher latitudes near the magnetic poles, the vertical component of the earth's magnetic field causing dip is stronger, and the horizontal component parallel to the surface of the earth is weaker – making the compass magnet less effective as an indicator of horizontal direction. At latitudes higher than 60° north or south, the magnetic compass is not very reliable.

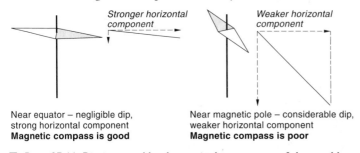

Near equator – negligible dip, strong horizontal component
Magnetic compass is good

Near magnetic pole – considerable dip, weaker horizontal component
Magnetic compass is poor

■ *Figure 27-11* **Dip is caused by the vertical component of the earth's magnetic field**

A freely swinging compass needle allowed to point down at the angle of dip would not be satisfactory in an aeroplane. To keep the magnet at least approximately horizontal, the pivot point is designed to be high, with the magnet suspended below – like a pendulum.

As the magnet tries to align itself with the field, the more it tries to dip down, the further out its centre of gravity moves. Its weight, acting through the CG, will try to move back into a position directly under the point of support, which is the pivot. Some sort of balancing couple will be set up – a couple formed by the supporting force of the pivot and the weight force acting through the CG.

The arm of the couple is the horizontal distance between the line of action of the pivot and the line of action of the magnet weight. This couple will act against the magnetic dip and, by finding an angle where the moment arm is sufficiently long for the pivot–magnet couple, will balance the magnetic dip. The result is a reasonably horizontal compass needle with only a small amount of *residual dip* (usually less than 3° from the horizontal).

Wherever the compass is located on (or above, as in the case of aircraft) the earth's surface, the magnet will find a level of residual dip where the pivot–magnet couple automatically balances the magnetic dip. Note that the CG is not directly under the pivot but is displaced slightly away from the nearer pole.

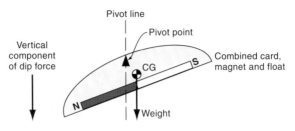

■ *Figure 27-12* **Pendulous suspension**

In the northern hemisphere, the CG of the magnet will be displaced south of the pivot. This displacement of the magnet's CG from directly under the pivot away from the nearer pole leads to transient indication errors in the compass when the aeroplane is accelerated in a straight line – (i.e. speed increase or decrease) or turned – (i.e. accelerated by changing the direction).

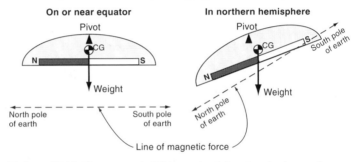

■ *Figure 27-13* **The magnet's CG is south of the pivot in the northern hemisphere**

The pivot is attached firmly to the aeroplane – if the aeroplane accelerates or turns, so does the pivot. The magnet, however, is not attached firmly to the aeroplane structure, but is suspended from the pivot – any motion of the magnet depends on this 'swinging' effect under the pivot, which is complicated by the fact that the magnet's CG (in the northern hemisphere) is displaced south of the pivot.

Acceleration Errors

If you change the airspeed, either accelerating or decelerating, transient indication errors occur with a magnetic compass, especially on easterly and westerly headings.

As the aeroplane accelerates, it takes the compass and the pivot along with it. The compass magnet, being suspended like a pendulum, is left behind due to its inertia. Its weight, not being directly under the pivot, will cause the needle to swing away from the correct magnetic direction as the pivot accelerates away. The compass card attached to the magnet rotates a little and indicates a new direction, even though there has been no change in direction.

Once a new steady speed is maintained, the magnet will settle down and the compass will read correctly.

ACCELERATING EAST. Accelerating towards the east, the CG (near the south-seeking end of the magnet) is left behind. This swings the compass card so that it indicates an 'apparent' turn to the north. During the acceleration, you will read a compass heading more northerly than the actual magnetic heading. Allow the compass to settle down after the acceleration is completed before adjusting the aircraft heading.

DECELERATING EAST. Decelerating towards the east, the pivot slows down with the rest of the aeroplane and the CG of the magnet, due to its inertia, tries to advance. The compass card rotates to indicate an 'apparent' turn to the south.

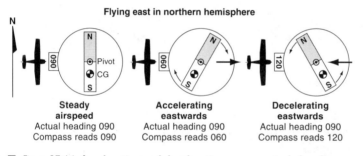

Flying east in northern hemisphere

Steady airspeed	Accelerating eastwards	Decelerating eastwards
Actual heading 090	Actual heading 090	Actual heading 090
Compass reads 090	Compass reads 060	Compass reads 120

■ *Figure 27-14* **Acceleration and deceleration on an easterly heading**

ACCELERATING WEST. Accelerating towards the west, the CG of the magnet and compass card (near the south-seeking end of the magnet) is left behind. This swings the compass card so that it indicates an 'apparent' turn to the north. The compass will indicate a more northerly heading than the aeroplane is actually on.

DECELERATING WEST. Heading west, a deceleration will cause the CG to advance ahead of the pivot, and the compass will indicate an 'apparent' turn to the south, i.e. it will appear, according to the compass, that the aeroplane has turned to a more southerly heading. After the speed has settled down, the compass will return to a more correct indication.

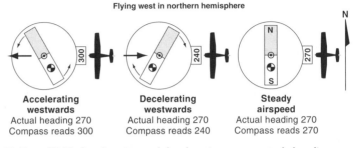

Flying west in northern hemisphere

Accelerating westwards	Decelerating westwards	Steady airspeed
Actual heading 270	Actual heading 270	Actual heading 270
Compass reads 300	Compass reads 240	Compass reads 270

■ *Figure 27-15* **Accelerating and decelerating on a westerly heading**

ACCELERATING NORTH OR SOUTH. Accelerating and decelerating on northerly or southerly headings will not cause 'apparent turns', because the pivot and the CG of the magnet will lie in the same north–south line as the acceleration or deceleration. On other headings, the acceleration errors will be greater the closer you are to due east or west.

Acceleration errors of the magnetic compass can be summarised in a small table:

HEADING	ACCELERATION ERROR	DECELERATION ERROR
Northerly	—	—
Easterly	*Apparent turn to north*	*Apparent turn to south*
Southerly	—	—
Westerly	*Apparent turn to north*	*Apparent turn to south*

These results are valid only for the northern hemisphere, where the magnetic dip is down towards the north magnetic pole and the compass magnet's CG is displaced from directly under the pivot towards the south.

The acceleration and deceleration errors in the northern hemisphere can be remembered with the mnemonic *ANDS:*

*Acceleration gives an apparent turn **N**orth*
*Deceleration gives an apparent turn **S**outh*

The situation in the southern hemisphere is reversed. Also, the closer to the pole you are, the greater the effect because the dip is greater. Magnetic dip is the major source of magnetic compass indication errors.

Turning Errors

Turning is also an acceleration due to the change in direction.

The aircraft has a centripetal force acting on it directed at the centre of the turn – i.e. in a turn, the centripetal force acts towards the centre of the turn and is therefore at right angles to the velocity. This force also acts on the pivot, which is attached to the aeroplane, and accelerates it towards the centre of the turn. The compass magnet (and compass card), being suspended like a pendulum, is left behind due to inertia. This leads to a transient error in the direction indicated by the compass.

TURNING THROUGH NORTH. When the aircraft is turning through a northerly heading the acceleration is at right angles – easterly or westerly, depending on which way you are turning. If you are turning right through north, the acceleration is towards the east, the CG is left behind so that the compass indicates less of a turn than is actually occurring.

> *Undershoot the heading when turning through north.*

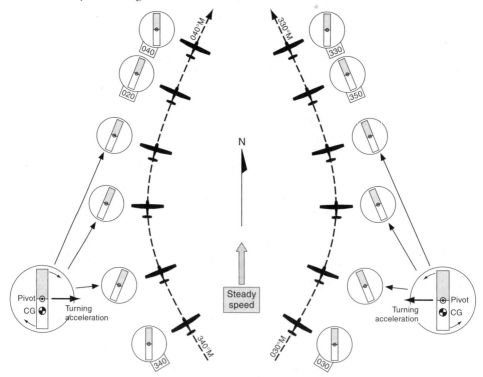

■ *Figure 27-16* **Undershoot the heading when turning through north**

Once the aeroplane takes up a steady heading, the compass will catch up with the turn and settle down. For this reason, under-shoot when turning through north. For example, turning from 340 to 040, level the wings before 040 is reached on the compass (say at an indicated 020), after which the compass will catch up and settle down on approximately 040.

If you are turning left through north, the acceleration is towards the west, the CG gets left behind and the compass will again lag behind. Therefore, undershoot when turning through north. For example, when turning from 030 to 330, level the wings when the compass indicates approximately 350, after which it should gradually settle down on about 330.

Overshoot the heading when turning through south.

TURNING THROUGH SOUTH. When turning left through south, the acceleration is towards the east and the CG is left behind so that the aeroplane appears to have turned further than what it really has. Therefore, you should overshoot the heading because, once the compass settles down, it will return to a more accurate reading. For example, turning from 200 to 140, do not level the wings until the compass indicates about 120. Once the compass settles down, it should indicate about 140.

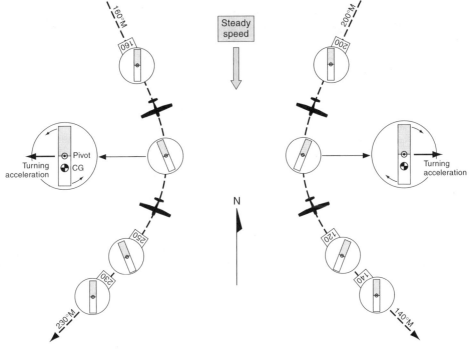

■ *Figure 27-17* **Overshoot the heading when turning through south**

When turning right through south, the acceleration is towards the west and the CG is left behind so that the aeroplane appears to have turned further than it really has. Again, you should over-shoot the heading. For example, turning from 160 to 230, do not level the wings until the compass indicates about 250. After it settles down, it should indicate about 230.

These turning and acceleration errors are a result of the CG of the compass magnet being displaced south of the pivot point (in the northern hemisphere) – the amount of displacement being greater the greater the magnetic dip, i.e. the nearer the magnetic pole you are, the more pronounced are these errors.

NOTE Turning errors in the southern hemisphere are reversed.

Aligning the HI with the Magnetic Compass

The heading indicator (HI) is a gyroscopic instrument, see page 267. Do not align the HI with the magnetic compass if you are changing speed or direction, as the magnetic compass will be experiencing acceleration or turning errors, i.e. keep the wings level and maintain a constant speed when aligning the HI with the compass.

One of the advantages of a heading indicator is that it is not subject to turning or acceleration errors. Its accuracy depends on it being aligned with magnetic north correctly, so this must be done when the magnetic compass is indicating correctly.

Now complete **Exercises 27 – The Magnetic Compass.**

Section **Four**

Airworthiness
and **Performance**

Airworthiness

The airworthiness requirements for aircraft in the UK are specified in the Air Navigation Order (Articles 7–16). The airworthiness documents that are of most importance to pilots are the:

☐ Certificate of Registration;
☐ Certificate of Airworthiness;
☐ Flight Manual; and
☐ Maintenance Documents.

Type Certificate

When a new type or model of aircraft is designed and built, the manufacturer applies for and, after suitable tests on the original test aeroplanes have been passed, is granted a Certificate of Type Approval. This document is issued to the manufacturer by the aviation authority in the country of manufacture.

Engineering and safety requirements, reliability and many other factors are considered in detail, with many inspections and flight tests being carried out prior to the issue of a Type Certificate. Once it is obtained, the manufacturer commences production and a new aeroplane type comes onto the market.

The pilot does not see the Type Certificate, which is retained by the manufacturer.

The Certificate of Registration

It is required that UK-owned or operated aircraft be registered with the Civil Aviation Authority (CAA). When this is done for an individual aircraft, the CAA issues a Certificate of Registration to the owner.

■ *Figure 28-1* **Part of a Certificate of Registration**

The aircraft is given a registration number of four letters to follow the UK nationality marking 'G' (e.g. G-AESE) and this must be displayed prominently on the aircraft in specific sizes and positions. The aeroplane may be identified in-flight by its registration, which in the above case is, *Golf Alpha Echo Sierra Echo.* The pilot should verify that the aircraft is registered – hiring from a reputable organisation or owner is usually sufficient.

Other nationality markings are: 'N–' for USA, 'F–' for France, 'D–' for Germany (Deutschland) and 'VH–' for Australia.

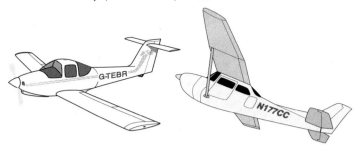

■ *Figure 28-2* **Examples of aircraft registrations**

Certificate of Airworthiness (CofA)

The Certificate of Airworthiness is issued by the CAA for an individual aircraft for a specified period and an aircraft shall not fly unless it has a valid CofA. (Note: there are some exceptions to this, such as during test flights or whenever an aeroplane has a Permit to Fly, but for a PPL pilot the rule generally holds.)

Part of the CofA for each individual aeroplane is the Flight Manual; the two documents are linked with an identification number.

The Certificate of Airworthiness is issued by the CAA for an individual aeroplane to operate in a particular **category,** provided it complies with the appropriate airworthiness requirements. Categories and their authorised purposes include:

▢ **Transport (Passengers)** – any purpose;
▢ **Transport (Cargo)** – any purpose except the public transport of passengers;
▢ **Aerial Work** – any purpose other than public transport;
▢ **Private** – any purpose other than public transport or aerial work;
▢ **Special.**

Note that the sample CofA in Figure 28-3 expires on the stated date (30th September 1997 in this case) and would normally be renewed prior to this date.

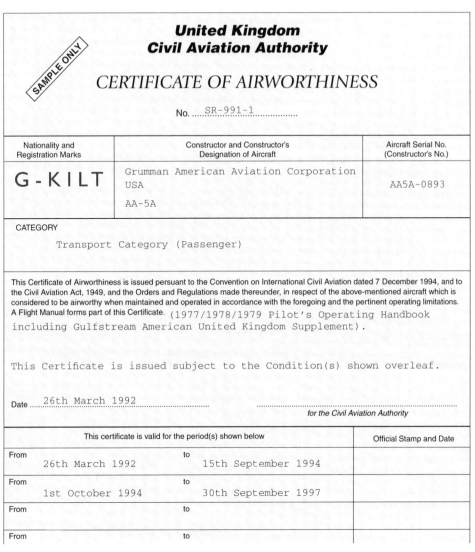

United Kingdom
Civil Aviation Authority

SAMPLE ONLY

CERTIFICATE OF AIRWORTHINESS

No. .....SR-991-1.....................

Nationality and Registration Marks	Constructor and Constructor's Designation of Aircraft	Aircraft Serial No. (Constructor's No.)
G - K I L T	Grumman American Aviation Corporation USA AA-5A	AA5A-0893

CATEGORY

Transport Category (Passenger)

This Certificate of Airworthiness is issued persuant to the Convention on International Civil Aviation dated 7 December 1994, and to the Civil Aviation Act, 1949, and the Orders and Regulations made thereunder, in respect of the above-mentioned aircraft which is considered to be airworthy when maintained and operated in accordance with the foregoing and the pertinent operating limitations. A Flight Manual forms part of this Certificate. (1977/1978/1979 Pilot's Operating Handbook including Gulfstream American United Kingdom Supplement).

This Certificate is issued subject to the Condition(s) shown overleaf.

Date ......26th March 1992.. ....
for the Civil Aviation Authority

This certificate is valid for the period(s) shown below		Official Stamp and Date
From 26th March 1992	to 15th September 1994	
From 1st October 1994	to 30th September 1997	
From	to	
From	to	

■ *Figure 28-3* **A Certificate of Airworthiness**

Aeroplanes are further categorised in a different manner according to the manoeuvres that they are permitted to perform:

▢ **Normal category** – below 5,700 kg and non-acrobatic: manoeuvres limited to stalls and steep turns of 60°. Typical limit load factors +2.5g and –1.0g.

▢ **Utility category** – as for a Normal category, plus limited aerobatics. Typical limit load factors are +4.5g and –1.8g.

▢ **Acrobatic category** – fully aerobatic. Typical limit load factors are +6.0g and –3.0g.

Do not intentionally carry out inappropriate manoeuvres for the category of your aeroplane – structural damage or destruction is a real possibility. Some aircraft in the normal category may be allowed to operate in the utility category within certain specified weight limits – usually with fuel/passenger restrictions – and these will be seen on the Weight and Balance Schedule as limits on the weight and position of the CG.

As well as being a physical piece of paper, the Certificate of Airworthiness, has other documents associated with it – in particular, the **Flight Manual** and the **Certificate of Maintenance Review.** An important part of the letter is the Certificate of Release to Service. It is stated on the CofA (Figure 28-3) that the aeroplane must be maintained and operated correctly for the CofA to remain valid. If the aeroplane is not maintained according to the approved maintenance schedule, the CofA becomes invalid until the required maintenance has been completed.

The Flight Manual

The Flight Manual must be approved by the CAA and it forms part of the CofA for a particular aeroplane. The CofA and the Flight Manual for a particular aeroplane carry the same identification number.

Since requirements in the country of manufacture (where the aeroplane and the Flight Manual originate), may differ from those in the UK, the CAA will often issue a **Flight Manual Supplement** that amends the original. This supplement may contain additional limitations, which must be observed even if in conflict with the manufacturer's Flight Manual. Performance information and operating limitations for a particular aeroplane are found in its Flight Manual and these are often areas which the CAA Supplement amends.

A pilot must comply with all the requirements, procedures and limitations with respect to the operation of the aeroplane as set out in its approved Flight Manual, as amended by the CAA Supplement. Placards placed in the cockpit reflect the Flight Manual and have the same status, i.e. the instructions should be followed.

The Flight Manual (and its CAA Supplement if there is one) must be carried in the aeroplane, which means that a pilot cannot take it home for reference. An easy-to-follow booklet derived from the Flight Manual and other operational documents is the **Pilot's Operating Handbook (POH),** which you should have for each type of aeroplane you fly. It does not have to remain with the aeroplane. The Pilot's Operating Handbook does not have the same legal standing as the Flight Manual.

The Maintenance Schedule

Each aeroplane must have a maintenance schedule approved by the CAA. The usual one is the **Light Aircraft Maintenance Schedule (LAMS).** This requires a system of regular checks and inspections by licensed and approved people. Logbooks must be kept for the airframe, the engine and the propeller if it has a constant-speed unit. Instrument Flight Rules aircraft will have a Radio and Navigation Aids Logbook.

A typical maintenance schedule will include:

☐ scheduled 'major inspections';
☐ 100-hour (or 150-hour) inspections;
☐ 25-hour or 50-hour inspections (in some cases);
☐ the daily inspection (or Check A) carried out by the pilot.

The **Certificate of Maintenance Review** is normally issued for aircraft below 2,730 kg after a 12-month period. It confirms that the aircraft has been maintained in accordance with its Maintenance Schedule and that any Airworthiness Directives (ADs) or Manufacturer's Service Bulletins promulgated during this period have been complied with.

A **Certificate of Release to Service** is issued by a licensed engineer following maintenance or an inspection.

A **Technical Log** may be kept for an aeroplane, in which the pilot can record any defect immediately following the completion of a flight, and the ground engineer can record the maintenance performed to correct that defect. Take-off and landing times will also be recorded in the Technical Log and there may be a small pocket to hold the Certificate of Maintenance Review and the Certificate of Release to Service. Each pilot should review these documents prior to flight.

An aeroplane structure subjected to severe turbulence in flight and/or a heavy landing may result in the aeroplane becoming unairworthy. Following such events, and prior to the next flight, the airframe should be checked for distortion, popped or sheared rivets, cracks, skin wrinkles, etc. Appropriate entries should be made in the Technical Log.

Maintenance Allowed by Pilots

Owners or operators who hold a Private Pilot's Licence or higher (student pilots are excluded) are permitted to carry out minor repairs and services on their aircraft not exceeding 2,730 kg (6,000 lb), which are in a category other than Public Transport. This permission is granted by Air Navigation Order, Article 11(3).

These minor repairs or replacement are listed in the Air Navigation (General) Regulations, number 16, which is reproduced in Figure 28-4.

Pilot maintenance – prescribed repairs or replacements

16 For the purposes of article 11(3), the following repairs or replacements are hereby prescribed:

(1) Replacement of landing gear tyres, landing skids or skid shoes;

(2) Replacement of elastic shock absorber cord units on landing gear where special tools are not required;

(3) Replacement of defective safety wiring or split pins excluding those in engine, transmission, flight control or rotor systems;

(4) Patch-repairs to fabric not requiring rib stitching or the removal of structural parts or control surfaces, if the repairs do not cover up structural damage and do not include repairs to rotor blades;

(5) Repairs to upholstery and decorative furnishing of the cabin or cockpit interior when repair does not require dismantling of any structure or operating system or interfere with an operating system or affect the structure of the aircraft;

(6) Repairs, not including welding, to fairings, non-structural cover plates and cowlings;

(7) Replacement of side windows where that work does not interfere with the structure or with any operating system;

(8) Replacement of safety belts or safety harness;

(9) Replacement of seats or seat parts not involving dismantling of any structure or of any operating system;

(10) Replacement of bulbs, reflectors, glasses, lenses or lights;

(11) Replacement of any cowling not requiring removal of the propeller, rotors or disconnection of engine or flight controls;

(12) Replacement of unserviceable sparking plugs;

(13) Replacement of batteries;

(14) Replacement of wings and tail surfaces and controls, the attachments of which are designed to provide for assembly immediately before each flight and dismantling after each flight;

(15) Replacement of main rotor blades that are designed for removal where special tools are not required;

(16) Replacement of generator and fan belts designed for removal where special tools are not required;

(17) Replacement of VHF communications equipment, being equipment which is not combined with navigation equipment.

■ *Figure 28-4* **Air Navigation (General) Regulation 16, listing maintenance (repairs or replacements) permitted by a PPL holder**

Pilots should record any minor work that they carry out in the appropriate logbook and certify it with their signature and licence number.

The **50-hour check** of an aircraft in the Private category may be carried out and signed for by a licensed pilot who is the owner or operator of the aeroplane. A pilot may only sign for the actual 50-hour check and for rectification work within the scope of Air Navigation (General) 16 Regulation as described in Figure 28-4, with the provisio that any CAA mandatory requirements due at that time must be certified by a licensed or authorised engineer.

The Daily Inspection or Check A

A daily inspection, which is known as **Check A** in the UK, must be carried out prior to the first flight of the day, and can be performed by the pilot. Each flying training organisation or operator will have a specific daily inspection procedure to follow. It will be available in written form and contain items closely resembling the list below.

CHECK A	LAMS Fixed Wing
General	**Remove** *frost, snow or ice, if present.*
	Check *that the aircraft documents are available and in order.*
	Ensure all loose equipment *is correctly stowed and the aircraft is free of extraneous items.*
	If the aircraft has not been regularly used, *ensure before resumption of flying that:* *(a) Either (i) the engine has been turned weekly or run fortnightly,* *or (ii) the manufacturer's recommendations have been complied with.* *(b) Compression appears normal when engine turned by hand.* *(c) Previously reported defects have been rectified.*
Powerplant/ Engine	**Check** *– oil level; security of filler cap and dipstick.*
	Inspect *– engine, as visible, for leaks, signs of overheating, and security of all items.*
	Inspect *– air filter/air intake for cleanliness.*
	Check *– security of cowlings, access doors and cowl flaps.*
Propeller	**Inspect** *– blades and spinner for damage and security.*
Windscreen	**Inspect** *– for damage and cleanliness.*
Fuel System	**Check** *– visually that quantities are compatible with indicator readings.*
	Drain *– fuel sample from each drain point into a transparent container and check for water, foreign matter and correct colour.*
Wings	**Inspect** *– skin/covering, bracing wires, struts and flying control surfaces for damage and security of all items.*
	Inspect *– pitot/static vents, fuel vents and drain holes for freedom from obstruction.*
	Test *– operation of stall warning device.*
Landing Gear	**Check** *– shock-absorber struts for leaks and that extension appears normal.*
	Check *– tyres for inflation, damage and creep.*
	Inspect *– brake installation for external evidence of leaks, and for damage and security.*
Fuselage and Empennage	**Inspect** *– skin/covering, bracing wires, struts and flying control surfaces for damage and security of all items.*
	Inspect *– drain holes and vents for freedom from obstruction.*
	Inspect *– radio aerials for damage and security.*

CHECK A	LAMS Fixed Wing

Cabin Area **Check** – *flying and engine controls, including trimmers and flaps, for full and free movement in the correct sense.*

Check – *brake operation is normal.*

Check – *instrument readings are consistent with ambient conditions.*

Perform – *manual override and disengagement check on auto-pilot.*

Check – *avionic equipment operation, using self-test facilities where provided.*

Inspect – *seats, belts and harnesses for satisfactory condition, locking and release.*

Check – *emergency equipment properly stowed and inspection dates valid.*

Test – *operation of electrical circuits.*

Inspect – *cabin and baggage doors for damage, security, and for correct operation and locking.*

Check – *that markings and full complement of placards are correctly positioned and legible.*

■ *Figure 28-5* **'Check A' items (from light aircraft maintenance schedule)**

Duplicate Inspection

Any adjustments that are made to either the **flight controls** and/or the **engine controls** of an aeroplane are normally required to be checked by two licensed personnel, either engineers or inspectors, before it is considered to be airworthy again.

The Airworthiness Requirements (BCAR (British Civil Airworthiness Requirements) Section A, Chapter 5-3) do, however, state that, should a **minor adjustment** of a vital point or control system be necessary when the aircraft is away from base, the second part of the Duplicate Inspection may be completed by a pilot licensed for the type of aircraft concerned.

The Insurance Document

While the Certificate of Insurance has no standing as an airworthiness document, it is common sense to confirm that the aeroplane you are about to fly is covered by adequate insurance.

Other Documents

Other documents associated with a particular aeroplane may include a:
☐ Noise Certificate;
☐ Certificate of Approval of Radio Installation;
☐ Aircraft Radio Licence;
☐ Weight and Centre of Gravity Schedule.

Now complete **Exercises 28 – Airworthiness.**

Airframe Limitations

Weight Limitations

The **gross weight** or **all-up weight** of the aeroplane is subject to certain limitations. Some of the limitations are *structural* in nature, as the aeroplane is designed and built to perform certain tasks and carry certain loads, up to a maximum. Other limitations are due to the *performance* limitations of the aeroplane – certain conditions of temperature and pressure, runway conditions, etc., may limit allowable weights for take-off, landing and so on.

Maximum Take-Off Weight (MTOW)

Maximum take-off weight is a structural limitation. The MTOW is the maximum gross weight according to the Certificate of Airworthiness or approved Flight Manual, at which that aeroplane is permitted to take-off. It is sometimes referred to as the maximum brakes release weight (MBRW).

NOTE The take-off weight for a particular take-off may not exceed the structural MTOW or the TOW as limited by aeroplane performance and runway considerations.

Maximum Landing Weight (MLW)

Maximum landing weight is also a structural limitation. The MLW is the maximum gross weight, according to the Certificate of Airworthiness or approved Flight Manual, at which that aeroplane is permitted to land.

NOTE The landing weight for a particular landing should not exceed the structural MLW or the LW as limited by aeroplane performance and runway considerations. The MLW is usually less than the MTOW because of the greater stresses expected in landing compared to taking off.

Maximum Zero Fuel Weight (MZFW)

Maximum zero fuel weight may be specified (but is not for many light aircraft). MZFW is the maximum allowable gross weight with no usable fuel in the wing tanks.

The wings provide the upwards lift force to balance the weight of the aeroplane. This upwards force tends to bend the wings upwards, which it will do, especially if there is no fuel in the wing tanks whose weight will tend to bend the wings down. The greatest upward bending of the wings will occur when the aeroplane is heavy and there is little fuel in the wing tanks – the maximum zero fuel weight places a structural limit on this.

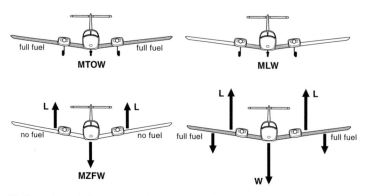

■ Figure 29-1 **MTOW, MLW, MZFW**

Speed Limitations

The aeroplane should only be flown in a specific operating speed range, limited by certain high and low speeds. Sometimes aerodynamic considerations provide the reason for the limit (e.g. stalling speed is the lower speed limit), and sometimes power considerations limit the speeds (e.g. maximum speed on the cruise is limited by the amount of power available to overcome the increasing parasite drag).

More important are the **structural limitations.** There might be sufficient power available for a very-high-speed cruise or dive, but the airframe may not be designed to withstand these stresses.

The airframe is subjected to forces of 1g in calm straight-and-level flight, i.e. the aeroplane and the pilot experience a force equal to their own weight. As you read this, sitting in your chair, you will be experiencing a force provided by the chair equal and opposite to your weight, i.e. 1g.

We already know that the important speed for aerodynamic considerations is the indicated airspeed (IAS) as shown on the airspeed indicator (ASI). The IAS is related to the dynamic pressure ½ *rho V-squared* which governs the generation of aerodynamic forces like lift and drag. Therefore all of these aerodynamically limiting speeds are indicated airspeeds.

NOTE You will find that advanced texts refer to a *calibrated airspeed* or *rectified airspeed*. This is simply indicated airspeed read off the ASI in the cockpit, corrected for any errors in the instrument reading, say due to imperfect positioning of the pitot tube and static vent. In most light aircraft this error is only a knot or two at the speeds we are considering and so we can assume that IAS and RAS/CAS are the same. There is no need for you to remember this for the examination.

The airframe is subjected to forces of 1g in calm, straight and level flight; you also experience a force of 1g exerted on your body by the seat, equal and opposite to your weight. This force, both on the airframe and on you, will change in manoeuvres.

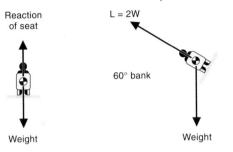

■ *Figure 29-2* **Experiencing 1g and experiencing 2g**

Any manoeuvring, such as turning, diving, or performing aerobatics, will increase or decrease this load on the structure and on you, e.g. a perfect 60° banked turn increases the structural load to 2g. You will experience a force (exerted by the seat) equal to double your weight, i.e. double the force of gravity – hence the expression 2g.

Turbulence and gusts provide almost instantaneous changes in the local angle of attack between the aerofoils and the relative airflow, which causes immense changes in the lift produced and places great stresses on the aeroplane structure. These stresses are described in terms of the **load factor** or *g-forces* – how many times greater than *g*, the force of gravity, they are.

$$\text{Load factor } (n) = \frac{\text{Lift produced by wing}}{\text{Weight of aeroplane}}$$

Avoid pulling excessive g when recovering from unusual attitudes.

It is important when recovering from the more unusual attitudes of flight (steep turns, steep dives, spiral dives) that you avoid pulling excessive *g*, because this may overstress the airframe, causing distortion, skin wrinkles, cracks, and popped or sheared rivets.

An aerobatic category aeroplane will be certificated for higher load factors than a normal or utility category aeroplane.

As well as the static load factor or *g-forces,* there are **dynamic strength considerations,** such as dynamic instability of the aeroplane in high-speed flight, 'flutter' in the control panels, which, if allowed to develop, can lead to structural failure.

There are **absolute limit speeds,** such as the never-exceed speed (V_{NE}) on the high side and the stalling speed (V_S) on the low side. Within these extreme limits are other more cautious limits, such as the normal operating limit speed (V_{NO}) on the high side, and the stall buffet on the low side.

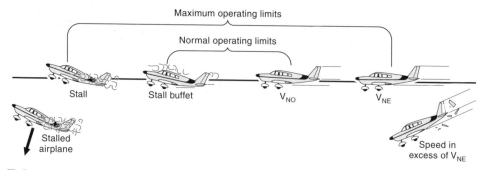

Figure 29-3 **The speed range of an aeroplane**

Never-Exceed Speed (V$_{NE}$)

V$_{NE}$ is the absolute maximum speed at which the aeroplane should be flown. It is indicated on the airspeed indicator (ASI) by a red line. Any gusts or manoeuvring at speeds higher than V$_{NE}$ can cause unacceptable load factors. A sensible pilot would not allow the aeroplane to approach this speed under normal operations.

Normal Operating Limit Speed (V$_{NO}$)

V$_{NO}$ is the maximum speed at which the aeroplane should be flown under normal operating conditions. The normal operating speed range is indicated on the ASI by a green arc. Above V$_{NO}$ (normal operating limit speed) is a yellow or orange caution arc, extending to the limiting red line at V$_{NE}$.

You should not exceed V$_{NO}$ – though it may be safe in smooth air, any gusts could over-stress the airframe.

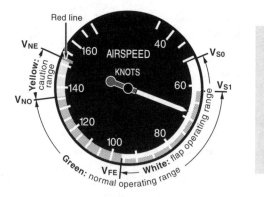

V$_{S0}$	Stall speed at max weight, landing gear down, flaps down, power off
V$_{S1}$	Stall speed at max weight, landing gear up (if retractable), flaps up, power off
V$_{FE}$	Maximum speed, flaps extended
V$_{NO}$	Maximum structural cruising speed (for normal operations)
V$_{NE}$	Never-exceed speed (max speed, all ops.)

Figure 29-4 **Colour coding on the airspeed indicator**

Manoeuvring Speed (V$_A$ or V$_{MAN}$)

When the pilot is manoeuvring the aeroplane, the control surfaces (ailerons, elevators and rudder), the wings and the tailplane are all subjected to increased loading. Manoeuvring speed (V$_A$) is the maximum speed for manoeuvres at which full application of the primary flight controls will not overstress the airframe.

NOTE The Aeroplane Flight Manual may specify varying speeds for V$_A$ because, at light weights, V$_A$ is lower than at higher weights.

Other Maximum Speeds

V$_{FE}$. As the flaps are extended, the airframe is subjected to extra stresses and so a maximum flap extended speed (V$_{FE}$) is usually specified to prevent possible structural damage.

V$_{LO}$,V$_{LE}$. For aeroplanes with retractable undercarriage (landing gear) one or two speed limitations will be specified, according to system design: V$_{LO}$ – the maximum airspeed for operating (extending or retracting) the landing gear, and V$_{LE}$ – the maximum airspeed at which you may fly with gear extended. Where both are specified, V$_{LO}$ will be slower than V$_{LE}$. This is because, while the undercarriage is in transit between retracted and extended, some gear doors may open out into the airstream and be subjected to air loads. In systems where these doors close again once the gear is extended, a higher airspeed (V$_{LE}$) is permitted (although not as high as when the gear is retracted and the doors are closed again). Also, small locking devices may be fitted to strengthen the under-carriage structure when it is extended.

Flying in Turbulence

Turbulent air or gusts can change the direction of the local relative airflow and the angle of attack almost instantaneously. Flying slowly (at a high angle of attack), an upwards gust could increase the angle of attack and the wing-loading (g-forces) such that the wing stalls. Flying slowly through gusts decreases the stresses on the aeroplane, but exposes it to the possibility of a stall.

Flying fast through turbulence gives a bumpier ride and puts more stress (higher load factors) on the structure than low speeds.

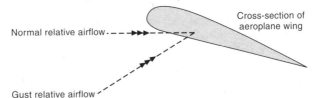

Normal relative airflow

Cross-section of aeroplane wing

Gust relative airflow

■ *Figure 29-5* **Gusts can increase or decrease the angle of attack, cause high wing loadings, or cause the wing's critical angle of attack to be exceeded (stall)**

The **turbulence penetration speed** (V_B or V_{TURB}), or the **rough air speed** (V_{RA}), are the recommended target speeds for flying through turbulence. They are compromise speeds to avoid *high-g* stalls on the low-speed side and excessive wing loading on the high-speed side. If no V_B or V_{RA} is specified (often the case for light aircraft), then use the manoeuvring speed (V_A) to avoid structural damage.

Refer to your instructor for techniques for flying in turbulence in your aeroplane. Some general comments on flying in turbulence follow.

☐ **Turbulence penetration speed** is a 'target speed'. In turbulence the airspeed may fluctuate rapidly and any attempt to chase a constant airspeed with elevator control and power changes may over-stress the aircraft. Allow the airspeed to fluctuate around V_{TURB}. If this speed is not specified, then the manoeuvring speed, V_A, is a good 'target speed' for turbulence penetration. V_{NO} should not be exceeded in turbulence.

☐ **Maintain wings level** with the ailerons, but be gentle with the elevators. Due to their long moment arm from the centre of gravity, the elevators can easily over-stress the structure if they are moved too violently or too far in turbulence.

☐ **Do not chase altitude** – allow the aeroplane to rise and fall with the air currents (provided that terrain clearance and separation from other traffic is adequate).

☐ **Ensure that any power changes** are made smoothly.

The Velocity/Load Factor (or V-n) Diagram

The V-n diagram illustrates the flight operating strength of an aeroplane. Limit load factors and limit speeds are specified by the CAA for different aeroplane categories, within which the aeroplane must be operated. Taken beyond these limits, the aeroplane may suffer structural damage or even structural failure.

The high speed limit is V_{NE}, the never-exceed speed, and speed on the low side is limited by the stall. The stalling speed is affected by the load factor, occurring at higher speeds when *g* is being pulled. V_{S1g} is the 1g stalling speed, i.e. when flying straight-and-level.

Full backward movement of the control column will increase the g-loading and cause a stall to occur – at low speeds the stall occurs before the limit load factor is reached. At high speeds, however, the limit load factor may be reached before the stall occurs and so full back-stick must not be applied. The manoeuvring speed (V_A) is the speed above which this is a consideration and full back control column should not be applied. In fact, above V_A you should avoid making any abrupt or large control movements.

Above V_A avoid making any abrupt or large control movements.

Gusts also cause changes in the load factor and care should be taken when flying in turbulence. V_{NO}, the normal operations limit speed, should not be exceeded except in very smooth air, when V_{NE} becomes the absolute limit. In strong turbulence, consideration should be given to flying at the turbulence penetration speed (if specified), otherwise at the manoeuvring speed V_A, to avoid excessive flight loads causing damage to the aeroplane structure.

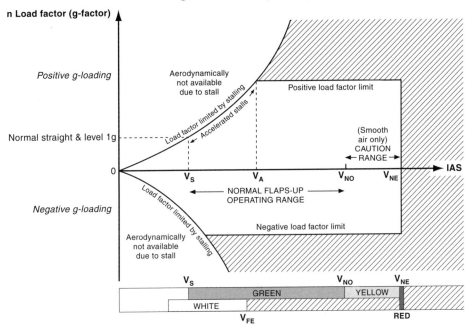

■ *Figure 29-6* **A typical V-n diagram related to ASI markings**

Checks following Excessive Stress on the Airframe

While you must not knowingly exceed the airframe limitations, excessive stress can be caused by unexpected severe turbulence or a particularly heavy landing. In both cases, the wing structure may be heavily loaded and, in the case of heavy landing, the landing gear and the areas where it is attached to the airframe will be heavily loaded.

Structural damage can exist even without external indications. If you overstress an aircraft you must ensure an engineer checks it.

One of the responsibilities of being a pilot is to ensure that following pilots will be presented with an airworthy aeroplane. The occurrence of heavy stress must be referred to an engineer. There could be damage not immediately apparent to you during an inspection, quite apart from those items already listed. For this reason, if an aeroplane has been overstressed, you must ensure that a qualified engineer carries out an inspection prior to the next flight.

Many light aircraft are of semi-monocoque construction, where the loads are carried, not only by the internal structure, but also by the skin. Damage of any of these will weaken the overall structure. In carrying out an inspection the engineer will look for indications of stress on the airframe, the main external items being:

- **distortion of the structure;**
- **cracks;**
- **popped or sheared rivets;** and
- **wrinkles in the skin,** especially in the areas surrounding the main structural attachments for the engine, wing, wing struts and tailplane.

Severe overload can distort or break the wings and associated struts or braces. In the case of a heavy landing, checks of the landing gear and the areas surrounding its attachment points would be made (e.g. the engine firewall to which a nosewheel may be attached).

Now complete **Exercises 29 – Airframe Limitations.**

The Atmosphere

For a safe take-off to be achieved, you must first have the skills to handle the aeroplane in flight. Then you must learn the skills involved in taking the aeroplane from one medium (the ground) to another (the atmosphere). Of course, even when on the ground the aeroplane is immersed in the air and so wind effects and pressure/temperature (i.e. density) affect it.

Pressure and temperature play an extremely important role in the performance of aeroplanes (both the performance of the airframe and performance of the engine). The critical element is **air density** (*rho* or ρ), which decreases as pressure falls and temperature rises.

On a hot day, the air is less dense and the aeroplane performance capabilities will also be less. If the pressure is low (e.g. for take-off at an aerodrome of high elevation), then the air is less dense, lowering the performance capabilities of the aeroplane.

The power delivered by the engine depends on the weight of the fuel/air charge – the less dense the air, the lower the power-producing capability of the engine.

Performance decreases when air density reduces.

The aerodynamic qualities of the airframe depend on air density (*rho*). Dynamic pressure is ½ *rho V-squared* and this appears in the aerodynamic relationship: Lift = $C_{Lift} \times$ ½ *rho V-squared* $\times$ S.

If air density (*rho*) decreases, then aerodynamic qualities decrease. High temperatures and low pressures (at altitude) cause a decrease in air density, as does high humidity (moisture content).

Factors affecting Air Density

Altitude

The atmosphere consists of a mixture of gases that surround the earth and are held to it by the force of gravity. For this reason, the atmosphere is densest near the earth's surface and the air density decreases as height is gained. Since both engine and aerodynamic performance depend on air density, they also decrease with altitude.

Performance decreases as altitude increases.

The pressure that the air exerts at any point depends on the weight of air pressing down from above, therefore pressure also decreases with altitude. If the pressure is reduced, then the air expands and becomes less dense. Performance is poorer at high altitudes.

Temperature

Heating of an air mass causes it to expand and decreases its density, therefore decreasing both engine and aerodynamic performance of an aeroplane, i.e. performance is poorer on hot days. Temperature generally decreases with altitude (the nominal standard rate being 2°C/1,000 ft).

Performance reduces as air temperature increases.

Cooling of an air mass increases its density, although this effect is not as great as height is gained as that of the decreased pressure, the overall effect being a decrease of density at higher altitudes.

Humidity

The mixture of gasses that we call 'air' consists mainly of nitrogen and oxygen and water vapour.

COMPOSITION OF AIR	
Gas	Volume (%)
Nitrogen	78%
Oxygen	21%
Other gases (argon, carbon dioxide, neon, helium, etc.)	1%
Total	100%

The amount of water vapour in the air is called **humidity**. Because water molecules are very light, a high humidity will cause the air density to be slightly less, but no account of this is taken in performance charts.

Performance reduces as humidity increases.

Just how much water a parcel of air is capable of holding depends on its temperature – warm air can hold more water than cold air. If a parcel of air is holding 70% of its maximum capacity of water vapour, then it has a *relative humidity* of 70%. If it cools, its capacity to hold water vapour is less and, even though the actual amount of water does not change, the relative humidity increases.

If the parcel of air cools until its capacity to hold water vapour is equal to that which it is actually holding, then its relative humidity is 100% and the parcel of air is said to be **saturated**. Any further cooling will cause some of the water vapour to condense as water droplets and form cloud, fog or dew.

Relative humidity is defined as the amount of water vapour present in a parcel of air compared to the maximum amount that it can support (i.e. when it is saturated) at the same temperature.

A rough measure of humidity is what happens to perspiration. If it evaporates, the air is 'dry' (low relative humidity) and can absorb more water vapour. If the perspiration remains as beads of sweat, the relative humidity is high and the air cannot absorb the extra moisture.

The International Standard Atmosphere (ISA)

Because the pressure and temperature in the real atmosphere are continually changing, a theoretical International Standard Atmosphere (the ISA, or the ICAO Standard Atmosphere) has been defined as a 'measuring stick' by the International Civil Aviation Organization (ICAO).

NOTE A unit of pressure for aviation known as the *hectopascal* has been adopted by ICAO. However, in the UK, the unit *millibar* has been retained for the foreseeable future. 1 millibar of pressure is equal to 1 hectopascal. Other countries also differ from the ICAO standard – in the USA the unit of pressure for aviation is *inches of mercury*, usually abbreviated to *inches*.

The International Standard Atmosphere has a mean sea level (MSL) pressure of 1013.2 mb(hPa), and an MSL temperature of 15° Celsius. They decrease at specified rates as altitude is gained.

The real and ever-changing atmosphere will differ from the ISA, and we can compare the real and actual atmosphere existing at the point under consideration with the conditions one would expect in the ISA.

Pressure Altitude

The standard ISA mean sea level pressure is 1013.2 mb(hPa) (in practice we use 1013 mb or hPa), and this decreases at about 1mb(hPa) per 30 feet increase in height.

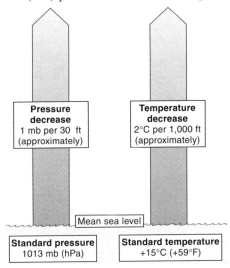

■ *Figure 30-1* **The International Standard Atmosphere (ISA)**

At 600 ft in the ISA, the pressure will have decreased by approximately (600 ÷ 30) = 20 mb, i.e. from 1013 mb it will have decreased to 993 mb. If the point where your aeroplane is situated has a pressure of 993 mb, then we say it has a *pressure altitude* of 600 ft, i.e. it is the equivalent of 600 ft above the 1013 mb(hPa) pressure level in the ISA.

> **Pressure altitude** is the height in the International Standard Atmosphere above the 1013.2 mb(hPa) pressure level at which the pressure equals that of the aircraft or point under consideration.

The easiest way to read pressure altitude in the cockpit is to set 1013 mb(hPa) in the altimeter subscale – the altimeter will then indicate pressure altitude. Knowing the pressure altitude allows us to compare the aeroplane performance against a known standard.

Pressure altitude can be calculated mathematically (using a decrease of 1 mb per 30 ft gain in height) or on your navigation computer.

EXAMPLE 1 QNH is 1005 mb and the aeroplane is on the ground at an aerodrome, elevation 20 ft. Find the pressure altitude.

Step 1.
QNH (MSL) is 1005 mb. Since pressure decreases with height, the standard pressure level of 1013 mb will occur (theoretically) below sea level.

To find pressure altitude (height above the standard 1013 mb level), we first find the height between MSL (QNH) and 1013. The 8 mb difference is equivalent to (8 × 30) = 240 ft.

Step 2.
The aeroplane is a further 20 ft above this, i.e. 260 ft above the 1013 mb pressure level. The pressure altitude is 260 ft.

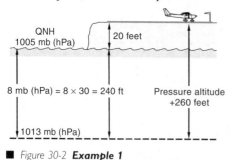

■ *Figure 30-2* **Example 1**

EXAMPLE 2 QNH is 1030 mb, and the aeroplane is on the ground at an aerodrome whose elevation is 20 ft. Find the pressure altitude.

Step 1.

Pressure decreases with altitude. Since MSL pressure is 1030 mb, the standard pressure level of 1013 mb, being less, must be higher than MSL on this particular day. The 17 mb pressure difference means that the height difference is about (17 × 30) = 510 ft.

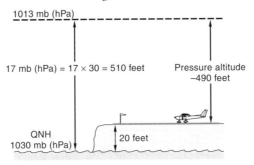

■ *Figure 30-3* **Example 2**

Step 2.

From Figure 30-3 you can see that the aeroplane is 490 ft below the standard 1013 mb pressure level. Thus, its pressure altitude is –490 ft or 490 ft *below* mean sea level (bmsl).

EXAMPLE 3 An aircraft is cruising at 5,000 ft with QNH (actual MSL pressure) 1027 mb set in the subscale. Find the pressure altitude.

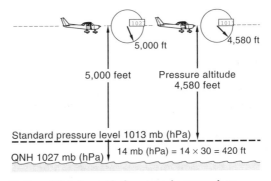

■ *Figure 30-4* **Example 3 – a good approach to pressure altitude problems**

The altimeter measures the height it is from the pressure level set in the subscale. A quick means of estimating pressure altitude (height in the ISA above the 1013 mb/hPa) pressure level is simply to wind the subscale around so that 1013 is set there.

From the above example you can see:

Wind off millibars (hectopascals) – wind off height.

Temperature

The higher the temperature the lower the density – and the lower the aeroplane performance.

The 'measuring stick' for temperature in the atmosphere is the International Standard Atmosphere (ISA). Standard sea level temperature is + 15° Celsius and it falls at approximately 2°C per 1,000 feet gain in altitude.

☐ At **1,000 ft** in the ISA, the temperature will have fallen to +13°C.

☐ At **2,000 ft** in the ISA, the temperature will have fallen to +11°C.

☐ At **3,000 ft** in the ISA, the temperature will have fallen to +9°C.

Now if the actual temperature at a pressure altitude of 3,000 ft is +16°C, i.e. 7° warmer than that expected in the ISA, we refer to it as ISA+7. The **temperature deviation** from ISA is +7.

If the actual temperature at 2,000 ft is +7°C, (i.e. 4° cooler than in the ISA), we refer to that as ISA–4. The temperature deviation from ISA is –4.

Aeroplane and engine performance depend on air density. It is impractical for the pilot to have the equipment necessary to measure air density, so we use two pieces of information already available in the cockpit and on which air density depends – pressure altitude and temperature.

Density Altitude

By considering pressure altitude (related to height in the International Standard Atmosphere) and temperature, we are really considering air density (*rho* or ρ). Most performance charts allow us to enter with these two, therefore there is usually no need to directly calculate density. On the rare occasion that it is, there is a quick method of doing it.

We already know that in the ISA, temperature is + 15°C at ISA MSL (i.e. pressure altitude 0 ft), and decreases at 2°C for every 1,000 ft gained in height. Therefore, at a pressure altitude of 3,000 ft, the ISA temperature should have dropped by 6° to be +9°C.

If the temperature at pressure altitude 3,000 feet exceeds this – (say it is +13°C), the air will be less dense than in the ISA and the aeroplane will perform as if it were higher than the 3,000 ft in the ISA – by an amount equal to:

120 ft for each 1°C deviation from the ISA temperature.

In this case, it is 4° warmer than ISA and so the aeroplane will perform as if it were (4 × 120) = 480 ft higher than the 3,000 ft pressure altitude. We say it has a **density altitude** of 3,480 ft. Performance will be poorer.

NOTE Navigation computers have the facility for finding density altitude.

Fahrenheit and Celsius Conversions

There are various temperature scales in use and, if you are flying in foreign countries, it may be necessary to convert from one to the other. The Celsius (centigrade) and Fahrenheit scales both use the boiling point and freezing point of water as standard temperatures – the difference between them is 100°C or 180°F. See Figure 30-5.

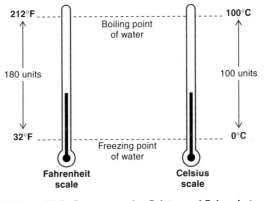

■ *Figure 30-5* ***Comparing the Celsius and Fahrenheit temperature scales***

Each 1°C is larger than 1°F by a ratio of ¹⁸⁰⁄₁₀₀ or ⁹⁄₅. The starting point of both scales is the freezing point of water, 0°C or 32°F. These can be combined into the one relationship connecting °F and °C:

Degrees F = ⁹⁄₅ degrees C + 32.

EXAMPLE 4 Convert 20°C to °F.

°F = ⁹⁄₅ × 20°C + 32 = 36 + 32 = 68°F.

To reverse the relationship, simply subtract 32 from both sides and then multiply both sides by ⁵⁄₉ to obtain:

°C = ⁵⁄₉ (°F − 32)

EXAMPLE 5 Convert 68°F to °C.

°C = ⁵⁄₉ (68°F − 32) = ⁵⁄₉ × 36 = 20°C.

NOTE You may be required to apply these formulae in the examination but, in practice, the easiest method of converting temperatures is to use conversion scale on a navigation computer.

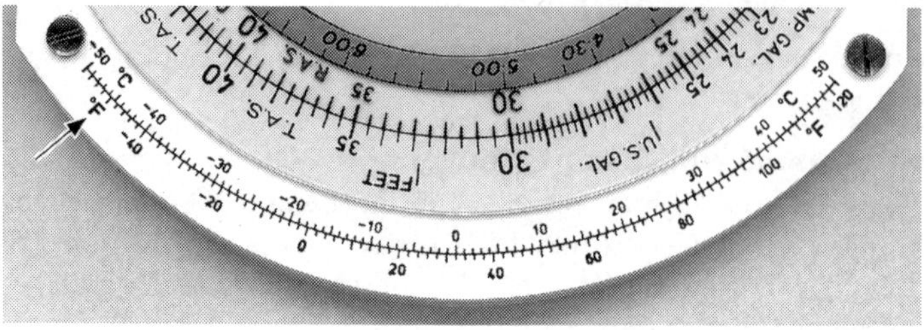

■ *Figure 30-6* **Temperature conversion scale on a navigation computer**

Now complete **Exercises 30 – The Atmosphere.**

Take-Off and Landing Performance

Take-offs and landings involve much more than smooth piloting skills. They involve careful prior consideration (planning) to ensure that the aeroplane is capable of the task. A very smooth take-off is of little value if the aeroplane, once airborne, is faced with obstacles impossible to avoid. The take-off performance of the aeroplane needs to be compared to the runway and surrounding obstacles in the existing conditions *prior* to actually taking off. Similarly, each landing must be carefully planned. A smooth touchdown is of little value if the aeroplane runs into the fence at the far end of a 'too-short' landing strip.

Aeroplane take-off and landing performance is subject to many variables including:

☐ **aeroplane weight;**
☐ **aerodrome pressure altitude;**
☐ **temperature** (which, together with pressure altitude, gives density altitude);
☐ **wind;**
☐ **runway length;**
☐ **runway slope;**
☐ **runway surface;**
☐ **flap setting;**
☐ **humidity.**

The supplied performance data for the aeroplane will usually allow adjustments to be made for these variables. Later in this chapter, typical percentage effects on the take-off and landing distances due to these variables are considered.

Competent pilots will know approximate take-off and landing distances required at maximum weight on a level, hard, dry surface for their particular aeroplanes. If the runway is long, say at Manchester International, and the conditions are good, then obviously sufficient distance will be available for a light aircraft and no precise performance calculation is needed. If, however, the strip is short, or conditions are poor (mud, snow, wet grass, tailwind, etc.), or some marginal situation exists (say a request to make an intersection departure using only part of a runway at a busy aerodrome), then the performance data should be checked carefully.

Where to find Performance Information

Performance figures may be given in a variety of publications and it is important for pilots to know where to find the data needed to predict the performance in the expected flight conditions. The appropriate documents are specified in the Certificate of Airworthiness and may be any one of the following:

- ☐ **The UK Flight Manual** for the aircraft;
- ☐ **The Owner's Manual** or Pilot's Operating Handbook, which may contain a CAA supplement or overriding data in the main document (the case for many light aeroplanes);
- ☐ **The Performance Schedule** (applies to some older aircraft);
- ☐ **For some imported aeroplanes,** an English Language Flight Manual approved by the Airworthiness Authority in the country of origin, but with a UK supplement containing performance data approved by the CAA.

Using Performance Data

The majority of modern light aeroplanes in the UK are certified in *Performance Group E.* The CAA-approved performance charts or tables for these aeroplanes enable the pilot to obtain **measured take-off distance** and **measured landing distance.** These are *unfactored* performance data, usually representing the measured performance achieved by the manufacturer using a new aeroplane flown by a test pilot in ideal conditions.

For some aeroplane types, the CAA has imposed a mandatory limitation, or **performance writedown,** on the manufacturer's performance data that requires certain corrections to be made to these data. For instance, one commonly used trainer has the following writedown applied by the CAA.

The corrections listed below must be applied to the Pilot's Operating Handbook performance information whenever it is used, in addition to any other corrections which may be applicable, as indicated by the text.
  Rate of Climb – subtract 40 ft/min. (applicable graph quoted);
  Take-Off Field lengths – add 5% (applicable graph quoted).

The performance figures extracted from the manual or handbook (with any CAA-imposed limitation applied) are the *absolute minimum* figures that may legally be used by a PPL pilot. They are, however, considered inadequate for normal operations. Since it is most unlikely that an average pilot in a well-used aeroplane in less favourable conditions will be able to achieve the certificated performance, the CAA strongly recommends that a safety factor of 1.33 for take-off and 1.43 for landing be applied to the performance data obtained from the manual or handbook.

Apply a safety factor of 1.33 for take-off and 1.43 for landing to 'book figures'.

While these safety factors are "strongly recommended" for Private flights, they are "mandatory" for Public Transport flights. A PPL pilot conscious of safety should always apply these factors, even though it is not a legal requirement, and maintain the same level of safety as a Public Transport flight.

NOTE Performance data in manuals for aeroplanes certified in the other light-aircraft Performance Groups (C and D) already include factoring, and the manuals and handbooks should clearly indicate this. If in any doubt, consult the Airworthiness Division of the CAA.

Be aware that it is your **legal obligation** to ensure that the aeroplane has adequate performance to carry out the proposed flight safely (see Article 35 of the Air Navigation Order), and one of the aims of this chapter is to remind you to:

☐ **read the published performance data** carefully and allow for the variables;

☐ **apply any mandatory** CAA-imposed limitations; and

☐ **consider adding** the strongly recommended safety factor.

Take-Off Performance

The **measured take-off distance** for a particular weight and flap setting is the measured distance to accelerate on a dry, hard surface with (all) engine(s) operating at maximum power from the starting point, to effect a transition to climbing flight and attain a *screen height* of 50 feet (15.2 meters) at a speed not less than the **take-off safety speed (TOSS)** or V_2. The TOSS provides at least a 20% margin over the stall, i.e. it is at least $1.2V_s$.

While the **take-off distance** and **take-off safety speed at 50 ft** are vital performance figures, some tables also detail the actual ground run from the starting point on the runway to the point of lift-off (or 'unstick') where the aeroplane's wheels leave the ground, as well as the **lift-off speed**.

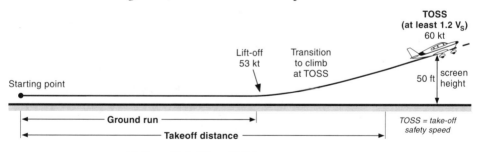

■ *Figure 31-1* **Take-off distance**

There are various presentations of take-off performance charts (tables and graphs). You must become familiar with those in your aeroplane's Flight Manual or Pilot's Operating Handbook, since they are the starting point for the calculation of **take-off distance required**.

| UNITED KINGDOM SUPPLEMENT | GULFSTREAM AMERICAN MODEL AA-5A CHEETAH |

TAKEOFF DISTANCE (AA-5A United Kingdom)

| Sample only Not to be used for operational purposes |

ASSOCIATED CONDITIONS:
  POWER – MAXIMUM
  FLAPS – UP
  RUNWAY – HARD SURFACE (LEVEL & DRY)
  FUEL MIXTURE – FULL THROTTLE CLIMB, MIXTURE LEANED ABOVE 5000 FT TO SMOOTH ENGINE OPERATION.

NOTES:
1. DECREASE DISTANCE 4% FOR EACH 5 KNOTS HEADWIND. FOR OPERATION WITH TAILWINDS UP TO 10 KNOTS, INCREASE DISTANCE BY 10% FOR EACH 2.5 KNOTS.
2. IF TAKEOFF POWER IS SET WITHOUT BRAKES APPLIED, THEN DISTANCES APPLY FROM POINT WHERE FULL POWER IS ATTAINED.
3. FOR TAKEOFF FROM A DRY, GRASS RUNWAY, INCREASE GROUND RUN AND TOTAL DISTANCE TO CLEAR A 50 FT OBSTACLE BY 12.5% OF THE HARD SURFACE RUNWAY TOTAL TO CLEAR 50 FT OBSTACLE.

WEIGHT KGS	TAKEOFF SPEED		PRESS. ALT FT	0°C (32°F) METRES		10°C (40°F) METRES		20°C (68°F) METRES		30°C (86°F) METRES		40°C (104°F) METRES	
	KIAS (MPH)			GND RUN	50 FT	GND RUN	50 FT	GND RUN	50 FT	GND RUN	50 FT	GND RUN	50 FT
	LIFT OFF	CLEAR 50 FT											
998	56 (64)	63 (73)	SL	230	419	255	464	282	512	311	564	341	618
			2000	273	495	304	549	336	606	370	667	407	732
			4000	326	587	362	651	401	719	442	791	485	868
			6000	391	698	434	774	479	854	529	940	581	1031
			8000	469	832	520	922	575	1018	634	1120	697	1229
907	53 (61)	60 (69)	SL	183	336	203	372	224	411	247	452	272	496
			2000	218	397	241	440	267	486	294	535	323	587
			4000	260	471	288	522	319	576	351	635	386	696
			6000	311	560	345	621	382	685	420	754	462	828
			8000	373	668	414	740	458	817	504	899	554	983
816	50 (58)	57 (66)	SL	142	263	158	292	174	322	192	355	211	389
			2000	169	312	187	345	207	381	229	419	251	460
			4000	202	369	221	409	247	452	273	497	300	546
			6000	241	439	268	486	296	537	326	591	359	649
			8000	290	523	321	580	355	640	392	704	430	773

■ *Figure 31-2* **Gulfstream AA-5A Cheetah take-off performance tables.** **There is no mandatory performance writedown to be applied to these particular figures by the CAA, because it is not mentioned in the Flight Manual or Pilot's Operating Handbook for this aeroplane.**

EXAMPLE 1 Figure 31-2 shows that, for an aeroplane weighing 907 kg at a sea level aerodrome with a temperature of +10°C (in nil-wind conditions), the measured take-off distance to 50 ft above the level of the runway for a zero-flap take-off is 372 metres.

Lift-off should occur at 53 kt, and a take-off safety speed of 60 kt should be achieved by the 50 ft point. The ground run will be 203 metres, but it is the **take-off distance to 50 ft** that is more important to the pilot.

The aeroplane should be lifted-off at 53 kt which should take a ground run of 203 metres, and then be flown so that it reaches the take-off safety of 60 kt by the 50 ft screen height which should occur approximately 372 metres from the starting point on the runway under the stated conditions.

The speeds are those which should be flown, but it is strongly recommended by the CAA that the take-off distance be factored by 1.33 to increase the level of safety, as well as the variables which must be allowed for (explained shortly). This means there should be more take-off distance available than the minimum required by the chart.

Take-Off Flap Setting

Small flap settings decrease the ground run.

Some aeroplanes offer a choice of flap setting for take-off. The use of small flap settings decreases the ground run. Flap has the effect of lowering the stalling speed, making the appropriate lift-off speed and take-off safety speed less. Provided that the flap setting used for take-off is small (so that the drag is not greatly increased), the aeroplane will reach lift-off speed after a shorter ground run. Hence a shorter runway may be used. If the ground surface is rough, using flap for take-off will allow you to leave the ground sooner.

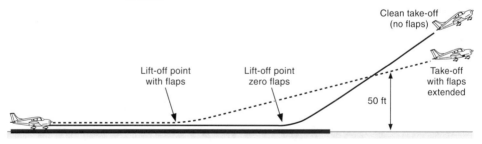

■ *Figure 31-3* **Flaps reduce take-off ground run, but often also reduce rate and angle of climb**

While the ground-run (take-off run) may be less with flap, the take-off distance (to 50 feet) may not be reduced significantly, because, as well as increasing lift, flap usually increases drag, thus reducing the lift/drag ratio, and thereby reducing both the rate and angle of climb.

This is the reason for only using small flap settings for take-off. A larger flap setting, even though it might reduce the stalling speed, would increase the aerodynamic drag during the ground run, causing a slower acceleration, and then, once airborne, would significantly degrade the climb performance due to the poor lift/drag ratio.

We cannot generalise too much in our statements here, as the precise effect of the use of flap on the take-off of a particular aeroplane depends on many things, including the flap setting, the engine–propeller combination, the airspeed flown, etc. You must become familiar with your own type of aeroplane and this is the job of your flying instructor.

Remember, large flap settings are good for landing, but bad news for take-off.

Factors Affecting Take-Off Performance

Many CAA-approved performance tables and charts allow you to account for weight, flap setting, wind effect, etc. An estimate of the effect that these variables have on take-off distance follows.

Weight

A higher weight has a number of effects that increase the take-off distance:

> *A heavier aeroplane requires a greater take-off distance.*

IN THE AIR. With increased weight, the stalling speed is increased. The lift-off speed is related to the stalling speed and so any increase in stalling speed must mean an increase in lift-off speed and in take-off safety speed.

After lift-off, the increased weight will degrade the aeroplane's climb performance (rate of climb and angle of climb) and so the distance to reach 50 feet above the runway will be greater. This is still part of the take-off distance, hence more distance is consumed.

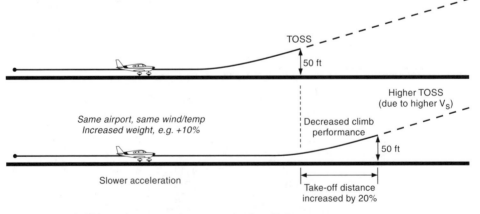

TOSS

50 ft

Higher TOSS
(due to higher V_S)

Same airport, same wind/temp
Increased weight, e.g. +10%

Decreased climb
performance

50 ft

Slower acceleration

Take-off distance
increased by 20%

■ *Figure 31-4* **A 10% increase in weight increases take-off distance by 20%**

ON THE GROUND. The greater mass means a slower acceleration by the thrust force from the engine–propeller, hence more distance is consumed. The greater weight on the wheels during the ground-run increases the frictional forces resisting acceleration, hence more distance is consumed.

The overall effect of a 10% increase in weight is to increase the take-off distance by 20%, i.e. a factor of 1.2. Most performance tables or graphs allow you to extract the performance figures applicable to the aeroplane's actual gross weight.

Density Altitude

An increased density altitude (lower air density *rho*) means a longer take-off distance. There are a number of things that will cause a decrease in air density:

A high aerodrome elevation decreases aeroplane performance.

☐ **Lower air pressure** will decrease the density and this can occur as a result of a different ground level pressure or as a result of a higher aerodrome elevation. This effect is covered by *pressure altitude,* which relates the actual pressure experienced by the aeroplane to a level in the International Standard Atmosphere (ISA) that has an identical pressure. High-elevation aerodromes lead to longer take-off distances.

High temperatures decrease aeroplane performance.

☐ **Higher air temperatures** will decrease the density.

The effect of decreased density (high pressure altitude and/or high temperature) on aeroplane performance is allowed for in one of two ways:

1. By adjusting the pressure altitude to allow for a temperature deviation from the standard ISA temperature at that particular pressure altitude (120 ft per 1°C deviation from ISA), thereby giving *density altitude* (the height in the ISA with an identical density); or

2. By using a graph that allows for the effects of both pressure and temperature separately.

If the air density (*rho*) decreases, the engine–propeller will not produce as much power and so the take-off distance will increase.

As well as the deterioration in power/thrust from the engine–propeller, the aerodynamic performance of the aeroplane will also decrease as air density becomes less. To produce the required lift force ($L = C_{Lift} \times \frac{1}{2}$ *rho V-squared* $\times S$), a decrease in air density (*rho*) means an increase in velocity (true airspeed *V*), hence a longer take-off distance. The indicated airspeed shown in the cockpit will not alter, as it is a function of the dynamic pressure (½ *rho V-squared*).

This is a little tricky to understand, but it is important and worth stating again. The lift-off speed you see in the cockpit is the IAS and it will remain the same irrespective of air density. (What does change with a low air density (*rho*) is the true airspeed (*V*), which will be greater for a lower air density, hence a longer take-off distance.)

Not only does a lower air density (*rho*) affect the aerodynamic performance of the airframe (controlled by ½ *rho V-squared*), it also decreases the mass of the fuel/air mixture in the engine cylinders, causing a decrease in engine power. 'Hot and high' penalises you both in terms of aerodynamics and engine power.

Many take-off performance tables or graphs allow for variations in the pressure altitude and the ambient temperature of the aerodrome (density altitude). The pressure altitude is easily determined in the cockpit by winding the altimeter subscale to 1013 mb and noting the altimeter reading.

In approximate terms:

- ☐ **a 1,000 ft increase** in pressure altitude will increase take-off distance by 10%, i.e. a factor of 1.1; and
- ☐ **a 10°C increase** in ambient temperature will increase take-off distance by 10%, also a factor of 1.1.

Humidity

Air is a mixture of gases, mainly oxygen and nitrogen whose molecules are reasonably heavy. When the humidity is high, some of these heavier molecules are replaced by very light water molecules, which has the effect of lowering the air density.

> High humidity decreases aeroplane and engine performance.

Humidity decreases aeroplane and engine performance. This effect is usually taken into account during certification; however, there may be a correction factor applicable to your aircraft. Check the Flight Manual or Pilot's Operating Handbook.

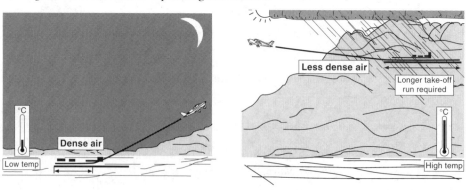

■ *Figure 31-5* **Hot, high and humid means decreased performance**

Headwinds and Tailwinds

A headwind reduces the take-off distance.

For flight, the aeroplane requires a certain speed relative to the air it is flying through. An aeroplane stopped at the end of the runway and facing into a 20 kt headwind is already 20 kt closer to the lift-off speed compared to the nil–wind situation. A 10 kt tailwind would worsen the situation considerably, as the aircraft would have to accelerate to a groundspeed (GS) of 10 kt before it had an airspeed of zero.

HEADWIND. In a headwind take-off, the aeroplane reaches lift-off airspeed at a lower groundspeed, and so less ground run is required. Once in the air, the angle or gradient relative to the ground is increased by a headwind, giving better obstacle clearance.

TAILWIND. With a tailwind, the effect is to lengthen the ground run and to flatten the climb-out over obstacles. As a guideline factor, the take-off distance will be increased by 20% for a tailwind component of 10% of the lift-off speed, i.e. a factor of 1.2. Tailwinds in excess of 5 kt should not normally be considered suitable for take-off. Obviously a take-off into the wind shows better airmanship.

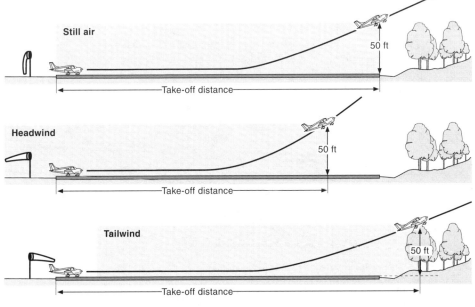

■ *Figure 31-6* **A headwind reduces take-off distance**

NOTE Where the published data allow adjustment for wind, it is recommended that not more than 50% of the headwind component and not less than 150% of the tailwind component of the reported wind be assumed. This allows for some variations in the wind effect during take-off – the headwind not being as strong or the tailwind being stronger than expected. In some manuals this factoring is already included (indicated, for instance, by different spacing on graphs or different percentage corrections on tables for the headwinds and tailwinds), and it is necessary to check the performance section of the manual. A sound briefing by a flying instructor on the performance data in the manual to be used is highly recommended.

WINDSHEAR. A further wind effect that was not often considered in the past is that of **windshear,** a term which means a wind that differs in strength or direction from place to place. Windshear is a complex subject and is still not fully understood; however, some of the basics should be considered by even the student pilot.

The following points apply to the effect of windshear on take-off and landing performance.

The wind usually increases in strength as you move further from the ground. This is a result of the friction forces between the ground and the wind causing the wind to slow down near the surface.

Taking off into a headwind would normally mean that you would climb into an increasing headwind, which tends to increase your airspeed (the speed of the aeroplane relative to the air) and increase the gradient of climb-out over obstacles on the ground. An increasing headwind leads to increased performance.

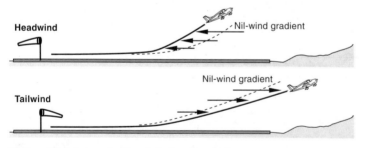

■ *Figure 31-7* ***Increasing headwind assists performance***

Taking off downwind would normally mean that you would climb into an increasing tailwind and the effect is a little like trying to catch a bus that is accelerating away from you. It tends to decrease your airspeed, hence the nose must be lowered to retain the desired IAS, and the climb-out angle over obstacles on the ground is degraded.

The effect of a tailwind in degrading climb-out angle or gradient relative to the ground is not considered in take-off charts. Once again, a take-off into the wind shows good airmanship.

For more on windshear, see Chapter 36.

Crosswinds

An aeroplane must not take off in a crosswind that exceeds the maximum crosswind limitation for that aeroplane.

Directional control is one problem – the aerodynamic lift force from the rudder has to overcome the effect of the keel surfaces trying to weathercock the aeroplane into wind. Lateral control is another problem – the crosswind tries to lift the into-wind wing, which then has to be held down with aileron. The deflected ailerons and rudder will cause a slight increase in drag with a consequent decrease in acceleration.

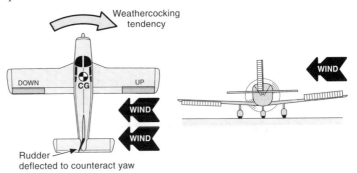

■ *Figure 31-8* **Crosswind take-off**

To estimate the strength of a crosswind component it will pay us to consider a 10 kt wind blowing from various directions:

☐ **If the wind is 30°** off the runway heading, then the crosswind component is ½ the wind strength.

☐ **If the wind is 45°** off the runway heading, then the crosswind component is ⅔ the wind strength.

☐ **If the wind is 60°** off the runway heading, then the crosswind component is 9⁄10 the wind strength.

☐ **If the wind is 90°** off the runway heading, it is all crosswind.

When calculating the crosswind angle, be sure to work in common units – usually °M. Wind directions given by the tower or ATIS are in °M, as is runway direction.

In crosswind conditions, the headwind or tailwind component has to be calculated to enter the performance charts or tables.

NOTE Navigation computers have the facility for calculating crosswinds (and head/tailwind components). See Vol. 3 of the *The Air Pilot's Manual.*

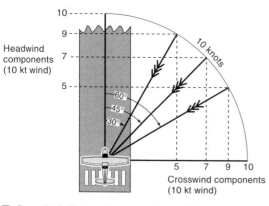

Figure 31-9 Estimating crosswind and headwind components

Runway Surface

Take-off performance information in the UK is based on a hard surface that is level and dry. Other surfaces, such as grass, will retard the acceleration on the ground and therefore lengthen the take-off distance. The rolling resistance or friction can seriously degrade the take-off acceleration:

Poor runway surfaces increases the take-off ground run.

- Short, dry grass increases the take-off distance by 20%.
- Long, dry grass or short, wet grass increase it by 25%.
- Long, wet grass increase it by 30%.

Soft ground or snow may increase the take-off distance by 25% or more i.e. a factor of at least 1.25; (such a surface may in fact make acceleration to the lift-off speed impossible, no matter how much length is available).

It is recommended that a take-off should not be attempted if the grass is more than 10 inches long (wet or dry).

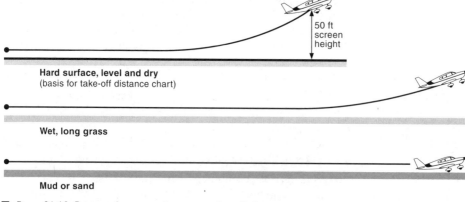

Figure 31-10 Poor surfaces may increase take-off distance

Runway Slope

Take-off distance is calculated for a level runway, so the take-off chart must allow for the effect of runway slope. A downslope of 2 in 100 (2% down) will allow the aeroplane to accelerate faster and so will decrease the take-off distance. An upslope of 2 in 100 (2% up) will make it more difficult for the aeroplane to accelerate and so the take-off distance will be greater.

Some charts allow for slope and others do not. In general terms, a 2% upslope will increase the take-off distance by 10%.

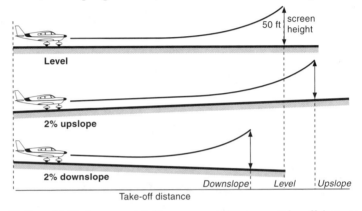

■ *Figure 31-11* **An upward sloping runway will increase take-off distance**

NOTE The corrections are for take-off distance from the starting point to the screen height of 50 ft. For the surface and slope factors the correction to the ground run will be greater.

Runway slope is calculated using the elevations at either end of the take-off run available (TORA); therefore, a runway with downslope may have a hump (involving upslope) somewhere along its length (and vice versa).

■ *Figure 31-12* **Each of these runways has a downslope of 1%**

22	Physical Characteristics											
RUNWAY					DECLARED DISTANCES				SURFACE ELEVATION (ft)			
°M	°T	DIMENSIONS (m)	S	PCN	THR ELEV (ft)	TORA (m)	ED (m)	TODA (m)	LDA (m)	START OF TORA	END OF TORA	END OF ED	END OF TODA
08/ 26	079 259	656 x 30†	A		331 303	656 656	656 830	656 830	656 656	331 303	303 332	303 332	303 331

Runway 26 stopway is not available for aircraft required to use a licensed aerodrome. The 18 m wide centre-line section of the surface to the west of threshold 08 is suitable for taxiing. †Normal operations are confined to the runway between the marked thresholds.

■ *Figure 31-13* **AIP AD contains runway threshold elevations, necessary for calculating slope**

Recommended Safety Factor for Take-Off

After taking account of the above variables and their *cumulative* effect, the CAA strongly recommends that a safety factor of 1.33 be used for take-off for all Group E aeroplanes – the majority of light general aviation aircraft. (It is necessary to check the manual or handbook of Performance Groups C and D aeroplanes to see if this factor is already included.)

EXAMPLE 1 Suppose the base figure for measured take-off distance is 400 metres for a take-off at a sea-level aerodrome at + 10°C at the particular aeroplane weight, and there is no CAA-imposed mandatory performance writedown for this type.

Situation A:
☐ Sea-level aerodrome
☐ Hard, dry runway with no slope
☐ Nil wind
☐ Temperature: 10°C
☐ Mandatory CAA writedown: nil
☐ Correction factors: nil
☐ Safety factor for take-off: × 1.33

ANSWER
Recommended take-off distance = 400 × 1.33 = **532 metres.**

Situation B:
☐ Aerodrome elevation 1,000 ft
☐ Wet, long-grass strip with 2% upslope
☐ Temperature 20°C
☐ Tailwind component 5 kt (lift-off speed 50 kt)
☐ Mandatory CAA writedown: nil
☐ Correction factors:
   elevation   × 1.1
   10°C temperature increase   × 1.1
   long, wet grass   × 1.3
   2% upslope   × 1.1
   tailwind 10% of lift-off speed × 1.2
☐ Safety factor for take-off: × 1.33

ANSWER
Recommended take-off distance =
400 × 1.1 × 1.1 × 1.3 × 1.1 × 1.2 × 1.33 = **1,105 metres.**

Note the significant increase in distance in situation B – more than double that of situation A. Good airmanship suggests that a take-off in the opposite direction would be preferable, taking advantage of a downslope and a headwind.

Using Take-Off Performance Charts

There are various presentations of take-off performance charts and tables. They are presented logically and allow you to enter with known data such as temperature and pressure altitude and proceed through the chart or table, to find the take-off distance, or the highest weight allowed for the conditions.

▢ Figure 31-14 shows the tabular style performance chart.

▢ Figure 31-15 shows an example of the graphical presentation.

UNITED KINGDOM SUPPLEMENT

GULFSTREAM AMERICAN MODEL AA-5A CHEETAH

TAKEOFF DISTANCE (AA-5A United Kingdom)

Sample only
Not to be used
for operational
purposes

ASSOCIATED CONDITIONS:
POWER – MAXIMUM
FLAPS – UP
RUNWAY – HARD SURFACE (LEVEL & DRY)
FUEL MIXTURE – FULL THROTTLE CLIMB, MIXTURE LEANED ABOVE 5000 FT TO SMOOTH ENGINE OPERATION.

NOTES:
1. DECREASE DISTANCE 4% FOR EACH 5 KNOTS HEADWIND. FOR OPERATION WITH TAILWINDS UP TO 10 KNOTS, INCREASE DISTANCE BY 10% FOR EACH 2.5 KNOTS.
2. IF TAKEOFF POWER IS SET WITHOUT BRAKES APPLIED, THEN DISTANCES APPLY FROM POINT WHERE FULL POWER IS ATTAINED.
3. FOR TAKEOFF FROM A DRY, GRASS RUNWAY, INCREASE GROUND RUN AND TOTAL DISTANCE TO CLEAR A 50 FT OBSTACLE BY 12.5% OF THE HARD SURFACE RUNWAY TOTAL TO CLEAR 50 FT OBSTACLE.

WEIGHT KGS	KIAS LIFT OFF	(MPH) CLEAR 50 FT	PRESS. ALT FT	0°C (32°F) GND RUN	0°C 50 FT	10°C (40°F) GND RUN	10°C 50 FT	20°C (68°F) GND RUN	20°C 50 FT	30°C (86°F) GND RUN	30°C 50 FT	40°C (104°F) GND RUN	40°C 50 FT
998	56 (64)	63 (73)	SL	230	419	255	464	282	512	311	564	341	618
			2000	273	495	304	549	336	606	370	667	407	732
			4000	326	587	362	651	401	719	442	791	485	868
			6000	391	698	434	774	479	854	529	940	581	1031
			8000	469	832	520	922	575	1018	634	1120	697	1229
907	53 (61)	60 (69)	SL	183	336	203	372	224	411	247	452	272	496
			2000	218	397	241	440	267	486	294	535	323	587
			4000	260	471	288	522	319	576	351	635	386	696
			6000	311	560	345	621	382	685	420	754	462	828
			8000	373	668	414	740	458	817	504	899	554	983
816	50 (58)	57 (66)	SL	142	263	158	292	174	322	192	355	211	389
			2000	169	312	187	345	207	381	229	419	251	460
			4000	202	369	221	409	247	452	273	497	300	546
			6000	241	439	268	486	296	537	326	591	359	649
			8000	290	523	321	580	355	640	392	704	430	773

■ *Figure 31-14* **Tabular take-off performance chart**

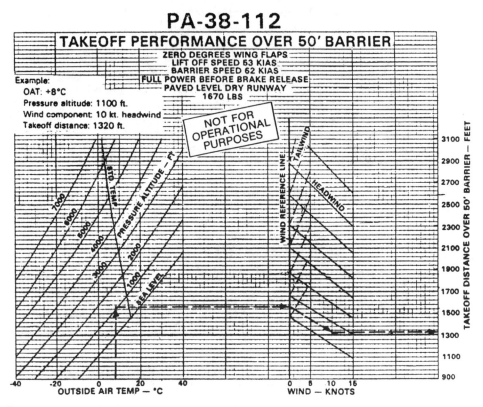

■ *Figure 31-15* **Graphical take-off performance chart**

Notice that this chart is for a fixed weight (1,670 lb) and that zero degrees of wing flaps is used. Ensure that you use the chart or table for the flap setting that you will be using for the particular take-off.

Figure 31–16 shows a chart which is already factored for take-off surface and runway slope (unlike Figure 31–15).

EXAMPLE 2 Using a flap setting of 0° for take-off and the procedures recommended on the chart (take-off power setting 2,700 rpm, which should be applied prior to rolling to achieve the chart distance), take-off safety speed 78 kt, find the highest take-off weight.

- ☐ Take-off distance available 800 metres;
- ☐ Pressure altitude 4,000 ft;
- ☐ Temperature + 14°C;
- ☐ 2% downslope;
- ☐ Short, dry grass;
- ☐ 10 kt headwind.

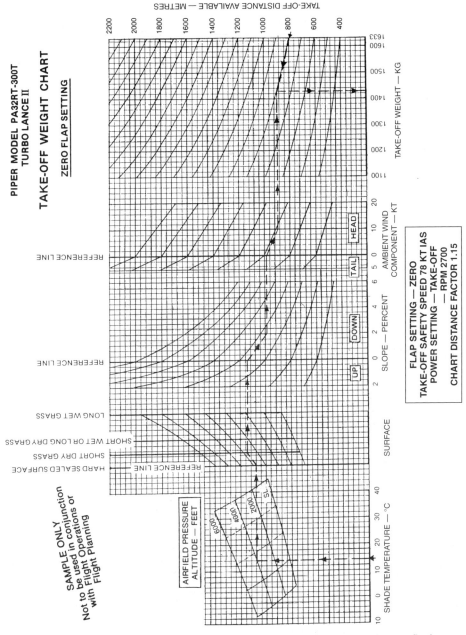

■ *Figure 31-16* **A typical take-off weight chart (zero degrees flap)**

Method:

As shown on the chart in Figure 31-16, we enter with a temperature of + 14°C and proceed vertically up to the airfield pressure altitude of 4,000 ft.

Proceed horizontally to the 'surface' reference line, following the guidelines up from it to the 'short dry grass' line (as we will be taking off this time on short, dry grass). Then proceed horizontally to the 'slope' reference line, and since our surface has a 2% downslope, we follow the guidelines down to the '2% down' line.

Continue across to the wind reference line and follow the guidelines down to the '10 kt headwind' line. (If you had a 5 kt tailwind, you would go horizontally to the reference line and then back up the guidelines until intercepting the 5 kt tailwind line. You will see later that this tailwind has the effect of lengthening the take-off distance required, whereas the headwind shortens it.)

Proceed horizontally until you intercept the 800 metre TODA line (take-off distance available), and then drop vertically to determine the highest take-off weight allowable for this take-off.

ANSWER 1,430 kg.

Ensure that Sufficient Take-off Distance is Available

You should always ensure that, having applied all the relevant factors, including the safety factor, to obtain the recommended take-off distance, there is sufficient take-off distance available (TODA). See *Runway Characteristics* on page 327.

The Climb-Away after Take-Off

So that aeroplane climb performance does not fall below the prescribed minimum, some manuals give take-off and landing weights that should not be exceeded at specific combinations of altitude and temperature, known as **WAT limits** (pronounced *wott*). Unless included in the limitations section of the manual, these weight restrictions are only mandatory for Public Transport flights. They are, however, recommended for Private flights and are calculated using the pressure altitude and temperature (i.e. density altitude) at the relevant aerodrome.

Where WAT limits are not given, it is recommended that a single-engine, fixed-undercarriage aeroplane should be capable of a 500 ft/min rate of climb in the en route configuration at the en route climb speed and using maximum continuous power.

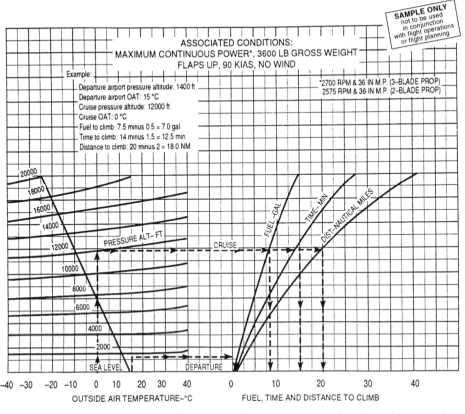

■ *Figure 31-17* **Example of a maximum rate of climb performance chart**

Runway Characteristics

TAKE-OFF DISTANCE AVAILABLE (TODA). A runway is a defined rectangular area on a land aerodrome prepared for the landing and taking off of aircraft. The surface of a runway may be sealed (e.g. bitumen, concrete) or natural (e.g. grass, clay).

The **take-off run available (TORA)** is the length of runway which is available and suitable for the ground run of an aeroplane taking off. In most cases this corresponds to the physical length of the runway.

■ *Figure 31-18* **Take-off run available (TORA)**

The take-off is not completed at lift-off when the wheels leave the runway. Take-off considerations apply until you are at least at the take-off safety speed at 50 feet above the take-off surface. There is no need for all of this air distance to be above an actual runway surface – some of the air distance from lift-off to 50 ft can be above an obstacle-free zone, called a *clearway.*

A **clearway** is a defined rectangular area on the ground or water at the end of a runway in the direction of take-off and under the control of the competent authority, selected or prepared as a suitable area over which an aircraft may make a portion of its initial climb to a specified height (50 ft in our case).

This means that the take-off distance available may exceed the take-off run available by the distance provided by the clearway. Thus, the **take-off distance available (TODA)** is the length of the runway available plus the length of clearway available (if clearway is provided). TODA is not to exceed 1.5 times TORA.

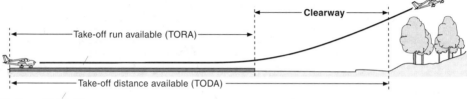

■ *Figure 31-19* **Clearway**

REJECTED TAKE-OFFS. Occasionally a take-off is rejected, say due to an engine failure. A rejected take-off (RTO) is also known as an *accelerate-stop,* because the aeroplane first accelerates as in every take-off and then, for some reason, the take-off manoeuvre is aborted and the aeroplane is stopped. The distance required for such a manoeuvre is called the accelerate-stop distance or the emergency distance (ED).

The **emergency distance (ED)** on the runway is the take-off run available (usually the physical length of the runway) plus the length of any stopway available (if stopway is provided).

A **stopway** is a defined rectangular area on the ground at the end of a runway in the direction of take-off, designated and prepared by the competent authority as a suitable area in which an aircraft can be stopped in the case of an interrupted take-off.

Note that a stopway must be on the ground, so that the aeroplane can brake and stop on it, whereas a clearway is provided as an obstacle-free zone over which the aeroplane can fly, hence it can be ground or water.

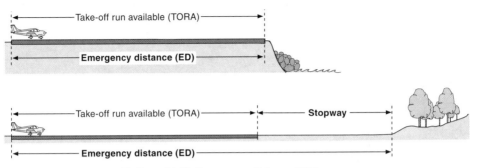

■ *Figure 31-20* **Emergency distance (ED)**

LANDING DISTANCE AVAILABLE (LDA). The landing distance available (LDA) is the length of runway available for landing, taking into account any obstacles in the approach path.

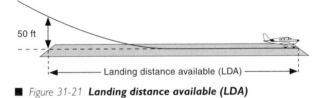

■ *Figure 31-21* **Landing distance available (LDA)**

The above lengths available are vital distances when calculating the performance limitations on an aeroplane for take-off or landing on a particular runway. TORA, ED, TODA and LDA are known as the declared distances for that runway.

The AD Section of the AIP

The **declared distances** and other important information regarding particular runways at certain aerodromes are obtainable from the Aerodromes (AD) section of the UK Aeronautical Information Publication (AIP). Any changes will be notified by NOTAM.

| Take-off run available | | Emergency distance | Take-off distance available | | Landing distance available |

22					Physical Characteristics								
		RUNWAY					DECLARED DISTANCES				SURFACE ELEVATION (ft)		
°M	°T	DIMENSIONS (m)	S	PCN	THR ELEV (ft)	TORA (m)	ED (m)	TODA (m)	LDA (m)	START OF TORA	END OF TORA	END OF ED	END OF TODA
08/ 26	072 252	1342 x 46	A		321 324	1237 1237	1237 1237	1237 1237	1102 1065	321 325	323 321	323 321	323 321
08/ 26	072 252	500 x 18	G		321 323	500 500	500 500	500 500	500 500	321 323	323 321	323 321	323 321

■ *Figure 31-22* **Example of distances available as published in AIP AD**

Another source of runway information is *Pooley's Flight Guide* which lists take-off run available (TORA) and landing distance available (LDA) for UK aerodromes. If using this guide, be sure your information is up to date. If in doubt, refer to AIP AD.

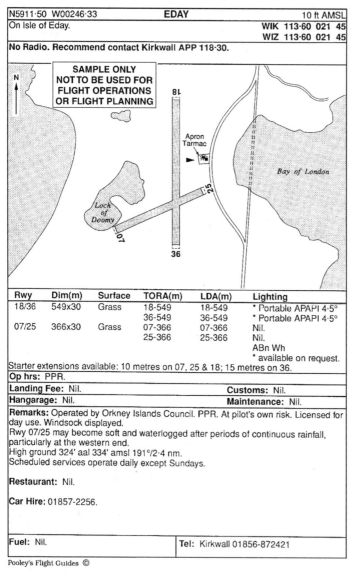

N5911·50 W00246·33	**EDAY**		10 ft AMSL

On Isle of Eday.	WIK 113·60 021 45
	WIZ 113·60 021 45

No Radio. Recommend contact Kirkwall APP 118·30.

Rwy	Dim(m)	Surface	TORA(m)	LDA(m)	Lighting
18/36	549x30	Grass	18-549	18-549	* Portable APAPI 4·5°
			36-549	36-549	* Portable APAPI 4·5°
07/25	366x30	Grass	07-366	07-366	Nil.
			25-366	25-366	Nil.
					ABn Wh
					* available on request.

Starter extensions available: 10 metres on 07, 25 & 18; 15 metres on 36.

Op hrs: PPR.	
Landing Fee: Nil.	**Customs:** Nil.
Hangarage: Nil.	**Maintenance:** Nil.

Remarks: Operated by Orkney Islands Council. PPR. At pilot's own risk. Licensed for day use. Windsock displayed.
Rwy 07/25 may become soft and waterlogged after periods of continuous rainfall, particularly at the western end.
High ground 324' aal 334' amsl 191°/2·4 nm.
Scheduled services operate daily except Sundays.

Restaurant: Nil.

Car Hire: 01857-2256.

Fuel: Nil.	**Tel:** Kirkwall 01856-872421

Pooley's Flight Guides ©

■ *Figure 31-23* **Extract of runway information as shown in Pooley's Flight Guide (reduced)**

Landing Performance

The measured landing distance is the distance established from a point where the aircraft is 50 ft over the runway (assumed to be hard, level, dry surface) at a speed not less than 1.3 V_{Stall} to the point where the aeroplane reaches a full stop, following a steady, full-flap, no-power approach and maximum braking.

The 1.3 V_{Stall} provides a 30% safety margin over stalling speed in the landing configuration. If the stalling speed is 50 kt, then the minimum approach speed should be 30% up on this at 65 kt.

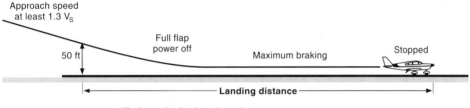

■ *Figure 31-24* **Landing distance**

Landing Performance Data

The aeroplane's Flight Manual or Pilot's Operating Handbook will contain performance data for landing in the form of a graph or table.

For example, using the chart in Figure 31–26, the landing distance from 50 ft for a *Cheetah* at landing weight 907 kg on a hard, dry, level surface at a sea-level aerodrome and +10°C in nil-wind conditions is 392 metres. The approach speed is 65 kt and the ground run will be 118 metres.

The actual landing performance from 50 ft to a stop will be affected by a number of variables which you must take into account.

Factors Affecting Landing Performance

Weight

A heavier aeroplane will need a greater landing distance.

Increased weight means a greater landing distance. A higher weight has a number of effects:

☐ **The stalling speed is increased,** so the minimum approach speed of 1.3 V_{Stall} must be greater. A higher speed requires more distance to land and stop.

☐ **The higher weight** means that the kinetic energy ($\frac{1}{2}mV^2$) is higher and the brakes have to absorb this greater energy, increasing the landing run. (There will be a slight increase in the retarding friction force due to the extra weight on the wheels).

As a guideline, the landing distance will be increased by 10% for each 10% increase in aeroplane weight, a factor of 1.1.

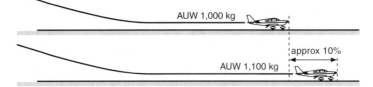

■ *Figure 31-25* **A 10% increase in weight requires a 10% increase in** **landing distance (approximately)**

GULFSTREAM AMERICAN
MODEL AA-5A CHEETAH

UNITED KINGDOM
SUPPLEMENT

LANDING DISTANCE (AA-5A United Kingdom)

ASSOCIATED CONDITIONS:
POWER — OFF
FLAPS — DOWN
RUNWAY — HARD SURFACE (LEVEL & DRY)
BRAKING — MAXIMUM

SAMPLE ONLY
Not to be used in conjunction
with Flight Operations or
Flight Planning

NOTES:
1. DECREASE DISTANCE 4% FOR EACH 5 KNOTS HEADWIND.
2. FOR OPERATIONS WITH TAILWINDS UP TO 10 KNOTS, INCREASE DISTANCE BY 9% FOR EACH 2.5 KNOTS.
3. WHEN LANDING ON A DRY GRASS RUNWAY, INCREASE GROUND RUN AND TOTAL DISTANCE OVER 50 FT. OBSTACLE BY 20% OF THE HARD SURFACE RUNWAY TOTAL DISTANCE OVER A 50 FT OBSTACLE.

WEIGHT KGS	SPEED AT 50 FT KIAS	SPEED AT 50 FT MPH	PRESS ALT FT.	0°C (32°F) METRES GND RUN	0°C (32°F) METRES CLEAR 50 FT	10°C (40°F) METRES GND RUN	10°C (40°F) METRES CLEAR 50 FT	20°C (68°F) METRES GND RUN	20°C (68°F) METRES CLEAR 50 FT	30°C (86°F) METRES GND RUN	30°C (86°F) METRES CLEAR 50 FT	40°C (104°F) METRES GND RUN	40°C (104°F) METRES CLEAR 50 FT
998	68	78	SL	123	410	127	422	130	434	133	445	137	458
			2000	130	434	134	447	138	460	141	473	145	487
			4000	138	461	142	476	146	490	150	504	155	519
			6000	147	492	151	507	156	523	161	539	165	555
			8000	157	526	162	543	167	560	172	578	177	595
907	65	75	SL	115	362	118	392	121	402	124	413	127	424
			2000	121	403	125	414	128	426	131	438	135	449
			4000	128	427	132	440	135	452	139	465	143	478
			6000	136	454	140	468	144	482	148	496	152	511
			8000	145	484	149	500	154	515	158	531	163	547
816	61	71	SL	107	353	110	362	112	371	115	380	118	390
			2000	112	371	115	381	118	392	121	402	121	412
			4000	118	393	122	404	125	415	128	426	131	438
			6000	125	416	129	429	132	441	136	454	140	467
			8000	133	443	137	457	141	471	145	485	149	499

■ *Figure 31-26* **A typical landing distance table (Gulfstream Cheetah)**

Density Altitude

Increased density altitude results in a longer landing distance.

An increased density altitude means a longer landing distance required. Low pressure, high elevation and high temperatures can decrease the air density (*rho*), giving what we call a higher density altitude (the height in the International Standard Atmosphere that has the same density as the point under consideration).

A decreased *rho* means an increased V (TAS) to provide the same lift force. Even though you see the same indicated airspeed in the cockpit, the true airspeed is higher in air of lower density.

Therefore, at high density altitudes the true airspeed will be greater than for lower density altitudes, the touchdown groundspeed will be higher, and therefore the amount of kinetic energy to be dissipated in the stop is greater – hence a longer landing distance.

In approximate terms, an increase in pressure altitude of 1,000 ft or an increase of 10°C will increase the landing distance by 5%, a factor of 1.05.

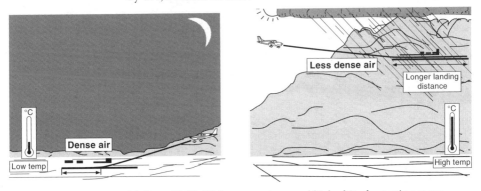

■ *Figure 31-27* **High temperature and high altitude requires more landing distance**

Headwinds and Tailwinds

A headwind reduces the ground run and landing distance.

A headwind reduces the landing distance because the groundspeed (GS) is reduced by the headwind for the same TAS (V).

A tailwind means that the groundspeed will exceed the TAS, and so the touchdown speed relative to the ground is higher and a longer landing distance will be required.

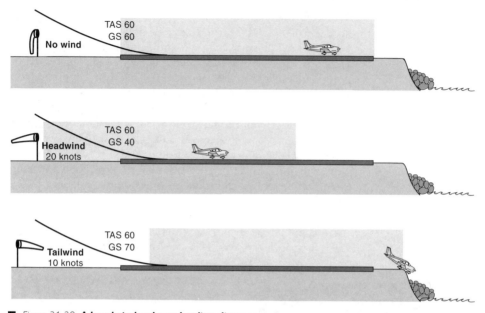

■ *Figure 31-28* **A headwind reduces landing distance**

As for take-off, a further wind effect to consider is windshear (discussed in detail in Chapter 36). If the headwind component increases, then the aircraft experiences a transient increase in performance.

There are advantages in approaching into wind (lower groundspeed, shorter landing distance required), however, as you near the ground, if the headwind decreases, then the aircraft will experience a loss of performance and tend to sink and possibly undershoot the aiming point.

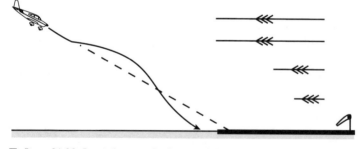

■ *Figure 31-29* **Be vigilant on final approach**

It is disadvantageous to approach in a tailwind due to the high touchdown groundspeeds and longer landing distances required.

Approaching the ground, the reducing tailwind has the same effect as an increasing headwind – the aircraft may experience an increase in performance and tend to float further down the runway.

As a guideline, a tailwind component of 10% of the landing speed will increase the landing distance by 20%, a factor of 1.2.

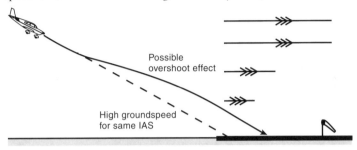

Possible overshoot effect

High groundspeed for same IAS

■ *Figure 31-30* **Downwind landings are not recommended**

NOTE Where the published data allow adjustment for wind, it is recommended that not more than 50% of the headwind component and not less than 150% of the tailwind component of the reported wind be assumed. This allows for some variations in the wind effect during the approach and landing – the headwind not being as strong or the tailwind being stronger than expected. In some manuals this factoring is already included (indicated, for instance, by different spacing on graphs or different percentage corrections on tables for the headwinds and tailwinds), and it is necessary to check the performance section of the manual. A sound briefing by a flying instructor on the performance data in the manual to be used is highly recommended.

Runway Surface

A wet runway will result in a longer landing distance.

A low-friction runway surface (wet, slick, icy) will not allow effective braking to occur and so the landing distance required will be longer.

Aquaplaning on a wet surface may occur and this can give extraordinary increases in the stopping distances. **Aquaplaning** is the phenomenon of a tyre skating along on a thin film of water and not rotating, even though it is free to do so. Wheel braking therefore has no effect when aquaplaning and directional control can easily be lost. Friction forces are practically zero.

As aquaplaning is more likely to occur at higher groundspeeds, landing into-wind on a wet runway (which keeps the groundspeed to a minimum) is recommended.

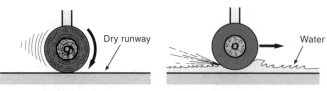

Dry runway
braking action slows wheel

Aquaplaning on wet runway
wheel skates on water,
braking action is ineffective

■ *Figure 31-31* **Low friction surfaces increase landing distance**

Typical increases in landing distance are:

- **short, dry grass** (under 5 inches) 20%, a factor of 1.2;
- **long, dry grass** (over 5 inches) 30%, a factor of 1.3;
- **short, wet grass** (under 5 inches) 30%, a factor of 1.3;
- **long, wet grass** (over 5 inches) 40%, a factor 1.4;
- **snow** 25% or more, a factor of at least 1.25.

Runway Slope

A downslope will require a longer landing distance. It will take longer for the aeroplane to touch down from 50 ft above the runway threshold, as the runway is falling away beneath the aeroplane, and of course braking while going downhill is not as effective as on a level or upward-sloping runway. A 2% downhill slope will increase landing distance by 10%, a factor of 1.1.

> *A downsloping runway will result in a longer landing distance.*

NOTE For surface and slope factors, the guideline factors are for landing distance from 50 ft. The correction to the ground roll will be greater.

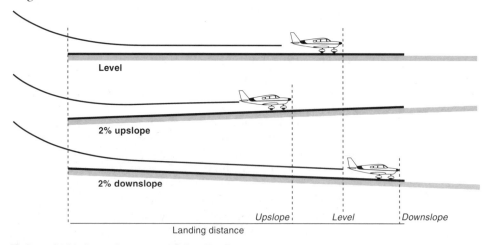

■ *Figure 31-32* **Downslope increases landing distance**

Flap Settings

Higher flap settings reduce the stalling speed and therefore the approach speed ($1.3V_s$) is less. High flap settings also give additional aerodynamic drag that helps to slow the aeroplane down, as well as allowing a steeper approach path.

Recommended Safety Factor for Landing

The CAA recommends that a landing safety factor of 1.43 be applied for Private flights (it is mandatory for Public Transport flights) in Group E aeroplanes. It is necessary to check the manual of Performance Groups C and D aeroplanes to see if it is already included.

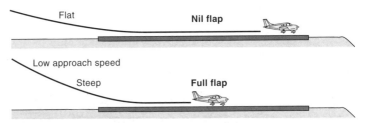

■ *Figure 31-33* **Increased flap – slower and steeper approach, shorter landing distance**

Landing Factors are Cumulative and should be Multiplied

The above factors are cumulative and, where several factors are relevant, they must be multiplied. The resulting distance can sometimes be surprisingly high.

EXAMPLE 3 In still air on a level, dry runway with an ambient temperature of 10°C, an aeroplane has a measured landing distance from a height of 50 ft of 400 metres.

Situation A:

The recommended landing distance in the above situation is:
400 × 1.43 = 572 metres.

Situation B:

The landing strip is long, wet grass with a downslope of 2% and a tailwind of 5 kt (landing speed 50 kt), +20°C, elevation 2,000 ft.

Recommended landing distance = 400 × 1.4 (surface); × 1.1 (slope); × 1.05 (temperature); × 1.1 (elevation); × 1.2 (tailwind); × 1.43 (safety factor) = 1,221 metres. Good airmanship should lead you to consider landing in the opposite direction, taking advantage of a headwind and an upslope.

Ensure that the Landing Distance Available is Sufficient

Having calculated the landing distance from 50 ft, you must ensure that the landing field chosen has sufficient **landing distance available (LDA).** This is obtained from AIP AD, as shown earlier. (*Pooley's Flight Guide* also provides values for LDA.)

Landing Data Presentation

As with take-off charts, there are various ways of presenting landing performance data. Figure 31-26 showed the tabular method of presentation; the next two examples show the graphical style.

Figure 31-34 shows a graphical landing performance chart. It is for a 40° flap landing approaching at 76 kt indicated airspeed and is based on power-off at 50 ft.

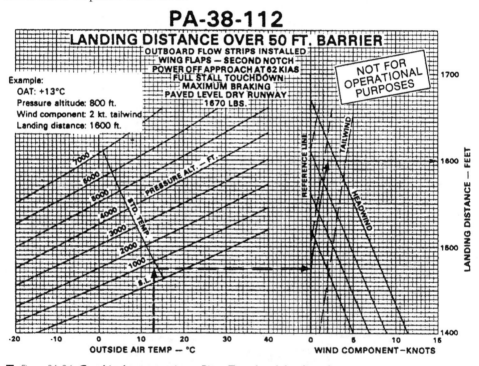

PA-38-112

LANDING DISTANCE OVER 50 FT. BARRIER

OUTBOARD FLOW STRIPS INSTALLED
WING FLAPS — SECOND NOTCH
POWER OFF APPROACH AT 62 KIAS
FULL STALL TOUCHDOWN
MAXIMUM BRAKING
PAVED LEVEL DRY RUNWAY
1670 LBS.

NOT FOR OPERATIONAL PURPOSES

Example:
OAT: +13°C
Pressure altitude: 800 ft.
Wind component: 2 kt. tailwind.
Landing distance: 1600 ft.

OUTSIDE AIR TEMP — °C

WIND COMPONENT — KNOTS

LANDING DISTANCE — FEET

■ *Figure 31-34* **Graphical presentation – Piper Tomahawk landing chart**

(Note that, although this is the method used for certification, it does not mean that you must take the power OFF at 50 ft in every landing – it is used simply as a standard method of determining landing distances.)

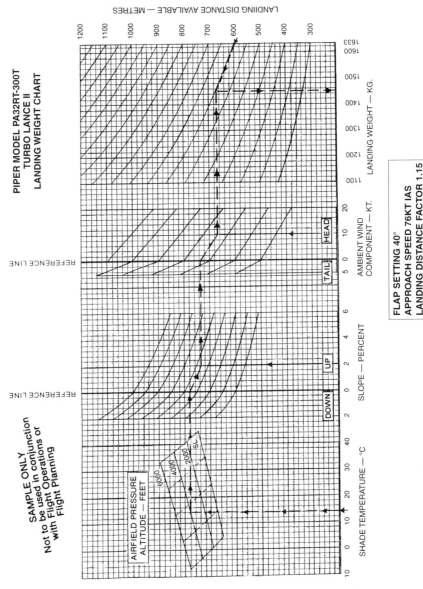

LANDING DISTANCE AVAILABLE — METRES

PIPER MODEL PA32RT-300T
TURBO LANCE II
LANDING WEIGHT CHART

REFERENCE LINE

REFERENCE LINE

SAMPLE ONLY
Not to be used in conjunction or
with Flight Operations or
Flight Planning

AIRFIELD PRESSURE
ALTITUDE — FEET

FLAP SETTING 40°
APPROACH SPEED 76KT IAS
LANDING DISTANCE FACTOR 1.15

LANDING WEIGHT — KG.

AMBIENT WIND
COMPONENT — KT.

SLOPE — PERCENT

SHADE TEMPERATURE — °C

■ *Figure 31-35* **Another type of landing performance chart**

EXAMPLE 4 Find the maximum landing weight possible on a
600 metre runway at a pressure altitude of 4,000 ft, temperature
+14°C, 2% upslope, 10 kt headwind.

Method:
Refer to the chart in Figure 31-35. Enter with + 14°C and move
vertically to intercept the pressure altitude 4,000 ft line.

Move horizontally to the slope reference line and from there follow the guidelines down to the '2% up' line (notice by a quick glance to the landing distance scale on the right-hand side that this has the effect of reducing it).

Next, proceed to the wind reference line – the 10 kt headwind being favourable.

Now move across to meet the 600 m landing distance available line, and drop vertically to the **maximum landing weight of 1,450 kg.**

Suppose your weight was 1,500 kg. Under the same meteorological conditions, the 1,500 kg line proceeding up the graph would intersect the horizontal line from the left at about 620 m landing distance, and this is what you then legally require to land.

If you were limited by the landing distance available being only 600 m, then you could look at the wind situation (by proceeding left from where the 1,500 kg line intersects the 600 m line). To be able to land legally, the headwind component would have to be at least 14 kt.

Notice that:

☐ **Higher temperatures** mean more landing distance or lower landing weight.

☐ A **higher pressure altitude** means more landing distance or lower landing weight.

☐ A **downslope** means more landing distance or lower landing weight.

☐ A **tailwind** means more landing distance or lower landing weight.

Fast Approach Speeds

Landing performance charts are based on specified approach speeds. If you approach for a landing at a speed higher than that specified, the landing distance may exceed that predicted by the chart.

An important point to note in 'too-fast' approaches is that the aeroplane is reluctant to settle onto the ground due to **ground effect.** This is the 'cushioning' of the aeroplane on the air between it and the ground when the aeroplane is close to the ground – as during the flare to land.

Ground effect is caused by the reduction in the amount of downwash behind the wings, and by the tendency of the aeroplane not to slow down (decreased drag) resulting from the reduction in the formation of wingtip vortices. (See Chapter 35 for more about ground effect.)

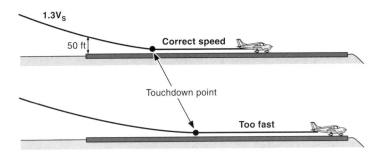

■ *Figure 31-36* **High approach speeds increase landing distance**

Performance Considerations

Incorrect performance calculations (or none at all) can result in aeroplanes failing to become airborne on take-off in the distance available, or colliding with obstacles owing to an inadequate climb-out, or over-running the landing distance available on landing. Contributing factors are often short strips, tailwind, slope, poor surfaces, poor airmanship and lack of recent experience.

The pilot has a legal obligation to check that aeroplane performance is adequate for all aspects of the proposed flight – take-off, climb-out, approach and landing. What you have read in this chapter, plus sound consideration of the performance charts of the aeroplane to be flown, should prepare you to undertake this responsibility prior to each flight. Some runways in certain weather conditions will be more than adequate for a particular operation in a light aircraft, in which case no precise calculations are necessary. In doubtful situations, the charts should definitely be referred to.

If there is no published information for the airfield to be used, then the distances should be paced out. The pace length can be established accurately or assumed to be no more than 2.5 ft.

A crude method of establishing slope is to taxi the aeroplane from one end of the strip to the other and note the difference in readings.

An altitude difference of 50 ft on a 1,000 metre strip (3,280 ft) gives a slope of $^{50}/_{3280} \times {}^{100}/_1 = 1.53\%$. Take care that the feet (height) and metres (distance) units are not confused.

You must always bear in mind the possibility of **engine failure,** which can occur at any stage in flight (although less frequently now than in years gone by). For a single-engined aeroplane, considerations are the gliding performance of the aeroplane and the availability of a field for forced landing. For instance, all other things being equal, a take-off over open fields is preferable to a take-off over a built-up area.

Always consider the possibility of engine failure.

For normal operations, the aeroplane must have sufficient performance and be flown so that it clears any obstacles in the take-off or landing path by a safe margin.

If any doubt exists on the source of data to be used or their application in given circumstances, advice may be sought from the CAA's Performance Section in the Airworthiness Division.

Now complete

Exercises 31 – Take-Off and Landing Performance.

En Route Performance

The total drag generated by an aeroplane is high at both high and low speeds – at high speeds because of the large amount of parasite drag and at low speeds because of the large amount of induced drag. Minimum drag occurs at an intermediate airspeed.

For the aeroplane to maintain straight and level flight at a constant airspeed, the thrust must balance this drag. Thrust is produced by the propeller's use of engine power – high power being required, therefore, to maintain both high and low airspeeds. The **power required** to maintain speed straight and level is illustrated in Figure 32-1.

The engine has a certain maximum power capability at various airspeeds and this is shown as the **power-available** curve. The excess power available over that required at any speed can be used, if desired, to accelerate or to climb. If there is no excess power available, then neither a climb at that speed nor acceleration in level flight is possible. If there is a deficiency of power, the aeroplane will decelerate or descend.

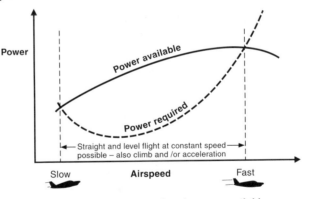

■ *Figure 32-1* **The power-required and power-available curves**

Climb performance depends on excess power.

The **greatest rate of climb** (most height in shortest time) can be achieved at the airspeed at which excess power is maximum. This speed is usually specified in the Flight Manual.

The speed for the **maximum angle** or **maximum gradient climb** (most height in shortest distance) is also specified and is usually some 5 to 10 kt less than that for maximum rate.

Aircraft weight, aircraft configuration and density altitude affect the power curves. A heavily laden aeroplane requires more lift to balance the weight, hence needs to be flown at a higher angle of attack to maintain a given airspeed. This means more drag, and an increased power requirement. Inefficient in-flight aircraft configuration (such as landing gear extended when it could be retracted, or even partial flap extended) increases the drag, especially at high speeds, thereby decreasing the acceleration and rate of climb capabilities of the aeroplane. High density altitudes (high altitudes and/or temperatures) increase the power required and decrease the power available.

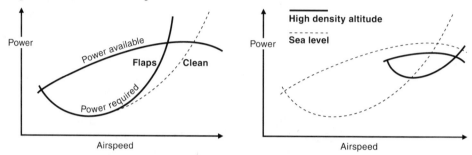

■ Figure 32-2 **Flaps and high density altitudes affect the power curves**

Range and Endurance

En route performance is an important consideration, especially in high-performance aeroplanes where incorrect selection of power settings, cruising speeds and altitudes can significantly affect the efficiency and economics of the operation.

Fuel consumption is a function of the power used, so minimum fuel consumption in straight and level flight will occur at the airspeed for minimum power. This airspeed is known as the **endurance airspeed,** since it allows the longest time of flight for the minimum amount of fuel burn. This speed is used for delaying action, for instance holding while waiting for a fog to lift at the destination aerodrome.

> *Maximum-endurance speed occurs at the TAS where power is minimum.*

It is more common to want to cover the maximum distance for a given amount of fuel, and the speed at which this can be achieved is the **best-range speed.** Since the *rate of covering distance* is airspeed, and the *rate of burning fuel* depends on power, the **maximum-range airspeed** will be that where the power/airspeed ratio is least. This occurs where the line from the origin is a tangent to the curve. At all other airspeeds, the line from the origin to the point on the curve will be steeper and the power/speed ratio greater, causing more fuel per mile to be burnt.

> *Maximum-range speed occurs at the TAS where drag is minimum and the L/D ratio maximum.*

In strong headwind conditions, the best-range speed will be a little faster – the increased fuel flow being compensated for by a higher speed allowing less time en route for the headwind to act. Conversely, the best-range airspeed will be a little slower when there is tailwind assistance. Wind will not affect endurance speed, since time and not distance is the important factor.

It must be emphasised that the manufacturer's cruise performance figures assume correct leaning of the mixture.

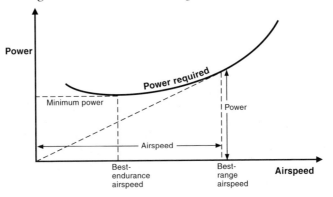

■ *Figure 32-3* **Best-endurance and best-range speeds**

The graphical analysis in Figure 32-3 is a theoretical approach.
In practice, the Flight Manual should be referred to, since it will
contain tables of cruise performance figures. By comparing the
groundspeed and the fuel flow, the speed and altitude for best
range can be calculated.

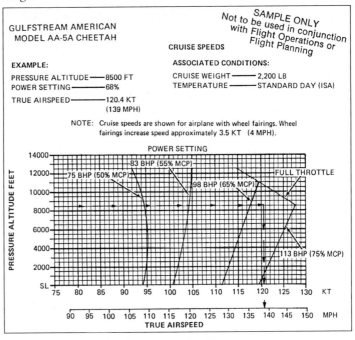

■ *Figure 32-4* **Example of cruise speeds table**

GULFSTREAM AMERICAN
MODEL AA-5A CHEETAH   CRUISE PERFORMANCE

Not to be used in conjunction with Flight Operations or Flight Planning — SAMPLE ONLY

CONDITIONS:
Recommended lean mixture, weight 2200 pounds.

NOTE:
Shaded area represents operation with full throttle. (F.T.)

RPM	20°C BELOW STD. TEMP				STANDARD TEMP				20°C ABOVE STD. TEMP			
	% BHP	TAS KT	TAS MPH	FUEL GPH	% BHP	TAS KT	TAS MPH	FUEL GPH	% BHP	TAS KT	TAS MPH	FUEL GPH
PRESSURE ALTITUDE 8000 FEET												
	21°C (−6°F)				−1°C (31°F)				19°C (67°F)			
2700	79	128	147	9.1	75	128	147	8.6	72	126	145	8.2
2600	73	123	142	8.3	69	121	140	7.9	65	119	137	7.4
2500	66	117	134	7.5	63	114	132	7.1	59	111	128	6.7
2400	60	110	126	6.8	67	107	123	6.5	55	104	120	6.2
2300	54	102	118	6.1	52	99	114	5.9	51	96	110	5.7
PRESSURE ALTITUDE 9000 FEET												
	−23°C (−9°F)				−3°C (27°F)				17°C (63°F)			
2700	75	126	145	8.7	73	126	145	8.3	70	125	144	8.0
2600	71	122	141	8.1	67	120	138	7.7	64	118	136	7.3
2500	64	116	133	7.3	61	113	130	7.0	59	111	128	6.6
2400	58	108	125	6.6	56	106	122	6.3	54	108	118	6.1
2300	53	101	116	6.0	51	98	112	5.8	50	93	107	5.7
PRESSURE ALTITUDE 10,000 FEET												
	−25° (−13°F)				−5°C (23°F)				15°C (59°F)			
F.T.	71	123	142	8.1	69	123	142	7.9	68	123	142	7.7
2600	70	122	140	8.0	66	119	137	7.5	62	116	134	7.1
2500	63	115	132	7.2	60	111	128	6.8	58	107	126	6.5
2400	57	107	123	6.5	66	106	120	6.2	53	101	116	6.0
2300	52	100	115	5.9	51	96	110	5.7	49	91	105	5.6
PRESSURE ALTITUDE 11,000 FEET												
	−27°C (−16°F)				−7°C (20°F)				13°C (45°F)			
F.T.	—	—	—	—	65	119	137	7.4	64	119	137	7.3
2600	57	119	137	7.6	64	118	136	7.3	61	116	133	7.0
2500	62	114	131	7.0	59	111	129	6.7	57	108	124	6.4
2400	56	107	123	6.4	54	108	118	6.1	53	99	114	6.0

■ *Figure 32-5* **Example of a cruise performance chart**

Now complete **Exercises 32 – En Route Performance.**

Weight and Balance

Aircraft Weight

Weight Definitions

Aircraft weights that we use in calculating the gross weight (or all-up weight) are as follows.

Basic Empty Weight

Basic empty weight includes the airframe, engine, fixed equipment (which is used for all operations), unusable fuel, full oil and other items necessary for all flights. The basic empty weight does not include:

☐ **pilot;**
☐ **payload** (passengers and freight);
☐ **any ballast** (for balance); or
☐ **usable fuel.**

Unusable fuel

■ *Figure 33-1* **We use basic empty weight**
for all our load sheet calculations

Empty Weight

The empty weight is the same as basic empty weight except that it includes only the undrainable oil rather than full oil. The empty weight and its centre of gravity (CG) are determined by a licensed weighing of the aeroplane and are specified in the Flight Manual.

> *For our purposes, since one normally flies with full oil, we will use basic empty weight in our problems, as it is simpler.*

Operating Weight

Some operators will determine an operating weight for a particular aeroplane. The operator can nominate what is included in operating weight – it may or may not include all items necessary for the flight (pilots, special equipment, etc.), but it will not include the usable fuel.

Different operators may define different operating weights for the same aeroplane depending on what they choose to include. If you use operating weight, then be sure you know exactly what is included and what is not.

If the operating weight is used then it will appear on the load sheet in place of the basic empty weight. Because basic empty weight is a clearly defined quantity and operating weight is not, we will use basic empty weight for our calculations on the load sheet.

Zero Fuel Weight (ZFW)

Zero fuel weight is the gross weight of the aeroplane excluding the usable fuel in the wing fuel tanks – i.e. it includes the pilot, payload and ballast, but none of the usable fuel.

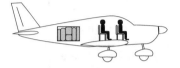

■ *Figure 33-2* **Zero fuel weight**

ZFW includes the basic empty weight of the aeroplane plus the pilot, plus passengers, plus baggage and cargo. Usable fuel is not included (unusable fuel which is always in the tanks is included). The zero fuel weight is used in your weight and balance calculations, although in reality (hopefully) the aeroplane would never be in the zero fuel situation of having everything on board except usable fuel.

Gross Weight (GW)

Gross weight is the total weight of the aircraft (and its contents) at that particular time. It is the basic weight plus pilot, plus payload (passengers and cargo), plus ballast (if any), plus fuel.

Usable fuel added

■ *Figure 33-3* **The gross weight**

The gross weight should not exceed the maximum weight permissible for that manoeuvre. On take-off, GW must not exceed MTOW (structural) or the performance-limited TOW. On landing, GW must not exceed MLW (structural) or the performance-limited LW.

Each aircraft has weight limitations placed on it. They depend on the structural strength of the aircraft, the operations for which it is designed, and the manoeuvre being considered.

Maximum Ramp Weight

Maximum ramp weight is the maximum gross weight permitted prior to taxiing. It may exceed the maximum take-off weight by the taxi fuel allowance. While this is not specified for many light aircraft, it is specified for some, and so you should be aware of ramp weight.

The *Cessna 172* (which we consider later) has a 3 kg taxi allowance (fuel burn-off during the taxi), so the ramp weight may exceed the maximum allowable take-off weight by this amount.

Maximum Take-Off Weight (MTOW) – Structural

Maximum take-off weight is the maximum allowable gross weight permitted for take-off.

Performance-Limited Take-Off Weight

Sometimes a performance limitation (short runway, high obstacle in the take-off path, unfavourable wind or slope, high temperature, high pressure altitude, i.e. high density altitude) will limit that particular take-off to a weight less than the structural MTOW. Refer to the performance charts in the aircraft's Flight Manual.

Maximum Landing Weight (MLW) – Structural

The maximum landing weight is the maximum permitted gross weight for landing. For many light aircraft the MLW is the same as the MTOW, and you can take off at maximum weight and return for an immediate landing without exceeding the limitations. The MLW of other aircraft may, for structural reasons, be less than the MTOW. In this case, the fuel burn-off must be sufficient to reduce the actual take-off gross weight to a figure less than the maximum landing weight.

NOTE The basic empty weight (and moment arm – which we consider later) will be different for each individual aeroplane, and is always specified in that particular aeroplane's Flight Manual.

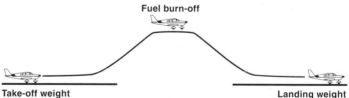

■ *Figure 33-4* **Landing weight equals take-off weight minus burn-off**

Performance-Limited Landing Weight

Sometimes a performance limitation (short runway, high obstacle in the approach path making a long touchdown necessary, unfavourable wind or slope, high density altitude) may limit that particular landing to a weight less than the structural MLW.

Why Aeroplane Weight is Restricted

The main force generated to balance the weight is the lift force. Its magnitude (size) depends on the wing, the airspeed and the air density (*rho* or ρ).

The airspeed is limited by the power available from the engine–propeller, the wing is fixed by the designer and the air density is outside the control of the pilot. If lift cannot be made to equal the weight, then the aircraft cannot maintain level flight.

An overweight aeroplane will perform and handle badly and may suffer structural damage if flown. From the performance point of view, an overweight aeroplane will have:

Never fly an overloaded aeroplane!

- a higher stalling speed;
- a higher take-off speed;
- poorer climb performance (angle and rate);
- a lower service ceiling;
- less endurance;
- a higher landing speed;
- greater braking requirements;
- less manoeuvrability;
- a longer take-off run;
- higher fuel consumption;
- shorter range;
- a longer landing distance.

Aeroplane Loading

The Air Navigation Order specifies the operational requirements for the loading of aircraft. The items that must be weighed in determining the loading of an aircraft are:

- all cargo;
- removable equipment;
- baggage;
- occupants, including their personal effects.

Knowing the exact weight of passengers is, of course, best, but approximate weights that can be used are:

- an infant 8 kg (17 lb) (under 2 years);
- a child 48 kg (105 lb) (under 15 years);
- an adult 77 kg (170 lb).

NOTE 1 kg = 2.2 lb (approximately); to convert kg to lb, multiply by 2.2; to convert lb to kg, divide by 2.2.

Other Weight Restrictions

There may be other weight restrictions, such as maximum baggage compartment loads, maximum floor loads (per unit area), etc., specified in the Flight Manual and on placards in the aircraft.

Know your aeroplane's weight limitations.

The Weight of Fuel

Fuel has a specific gravity of 0.72 Avgas (100/130).
Oil has a specific gravity of 0.96 (synthetic), 0.90 (mineral).

A specific gravity of 0.72 means that 100/130 Avgas weighs only 0.72 times as much as an equal volume of water. 1 litre of water weighs 1 kg, therefore 1 litre of 100/130 Avgas weighs 0.72 kg. 1 imperial gallon of water weighs 10 lb, therefore:

◻ **1 imperial gallon of Avgas** weighs 7.2 lb; and
◻ **1 US gallon of Avgas** weighs 6.0 lb.

It is the pilot's responsibility to ensure weight limitations are not exceeded. In many light aeroplanes it is not possible to carry both a full fuel load and a full passenger and baggage load.

Aeroplane Balance

Forces, Moments and Datums
The turning moment of a force depends on two things:

1. The size of the force;

2. Its moment arm.

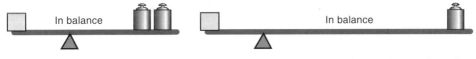

■ *Figure 33-5* **Balancing (or turning) moment depends on weight and moment arm**

If a body (object) does not turn, then the moments wanting to turn it clockwise must be perfectly balanced by the moments wanting to turn it anticlockwise.

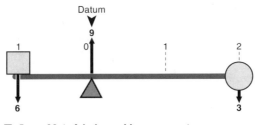

■ *Figure 33-6* **A balanced beam experiences no resultant turning moment**

Using the pivot as the datum:
◻ Clockwise moments = 3 × 2 = 6.
◻ Anticlockwise moments = 6 × 1 = 6.

Because they balance, there is no resultant turning moment. We can calculate turning moment about any datum point.

Suppose we choose the left-hand side of the beam as our datum.

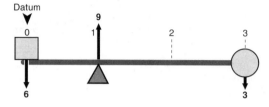

■ *Figure 33-7* **Choice of datum point does not affect the balance**

☐ Clockwise moments = 3 × 3 = 9.
☐ Anticlockwise moments = 9 × 1 = 9, i.e. no resultant turning moment.

Suppose we choose a point 1 unit to the left of the beam as the datum.

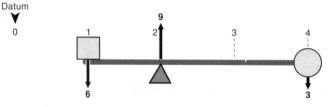

■ *Figure 33-8* **An external datum is also acceptable**

☐ Clockwise moments = (6 × 1) + (3 × 4) = 18.
☐ Anticlockwise moments = 9 × 2 = 18.

You can see that the choice of a datum point makes no difference to the results. If the system is in balance, the moments taken about any datum point will have a zero resultant.

In the same sense, when considering the balance of an aeroplane it does not matter where the datum point is chosen to be. The designer nominates one, specifies it in the Flight Manual, and bases all his charts on it.

Index Units (IU)

The units of a turning moment are those of *force × distance* and may be pound.inch or kilogram.millimetre. For a force of say 200 kg acting 300 mm from the datum, its moment is (200 kg × 300 mm) = 60,000 kilogram.mm. Since large numbers often result, it is usual to divide them by 1,000 and instead of 60,000 kg.mm, we have 60 **index units** (where 1 IU = 1,000 kg.mm).

1 index unit (IU) equals 1,000 kg.mm

Effect of CG Position on Aeroplane Handling

In straight and level flight, lift equals weight and thrust equals drag. These four main forces provide two couples which have turning moments that are not always perfectly in balance. Extra forces are provided by the tailplane to make up for this. The tailplane force has a turning moment in the pitching plane (nose-up or nose-down) about the centre of gravity (CG). Its effectiveness depends on its magnitude (size) and the length of its moment arm from the CG.

Any movement of the centre of pressure on the wings (through which the lift force acts), or of the centre of gravity (through which the weight acts), will require a different balancing force from the tailplane.

The lift force that the tailplane can produce depends on its airspeed. Its effectiveness at low speeds, therefore, determines just how much the length of its moment arm to the CG can change, by movement of the CG. The reasons for limiting the forward and aft movement of the CG were discussed in Chapter 7, *Stability*. Briefly, they are:

▢ **If the CG is forward,** the tailplane has a long moment arm and the aeroplane is very stable in the pitching plane, i.e. naturally resistant to any pitching motion. The forward position of the CG is limited to ensure that the elevator has a sufficient turning moment available to overcome the natural stability and flare the nose-heavy aeroplane for take-off and landing, which occur at relatively low speeds when the elevator is less-effective.

▢ **With an aft CG,** the aeroplane is less stable in the pitching plane. The aft position of the CG is limited so that the static stability of the aeroplane (its ability to retain a steady nose attitude) and the elevator 'feel' experienced through the control column by the pilot both remain satisfactory.

Movement of the CG Position

The CG position must remain within limits throughout the flight.

As fuel is burned in the course of a flight, the resulting weight change affects both the gross weight and the CG position of the aeroplane. Prior to flight, you must consider these two items at both:

▢ **take-off weight** (the highest gross weight of the flight); and
▢ **zero fuel weight** (as if all usable fuel had been burned-off; not that you will reach this point in flight – hopefully!)

CG position at landing weight may also be found if desired.

Fuel tanks are normally designed to be near the CG, so that as the weight burns down, the CG will not move greatly. In aeroplanes with swept-back wings there will be some difficulties in achieving this. Of course, movement of passengers and cargo will also change the CG position.

The actual forward and aft limits of the CG will be different for different gross weights of the aeroplane. The manufacturer usually shows this in the Flight Manual with a graph of gross weight versus CG position. It is often labelled *centre of gravity moment envelope.*

Aircraft manufacturers will specify a datum point on which their graph is based and from which all the moment arms are measured. If we can calculate the turning moment for a particular gross weight about this datum, calculate the position of the CG and plot it on the manufacturer's graph, we can see if it guarantees the balance of the aeroplane or not.

If our *CG versus GW* point falls within the envelope, then all is fine. If it does not fall within the envelope, then we must alter the loading of the aeroplane – shift the load, reduce it, add ballast – until the weight and balance requirements are satisfied.

Following an aircraft accident, two of the first things investigated are that the pilot was licensed and that the aircraft was being operated within correct weight and balance limitations.

Mathematical Approach to Weight and Balance

We obtain the gross weight by adding up the various component weights – in this case, 2,200 lb.

We obtain the total moment by adding up the various component moments. The various component weights act at known positions relative to the fixed datum. Each of these has a moment, which we can calculate by multiplying the individual weight by its arm from the datum. For example:

$$222 \text{ lb of fuel} \times 90.9 \text{ inches} = 20,180 \text{ lb.in}$$
$$= 20.18 \text{ lb.in}/1,000$$
$$= 20.18 \text{ IU}$$

We obtain the total moment by summing (adding up) all of the moments due to these component weights. It adds up to 202.72 lb.in/1,000.

Referring to the loading graph, we see that 2,200 lb and 202.72 lb.in/1,000 lie within the Normal Category envelope.

If we want to calculate the position of the CG through which all of these weights, combined into the gross weight, may be considered to act, we do a small sum:

$$\text{Sum of individual moments} = \text{total moment}$$
$$= \text{gross weight} \times \text{moment arm}$$
$$202,720 \text{ lb.in} = 2,200 \text{ lb} \times \text{moment arm}$$
$$\text{moment arm} = \frac{202,720}{2,200}$$
$$\text{moment arm} = 92.15 \text{ inches}$$

Aircraft weight and balance calculations are straightforward, especially after a bit of practice.

1. Total-up the weights and ensure no weight limitations are exceeded.

2. Total-up the moments and divide this total by the gross weight to find the CG position.

3. Verify that the CG versus GW point lies within the approved envelope.

Graphical Approach to Weight and Balance

Some (thoughtful) manufacturers provide a small loading graph that allows us to enter with weight, take it across horizontally to the appropriate guide line, travel vertically and read off the moment (in index units).

Load Sheet Method

Using a load sheet to calculate weight and balance is even easier than the mathematical or graphical methods. A sample load sheet follows.

Data:

- Basic weight of aircraft 830 kg, −270 index units
- 1 pilot, 4 passengers
- Maximum baggage allowed in lockers: 90 kg (45 kg in each)
- Maximum fuel: 356 litres (252 kg)

LOAD SHEET	
Basic empty weight	830 kg
Row 1: 1 pilot, 1 passenger	154
Row 2: 1 passenger	77
Row 3: 2 passengers	154
Forward baggage	45
Rear baggage	45
ZFW	**1,305**
Fuel	**252**
Take-off weight	**1,557 kg**

NOTE We have done the weight calculation above separate to the load sheet, to make it clearer. There is no need for you to do this as space is available down the right-hand side of the aircraft loading system sheet and you can enter the figures directly onto it.

SAMPLE LOADING PROBLEM	SAMPLE AIRPLANE			YOUR AIRPLANE		
	WEIGHT (LBS.)	ARM (IN.)	MOMENT (LB.-IN. /1000)	WEIGHT (LBS.)	ARM (IN.)	MOMENT (LB.-IN. /1000)
*1. Licensed Empty Weight (Typical)	1262	83.4	105.25	——		——
2. Oil (8 qts.) 1 qt. = 1.875 lbs.	15	32.0	.48	——	32.0	——
3. Fuel (in excess of unuseable) Standard Tanks (37 gal.)	222	90.9	20.18	——	90.9	——
Long Range Tanks (51 gal.)		94.81		——	94.81	——
4. Pilot and Co-Pilot	340	90.6	30.80	——	90.6	——
5. Rear Seat Passengers	340	126.0	42.84	——	126.0	——
*6. Baggage (in baggage compartment) Max. allowable 120 lbs.	21	151.0	3.17	——	151.0	——
7. Cargo Area Max. allowable 340 lbs.		116.4		——	116.4	——
8. Total Airplane Weight (loaded)	2200	92.17	202.72			
9. Usable Fuel	222	90.9	20.18			
10. Zero Fuel Weight	1978		182.54			

NOTE: If desired, the **Landing Weight and CG position** can be calculated by subtracting from the Take-Off Weight values the weight and moment of the fuel consumed.

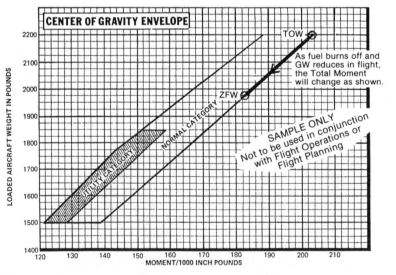

■ Figure 33-9 *Mathematical approach to weight and balance* **calculations**

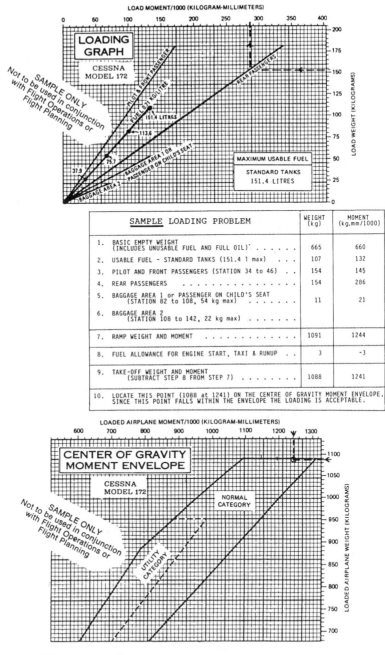

LOAD MOMENT/1000 (KILOGRAM-MILLIMETERS)

LOADING GRAPH

CESSNA MODEL 172

MAXIMUM USABLE FUEL
STANDARD TANKS
151.4 LITRES

LOAD WEIGHT (KILOGRAMS)

SAMPLE LOADING PROBLEM	WEIGHT (kg)	MOMENT (kg.mm/1000)
1. BASIC EMPTY WEIGHT (INCLUDES UNUSABLE FUEL AND FULL OIL)'	665	660
2. USABLE FUEL - STANDARD TANKS (151.4 1 max) . . .	107	132
3. PILOT AND FRONT PASSENGERS (STATION 34 to 46) . .	154	145
4. REAR PASSENGERS	154	286
5. BAGGAGE AREA 1 or PASSENGER ON CHILD'S SEAT (STATION 82 to 108, 54 kg max)	11	21
6. BAGGAGE AREA 2 (STATION 108 to 142, 22 kg max)		
7. RAMP WEIGHT AND MOMENT	1091	1244
8. FUEL ALLOWANCE FOR ENGINE START, TAXI & RUNUP . .	3	-3
9. TAKE-OFF WEIGHT AND MOMENT (SUBTRACT STEP 8 FROM STEP 7)	1088	1241
10. LOCATE THIS POINT (1088 at 1241) ON THE CENTRE OF GRAVITY MOMENT ENVELOPE. SINCE THIS POINT FALLS WITHIN THE ENVELOPE THE LOADING IS ACCEPTABLE.		

LOADED AIRPLANE MOMENT/1000 (KILOGRAM-MILLIMETERS)

CENTER OF GRAVITY MOMENT ENVELOPE

CESSNA MODEL 172

NORMAL CATEGORY

UTILITY CATEGORY

LOADED AIRPLANE WEIGHT (KILOGRAMS)

■ *Figure 33-10* **The graphical approach**

With the above passenger arrangement, the CG position is just inside the rear limit. A better arrangement would be to have two passengers in Row 2, one passenger in Row 3, as this would move the CG position well into the envelope and provide you with a more stable aeroplane to fly.

You must be very careful that the correct figures, especially for basic empty weight and its index unit, are entered onto the load sheet. This is the starting point for the whole thing. Always check this.

We have used the **77 kg standard weight** for an adult. The designer of the chart has made our task easier by dividing the scale line into 77 kg divisions along the bottom, each division representing one adult person. Two adults in the one row gives us 154 kg for the weight column and two divisions on the index unit (moment) scale.

Along the top of the scale line he has placed 50 kg divisions to ease our task if we are carrying baggage or other items in the seat rows. Notice that loading row 1 (R1) and loading the forward baggage compartment both have the effect of moving the CG forward.

Loading row 2 and aft of it, including the rear baggage locker, will move the CG rearwards. In this aeroplane, the fuel has an IU of zero, i.e. the tanks are on the datum, so, as fuel is consumed in flight, the moment will remain unchanged.

Dangerous Goods

There are many goods which should not be carried in an aeroplane. There are some items which are illegal to carry and others which, while legal, are better not carried. You must show responsibility and common sense in accepting or rejecting particular items. The following are some of the dangerous goods that are hazardous to aviation:

Do not carry dangerous goods in an aeroplane.

- explosives;
- flammable goods (including chemicals which may evaporate as altitude is gained, cigarette lighters, matches, alcohol, etc.);
- radioactive materials;
- infectious substances;
- corrosive substances (e.g. the weak sulphuric acid in a spare battery);
- magnetic materials (that could affect the magnetic compass – so do not place a headset or radio near it).

LOAD DATA SHEET

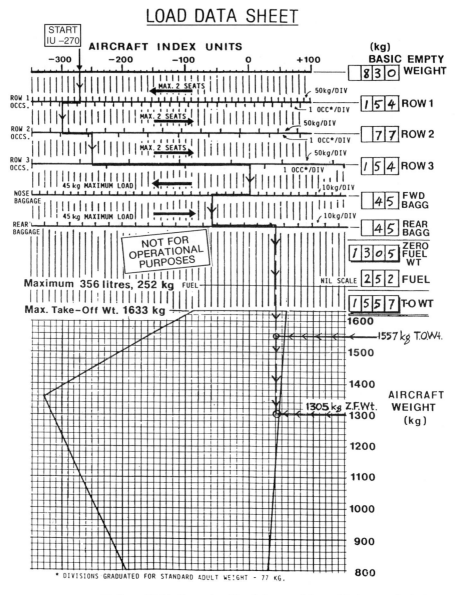

■ Figure 33-11 **Example of load sheet weight and balance calculation**

Baggage and Cargo Restraint

Baggage should be restrained so that it cannot move in flight and cause a shift in the centre of gravity which, in extreme cases, could lead to loss of control, or, if it is thrown around the cabin in turbulence, cause personal injury, damage to the aeroplane or obstruction of the controls. The same applies to other heavy items such as a fire extinguisher.

Restrain baggage, cargo or other cabin items that could move in turbulence. Do not take chances!

Most baggage compartments have tie-down points to which the load may be secured by ropes or a security net. If baggage is loaded onto a seat, restraining it by passing a seat belt through it may be sufficient. If not, use additional tie-downs. Do not leave loose parcels or suitcases on the seats. Similarly, ensure that everyone has their seat belt on for take-off, landing and in turbulence.

*Now complete **Exercises 33 – Weight and Balance.***

Wake Turbulence

As a wing produces lift, the higher static pressure area beneath it forces an airflow around the wingtip into the lower pressure area above. The greater the pressure differential, the greater is this flow around the wingtips.

At the high angles of attack necessary to produce the required lift force at low speeds, very large and strong trailing vortices are formed. As the aeroplane is moving forward, a trail of wingtip vortices is left behind. This effect was discussed under *Induced Drag* – the drag generated by the production of lift (see page 31).

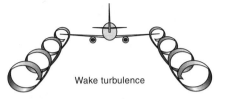
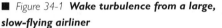

Wake turbulence

■ *Figure 34-1* **Wake turbulence from a large, slow-flying airliner**

> *Wake turbulence will be strongest behind a heavy aircraft flying with its flaps up.*

As a large and heavy aircraft is rotated for take-off or flared for landing, the angle of attack is large. The trailing wingtip vortices formed can be strong enough to upset a following aeroplane if it flies into them. They are invisible but real. This effect is known as **wake turbulence.**

> *The main danger from wake turbulence is loss of control caused by induced roll.*

The wake turbulence behind a *Boeing 747* can significantly affect, for example, a *737* or a *DC-9,* and can cause lighter aircraft to become uncontrollable.

To avoid wake turbulence accidents and incidents, Air Traffic Control delays the operation of light aircraft on runways behind heavy jets for up to five minutes to allow the vortices to drift away and dissipate.

All pilots must be aware of wake turbulence because even the Air Traffic Control procedures occasionally provide insufficient separation from the wingtip vortices behind another aircraft. Air Traffic Controllers are experts at their job – do not expect them to be experts at yours as well. As pilot you have the ultimate responsibility for the safety of your aeroplane – so learn to visualise the formation and movement of invisible wingtip vortices.

Heavy aircraft will also leave vortices in their wake in flight, especially in the circuit area where they are flying slowly at high angles of attack – make sure that you provide your own separation in the circuit.

The vortices will tend to lose height slowly (drift downwards) and drift downwind. To be able to avoid these invisible danger areas when following heavier aircraft, you must be able to visualise the movement of the vortices and take steps to avoid them.

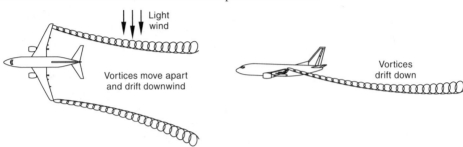

Light wind

Vortices move apart and drift downwind

Vortices drift down

■ *Figure 34-2* **Wingtip vortices drift downwind (as well as backwards)**

☐ **A crosswind** will cause the vortices to drift off the downwind side of the runway.

☐ **A headwind or a tailwind** will carry them down the runway in the direction of the wind.

☐ **In nil-wind** or light and variable conditions, the vortices will 'hang around'. Calm conditions can be very dangerous – delaying your take-off or changing runway is worth considering.

Be extra careful in calm conditions, as the vortices will not be blown away.

Avoiding Wake Turbulence
The main aim of wake turbulence avoidance is to avoid passing through it at all, especially in flight.

Avoid wake turbulence by flying above and upwind of the path of other aircraft.

On Take-Off
When taking off behind a large aircraft which has itself just taken off, commence your take-off at the end of the runway so that you will become airborne in an area well before where the heavy aircraft rotated or to where its vortices may have drifted. If doubtful, delay your take-off.

Do not use an intersection departure (less than the full length of the runway) behind a heavy aircraft, as this may bring your flightpath closer to its wake turbulence.

Manoeuvre to avoid the vortices in flight by climbing steeply (but not too slowly, as speed is a safety factor if you strike wake turbulence) or turning away from where you think the wake turbulence is.

When taking off after a heavy aircraft has landed, plan to become airborne well past the point where it flared and landed.

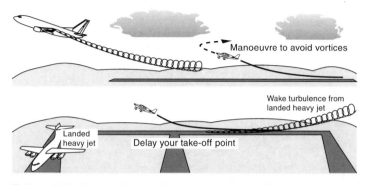

■ *Figure 34-3* ***Avoid wake turbulence on your take-off***

If a heavy aircraft has taken off on a different runway and you expect to be airborne prior to the intersection of the runways, observe that the heavy aircraft was still on the ground until well past the intersection, before you commence your take-off.

Always avoid flying through the wake of a heavy aircraft, especially at low speed near the ground.

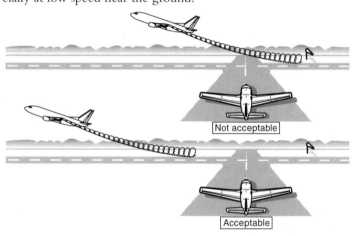

■ *Figure 34-4* ***Awareness of wake turbulence for your take-off***

In the Circuit

Avoid flying below and behind large aircraft. Fly a few hundred feet above them, a thousand feet below them or to windward of them. Calm days where there is no turbulence to break up the vortices are perhaps the most dangerous.

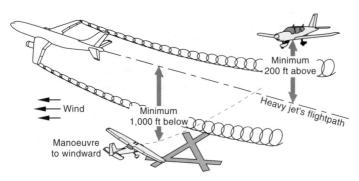

■ *Figure 34-5* **Avoidance of wake turbulence in the circuit area**

On Approach to Land

When following a preceding landing heavy aircraft, fly above its approach path and land well beyond its touchdown point. This is usually possible in a light aircraft landing on a long runway where heavy aircraft are landing.

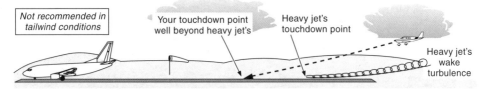

■ *Figure 34-6* **Avoidance of wake turbulence on your approach**

When landing on a runway where a heavy aircraft has just taken off, touchdown well short of its lift-off point or where you think the vortices may have drifted to. The normal touchdown zone will probably ensure this.

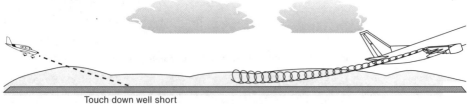

■ *Figure 34-7* **Landing behind a heavy aircraft that has taken off**

If a preceding heavy aircraft has discontinued its approach and gone around, its turbulent wake will be a hazard to a following aircraft. You should consider changing your flightpath in these circumstances.

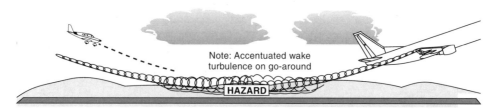

Note: Accentuated wake turbulence on go-around

HAZARD

■ Figure 34-8 **Making an approach behind a heavy aircraft that has gone around**

Jet Blast

Do not confuse wake turbulence (wingtip vortices) with **jet blast** (sometimes referred to as thrust stream), which is the high-velocity air exhausted from a jet engine or a large propeller-driven aircraft, especially a turbo-prop. Jet blast can be dangerous to a light aircraft taxiing on the ground behind a jet or large propeller-driven aircraft. Always position your aeroplane when taxiing or when stopped to avoid any potential jet blast.

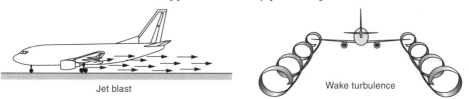

Jet blast

Wake turbulence

■ Figure 34-9 **Wake turbulence is different from jet blast**

Helicopter Rotor Tip Vortices

Avoid helicopters by a wide margin, especially if they are hover-taxiing.

Helicopters generate significant and powerful rotor tip vortices, particularly when hover-taxiing and hovering, as the rotors are supporting the full weight of the helicopter.

Take extra care when taking off and landing near air-taxiing helicopters, as their rotor tip vortices will drift downwind, and may drift across your runway. When on final approach, it may not be apparent to you which stage of flight the helicopter is at – so allow a larger space between yourself and the helicopter than you would for an aeroplane of similar size. If in doubt, go around.

More Information

Read the CAA's *General Aviation Safety Sense* leaflet No. 15 – it contains excellent practical information on wake turbulence and rotor tip vortices. See also Aeronautical Information Circular AIC 178/1993 (Pink 95) dated 16 December.

Now complete **Exercises 34 – Wake Turbulence.**

Ground Effect

An aeroplane's flight characteristics change when it is very close to the ground or any other surface, because:
- it can fly at a **slower speed** than when it is at altitude, and
- it can fly at the **same speed** using less thrust than when it is at altitude.

The better 'flyability' of an aeroplane when it is just above a surface is known as **ground effect.**

Birds know all about ground effect and it is common to see large water-birds, for example, skimming leisurely just above the waves with no apparent effort. Birds may not understand the physics of ground effect but they certainly know how to use it. Many pilots fall into the same category – of knowing that the effect is there but not really understanding why. These few pages will explain ground effect in simple terms.

In the chapters on lift and drag in Section One we considered an aeroplane to be flying well away from the ground. There was no restriction to the downwash of the airflow behind the wings, nor to the upwash ahead of the wings. There was also no restriction to the formation of wingtip vortices.

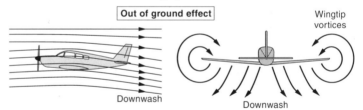

■ *Figure 35-1* **In free air, the upwash and downwash are not restricted and the formation of wingtip vortices is not restricted**

When an aeroplane is flying close to the ground the ground surface interferes with the airflow around the wings, restricting it in a number of ways. A nearby surface:
- **restricts** the upwash and downwash, and
- **restricts** the formation of wingtip and line vortices.

When an aeroplane is *in ground effect,* the total reaction on the wing is more perpendicular to the remote free airstream and the induced drag is less, compared with *out of ground effect.*

Ground effect becomes noticeable when the aeroplane is at a height above the surface of less than one wingspan. The effect is greater the closer the wing is to the surface.

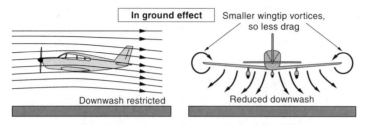

■ *Figure 35-2* **Near the ground, the upwash and downwash are restricted and the formation of wingtip vortices is restricted**

By definition the term **ground effect** refers to the general aerodynamic influence on an aeroplane when it is in proximity to a surface. Although the wing, fuselage and tailplane will all be affected by ground effect, by far the most significant effect is on the wing.

Ground effect reduces upwash and downwash of the airflow, and the cushioning effect produces more lift.

By reducing the upwash in front of the wing and the downwash behind the wing, the ground surface acts like a cushion, causing the wing to develop more lift (i.e. a higher coefficient of lift or greater lifting ability), even though the actual pitch attitude of the aircraft may not have changed.

Ground effect causes reduced wingtip and line vortices and less induced drag than in free air.

You will recall from Chapter 4, *Drag,* that we break up the total drag on an aeroplane into two main types – **induced drag** that is a by-product of the production of lift, and **parasite drag** that is not directly associated with the production of lift.

Wingtip vortices, and line vortices behind the trailing edge, are a major cause of induced drag. So when a nearby surface restricts their formation, the induced drag will be less and therefore the total drag on the aeroplane will be less.

You know that, in level flight, drag is balanced by thrust. The reduction in drag when near the ground or water means that the same airspeed can be maintained using less thrust. Therefore, underpowered aircraft may be able to maintain flying speed while in ground effect, even if they cannot maintain that speed in free air well away from the ground.

There are many 'Biggles' stories of multi-engined aircraft losing power from one or more of their engines and, flying on severely limited power, not being able to climb away from the ground or water, but relying on ground effect to maintain flight.

Induced drag is greatest at high angles of attack, so is significant at the high angles of attack and slow speeds common in take-offs and landings. The ground (hopefully) is reasonably close in these particular manoeuvres, so ground effect will play a major role.

At one wingspan height above the ground there is about a 1% reduction in induced drag and this reduction becomes more significant the closer the aeroplane is to the ground. At a height equal to only $\frac{1}{10}$ of a wingspan, the induced drag is reduced by about 50%. (There is no need to remember these figures, they are included just to give you an idea of how significant ground effect can be.)

Ground Effect during Landing

On an approach to land, as the aeroplane enters ground effect at about one wingspan high, you will experience a floating sensation – a result of the extra lift (from the increased coefficient of lift) and the slower deceleration (due to less drag).

In most landings there is no desire to maintain speed – indeed the aim is to lose speed. It is therefore usually important at flare height and in ground effect to ensure that the power is throttled back, especially considering the reduction of drag due to ground effect.

Excess speed at the commencement of the landing flare and the better 'flyability' of an aeroplane in ground effect may incur a considerable float distance prior to touchdown. This is not desirable, especially on landing strips of the minimum required length.

Ground Effect on Take-Off

As the aeroplane climbs out of ground effect on take-off, the lift coefficient will decrease for the same aeroplane pitch attitude (the lifting ability of the wing will be less). The induced drag will increase due to the greater wingtip vortices and line vortices, and the total reaction now 'leans' further back from the perpendicular to the remote free airstream. With this increase in drag, airspeed will tend to decrease for the same thrust.

Thus the aeroplane will not perform as well in free air as it will in ground effect. You will feel a sagging in climb-out performance as the aircraft flies out of ground effect.

It pays to bear this in mind if ever you are operating on short strips or strips which finish on the edge of a cliff. Once away from the take-off surface the climb performance will be less – a good reason for not forcing the aeroplane to become airborne at too low a speed because, while it might manage to fly in ground effect, it will be unable to climb out of it, possibly even settling back onto the ground. Some pilots have found this a little embarrassing, especially if they have retracted the landing gear!

Summary

In summary, the two main results of ground effect are:

1. An increased lifting ability of the wing (i.e. increased C_{Lift}).

2. A reduction in drag (less formation of vortices and less induced drag).

Both of these cause a floating effect near the ground. There are two further points to note about ground effect:

1. The disturbance in airflow may cause the airspeed indicator (ASI) and the altimeter to read inaccurately when flying near the ground.

2. The disturbance of normal airflow as compared to free air may cause a change in the stability characteristics of the aeroplane near the ground.

Now complete **Exercises 35 – Ground Effect.**

Windshear

> *This chapter goes beyond the syllabus requirements for the Aeroplane –*
> *Technical examination, but the information it contains is of practical use.*
> *It helps explain why alterations of pitch attitude and/or power are*
> *continually required to maintain a desired flightpath, just as changes*
> *in heading are required to maintain a steady track.*

The study of windshear and its effect on aeroplanes and what protective measures can be taken to avoid unpleasant results is still in its infancy and much remains to be learned. What is certain is that every aeroplane and every pilot will be affected by windshear – usually the light windshears that occur in everyday flying, but occasionally a moderate windshear that requires positive action from the pilot and, on rare occasions, severe windshear that can put an aeroplane out of control.

Severe windshears have caused the loss of a number of aircraft, some of them large passenger aircraft. A little knowledge will help you understand how to handle windshear and how to avoid unnecessary problems with it.

Windshear Terminology

Windshear is a change in wind direction and/or wind speed.

A **windshear** is defined as a change in wind direction and/or wind speed, including updrafts and downdrafts, in space. Any change in the wind velocity (be it a change in speed or in direction) as you move from one point to another is a windshear. The stronger the change and the shorter the distance within which it occurs, the stronger the windshear.

Updrafts and **downdrafts** are vertical components of wind. The most hazardous updrafts and downdrafts are usually those associated with thunderstorms.

The term **low-level windshear** is used to specify the windshear, if any, along the final approach path prior to landing, along the runway and along the take-off/initial climb-out flightpath. Windshear near the ground (i.e. below about 3,000 ft) is often the most critical in terms of safety for the aeroplane.

Turbulence is eddy motions in the atmosphere which vary with time and from place to place.

Effects of Windshear on Aircraft

Most of our studies have considered an aeroplane flying in a reasonably stable air mass which has a steady motion relative to the ground, i.e. in a steady wind situation. We have seen how an aeroplane climbing out in a steady headwind will have a better climb gradient over the ground compared to the tailwind situation, and how an aeroplane will glide further over the ground downwind compared to into wind.

In reality an air mass does not move in a totally steady manner – there will be gusts and updrafts and changes of wind speed and direction which the aeroplane will encounter as it flies through the air mass. In this chapter, we look at the *transient* effects that these windshears have on the flightpath of an aeroplane.

A Typical Windshear Situation

Often when the wind is relatively calm on the ground, at several hundred feet above the ground the light and variable wind conditions change suddenly into a strong and steady wind. If we consider an aeroplane making an approach to land in these conditions, we can see the effect the windshear has as the aeroplane passes through the shear.

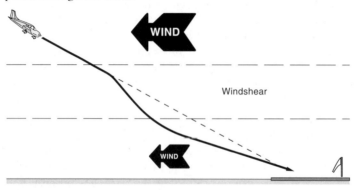

■ *Figure 36-1* **A typical windshear situation – calm on the ground with a wind at altitude**

An aeroplane flying through the air will have a certain inertia depending on its mass and its velocity relative to the ground. If the aeroplane has a true airspeed of 80 knots and the headwind component is 30 knots, then the inertial speed of the aeroplane over the ground is $(80 - 30) = 50$ knots.

When the aeroplane flies down into the calm air, the headwind component drops off quickly to say 5 knots. The inertial speed of the aeroplane over the ground is still 50 knots, but the new headwind of only 5 knots will mean that its true airspeed has suddenly dropped back to 55 knots.

The pilot would observe a sudden drop in indicated airspeed and a change in the performance of the aeroplane – at 55 knots airspeed the performance will be quite different to when it is at 80 knots airspeed. The normal reaction would be to add power or to lower the nose to regain airspeed, and to avoid undershooting the desired flightpath.

The pilot can accelerate the aeroplane and return it to the desired flightpath by changes in attitude and power. The more the windshear, the more these changes in power and attitude will be required. Any fluctuations in wind will require adjustments by the pilot, which is why you have to work so hard sometimes, especially when approaching to land.

In gusty conditions, use a power-on approach and landing, and consider adding a few knots to the approach speed.

Overshoot and Undershoot Effect

The effects of windshear on an aeroplane's flightpath depend on the nature and location of the shear, as follows.

Overshoot Effect

Overshoot effect is caused by a windshear which results in the aeroplane flying above the desired flightpath and/or an increase in indicated airspeed. The nose of the aircraft may also tend to rise. Overshoot effect may result from flying into an increasing headwind, a decreasing tailwind, from a tailwind into a headwind, or an updraft.

Undershoot Effect

Undershoot effect is caused by a windshear which results in an aircraft flying below the desired flightpath and/or a decrease in indicated airspeed. The nose of the aircraft may also tend to drop. Undershoot effect may result from flying into a decreasing headwind, an increasing tailwind, from a headwind into a tailwind, or into a downdraft.

Note that the actual windshear effect depends on:

1. The nature of the windshear.

2. Whether the aeroplane is climbing or descending through that particular windshear.

3. The direction in which the aeroplane is flying.

Windshear Reversal Effect

Windshear reversal effect is caused by a windshear which results in the initial effect on the aeroplane being reversed as the aircraft proceeds further along the flightpath. It would be described as overshoot effect followed by undershoot, or undershoot followed by overshoot effect, as appropriate.

Windshear reversal effect is a common phenomenon often experienced on approach to land, when things are usually happening too fast to analyse exactly what is taking place in terms of wind. The pilot can, of course, observe undershoot and overshoot effect and react accordingly with changes in attitude and/or thrust.

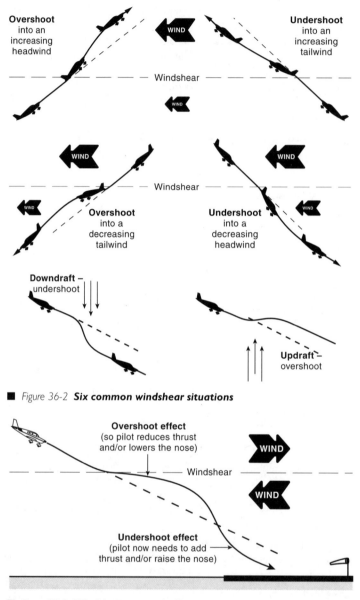

■ Figure 36-2 **Six common windshear situations**

■ Figure 36-3 **Windshear reversal effect**

Crosswind Effect

Crosswind effect is caused by a windshear which requires a rapid change of aircraft heading to maintain a desired track (not uncommon in a crosswind approach and landing because the crosswind component changes as the ground is neared).

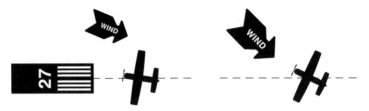

■ Figure 36-4 **Crosswind effect**

The Causes of Windshear

Causes of windshear include the wind being slowed down by ground surface roughness, abrupt changes in terrain, thunderstorms, cumulonimbus clouds, large cumulus clouds (downbursts and gust fronts), low-level jet streams, fronts, thermal activity, sea breezes, etc.

Avoid thunderstorms and cumulonimbus clouds as windshear effects near them can be severe. A strong downburst out of the base of one of these clouds will spread out as it nears the ground. The initial effect may be an overshoot effect followed by what may be an extremely severe undershoot.

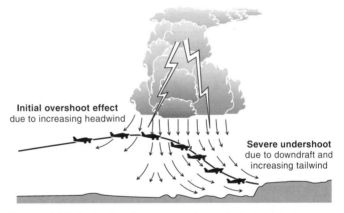

■ Figure 36-5 **Avoid thunderstorms and cumulonimbus clouds**

Now complete **Exercises 36 – Windshear.**

Aircraft (Type) – Aeroplanes

Introduction

The basic principles of flight, of engines, of systems and of performance apply to all aeroplanes, but there are differences between one aeroplane type and another. It is a requirement that pilots be thoroughly familiar with the type of aeroplane that they are about to fly.

For this reason, applicants for a UK Private Pilot's Licence (aeroplanes) must demonstrate a sound knowledge of the specific aeroplane on which they have trained and which will be used during the flight test. This aeroplane will normally be a **Group A** aeroplane (a single-engined aeroplane of 5,700 kg or less).

The primary source of this specific knowledge is the CAA approved Flight Manual, which is associated with the aeroplane's certificate of airworthiness.

Applicants should also have an understanding of what maintenance pilots are permitted to perform on the aeroplane, and what responsibility they can take in signing off the duplicate inspection form for adjustments made to *flight controls* and/or *engine controls*. These items are discussed in Chapter 28 of this volume and in Chapter 12 of Aviation Law, Flight Rules and Procedures in Vol. 2 of this series. The primary source of the information is the Air Navigation Order (ANO) Article 10(3), the Air Navigation (General) Regulation (ANR) 16, and the British Civil Airworthiness Requirements (BCAR) Section A, Chapter 5-3.

Having learnt to fly one specific type of aeroplane, it is a relatively straightforward matter to be trained (or endorsed) onto another. Following an endorsement training programme, the pilot must display not only an ability to fly the aeroplane but also a sound knowledge of it, along the same lines as described in this Appendix.

The PPL(A) aircraft (type) examination will normally take the form of an oral test, (usually combined with the General Flight Test for the Private Pilot's Licence itself), and will be confined to the type of aeroplane in which you are being flight tested.

You should be prepared to answer questions similar to those asked here. Since each specific type of aeroplane may require a different answer to the questions asked below, no answers are provided here. You should research them in the primary reference documents mentioned above, and discuss them with your flying instructor.

The Flight Manual

1 The Flight Manual is for a (manufacturer's name and model) type of aeroplane.

2 This particular Flight Manual (has/does not have) a UK CAA supplement.

3 A CAA supplement (amends/does not amend) information contained in the original Flight Manual supplied by the manufacturer.

4 The Flight Manual (should/need not) remain with the particular aeroplane.

Weight and Balance Limitations

1 The maximum take-off weight is .... kg.

2 The maximum landing weight is .... kg.

3 The maximum passenger load (excluding the pilot) is ..... passengers.

4 The maximum number of persons on board (POB), including the pilot, is ....

5 The maximum baggage weight that can be carried is ..... kg.

6 The empty weight of the aeroplane is .... kg.

7 In which category (or categories) is the aeroplane permitted to fly?

8 Do these weight limitations vary if the aeroplane is certificated to fly not only in the normal category but also in another category, such as the utility category, semi-aerobatic category or aerobatic category? If so, what are their values?

9 Calculate the weight and balance situation (i.e. the gross weight and centre of gravity position), given certain requirements, e.g. a certain number of passengers, a given amount of fuel, a given amount of baggage, etc., using the aeroplane weight schedule found in the Flight Manual.

Airspeed Limitations

1 The normal operating airspeed range is marked on the airspeed indicator with a ..... arc.

2 The caution airspeed range is marked on the airspeed indicator with a ..... arc.

3 The flap operating airspeed range is marked on the airspeed indicator with a ..... arc.

4 V_{NE} is known as the ..... airspeed and its value is ..... kt. It is marked on the airspeed indicator as a ....

5 V_{NO} is known as the ..... airspeed and its value is ..... kt. It is marked on the airspeed indicator as a ....

6 V_A is known as the ..... airspeed and its value is ..... kt. It (is/is not) marked on the airspeed indicator.

7 V_{RA}, if specified, is known as the ..... airspeed and its value is ..... kt. It (is/is not) marked on the airspeed indicator.

8 V_S is known as the ..... speed wings level and flaps up, and its value is ..... kt. It (is/is not) marked on the airspeed indicator as the (high/low) speed end of the ..... arc.

9 V_{FE} is known as the ..... airspeed and its value is ..... kt. It (is/is not) marked on the airspeed indicator as the (high/low) speed end of the ..... arc.

10 The stalling speed with full flap extended and the wings level is ..... kt.

11 The published stalling speeds are for when the aeroplane (is/is not) at maximum gross weight.

12 Stalling speed (increases/decreases/does not change) if the aeroplane is at less than maximum weight.

13 Stalling speed (increases/decreases/does not change) if the aeroplane is banked.

14 Stalling speed (increases/decreases/does not change) if the aeroplane is manoeuvring, for instance when pulling out of a dive.

15 In a 30° banked turn, the stalling speed will increase by .....%.

16 In a 60° banked turn, the stalling speed will increase by .....%.

17 The maximum airspeed at which you may use abrupt and full elevator travel is ..... kt.

Aerodynamic Load Limitations

1 Maximum load factor (flaps up) is +..... g and -..... g.

2 Maximum load factor (flaps extended) is +..... g and -..... g.

3 Are there any other handling limitations if, for instance, the aeroplane has a full complement of passengers, maximum baggage, maximum fuel load, etc?

4 What precautions should be observed if recovering from a steep dive?

5 What precautions should be observed if recovering from a steep turn?

Authorised Operations

1 The aeroplane (is/is not) certificated to fly during the day.

2 The aeroplane (is/is not) certificated to fly at night.

3 The aeroplane (is/is not) certificated to fly under the Visual Flight Rules (VFR).

4 The aeroplane (is/is not) certificated to fly under the Instrument Flight Rules (IFR).

5 The aeroplane (is/is not) certificated to fly in icing conditions.

Take-off Performance Limitations

1 The maximum structural take-off weight is ..... kg.

2 Be able to use the take-off chart(s) in the Flight Manual to calculate the performance figures (performance-limited take-off weight, or runway length required) given a specific situation.

3 The runway length required, under ISA MSL conditions, for a take-off at maximum weight is..... metres.

4 Compared to a take-off at a sea level aerodrome, the take-off at a high-elevation aerodrome will require (the same/more/less) runway length.

5 Compared to a take-off at ISA temperature, the take-off at a higher temperature will require (the same/more/less) runway length.

Landing Performance Limitations

1 The maximum structural landing weight is..... kg.

2 Be able to use the landing charts(s) in the Flight Manual to calculate the performance figures (performance-limited landing weight, or runway length required) given a specific situation.

3 The runway length required, under ISA MSL conditions, for a landing at maximum weight is ..... metres.

4 Compared to a landing at a sea-level aerodrome, landing at a high-elevation aerodrome will require (the same/more/less) runway length.

5 Compared to a landing at ISA temperature, landing at a higher temperature will require (the same/more/less) runway length.

Range Flying

1 Be able to use any tables or graphs in the Flight Manual to calculate range, i.e. the distance that the aeroplane can fly under given conditions.

Endurance Flying

1 Be able to use any tables or graphs in the Flight Manual to calculate endurance, i.e. the time that the aeroplane can remain airborne under given conditions.

Flying Controls

1 Understand how the elevator (or stabilator) system works: e.g. moving the control column back will cause the nose of the aeroplane to (rise/drop) as a result of the elevator moving (up/down).

2 Understand how the aileron system works: e.g. moving the control column to the left will cause the aeroplane, at normal flying speeds, to roll towards the (left/right) by moving the left aileron ..... and the right aileron ....

3 Understand how the rudder system works:
   (a) Moving the left rudder pedal in will cause the right rudder pedal to move ....
   (b) Moving the left rudder pedal in will cause the nose of the aeroplane to yaw (left/right), as a result of the trailing edge of the rudder moving (left/right).
   (c) The main function of the rudder in normal flight is to (balance/yaw) the aeroplane.
   (d) There (is/is not) an interconnection between the rudder and the aileron systems.

4 Understand how the trim system works:
   (a) Is there an elevator trim?
   (b) Is there a rudder trim?
   (c) Is there an aileron trim?
   (d) The elevator trim is a (servo/balance/anti-servo) type.
   (e) The main function of a trimming device is to (relieve steady pressures/manoeuvre the aeroplane).

5 Understand how the flap system works:
   (a) The flap system is (mechanical/electric/hydraulic).
   (b) The flaps are operated with a (switch/lever).
   (c) The flap indicating system is (mechanical/electric).
   (d) The flap range is from 0° to .....°.

6 The aeroplane (has/does not have) a stall warning device.

7 The stall warning device, if fitted, (is/is not) interconnected with the flap system.

The Propeller

1 The propeller is a (fixed-pitch/constant-speed unit) propeller.

2 Will nicks, mud, insects or other contamination affect the performance of the propeller?

3 Should new nicks or damage to the propeller be referred to an engineer if possible prior to flight?

4 Most training aeroplanes used for initial PPL instruction have a fixed-pitch propeller, but if yours has a variable-pitch propeller controlled by a constant-speed unit (CSU), then you should know how it works, how to control the rpm/manifold pressure with the pitch lever and the throttle, and the rpm/MAP limits.

Landing Gear and Brakes

1 The aeroplane is fitted with a (tricycle/tailwheel) type undercarriage.

2 The aeroplane (has/does not have) nosewheel steering.

3 The rudder and the nosewheel steering (are/are not) interconnected.

4 The rudder pedals (can/cannot) be used to provide directional control when taxiing on the ground

5 The undercarriage (is/is not) retractable.

6 Shocks on the nosewheel during taxiing, take-off and landing are absorbed by a (leaf spring/bungee/oleo-pneumatic strut).

7 Shocks on the main wheels during taxiing, take-off and landing are absorbed by (leaf springs/bungees/oleo-pneumatic struts).

8 The brakes are fitted to the (main wheels/nosewheel).

9 The brakes are operated from the cockpit using ..... .

10 The wheel brakes are operated (mechanically/hydraulically).

11 The wheel brakes are (disc/drum) type.

12 Normal tyre pressure is ..... .

13 Know what defects in the tyres are acceptable or unacceptable for flight, e.g. cuts, wear, bald spots, etc.

The Electrical System

1 The DC electrical system operates at (12/24) volts.

2 The battery is located ..... .

3 Once the engine is running, electrical power is supplied by (an alternator/a generator).

4 A serviceable battery (is/is not) required for the alternator (if fitted) to come on-line.

5 If a battery is almost flat, a high charging rate following start-up (may/will not) cause 'boiling' within the battery.

6 Understand how to manage the electrical system, e.g. the indications and actions to take if the alternator (or generator) system fails or malfunctions.

7 If the alternator (or generator) fails in flight, then as much electrical load as possible (should/need not) be shed by switching non-essential services off.

8 A fully-charged battery should supply emergency power for a period of ..... if required.

9 Know the function and location of circuit breakers and fuses, and what to do if they 'pop' or fail, as applicable.

10 Is it possible to use external power to operate the electrical system whilst the aeroplane is parked and, if so, what is the procedure for connecting it?

11 The stall warning device, if fitted, operates (electrically/mechanically).

Flight Instruments

1 Name the flight instruments operated by the pitot-static system and state whether they use pitot pressure, static pressure or both.

2 Know the position of the pitot tube(s) and static vent(s), and any associated drains to eliminate water from the lines.

3 Is there electric-powered pitot-heat to prevent ice forming on the pitot head and causing incorrect instrument indications?

4 Is there an alternate static source and, if so, where is it located? What is its purpose and what effect does it have on the instrument indications if the static source is changed by the pilot from normal to the alternate?

5 Name the gyroscopic flight instruments.

6 Name the flight instruments that are operated electrically.

7 Name the flight instruments that are operated by the vacuum system, if fitted, and know how the vacuum system works (venturi or vacuum pump) and the maximum/minimum suction required for correct operation.

8 The airspeed indicator is operated by ....

9 The attitude indicator (artificial horizon) is operated by ....

10 The altimeter is operated by ....

11 The vertical speed indicator is operated by ....

12 The heading indicator is operated by ....

13 The turn coordinator (or turn indicator) is operated by ....

14 The flap indicator is operated by ....

15 The magnetic compass is operated by ....

16 The clock is operated by ....

Fuel

1 The correct grade of fuel is ..... , which is coloured ....

2 Fuel fittings for Avgas (which is used in piston engines) are usually coloured ....., whereas fuel fittings for Avtur (which is used in turbine engines) are usually coloured ....

3 How many fuel tanks does the aeroplane have, where are they located, and what is their capacity in terms of usable fuel?

4 How can the aeroplane be refuelled? Where are the filler caps and what precautions need to be taken?

5 Is it advisable to fill the fuel tanks prior to parking the aeroplane overnight?

6 Where are the fuel drains located and why are they used? When should fuel be drained?

7 Where are the fuel tank vents located and why are they important?

8 How can fuel quantity be measured, both on the ground and in flight?

9 Does the engine have a carburettor or a fuel injection system? How does it work?

10 Does the engine require priming prior to start-up and, if so, how is it done?

11 Does the aeroplane have fuel pumps and, if so, where are they located, what is their function, are they electrical or engine-driven, what are their maximum and minimum acceptable operating pressures, and when should they be used?

12 Know the correct fuel management procedure, such as which tank(s) to use for take-off and landing, when to use fuel pumps if fitted, when and how to switch tanks, etc.

Oil

1 The correct grade of oil is ....

2 The oil is stored in a tank or sump which is located ....

3 Explain how the oil quantity can be measured.

4 Minimum acceptable oil quantity prior to flight is ....

5 The maximum quantity of oil is ....

6 The oil is used to (lubricate/cool/both lubricate and cool) the engine.

The Engine

1 The engine has ..... cylinders, which are arranged (in line/horizontally opposed/.....).

2 The engine is (air-cooled/water-cooled).

3 Cooling of the engine can be increased by opening cowl flaps. (Yes/No).

4 The cockpit gauges used to monitor engine operation are ..... , ... , ... , ...

5 Maximum engine rpm is ....

6 Normal engine rpm is ....

7 Engine rpm is controlled with the ....

8 Maximum oil pressure is ....

9 Minimum oil pressure is ....

10 Normal oil pressure is approximately ....

11 Maximum oil temperature is ....

12 Minimum oil temperature is ....

13 Normal oil temperature is approximately ....

14 The aeroplane (is/is not) fitted with a cylinder head temperature gauge and, if so, the CHT limits are ....

15 During ground operations of the engine, it is usual to perform a magneto check, which should be done according to procedures specified by your training organisation.

(a) Specify the maximum acceptable rpm drop when one magneto is switched to OFF, the maximum difference between magnetos, and (if permitted) the significance of the 'dead-cut' check during which both magnetos are switched to OFF briefly.

(b) What is the probable cause if the engine keeps running even though the magneto switch has been placed to OFF?

16 Specify the action to be taken if an engine fire occurs in flight.

17 Specify the action to be taken if an engine fire occurs on the ground.

18 What services are no longer available if the engine fails in flight?

19 What instruments are rendered inoperative if the engine fails in flight?

20 Moving the throttle in will ....

21 Moving the throttle out will ....

22 Explain the functioning of the mixture control and how to operate it correctly. If an exhaust gas temperature gauge (EGT) is fitted, explain how it may be of use.

23 Under what condition is it permissible to lean the mixture?

24 To lean the mixture, the mixture control should be moved (in/out).

25 To richen the mixture, the mixture control should be moved (in/out).

26 Explain how to lean the mixture to obtain maximum power.

27 Explain how to lean the mixture to obtain maximum economy.

28 The fully-out position of the mixture control is called .... position and is used to (stop/start) the engine.

29 What are the indications if ice forms in the carburettor?

30 How do you melt carburettor ice and prevent it forming again?

31 What effect does applying carburettor heat have on the mixture, i.e. does it lean, richen or not alter the mixture?

32 Does the hot air used to eliminate carburettor ice pass through a filter or not?

33 Why should you not use carburettor heat when taxiing if it is not absolutely necessary?

Ventilation and Heating

1 Know how to ventilate the cockpit adequately.

2 Know how to heat the cockpit adequately.

3 Know how the heating system works and where the heated air comes from, e.g. from exhaust muffs which allow air to circulate near the very hot exhaust system, thereby raising its temperature, before being channelled into the cabin.

4 The engine exhaust contains a poisonous gas (carbon dioxide/carbon monoxide), which is colourless and odourless and should be excluded from the cockpit.

5 The presence of carbon monoxide in the cabin (may/will not) give pilots a sense of well-being, even though it causes their performance to deteriorate and (may/will not) lead to unconsciousness.

6 What precautions would you take if you suspect the presence of carbon monoxide in the cabin?

7 What action would you take in the event of a fire occurring in the cabin?

The Air Pilot's **Manual**

Volume 4

Exercises and Answers

Principles of Flight

Exercises 1

The Forces Acting on an Aeroplane

1 The downwards force of attraction between the aeroplane and the earth is called the w...... .

2 The force produced by the wings which supports the aeroplane in flight is called the l... .

3 The force produced by the engine–propeller is called the t...... .

4 The force that resists the motion of the aeroplane through the air is called the d... .

5 In straight and level cruising flight the aeroplane is in equilibrium, with the weight balanced by the ...., and the drag balanced by the ....

6 The lift force is generally much (greater/smaller) than the drag force in flight.

Exercises 2

Weight

1 The weight of an aeroplane can be considered as a single force acting through the c..... of g...... .

2 Define the term 'wing loading'.

3 An aeroplane weighs 3,000 lb and has a wing area of 200 square feet. What is its wing loading?

Exercises 3

Aerofoil Lift

1 Airflow past an aerofoil such as the wing of an aeroplane can produce a l... force.

2 The most important airflow is that nearest the surface of the aerofoil and which is called the b....... l..... .

3 A steady flow of molecules around the aerofoil where succeeding molecules follow each other is called s......... flow.

4 A disturbed flow with eddying is called t........ flow.

5 Daniel B........ showed that in a streamline flow the total energy remains constant.

6 Static pressure in the air is exerted (in all directions/down/up).

7 Dynamic pressure is the pressure (due to motion/due to no motion).

8 Bernoulli's principle describes the natural effect that 'in a streamline flow, the total pressure energy remains c.......' .

9 Total pressure energy = s..... pressure + d...... pressure.

10 In streamline flow, if dynamic pressure increases then, for the total pressure energy to remain constant, the static pressure will ....

11 If the relative velocity between the airflow and the aerofoil increases, then the dynamic pressure, which is due to motion, will (decrease/increase).

12 If velocity increases, then dynamic pressure increases. For the total pressure to remain the same, the static pressure will ....

13 If velocity increases, static pressure ....

14 Increasing the curvature of the upper surface of the wing causes the airflow over it to (speed up/slow down).

15 If the velocity over the upper surface of the wing increases, then the static pressure will ....

16 Curvature of the wing surfaces is called c...... .

17 The line drawn half-way between the upper and lower surfaces of the wing, which gives an indication of its curvature, is called the m... c..... l... .

18 The straight line joining the leading edge and the trailing edge of an aerofoil section is called the c.... l... .

19 The length of the straight line joining the leading edge and the trailing edge is the c.... .

20 The greatest distance between the upper and lower surfaces of the wing is called the t........ .

21 As the airflow accelerates across the upper surface of a well-cambered wing, the static pressure (increases/decreases).

22 In normal flight, the static pressure over the top surface of a well-cambered wing is (less than/greater than/the same as) the static pressure beneath the wing.

23 The difference between the static pressure above and below the wing generates a l... force.

24 As well as the lift force being generated by the aerofoil, it also generates a force opposing the relative motion of the aerofoil through the air – and this force opposing motion is called ..... .

25 The total force produced by an aerofoil is called the t.... r......., which can be resolved into two components: l... and d... .

26 The angle between the chord line of an aerofoil and the direction of the relative airflow well ahead of the aerofoil is called the a.... of a...... .

27 Even at zero degrees angle of attack, a wing with a well-cambered upper surface will cause the airflow to accelerate across it. The increase in velocity will cause a (decrease/increase) in static pressure over the upper surface, resulting in the generation of a l... force.

28 If the angle of attack is increased gradually, the lifting ability of the wing (increases/decreases).

29 At a critical angle of attack known as the stalling angle, the streamline airflow breaks down and becomes turbulent and the lifting ability of the wing (increases/remains good/decreases).

30 The forces acting on an aerofoil in-flight as a result of the changes in static pressure around it, may be considered to act through a point known as the c..... of p....... .

31 As the angle of attack is gradually increased in the normal flight range, the lifting ability of the wing increases and the centre of pressure (moves forwards/stays in the same place/moves rearwards) on the wing.

32 Beyond the stalling angle of attack (the critical angle when the streamline airflow breaks down and becomes turbulent), the lifting ability of the wing decreases markedly and the CP (moves forwards/moves rearwards/remains stationary) on the wing.

33 Name five items that the lift force generated by an aerofoil depends on: w... shape, a.... of a....., air d...... (rho), v....... of the airflow, w... area.

34 The wing shape and the angle of attack determine the profile that the aerofoil presents to the airflow and determines the lifting a...... of the wing.

35 The 'lifting ability' of the wing is given the technical name 'c.......... of l...' .

36 The velocity of the airflow and the air density (rho) are combined in the one expression ½ rho V-squared which is called the d...... p....... .

37 Write down the formula that neatly describes the lift force that a wing can produce.

38 The C_{Lift} of an aerofoil is determined by the wing shape and the angle of attack. The designer fixes the wing shape, but the pilot can change the ..... of a...... .

39 As the pilot increases the angle of attack by backwards pressure on the control column, the lifting ability (coefficient of lift) of the wing gradually (increases/decreases) until the critical angle of attack (the stalling angle) is reached.

40 If the pilot increases the angle of attack so that the lifting ability (C_{Lift}) of the wing is increased, the same lift force can be generated by the wing at a (higher/lower) velocity.

41 The airflow around a well-cambered wing at zero angle of attack will still have to accelerate over the upper surface. Increased velocity = decreased static pressure, so there (will/will not) be some lift produced.

42 A symmetrical aerofoil (upper and lower surfaces are the same shape) at zero angle of attack will have similar airflows over both upper and lower surfaces. Therefore at zero angle of attack, the lift generated by a symmetrical aerofoil will be (positive/zero/negative).

43 A symmetrical aerofoil moving through the air at zero degrees angle of attack:
  (a) will generate a low static pressure above the wing and a high static pressure beneath the wing.
  (b) will produce a high pressure above the wing and a low pressure beneath the wing.
  (c) will cause a similar acceleration of the airflow over both upper and lower surfaces, similar velocities of flow generating similar pressures and therefore no lift.
  (d) will cause the air over the upper surface to travel faster than the air over the lower surface.

44 As the angle of attack of a symmetrical aerofoil is gradually increased from zero, the lifting ability (increases/decreases/stays the same).

45 Lift acts at ....° to the remote relative airflow.

46 The coefficient of lift depends upon the shape of the wing chosen by the designer and the a.... of a....., which the pilot has control over.

47 In normal flight, as the angle of attack is increased, the lifting ability of the wing known as its coefficient of lift (increases/decreases).

48 The lift generated by an aerofoil is:
  (a) proportional to the square of the velocity of the relative airflow.
  (b) proportional to the velocity of the relative airflow.
  (c) inversely proportional to the air density.
  (d) inversely proportional to the wing surface area.

Exercises 4

Drag

1 Drag (opposes/encourages) motion through the air.

2 Drag acts (parallel to/at 90° to) the relative airflow.

3 The force used to overcome the drag in straight and level cruising flight is the t..... produced by the engine–propeller combination.

4 If drag can be kept low, then t..... can be kept low.

5 Total drag is the sum total of the various drag forces acting on the aeroplane which act (parallel to/perpendicular to) and (in the same direction as/opposite to) the direction of flight.

6 Total drag is considered in two basic groups:
   (a) Drag which comes about in the generation of lift, known as i...... drag; and
   (b) Drag which is not associated with the generation of lift, known as p....... drag.

7 Parasite drag consists of s... f......., f... d... and inter....... drag.

8 Flush riveting and polishing the surface of an aeroplane reduce ....

9 Roughness on a surface, such as an accumulation of insects or ice-accretion, will increase s... f....... .

10 As airspeed increases, drag due to skin friction (increases/decreases).

11 Form drag occurs when the airflow actually sep...... from the surface of the aerofoil and becomes turb..... .

12 To reduce form drag, separation of the boundary layer airflow from the wing surface should be (delayed/encouraged).

13 Streamlining of shapes reduces ....

14 The additional turbulence caused by interference between various airflows around the aeroplane is called inter....... d... .

15 As the aeroplane flies faster, parasite drag (increases/decreases).

16 The drag produced as a by-product in the generation of lift is called i...... d... .

17 For a wing to produce an upwards lift, the static pressure on the upper surface must be (higher/lower) than on the lower surface.

18 Air flows around the wingtips from the higher pressure area on the (upper/lower) surface of the wing into the area of lower pressure. This forms wingtip v....... .

19 The spanwise flow of air on the lower surface of the wing is (outwards to the wingtip/inwards to the wing root).

20 The spanwise flow of air on the upper wing surface is (outwards towards the tip/inwards towards the root).

21 As well as the strong wingtip vortices, where the two airflows from the upper and lower surfaces of the wing meet behind the wing, because of their different spanwise flows, they form a sheet of trailing edge v....... .

22 The pressure difference between the upper and lower surfaces of the wing is greatest at (high/low) angles of attack.

23 Therefore, the formation of wingtip vortices and induced drag is greatest at (high/low) angles of attack.

24 High angles of attack are associated with (high/low) speeds in straight and level flight.

25 Therefore, induced drag is greatest at high angles of attack and (high/low) airspeeds in straight and level flight.

26 Vortices that are generated at the wingtips:
   (a) cause much of the drag at low speed;
   (b) cause much of the drag at high speed;
   (c) cause a decrease in drag.

27 The designer can help minimise the formation of wingtip vortices and induced drag by using wings of (high/low) aspect ratio, w...out or wingtip modification.

28 A high aspect ratio wing has a (short/long) span and a (short/long) chord.

29 A wing with washout has a lower angle of attack at the (wingtip/wing root).

30 Induced drag increases at (high/low) speeds.

31 Parasite drag increases at (high/low) speeds.

32 The total drag is at a minimum at (high speed/low speed/at a speed where the parasite drag and induced drag are equal).

33 At the minimum total drag speed, the propeller has only to provide minimum t...... .

34 At low speeds and high angles of attack, because of the greater .... drag, the thrust must be (greater/less).

35 At high speeds and low angles of attack, because of the greater .... drag, the thrust requirement is (greater/less).

36 To maintain a steady speed straight and level, the thrust required is:

(a) the same at all speeds.

(b) greatest at normal cruise speed.

(c) greater at a speed just above the stall than at cruise speed.

37 At high angles of attack and low air-speeds:

(a) the induced coefficient of drag is high.

(b) the induced coefficient of drag is low.

(c) the parasite coefficient of drag is high.

(d) all of the above are incorrect.

Exercises 5

Lift/Drag Ratio

1 If you require 1,200 units of lift to support the aeroplane, and the drag is 100 units, then the L/D ratio is (10:1/12:1/120:1/5:1).

2 At high angles of attack, the drag is high due to i...... d.... . For 1,200 units of lift, the cost might be 240 units of drag. The L/D ratio is .... .

3 At low angles of attack and high speeds, the total drag is high due to p....... drag. if the required 1,200 units of lift is generated at a cost of 200 units, the L/D ratio is ..... .

4 If at say 4° angle of attack, where the total drag is a minimum for the particular aerofoil we are considering, the 1,200 units of lift is obtained for a cost of only 80 units drag, then the L/D ratio is ..... .

5 The angle of attack that gives the best L/D ratio is the (most/least) efficient angle of attack.

6 If you fly at the airspeed obtained at the best L/D ratio, then the required lift is obtained for the (minimum/maximum) drag.

7 Minimum drag means (minimum/maximum) thrust to maintain airspeed.

8 The term *lift/drag ratio:*

(a) can be used to describe the aerodynamic efficiency of the wing.

(b) is the ratio of the lift produced from an aerofoil compared to the drag produced from the aerofoil.

(c) varies as the angle of attack of the aerofoil changes.

(d) all the above statements are correct.

Exercises 6

Thrust from the Propeller

1 A propeller converts engine torque into t...... .

2 A propeller is similar to a wing in that it is an aero..... .

3 The angle that the propeller blade makes with the plane of its rotation is called the b.... a..... .

4 To ensure that it operates at an efficient angle of attack over its full length, the propeller blade is (twisted/straight).

5 The blade angle is greatest near the (hub/tip).

6 The fastest moving part of the propeller blade is near the (hub/tip).

7 The fastest moving part of the aeroplane is the p........ t.. .

8 The total reaction aerodynamic force on a wing is resolved into two components: lift and drag. The total reaction on the propeller blade is resolved into two components: t..... and engine torque.

9 A fixed-pitch propeller is efficient at only one set of r.. and air..... conditions.

10 For operating at high rpm and low forward airspeeds, the most efficient propeller would have a (fine/coarse) pitch.

11 For operating at very high airspeeds and low rpm, the most efficient propeller would have a (fine/coarse) pitch.

12 A variable-pitch propeller (constant-speed unit) is efficient over a wide range of pow.. and airspeed conditions.

13 The slipstream effect from the propeller can cause the nose to y...This is because the slipstream hits one side of the r..... more than the other.

14 When power is applied in an aeroplane fitted with a propeller that turns clockwise when viewed from behind, the aeroplane will tend to roll to the (left/right) and yaw to the (left/right).

15 As the forward speed of an aeroplane with a fixed-pitch propeller increases, what happens to the angle of attack of the propeller blades if the rpm remains constant:

(a) angle of attack decreases as forward speed increases.

(b) angle of attack increases as forward speed increases.

(c) angle of attack remains unaltered as forward speed increases.

(d) none of these.

16 If the airspeed of an aeroplane fitted with a fixed-pitch propeller is increased at constant power (say by entering a dive), the rpm will:

(a) remain constant.

(b) increase.

(c) decrease.

Exercises 7

Stability

1 If the centre of pressure is aft of the centre of gravity, then the lift–weight couple will have a (nose-down/nose-up) pitching moment. Draw this.

2 If the thrust line is lower than the drag line, then the thrust–drag couple will have a (nose-up/nose-down) pitching moment. Draw this.

3 In the above situation (questions 1 and 2), if there was a sudden loss of thrust from the engine–propeller, the nose would (pitch up/pitch down/neither).

4 If the L–W and T–D couples do not balance each other out, then there is a resultant pitching moment that will raise or lower the nose of the aircraft. A small balancing force with a long moment arm is provided by the t........ or the h......... s......... .

5 For an aeroplane to be in equilibrium in level flight:

(a) Lift exceeds weight, and thrust equals drag.

(b) Lift equals weight, and thrust equals drag.

(c) Lift equals drag, and thrust exceeds weight.

(d) Lift, drag, thrust and weight are all equal.

6 If, as is usual, the thrust line is not aligned with the drag line, then any power change (will/will not) cause a tendency for the nose to pitch.

7 Stability is the natural ability of the aeroplane to return to its original condition after a disturbance like a gust (with/without) any action being taken by the pilot.

8 The axis that runs along the aeroplane from nose to tail is called the l........... axis, and rotation about this axis is called r....... .

9 The axis that runs 'across-ship' is called the .... axis, and rotation about this axis is called ....

10 The axis that is perpendicular or normal to the longitudinal and lateral axes is called the ...... axis, and rotation about it is called ....

11 The most important factor contributing to longitudinal stability is the t........ .

12 The restoring moment arm of the tail-plane is greatest when the centre of gravity is (well forward/somewhat aft).

13 Therefore, longitudinal stability is greater with a (forward/aft) CG.

14 In most training aeroplanes, the centre of pressure is (ahead of/behind/at the same position as) the centre of gravity and the tailplane produces (an upward/zero/a downward) force.

15 If the aeroplane is loaded incorrectly so that the CG is forward of the allowable range, then the elevator force required to flare the aeroplane for landing will be:
 (a) the same as usual.
 (b) greater than usual.
 (c) less than usual.

16 Directional stability is improved with a (large/small) fin or v....... stabiliser.

17 Lateral stability is increased if a wing has di....... .

18 A high-wing aircraft is laterally stable with a high CP and a (high/low) CG.

19 If an aircraft is displaced in roll by a gust, i.e. a wing drops, the aircraft will start to s...s.... . The high keel surfaces, like the fin, will cause the nose to y.. .

20 If an aircraft is yawed, then it will sideslip and the dihedral will cause it to r.... .

21 R... and y.. are closely inter-related.

22 On the ground, the CG for a tricycle undercarriage aircraft (i.e. nose-wheel) must be (forward/aft) of the main wheels.

23 On the ground, the CG of a 'taildragger' must be (forward, aft) of the main wheels.

24 When taxiing fast and the brakes are applied heavily, a tailwheel aircraft (is/is not) more directionally stable than a nosewheel aircraft.

Exercises 8

Control

1 The primary control in pitch is provided by the ....

2 Nose movement up and down is in the pitching plane. It involves angular movement of the aeroplane around its centre of gravity and its (lateral/longitudinal/normal) axis.

3 To raise the nose, the pilot exerts backwards pressure on the control column. The elevators move so that the tail of the aeroplane goes (up/down).

4 To raise the nose and lower the tail of the aeroplane, the trailing edge of the elevator moves (up/down).

5 A stabilator is:
 (a) a balancing weight.
 (b) a vertical fin.
 (c) a fixed-tailplane and movable elevator.
 (d) a movable horizontal stabiliser.

6 When the pilot moves the control column aft to raise the nose of the aeroplane, the leading edge of a stabilator will (rise/fall/remain stationary).

7 The primary control in roll is by the a........ .

8 Rolling is angular motion about the .... axis running through the CG.

9 For the right wing to rise, the pilot moves the control column to the ..... .

10 At normal flight speeds for the right wing to rise, the right aileron will (go down/rise).

11 For the right wing to rise, the right aileron goes down. The left aileron goes (up/down).

12 The area below the wing has (higher/lower) static pressure than the area above the wing.

13 The aileron going down (i.e. on the rising wing) goes into an area of (higher/lower) pressure and will experience (more/less) drag than the other aileron.

14 As an aeroplane is banking to the left for a left turn, the extra drag on the right aileron will tend to yaw the nose (in the direction of/away from) the turn.

15 The aileron drag that yaws the nose away from a turn as an aeroplane is banking is called a...... a...... y.. .

16 Aileron drag or adverse aileron yaw can be designed out of the aeroplane by the use of d.......... a....... or by F....-type ailerons.

17 If differential ailerons are used to counteract the effect of adverse aileron yaw, one aileron will rise by an amount (greater than/less than/the same as) the other aileron is lowered.

18 If differential ailerons are used to counteract the effect of adverse aileron yaw then, compared to the aileron on the down-going wing, the aileron on the up-going wing will be (raised/lowered) to a (greater/lesser/similar) extent.

19 The primary control in yaw is provided by the ....

20 Yawing is about the ...... axis that passes through the CG.

21 Yawing increases the speed of the outer wing, causing its lift to (increase/decrease), leading to a r... .

22 Yaw also generates a sideslip, and the dihedral on the more forward wing will cause it to (rise/fall).

23 A yaw leads to a r... .

24 Movement of the flight control surfaces is:
(a) limited by air loads.
(b) limited by mechanical stops.
(c) not limited.

25 Increased airflow over control surfaces (increases/decreases) their effectiveness.

26 At high airspeeds the control surfaces are (more/less) effective than at low airspeeds.

27 Slipstream from the propeller over the rudder and elevators (increases/decreases) their effectiveness.

28 At low speeds near the stalling angle, high thrust from the propeller sends a slipstream over the (elevator/rudder/ailerons).

29 An aeroplane designer may use *aerodynamic balance,* such as the balance tab, horn balance or inset hinge, to reduce the control pressures required of a pilot. (True/False)?

30 Aerodynamic balance designed to assist a pilot in deflecting a flight control surface may be:

   (a) a trim tab.

   (b) an anti-balance tab.

   (c) a mass placed forward of the hinge line.

   (d) a balance tab or some part of the surface placed ahead of the hinge line.

31 If a pilot is exerting a steady backwards pressure on the control column, then he can remove this steady load by using the elevator t... t.., which may be controlled by a small wheel in the cockpit known as the t... wh... .

32 The pressure that a pilot feels through the controls is determined by the hinge moment of the control surface. The pressure distribution around the control surface can be altered to reduce the hinge moment by the use of t... t... .

33 Trim tabs are very effective. A small movement of a trim tab can have a (large/small) effect because of its moment arm to the control hinge.

34 Once a simple elevator trim tab has been set by the pilot to remove any steady pressure on the control column, the tab position (will/will not) remain fixed relative to the elevator when the pilot moves the control column fore and aft.

35 The correct method of using an elevator trim in an aircraft is to:

   (a) change the attitude with the elevator and/or the power with the throttle, allow the aeroplane to settle down, and then use the trim to remove steady control column pressure.

   (b) change the attitude with the trim.

   (c) change attitude, power and trim simultaneously.

36 Ailerons on some light aircraft have a fixed trim tab in the form of a metal strip that (may/must not) be adjusted on the ground following a test flight so that (lateral/longitudinal) level flight is more easily achieved.

37 An anti-balance tab may be designed into a flight control surface to:

   (a) provide 'feel' to the pilot and prevent excessive control movements.

   (b) prevent control surface flutter.

   (c) reduce the balancing moment required from the tailplane.

   (d) aerodynamically assist the pilot in moving the flight control surface.

38 If the stabilator is moved in the pre-flight external inspection, then the anti-balance tab should:

   (a) move in the same direction.

   (b) move in the opposite direction.

   (c) not move.

39 If the elevator is moved in the pre-flight external inspection, then the balance tab should:

   (a) move in the same direction.

   (b) move in the opposite direction.

   (c) not move.

40 A mass balance is used to:

   (a) stop flutter of the control surface when the aeroplane is parked.

   (b) prevent control surface flutter in flight.

   (c) keep the control surface flared in flight.

   (d) relieve control pressures on the pilot.

Exercises 9

Flaps

1 Flaps can (increase/decrease) the lifting capability, or C_{Lift}, of a wing.

2 If flaps increase the lifting ability of a wing, then the required lift can be generated at a (higher/lower) airspeed.

3 The extension of flap (lowers/raises) the stalling speed.

4 The approach speed with flap extended may be (lower/higher) than the approach speed for a flapless landing.

5 Trailing edge flaps not only increase lift – flaps also increase d... .

6 In the early stages of their extension, such as at the take-off flap settings, the flaps may be thought of as l... flaps. At their full extension, such as on approach to land, they may be thought of as d... flaps.

7 The percentage increase in drag usually exceeds that in lift when the flaps are extended, therefore the lift/drag ratio is (less/more).

8 The extension of flaps on a glide approach allows a (steeper/flatter) approach flightpath or approach angle.

9 With flaps extended, the nose attitude of the aeroplane is (lower/higher).

10 Cruising with flaps extended may be achieved at a (higher/lower) airspeed than when clean.

11 Cruising with flap extended, such as in a low speed precautionary search to inspect a possible landing field, allows the pilot (better/worse) visibility of the ground because of the (higher/lower) nose attitude.

12 Extending the flaps to an appropriate take-off setting (shortens/lengthens) the ground run.

13 Extending full flap for landing allows for (faster/slower) approach speeds and a (longer/shorter) landing run.

14 Wing flaps at the recommended take-off setting:
- (a) increase lifting ability for a small penalty in drag.
- (b) increase lifting ability for a large penalty in drag.
- (c) significantly increase drag for a small decrease in lifting ability.
- (d) will not affect lift or drag.

15 Wing flaps set to the recommended landing setting:
- (a) increase lifting ability for a small increase in drag.
- (b) cause a large drag increase and a small increase in lifting ability.
- (c) significantly increase drag for a small decrease in lifting ability.
- (d) will not affect lift or drag.

16 Extending the wing flaps will (increase/decrease/not alter) the stalling speed.

17 Slats installed on the leading edge of a wing will (delay/promote/prevent/not affect) the stall.

18 Slots increase the angle of attack at which a wing stalls by delaying the separation and break up of the smooth airflow over the upper surface of the wing. (True/False)?

Exercises 10

Straight and Level

1 In steady straight and level flight, the aeroplane (is/is not) in equilibrium.

2 In steady straight and level flight, the four main forces acting on the aeroplane are ...., ..., ... and ....

3 In steady straight and level flight, the lift force is (equal/not equal) to the weight.

4 In steady straight and level flight, the thrust from the engine–propeller is (equal/not equal) to the drag.

5 The four main forces acting on an aeroplane in flight are balanced by an aerodynamic force generated by the:
   (a) propeller.
   (b) horizontal stabiliser.
   (c) flaps.
   (d) fin.

6 Write down the formula that makes it easy for us to remember the important factors influencing the production of lift by an aerofoil.

7 If V represents the true airspeed, then $\frac{1}{2}$ *rho* *V-squared* represents the i........ a..s..... .

8 The coefficient of lift (C_{Lift}) represents the shape of the aerofoil and the a.... of a...... .

9 The lift produced by a wing can be altered by the pilot changing the a.... of a..... or by changing the i........ a..s..... . If you want the lift generated to remain the same, then as one increases, the other must be made to (decrease/increase).

10 If indicated airspeed is increased, then for the same lift to be generated in straight and level flight, the angle of attack must be (increased/reduced).

11 If indicated airspeed is decreased, then for the aeroplane to remain in straight and level flight, the angle of attack must be (increased/reduced).

12 Low indicated airspeeds are associated with (high/low) angles of attack.

13 High indicated airspeeds are associated with (low/high) angles of attack.

14 Straight and level flight at a high speed is associated with a (high/low) nose attitude.

15 Straight and level flight at a low airspeed is associated with a (high/low) nose attitude.

16 In steady straight and level flight, the weight is balanced by the ..... .

17 If the weight decreases, then, for straight and level flight to continue, the lift must ....

18 The lift generated can be decreased by flying at the same angle of attack but a (higher/lower) indicated airspeed.

19 The lift generated can be lowered by flying at the same airspeed, but a (higher/lower) angle of attack.

20 In steady straight and level flight, the drag is balanced by the t..... .

21 For steady straight and level flight to be maintained, a large drag needs to be balanced by a large ....

22 At very high speed for your aircraft (say well in excess of the normal cruise speed), the drag is (high/low).

23 At very low speeds (say just above the stalling speed), the drag is also very (high/low).

24 Straight and level flight at very high speeds requires (high/low) power.

25 Steady straight and level flight at very low speeds (say just above the stalling speed) requires (high/low) power.

26 To generate the same lift in straight and level flight at a higher altitude, fly at the same i........ a..s..... .

27 At the same IAS, but at different altitudes, the a.... of a..... will be the same.

28 The indicated airspeed is associated with the dynamic pressure $\frac{1}{2}$ *rho* *V-squared,* where *rho* is the air density and V is the velocity or true airspeed. If indicated airspeed remains the same as air density (*rho*) decreases, say with a gain in altitude, then the velocity or true airspeed must (increase/stay the same/decrease).

29 In climbing at the same IAS as shown on the cockpit airspeed indicator, the TAS will be gradually (increasing/decreasing).

Exercises 11

Climbing

1 In straight and level flight at a steady speed, the thrust is equal to the drag. For a steady climb, thrust must (exceed/equal/be less than) drag.

2 In a steady climb, the thrust not only helps overcome the drag, but also part of the ...... of the aeroplane.

3 The angle of climb that the aeroplane is capable of depends upon the *excess thrust,* i.e. the amount of thrust over and above that required to balance the d.... .

4 The angle of climb of the same aeroplane with the pilot and three passengers will be (greater/less) than the angle of climb when only the pilot is on board.

5 Rate of climb (RoC) is expressed in (feet per minute/mph/knots/litres).

6 An aeroplane that climbs 350 ft in 1 minute has a RoC of (20/100/700/350) fpm.

7 An aeroplane that climbs 700 ft in 2 minutes has a RoC of (50/260/350/700) fpm.

8 An aeroplane that climbs 200 ft in ½ minute should climb ... ft in 1 minute.

9 An aeroplane that climbs 250 ft in 30 seconds has a rate of climb of ..... fpm.

10 To climb 500 ft in 1 minute, your rate of climb needs to be .... fpm.

11 To climb 1,200 ft in 2 minutes, your RoC needs to be ... fpm.

12 Rate of climb is shown in the cockpit on the v....... s.... i......... .

13 Rate of climb depends upon the *excess power,* i.e. the power in excess of that required to overcome the ..... .

14 The altitude at which the climb performance of an aeroplane falls close to zero is called its ....

15 Climb performance at sea level is (better/worse) than climb performance at high altitudes.

16 Climb performance on a hot day is (better/worse) than climb performance on a cold day.

17 If the aeroplane has a rate of climb of 500 fpm, it will climb 500 ft in 1 minute. How much will it climb in 1 minute if there is a headwind?

18 An aeroplane will reach a given altitude in the minimum time if it climbs at the (best-gradient or best-angle climb speed/the best rate of climb speed/the cruise-climb speed).

19 An aeroplane will clear obstacles by a greater margin at (the best-gradient or best-angle speed/the best rate of climb speed/the cruise-climb speed).

20 The aeroplane will travel furthest horizontally over the ground at the (best gradient climb speed/best rate climb speed/cruise-climb speed).

21 If the aeroplane is climbing in a headwind following take-off, will its climb angle relative to the ground and obstacles on the ground be steeper than if there was no wind?

22 Would an aeroplane taking off in a tailwind have less clearance over obstacles in the climb-out than if a headwind were present?

23 Which statement correctly describes an aeroplane in a steady climb?

    (a) Lift is equal to weight, and thrust is equal to drag.

    (b) Lift is less than weight, and thrust is greater than drag.

    (c) Lift is less than weight, and thrust is less than drag.

    (d) Lift is greater than weight, and thrust is less than drag.

24 The climb performance of a heavy aeroplane compared to when it is light is (better/worse/the same).

25 The climb performance of an aeroplane with low power set compared to high power is (better/worse/the same).

26 The climb performance of an aeroplane flown at a non-recommended climbing speed is (better than/worse than/the same as) the climb performance when flown at the recommended speed for the desired type of climb.

27 A prolonged en route climb is best flown:

    (a) at a relatively low airspeed to gain height quickly.

    (b) at a relatively low airspeed for better engine cooling and improved visibility.

    (c) at a relatively high airspeed for better engine cooling.

28 The take-off ground run may be shortened by using a small flap extension, but once in flight, the climb angle through the air is (steeper/flatter/the same) when compared to a clean (un-flapped) aeroplane.

29 The angle of climb through the air and the rate of climb of an aeroplane are not affected by wind. What is affected is the f.....p... relative to the gr..... .

Exercises 12

Descending

1 In a glide, three of the four main forces are acting on the aeroplane. They are ...., ..., ...

2 In a steady glide the aeroplane (is/is not) in equilibrium.

3 In a glide the weight is balanced by the .... and ..... .

4 In a descent, a component of the weight acts along the flightpath, counteracting the drag and contributing to the aeroplane's forward speed. (True/False)?

5 If drag is increased, the glide becomes (steeper/shallower).

6 If power is added, the descent becomes (steeper/shallower).

7 If flaps are lowered, the drag is (increased/decreased).

8 If flaps are lowered, the descent becomes (steeper/shallower).

9 A heavy aeroplane will glide (further/not as far/the same distance), compared with when it is light. To glide the same distance as when it is light, a heavy aeroplane will need a (higher/lower) airspeed on descent.

10 A headwind will (increase/decrease) glide distance over the ground.

11 A tailwind will (increase/decrease) glide distance over the ground.

12 If you glide with a rate of descent (RoD) of 500 fpm, then how long will it take you to descend 3,000 ft?

13 If you have a RoD of 500 fpm, how long will it take you to descend 3,000 ft in a 20 kt headwind?

14 If ice forms on the aeroplane, the drag will (increase/decrease).

15 Increased drag will make the glide (steeper/shallower).

16 Ice accretion will make a glide (steeper/shallower).

17 The addition of power will (steepen/flatten) the descent.

18 Adding power will (increase/decrease/not alter) the rate of descent.

19 Flying faster than or slower than the correct descent speed will (steepen/flatten) the descent angle through the air.

20 Lowering flap in a glide will (steepen/flatten/not alter) the descent angle through the air.

21 The rate of descent will (increase/decrease/remain the same) when descending into wind.

22 Wind does not affect descent through the air, but it does affect flightpath o... the gr..... .

23 Reduced weight does not change the glide angle, but (increases/reduces) the best gliding speed.

Exercises 13

Turning

1 The force that causes turning is called the cen........ force.

2 For a turning aeroplane, the centripetal force is provided by banking the aeroplane and tilting the l... force produced by the wings.

3 The pilot banks the aeroplane by using the a......s.

4 To retain a vertical component to balance the weight, the lift force required in a level turn must be (greater than/equal to/less than) the lift required when straight and level.

5 To develop the increased lift force required in a turn at the same speed, the a.... of ...... must be increased by the pilot applying back pressure to the control column.

6 The steeper the level turn, the greater the l... force required, the greater the a.... of a..... needed to produce it, and the greater the b.... pressure the pilot needs to apply to the control column.

7 Load factor is the ratio of l... produced by the wings/aircraft w..... .

8 If the load factor when straight and level is 1 (which it must be), then the load factor in a level turn will be (greater than/equal to/less than) 1.

9 In a 60° level banked turn, the required lift is twice that in straight and level flight. The load factor is .... .

10 Rudder is used by the pilot to b...... the turn.

11 In a turn, due to the requirement for increased lift, there is also increased d... .

12 To maintain airspeed in a turn, the pilot must apply p.... to overcome the increased drag.

13 At the same airspeed, the a.... of a..... is greater in a turn than in straight and level flight.

14 In a turn, for the same airspeed the angle of attack is higher, and therefore the stalling angle of attack will be reached at an airspeed (higher than/lower than/the same as) in straight and level flight.

15 In straight and level turns there is a tendency to (overbank/underbank).

16 In climbing turns, there is a tendency to (overbank/underbank).

17 In descending turns, there (is/is not) a strong tendency to underbank or overbank.

18 The ball out to the left means more (left/right) rudder pedal pressure from the pilot is required to balance the turn.

19 Bank angle is controlled by the a......s.

20 Nose position and height are controlled by the e......... .

21 The turn is balanced by keeping the ball in the centre with the r..... .

Exercises 14

Stalling

1 Stalling occurs at high angles of attack when the airflow around the aerofoil is unable to remain streamline, separates from the aerofoil surface and becomes t......... .

2 Turbulent flow upsets the formation of the areas of low s..... pressure so necessary to the production of l.... .

3 The lowering of the lifting ability of the wing beyond this critical or stalling angle of attack is described as (increasing/ decreasing) the coefficient of lift.

4 At angles of attack beyond the stalling angle, the lift force produced by the wing is markedly (lower/higher).

5 Beyond the stalling angle, the centre of pressure for the diminished lift force moves (rearwards/forwards), causing the nose to drop.

6 If the wings stall, the turbulent airflow over the tailplane may cause control b...... .

7 The stalling angle on a typical light training aircraft could be (0°/4°/16°) angle of attack.

8 Stalling is associated with a particular a.... of a...... .

9 Write down the formula that summarises the factors involved in the production of lift. Lift $= C_{Lift} \times$ ....

10 Of the factors involved in the production of lift, the pilot can change a.... of a..... and i........ a..s..... .

11 Stalling occurs at a particular angle and is associated with an a.... of a..... , but in straight and level flight at a given weight, every angle of attack is associated with a particular i........ a..s.... .

12 Lift is a direct function of (airspeed/airspeed-squared).

13 Airspeed is a direct function of (lift/the square root of lift).

14 S....... s.... depends upon the square root of the lift required.

15 Lift required depends upon the w..... and/or the l... f..... .

16 If the weight is lower, the lift required is (higher/lower) and the stalling speed straight and level is (higher/lower).

17 If the weight of an aeroplane was increased in flight, say by the formation of ice, its stalling speed would (increase/ decrease).

18 If the lift required from the wings is increased due to the pilot banking the aeroplane and applying back pressure to the control column to maintain height, then the stalling speed compared to that straight and level will (increase/stay the same/decrease).

19 In a banked turn at a constant height, the load factor is (increased/decreased/ equal to 1).

20 The steeper the turn, the (greater/ smaller) the load factor.

21 The steeper the turn, the (higher/lower) the stalling speed.

22 Stalling speed (increases/decreases/ remains unaltered) with an increase in angle of bank.

23 Pulling out of a fast and steep dive, the load factor (is increased/is decreased/ remains at 1 as in smooth straight and level flight).

24 Pulling out of a fast and steep dive, the stalling speed (is increased/is decreased/ remains the same as straight and level).

25 If the bank angle is 30°, using the graphs in our notes, determine the increase in stalling speed over that for straight and level flight.

26 In a 60° steep turn, the stalling speed will be ....% greater than that for straight and level flight.

27 Using the 'g-factor' graph in Figure 14-6, what percentage increase in stalling speed would you expect if you pulled out of a dive and experienced 4g?

28 Stalling speed varies with the square root of the l... force required to be generated by the wings.

29 At higher weights, the wings need to produce (more/less/the same) lift.

30 At higher weights, the stalling speed straight and level is (higher/the same/ lower).

31 Stalling occurs at a critical ..... for an aerofoil.

32 Lift is a function of *angle of attack* and *indicated airspeed*. If the aeroplane flies at different altitudes, its lift requirement straight and level at the same weight remains the same. Therefore at the stalling angle of attack the indicated airspeed will be (the same/higher/lower) at all altitudes.

33 The stalling IAS (varies/does not vary) with altitude.

34 If the aeroplane approaches the stalling angle with a lot of power on, the slipstream adds a lot of kinetic energy to the airflow and separation and stalling is delayed. The stalling speed power-on is (less than/the same as/greater than) the power-off stalling speed.

35 It is preferable to have a wing designed so that it stalls first near the (wingtip/ wing root/trailing edge).

36 Washout designed into a wing (causes/ does not cause) the inner section of the wing to stall first.

37 Stalling first towards the inner section of the wing is preferable because:

(a) it sends turbulent air over the tail-plane causing buffet which acts as a warning to the pilot before the whole wing stalls.

(b) the tendency for the aeroplane to roll is less if one wing stalls ahead of the other.

(c) the ailerons may not lose their effectiveness as early.

(d) all of the above.

38 Flaps (lower/increase) the stalling speed.

39 Stalling indicated airspeed when flying into a headwind is (higher than/lower than/the same as) stalling IAS when flying in a tailwind.

40 If the aeroplane is flying at a high angle of attack near the stall and a wing drops, then:

(a) the dropped wing will have a smaller angle of attack and a greater possibility of stalling.

(b) the dropped wing will have a higher angle of attack and a greater possibility of stalling.

(c) the dropped wing will have a higher angle of attack and a lesser possibility of stalling.

(d) the dropped wing will have a smaller angle of attack and a lesser possibility of stalling.

41 Attempting to pick-up a dropped wing with aileron near the stall on some aeroplanes can:

(a) stall the dropped wing by increasing its angle of attack beyond the stalling angle.

(b) stall the upper wing by increasing its angle of attack beyond the stalling angle.

(c) stall the upper wing by decreasing its angle of attack.

42 During the entry to a spin, the angle of attack of the dropping wing (increases/decreases) and that of the rising wing (increases/decreases).

For your own summary draw diagrams to indicate:

1 Camber.

2 Aspect ratio.

3 Relative airflow.

4 Angle of attack.

5 Angle of incidence.

6 Chord.

7 Span.

8 Lift.

9 Thrust.

10 Centre of pressure.

11 Centre of gravity.

12 Dihedral.

13 Sweepback.

14 Indicated airspeed (IAS).

15 True airspeed (TAS).

16 Stalling angle of attack.

17 Stalling speed straight and level.

18 Stalling speed with increased load factors – turning, pulling out.

19 Stalling speed at higher weights.

20 Induced drag.

21 Parasite drag.

22 Primary flight controls.

23 The major axes of movement.

24 Initial and further effects of the primary flight controls.

25 The effect of lowering flap on lift, drag, attitude, and approach angle, of an aeroplane in flight.

26 The function of trim tabs.

27 The lift curve as angle of attack increases.

28 The drag curve.

29 The effect on stalling speed of weight, angle of bank, load factor, power, flap setting and height.

30 The effect on climb performance resulting from changes in weight, power, airspeed, wind and flap setting.

31 Repeat the same for descent performance.

32 Aileron drag.

Airframe, Engines and Systems

Exercises 15

The Airframe

1 The main structural component of the wing is the ..... .

2 The aerofoil shape of the wing surface is due to the ..... .

3 The most usual form of fuselage construction in training aeroplanes where the skin covers a light structure and carries much of the stress is called ....-......... .

4 Should an aeroplane be tied down so that ropes are taut?

5 Should pitot covers be used when over-night parking?

6 A flight control surface lock is used:
  (a) to lock the flight control in a fixed position when the aircraft is parked to prevent damage by strong and/or gusty winds.
  (b) to lock the flight control in a fixed position during steady straight and level flight.
  (c) to lock trim tabs into a fixed position.

7 Recall suggested actions in handling a cabin fire.

8 Recall suggested actions following an engine fire in flight.

9 Ventilating air (should/need not) always be used.

10 Air from a heat exchanger around the (engine air intake/exhaust manifold) is used in many light aircraft cabin heating systems.

11 Regular inspections of the engine exhaust system should be made to ensure that there are no leaks or cracks in the heat exchanger/exhaust manifold area that might allow dangerous exhaust gases such as .... into the cabin.

12 If a leak of engine gases into the cabin heating system is suspected the cabin heating air should be turned (FULL ON/ OFF) and the ventilation air (reduced/ increased).

Exercises 16

The Aeroplane Engine

1 Name the four strokes of a piston engine commencing with the induction stroke.

2 During the induction stroke the i.... valve is open to allow the fuel/air mixture into the c........ .

3 During most of the compression stroke the inlet valve is ...... and the exhaust valve is ....

4 During most of the power stroke the inlet valve is ...... and the exhaust valve is ....

5 During most of the exhaust stroke the inlet valve is ...... and the exhaust valve is .... .

6 TDC and BDC refer to ... . and .... of the piston movement in the cylinder.

7 The inlet valve opening just prior to TDC and the commencement of the induction stroke is called v.... l.... .

8 The inlet valve not closing until just after BDC on the completion of the induction stroke is called v.... l.. .

9 The exhaust valve opens just (before/after) BDC and the commencement of the exhaust stroke.

10 The exhaust valve closes just (before/after) TDC and the completion of the exhaust stroke.

11 The period when both inlet and exhaust valves are open simultaneously is called v.... o....... .

12 Compressing a gas causes its pressure to (increase/decrease/remain the same).

13 Compressing a gas causes its temperature to (increase/decrease/remain the same).

14 Ignition occurs in each cylinder just before the end of the .... stroke.

15 Ignition occurs in each cylinder just (as/before/after) the piston reaches top dead centre.

16 The function of the piston aeroplane engine is to:
(a) convert chemical energy to heat energy to mechanical energy.
(b) use a mixture of fuel and air and the process of combustion to create power.
(c) burn fuel only without the air being necessary to create power.
(d) both (a) and (b) are correct.

17 To ignite the fuel/air mixture in the cylinder, just prior to TDC and the commencement of the power stroke there is a high-voltage s.... .

18 The s.... is produced by the i....... system.

19 Two important components of the ignition system are the m...... and d........... .

20 Each cylinder receives a spark and fires (once/twice) in every two revolutions of the crankshaft.

21 Most aircraft have (one/two) magneto systems.

22 The magnetos are engine-driven and act as self-contained generators of electrical power to the spark plugs. (True/False)?

23 If one of the magneto switches is turned to OFF, there (should/should not) be an rpm drop.

24 Two separate ignition systems provide a higher level of s..... and more efficient c......... in the combustion chamber.

25 Switching the ignition OFF connects the magneto systems to *earth*. (True/False)?

26 If a magneto earth wire is broken, switching the ignition to OFF (will/will not) stop the magneto producing electrical power.

27 The primary winding of a magneto is earthed when the ignition switch is placed to:
(a) START.
(b) ON.
(c) OFF.

28 If a magneto earth wire comes loose in flight, the engine (will/will not) stop.

29 The spark plugs in a piston engine are provided with a high-energy (or high-tension) electrical supply from:
(a) the battery at all times.
(b) the magnetos, which each have a self-contained generation and distribution system.
(c) the battery at start-up, and then the magnetos.

30 Moving the ignition switch in the cockpit to START:
(a) directly completes the starter circuit connecting the battery to the starter motor.
(b) energises a solenoid-operated switch which completes the starter circuit connecting the battery to the starter motor.
(c) earths the starter motor.

31 Compared to the current flow through the starter circuit that connects the battery to the starter motor, the current flow through the ignition switch in the START position is (low/high/the same).

32 The heavy duty starter circuit is activated by a solenoid-activated switch remotely controlled from the cockpit through a low current circuit:

(a) to avoid the energy losses that would occur in additional heavy duty cable to the cockpit.

(b) to avoid the extra weight of heavy duty cable to the cockpit.

(c) to avoid the unnecessary fire risk caused by heavy current in the cockpit.

(d) all of the above.

33 Because of the very low revs as you start the engine the spark needs to be delayed. This is done automatically in some magnetos by an i...... c........ .

34 If the starter relay sticks after the starter switch has been released, the starter motor (will/will not) remain engaged and the starter warning light (will/will not) remain illuminated.

35 The pilot should monitor oil pressure when an engine is started. If the engine is cold prior to start-up, the engine should be:

(a) shut down immediately if oil pressure does not rise immediately on start-up.

(b) shut down if oil pressure is not seen to rise within approximately 30 seconds of start-up.

(c) shut down if oil pressure has not reached normal limits by the time the aeroplane is ready for take-off.

(d) operated normally, since it may take 10 minutes for oil pressure to rise.

36 It is important that there are no leaks in the exhaust system which may allow (oxygen/carbon monoxide/carbon dioxide), which is a colourless, odourless and dangerous gas, into the cabin.

37 If an engine failure is accompanied by a mechanical noise and the propeller stops rotating, the cause of the engine failure is most likely:

(a) fuel starvation.

(b) failure of a magneto.

(c) break-up of a piston or valve.

38 Following a sudden and complete loss of power from the engine, there is no mechanical noise and the propeller continues to windmill. The likely cause of the power loss is:

(a) fuel starvation.

(b) failure of a magneto.

(c) break-up of a piston or valve.

Exercises 17

The Carburettor

1 Fuel and air need to mixed in a correct ratio to burn properly and this may be done by a c.......... .

2 A carburettor is used to supply:

(a) air to the engine cylinders.

(b) fuel to the engine cylinders.

(c) a fuel/air mixture to the engine cylinders.

3 The amount of fuel that flows through the carburettor is directly controlled by the:

(a) fuel pump.

(b) accelerator pump.

(c) throttle.

(d) airflow through the carburettor venturi.

4 In a *chemically correct* mixture, following combustion all of the fuel and all of the air in the combution chamber (is/is not) burned.

5 In a rich mixture, following combustion excess .... remains.

6 In a lean mixture, following combustion excess ... remains.

7 Moving the throttle in the cockpit moves the b........ v.... in the carburettor.

8 To give a little squirt of fuel to match the increased airflow when the throttle is opened quickly, a carburettor has an a.......... p... built into it.

9 The accelerator pump on a carburettor is used to:

   (a) control the fuel/air mixture during the cruise.

   (b) shut the engine down.

   (c) prevent an over-lean mixture, or even a 'weak cut', if the throttle is opened quickly.

10 To ensure sufficient fuel is fed to the cylinders when idling at low rpm, the carburettor has an i.....j... .

11 As air density decreases, the weight of fuel introduced into the cylinders needs to be (increased/reduced) to match the decreased weight of air. This is done from the cockpit using the m...... c......, which is usually a r.. knob.

12 The mixture control is used to:

   (a) alter the fuel flow to the main jet of the carburettor.

   (b) increase the volume of air through the carburettor.

   (c) increase the fuel flow through the accelerator pump.

   (d) alter the level of fuel in the float chamber.

13 As an aeroplane climbs to higher altitudes with the mixture control set in RICH, the fuel/air mixture:

   (a) does not change.

   (b) becomes leaner.

   (c) becomes richer.

14 For take-off at sea level and +15°C, the mixture control should normally be in f.. r... .

15 An over-rich mixture may cause a loss of p...., high f... consumption, fouling of the s.... p.... and formation of c..... deposits on the piston heads and valves.

16 The extra fuel in a rich mixture causes extra (heating/cooling) in the cylinder by its evaporation.

17 A too-lean mixture may lead to excessively (high/low) cylinder head temperatures and explosive d......... .

18 The usual method of shutting an engine down is to pull the mixture control out into the i... cut-off position.

19 This (leaves/does not leave) fuel in the system, which would not be the case if the engine was shut down by switching the ignition to OFF.

20 Progressive burning that commences prior to the ignition spark is called p..-......... .

21 A great danger to correct functioning of the carburettor, especially in moist conditions, is c.......... i.. .

22 Ice can form in the .... even at high outside air temperatures, due to expansion and cooling as evaporation of fuel occurs.

23 The remedy for suspected carburettor ice is to apply c.......... h.... .

24 The pressure drop (and consequent temperature drop) near the throttle butterfly is *greatest* at (large/small) throttle openings, causing a greater likelihood of carburettor ice forming.

25 The correct procedure to achieve the best fuel/air mixture when cruising at altitude is to move the mixture control towards LEAN until the engine rpm:

(a) drops to a minimum value.

(b) reaches a peak value.

(c) passes through a peak value at which point the mixture control is returned to a slightly richer position.

(d) reaches a minimum value.

26 Normally you should avoid using carburettor heat during ground operations because the hot air source is ....

27 An engine that does not have a carburettor, but instead metered fuel that is fed under pressure into the induction manifold, is said to have:

(a) fuel injection.

(b) supercharging.

(c) metered carburation.

28 If, during start-up, a fire occurs in the engine air intake, a generally suitable procedure is to:

(a) place the starter switch to OFF.

(b) continue with a normal start.

(c) keep turning the engine, but move the mixture control to IDLE CUT-OFF and open the throttle.

Exercises 18

The Fuel System

1 Some aeroplanes have auxiliary fuel boost pumps to provide fuel at the required p......., to purge the fuel lines of any v....., to p.... the cylinders for start-up, and to supply fuel if the e.....-driven pump fails.

2 A cold engine needs to be primed for start-up. The fuel priming pump operated by the pilot delivers fuel:

(a) through the carburettor to the induction manifold or inlet valve ports.

(b) through the carburettor and directly into each of the cylinders.

(c) to the induction manifold or inlet valve ports, bypassing the carburettor.

3 Using a fuel of lower grade than specified may lead to d......... .

4 Using a fuel of higher grade than specified may lead to l...-fouling of the spark p...., and the exhaust valves and their sealing faces could be e..... by the higher-performance fuel exhausting.

5 Motor gasoline (should/should not) be used.

6 Motor gasoline is more prone to p..-i....... and d......... .

7 Motor gasoline contains higher amounts of l.... .

8 Motor gasoline may cause l...-fouling of the spark plugs and a strong possibility of d......... .

9 Fuel should be checked for contamination, especially water, prior to the f.... flight of the day, and after each re-f....... .

10 Water tends to collect at the (highest/lowest) points in the fuel system.

11 To minimise condensation of water in the fuel tanks when the aeroplane is parked, especially in cold conditions:

(a) the fuel tanks should be kept full.

(b) the fuel tanks should be kept as empty as possible.

12 Regular checks for water in the fuel system are important since the presence of water in the fuel may cause:

(a) a loss of engine power because of contamination of the fuel system.

(b) a loss of engine power because of carburettor icing.

(c) freezing of the fuel at high altitudes and/or low temperatures.

13 Aviation gasoline can be distinguished from aviation turbine fuel (kerosene) by col... and s..... .

14 100/130 fuel is coloured g.... .

15 100 LL (low lead) is b... .

16 Avgas equipment should normally be coloured ..., whilst Avtur equipment should normally be coloured ..... .

17 If the fuel strainer drain valve is left open following the pre-flight inspection of a low-wing aeroplane:

(a) the fuel tanks will empty.

(b) the effect will be negligible.

(c) the engine-driven fuel pump may not be able to supply sufficient fuel to the engine, resulting in fuel starvation unless an electric fuel pump is in use.

18 Recall the advantages and disadvantages of refilling aircraft fuel tanks prior to overnight parking.

19 Recall the precautions that should be taken when refuelling an aircraft directly from fuel company sources (i.e. tanker, bowser) or from drums.

Exercises 19

The Oil System

1 Oil lowers friction between moving parts and so prevents high t.......... and what heat is formed can to some extent be carried away by circulating o.. .

2 Oil is used both for lubrication and cooling. (True/False)?

3 Oil is circulated around an engine by:

(a) an engine-driven pressure pump.

(b) a scavenge pump.

(c) a vacuum pump.

(d) an electric pump.

4 Oil grades (may/may not) be mixed.

5 The same oil grade, but of different brand-names, (may/may not) be mixed.

6 Impurities in the oil should be removed by the o.. f..... .

7 If the oil filter clogs up, then the unfiltered oil is forced through an o.. f..... b..... valve. Dirty and contaminated oil (is/is not) better than no oil at all.

8 To aid in cooling the oil, most systems have an oil-c...... .

9 With too little oil, you may observe a (high/low) oil temperature and/or a (high/low) oil pressure.

10 If the oil quantity is too great, excess oil may be forced out through various parts of the e......, such as the front shaft s..... .

11 On start-up of a cold engine, the oil pressure gauge should indicate a rise (immediately/within 5 seconds/within 30 seconds/within 5 minutes).

Exercises 20

The Cooling System

1 Most aero-engines have cooling-f... to aid in cooling.

2 High airspeeds allow (better/worse) engine cooling.

3 Low airspeeds cause (worse/better) engine cooling.

4 A lean mixture leads to (higher/lower) engine temperatures.

5 A blocked oil cooler leads to (higher/lower) oil temperatures.

6 A high power setting leads to (higher/lower) engine temperatures.

7 Open cowl flaps encourage (better/ poorer) engine cooling.

8 High outside air temperatures lead to (higher/lower) engine temperatures.

Exercises 21

Engine Handling

1 If the oil quantity gauge suddenly drops to zero, immediately monitor the o.. t.......... g..... .

2 If the oil temperature gauge shows a rapid increase in temperature, then there (may/may not) be a serious loss of oil.

3 If the oil temperature remains normal, there is probably (sufficient/insufficient) oil circulating.

4 If you suspect a serious loss of oil, then consideration should be given to (an immediate landing/a landing at the next suitable aerodrome which is about half an hour away).

5 Increasing power with a constant-speed unit, increase rpm first followed by manifold pressure. (True/False)?

6 Decreasing power with a CSU, decrease MP first, followed by rpm. (True/False)?

7 Prior to shutting an engine down, you should allow a brief c...... period.

8 Why do most engine manufacturers recommend that the use of carburettor heat during ground operations be minimised?

Exercises 22

The Electrical System

1 Normal in-flight electrical power is provided by an a......... or g......... .

2 A distribution point for electrical power to various services is called a:
(a) circuit breaker.
(b) fuse.
(c) distributor.
(d) bus bar.

3 Electrical power for start-up and as an emergency source of electrical power is the b....... .

4 An a......... requires an initial current from the b...... to activate it.

5 A typical lead-acid battery contains a solution of weak s......... acid.

6 When the engine is stopped, the main source of electrical power is the:
(a) battery.
(b) magneto.
(c) generator or alternator.
(d) circuit breaker.

7 When the engine is running, the main source of electrical power is the:
(a) battery.
(b) magneto.
(c) generator or alternator.
(d) circuit breaker.

8 An ammeter measures (current in amps/ voltage).

9 A centre-zero ammeter measures current in and out of the b......, whereas a left-zero ammeter measures only the o..... of the alternator. It has zero amps on the l... end of the scale and increases in amps to the right end of the scale.

10 Immediately after starting, ammeter indication will be (high/low) as the battery is re-charged.

11 An alternator is capable of a (high/low) output, and there (is/is not) a risk that the charging rate of a partially-flat battery could cause damage to the battery.

12 The ammeter reading zero may mean that the alternator is not supplying electrical power. (True/False)?

13 The illumination of a warning light for the electrical system may mean that the alternator is not supplying electrical power. (True/False)?

14 A split master switch controls the b...... and the ....

15 A voltage regulator maintains correct output v...... from the alternator.

16 Electrical circuits are protected by f.... and c...... b........

17 Fuses and circuit breakers are protection against excessive electrical (current/voltage).

18 A blown fuse (may/should not) be replaced by a fuse of a higher rating so that it will not blow again.

19 A popped CB may be reset, or a blown fuse replaced by one of the same value, while the aircraft is in flight. It is not necessary to wait until the aircraft has landed to replace the fuse. (True/False)?

20 Blown fuses or popped CBs (should/should not) be replaced more than once.

21 If the alternator (or generator) fails in flight, the electrical loads (should/need not) be reduced to a minimum and an early landing (should/need not) be made.

22 A 28 volt DC electrical system in an aircraft has a 24 volt battery:
(a) for no particular reason.
(b) to allow the alternator to fully recharge the battery once the engine is running.
(c) so that the battery will not burn the alternator out.

23 A battery rated at 15 amp-hours is capable of providing 5 amps for a period of .... hours without recharging.

24 If the alternator fails in flight:
(a) the electrical system will not be affected.
(b) the battery will be able to supply normal electrical power to all services, even if the flight is of long duration.
(c) electrical services (such as lighting and unnecessary radios) should be reduced to a minimum to conserve battery power, and an early landing considered.

25 During engine start, a large current-draw (is/is not) made on the battery.

26 The battery master switch should be turned to OFF after the engine is stopped to avoid the battery discharging through:
(a) the magnetos.
(b) the alternator or generator.
(c) electrical services connected to it.
(d) the ignition switch.

27 Which of the following instruments and gauges would normally be electrically powered? Airspeed indicator, altimeter, vertical speed indicator, attitude indicator, turn coordinator, heading indicator, fuel quantity gauges, engine rpm gauge, oil temperature gauge. (Check for your own particular aeroplane).

Exercises 23

The Vacuum System

1 The vacuum system induces, or draws, a high-speed airflow onto the 'buckets' on the edge of the gyro rotors causing them to spin. (True/False)?

2 The suction (or vacuum) gauge reads the pressure (above/below) atmospheric pressure.

3 A vacuum pump may be used to operate the (gyroscopic/engine/pitot-static) instruments.

4 A vacuum pump (draws/blows) air through the suction-operated flight instruments to operate (gyro rotors/pressure valves/regulators).

5 The vacuum pump, if fitted to a modern aeroplane, is most likely to be (electrically/engine/hydraulically) driven.

6 Air-driven gyro rotors are prevented from spinning too fast by the (air filter/vacuum relief valve/suction gauge).

7 A zero reading on the suction gauge when the engine is running could indicate:

(a) a failure of the vacuum pump.

(b) a failure of the gauge itself.

(c) either of the above.

8 A reading of 2″Hg (2 inches of mercury) on the suction gauge indicates a (low/normal/high) vacuum and a (low/normal/high) airflow.

9 Insufficient suction (may/will not) cause gyroscopic instruments (such as the artificial horizon or the heading indicator) to indicate incorrectly, erratically, or respond slowly.

10 A reading of 5″Hg on the suction gauge indicates a (low/normal/high) vacuum and a (low/normal/high) airflow.

11 Gyroscopic instruments driven by 'suction' created in an externally mounted venturi-tube will be usable:

(a) immediately the engine starts.

(b) as soon as the aeroplane rolls for take-off.

(c) if there is any airflow through the venturi caused by wind.

(d) not until after the aircraft has been at flying speed for several minutes after take-off.

12 Name the two methods used to provide suction for the vacuum systems found in aircraft.

Exercises 24

Landing Gear, Tyres and Brakes

1 A cracked or severely corroded landing gear strut found by a pilot during his pre-flight inspection (should/need not) be inspected by a qualified engineer before the aeroplane flies.

2 The damping agent used to dampen the rebound action in the oleo-pneumatic unit following a shock is the (compressed air/oil).

3 The oleo strut will extend (further/the same/less) in flight than on the ground.

4 The state of charge of the oleo-pneumatic unit (is/is not) indicated by how much of the strut extends while the nosewheel is supporting its normal load on the ground.

5 Why should mud or dirt noticed in a pre-flight inspection be cleaned off the polished section of an oleo strut prior to taxiing?

6 The nosewheel is held aligned with a ...... link and nosewheel oscillations either side of centre are damped by a ......-........ .

7 A nosewheel which is free to turn, but is not connected to the cockpit by any control rods or cables for turning, is said to be of the .... type.

8 Nosewheel steering in light aircraft is usually operated by:

(a) control rods or cables operated by the rudder pedals.

(b) a steering wheel.

(c) the brakes.

9 A castoring nosewheel can be made to turn by:

(a) a steering wheel.

(b) differential braking.

(c) control rods or cables connected to the rudder pedals.

10 The relative movement between the tyre and the wheel flange is called ..... .

11 If a tyre has moved so that the creep marks are out of alignment, then:

(a) it is serviceable.

(b) it should be inspected and possibly re-fitted or replaced.

(c) tyre pressure should be checked.

(d) the brakes will be unserviceable.

12 A tyre that has some shallow cuts in the sidewalls and a number of small stones embedded in its tread (should/need not) be rejected by a pilot.

13 A tyre that has a deep cut that exposes the casing cords (should/need not) be rejected for further flight.

14 A tyre with a large bulge in one of its sidewalls (should/need not) be rejected for further flight.

15 Braking of an individual main wheel is known as:

(a) individual braking.

(b) directional braking.

(c) differential braking.

16 Most light aircraft braking systems are operated:

(a) by cables.

(b) pneumatically.

(c) hydraulically.

(d) electrically.

17 Hydraulic fluid leaks from the brake lines or other parts of the brake system (are/are not) acceptable.

18 A severely corroded or pitted brake disc (will/will not) be structurally weak and (will/will not) reduce braking efficiency.

19 The brake pads may suffer unnecessary wear if:

(a) the tyre pressure is too high.

(b) the tyre pressure is too low.

(c) the parking brake is left on over-night.

(d) the brake disc is corroded or pit-ted.

20 Wheel brakes (should/should not) be tested early in the taxi.

Flight Instruments

Exercises 25

Pressure Instruments

1 Pressure instruments make use of static pressure and/or total or p.... pressure.

2 The altimeter requires ...... pressure.

3 Static pressure is sensed by the (pitot tube/static vent/static tube).

4 The pitot tube senses (total pressure/ static pressure/dynamic pressure).

5 Some aeroplanes are fitted with an electrical p.... h..... as a precaution against ice forming in the pitot tube.

6 The pitot cover, used to prevent water, insects, dust, etc., accumulating in the pitot tube (should/should not) be removed prior to flight.

7 Water that has entered the pitot-static system lines (could/will not) cause incorrect readings on the pressure instruments.

8 From static pressure and pitot (total) pressure, we can obtain d...... pressure.

9 The ASI uses p.... (total) pressure and s..... pressure to find dynamic pressure, to which indicated airspeed is closely related.

10 The VSI measures the rate of change of (static/dynamic/total) pressure.

11 If a static vent ices over, the altimeter will show (an increasing/a decreasing/ the same) altitude.

12 The altimeter has a subscale on which to set a pressure datum. (True/False)?

13 The VSI has a subscale on which to set a pressure datum. (True/False)?

14 With QNH set, the altimeter reads height:
(a) above mean sea level (amsl).
(b) above aerodrome level (aal).
(c) above the 1013 mb(hPa) pressure level.

15 With QFE set, the altimeter reads height:
(a) above mean sea level (amsl).
(b) above aerodrome level (aal).
(c) above the 1013 mb(hPa) pressure level.

16 When landing at an aerodrome other than the one of departure, a new QFE pressure setting (is/is not) required.

17 The altimeter subscale of a parked aeroplane is turned until the altimeter reads zero. The subscale setting will be the aerodrome (QFE/QNH/elevation).

18 The altimeter subscale of a parked aeroplane is turned until the altimeter reads the aerodrome's elevation. The subscale setting will be the aerodrome (QFE/ QNH/pressure altitude).

19 The altimeter subscale is wound to 1013. The altimeter will indicate:
(a) elevation.
(b) height.
(c) pressure altitude.
(d) flight level.

20 V_{NE} is known as the .... speed and is marked on the ASI with a ...-coloured line.

21 The stalling speed, wings-level and full flap extended, is indicated on the ASI as the (high/low) speed end of the (white/ green/yellow) arc.

22 The stalling speed, wings-level and no flap extended, is indicated on the ASI as the (high/low) speed end of the (white/green/yellow) arc.

23 V_{NO} is known as the .... speed and is indicated on the ASI as the (high/low) speed end of the (white/green/yellow) arc.

24 Which instruments are connected to the static source?

25 Which instrument is connected to the pitot tube, where the total pressure (i.e. dynamic plus static) is sensed?

Exercises 26

Gyroscopic Instruments

1 The gyroscopic heading indicator should be regularly re-aligned with the magnetic c....... .

2 A vacuum pump fitted to an aeroplane may operate the (ASI/VSI/AI/HI/compass/turn coordinator).

3 Slip or skid is indicated on the:
   (a) turn coordinator.
   (b) balance ball.
   (c) attitude indicator.
   (d) heading indicator.

4 A low vacuum may be indicated by a low suction reading and slow or erratic gyroscopic instruments. (True/False)?

5 Failure of the electrical supply to an electrically driven attitude indicator may be indicated by:
   (a) a low ammeter reading.
   (b) a red warning flag.
   (c) low suction.

6 The turn indicator provides information resulting from the precession of a gyro that has its spin axis (vertical/horizontal).

7 The attitude indicator has a gyro with a (vertical/horizontal) spin axis.

Exercises 27

The Magnetic Compass

1 The lubber line of the magnetic compass indicates:
   (a) true north.
   (b) magnetic north.
   (c) the magnetic heading of the aeroplane.
   (d) the true heading of the aeroplane.
   (e) the track of the aeroplane over the ground.

2 The difference between true north and magnetic north is called v........ .

3 Corrections that need to be made to an individual magnetic compass to obtain its magnetic heading can be found in the cockpit on the d........ card.

4 May magnetic materials be placed near the compass?

5 Is a magnetic compass more reliable near the equator or near the poles?

6 In the northern hemisphere, turning through north you should .... the magnetic heading.

7 In the northern hemisphere, you should .... the magnetic heading turning through south.

8 In the northern hemisphere, accelerating on a westerly heading will cause an apparent turn to the ....

9 Recall the pilot serviceability checks on a magnetic compass.

10 Runway 32 at a particular aerodrome in the UK could have a bearing of:
   (a) 032°M.
   (b) 322°M.
   (c) 322°T.
   (d) 032°T.

Airworthiness and Performance

Exercises 28

Airworthiness

1 The document to show that an aircraft is registered is the Certificate of
....

2 The document issued to indicate that a particular aeroplane complies with the appropriate airworthiness requirements is the C.......... of ....

3 The CofA is issued for a specified period. (True/False)?

4 Any maintenance required by the approved Maintenance Schedule that forms part of the aeroplane's Certificate of Airworthiness (must/need not) be completed for the CofA to become valid again.

5 May spins and loops be carried out in an aeroplane in the Normal category?

6 The Flight Manual (must/need not) be carried in the aircraft, while the Pilot's Operating Handbook (must/need not) remain with it.

7 The CAA Supplement takes precedence over the manufacturer's Flight Manual. (True/False)?

8 Placards in the cockpit have the same status as instructions in the .... and should be adhered to.

9 The time remaining to the next major inspection can be determined from:
   (a) the Certificate of Airworthiness.
   (b) the Flight Manual.
   (c) the Certificate of Maintenance Review.
   (d) Air Navigation (General) Regulations.

10 A daily inspection shall be carried out:
   (a) before the first flight of the day.
   (b) at least daily, not necessarily before the first flight of the day.

11 Should the oil quantity be checked in a daily inspection?

12 Should tyre inflation and their condition be checked in the daily inspection?

13 Minor maintenance and replacements that can be performed by a qualified pilot are listed in the:
   (a) Flight Manual.
   (b) CAA Supplement to the Flight Manual.
   (c) Certificate of Airworthiness.
   (d) Air Navigation (General) Regulations.
   (e) Maintenance Schedule.
   (f) Pilot's Operating Handbook.

14 Aeroplanes on which a qualified pilot can perform minor maintenance tasks must be:
   (a) less than 5,700 kg and not used for aerial work.
   (b) less than 5,700 kg.
   (c) less than 2,730 kg and not used for public transport.
   (d) less than 2,730 kg.

15 The legal responsibility to ensure that the aeroplane's maintenance documents are in order prior to flight is the:
   (a) engineer's.
   (b) pilot's.
   (c) chief flying instructor's.
   (d) CAA's.

16 Defects requiring maintenance after flight should be entered by the pilot in the:

   (a) Technical Log.

   (b) Certificate of Airworthiness.

   (c) Flight Manual.

   (d) Certificate of Maintenance release.

17 Can a pilot legally replace a landing gear tyre?

18 Can a pilot legally change the engine oil?

19 Can a pilot legally change the spark plugs and set their gaps?

20 May a pilot who is not qualified as an aero-engineer replace a propeller?

21 Having completed approved maintenance, the pilot:

   (a) need not record it.

   (b) should record it in the appropriate place, but not sign for it.

   (c) should record it in the appropriate place and certify it with his signature and licence number.

   (d) should notify the CAA.

22 Aircraft performance data are contained in the ....

23 Some aircraft in the Normal Category are permitted to operate in the Utility Category and perform limited aerobatics provided:

   (a) certain weight and CG limitations are satisfied.

   (b) the weight is less than 3,000 kg.

   (c) stalls are not performed.

   (d) a flying instructor is on board.

24 Specify the conditions that must be satisfied before a pilot can sign the second part of a Duplicate Inspection for a flight or engine control system.

Exercises 29

Airframe Limitations

Define the following:

1 Maximum take-off weight.

2 Maximum landing weight.

3 Normal operating limit speed.

4 Never-exceed speed.

5 Manoeuvring speed.

6 Turbulence penetration speed.

7 Severe turbulence (can/will not) cause limit load factors to be exceeded and result in structural damage or failure.

8 At speeds in excess of the manoeuvring speed, full backward movement of the control column can cause the limit load factor to be exceeded. (True/False)?

9 At speeds in excess of the manoeuvring speed (V_A), the pilot should avoid abrupt or large control movements mainly because:

   (a) the aeroplane will stall.

   (b) the limit load factor may be exceeded.

   (c) the aeroplane will be out-of-balance.

10 The normal operating limit speed (V_{NO}) should:

   (a) only be exceeded in smooth air.

   (b) never be exceeded.

   (c) be less than the manoeuvring speed (V_A).

11 List the specific items that a pilot or an engineer should check on an aeroplane following a heavy landing.

Exercises 30

The Atmosphere

1 What are the three main constituents of the earth's atmosphere?

2 High humidity causes air density to (increase/decrease/remain the same).

3 The amount of water vapour in the air is called:
(a) dampness.
(b) relative humidity.
(c) humidity.
(d) the degree of saturation.

4 The amount of water vapour that the air is actually carrying compared to what it is capable of carrying at that temperature is called:
(a) dampness.
(b) relative humidity.
(c) humidity.
(d) the degree of saturation.

5 As the temperature of a parcel of air drops, its relative humidity:
(a) increases.
(b) decreases.
(c) stays the same.
(d) gradually falls to zero.

6 If the temperature of a given parcel of air increases at a constant pressure, the density of the air:
(a) increases.
(b) decreases.
(c) stays the same.

7 If the temperature increases, the take-off distance required:
(a) increases.
(b) decreases.
(c) stays the same.

8 Compared to a sea-level aerodrome, the take-off distance required at a high-elevation aerodrome is:
(a) greater.
(b) less.
(c) the same.

9 Engine performance and airframe aerodynamic performance are poorer at high altitudes mainly because of:
(a) the lower temperature.
(b) the higher pressure.
(c) the lower density.
(d) the higher relative humidity.

10 If the pressure altitude increases, the take-off distance required:
(a) increases.
(b) decreases.
(c) stays the same.

11 As air expands, its pressure and density:
(a) remain the same.
(b) increase.
(c) decrease.

12 Aeroplane performance deteriorates at (high/low) temperatures.

13 The lower the air density *(rho)* the (poorer/better) the performance of the airframe and the engine.

14 The 'measuring stick' for atmospheric variables such as pressure, temperature, density is the Inter........ St...... At......... .

15 ISA mean sea level standard pressure is ...... mb(hPa).

16 ISA MSL temperature is ....° Celsius.

17 Pressure in the ISA falls at approximately 1 mb(hPa) per .... ft.

18 Temperature in the ISA falls at approximately ....°C per 1,000 ft gain in altitude.

19 If MSL atmospheric pressure is 1013 mb(hPa), what is the pressure at:
(1) 30 ft amsl?
(2) 60 ft amsl?
(3) 3,000 ft amsl?

20 What is the ISA temperature at the following pressure altitudes?
(1) PA 2,000 ft
(2) PA 5,000 ft
(3) PA 10,000 ft

21 Convert 15°C to °F and write down the formula to use.

22 Convert 77°F to °C and write down the formula to use.

Exercises 31

Take-off and Landing Performance

1 Take-off distance is established on a h... surface that is ..... and .... .

2 Higher weights (increase/decrease) take-off distance required.

3 Higher temperatures (increase/decrease) take-off distance required.

4 Higher aerodrome elevations, with their decreased air density, result in poorer aerodynamic and engine performance, and require (increased/decreased) take-off distances.

5 A tailwind (increases/decreases) take-off distances.

6 A 10 kt wind at 60° off the runway heading gives a (0/4/9) kt crosswind.

7 A 20 kt wind at 60° off the runway gives a (0/9/18) kt crosswind.

8 A 10 kt wind at 30° off the runway heading gives a (0/5/9) kt crosswind component.

9 A 20 kt wind at 30° off the runway heading gives a (0/5/10) kt crosswind component.

10 In crosswind conditions, the headwind or tailwind component (should/need not) be applied when calculating the take-off or landing distances.

11 A 10 kt wind at 30° off the runway heading gives a (0/5/9) kt headwind component.

12 A 20 kt wind at 30° off the runway heading gives a (0/5/18) kt headwind component.

13 Take-off distance is measured to:
(a) the lift-off point on the runway.
(b) to 100 ft above the runway level.
(c) to 50 ft above the runway level.

14 Soft, sandy surfaces may (increase/decrease) take-off distance.

15 Up-slope will (increase/decrease) take-off distance.

16 A 10% increase in aircraft weight is likely to cause an increase in take-off distance to a height of 50 ft of ....%, i.e. a factor of ....

17 An increase of 1,000 ft in aerodrome elevation is likely to cause an increase in take-off distance to a height of 50 ft of ....%, i.e. a factor of ....

18 An increase of 10°C in ambient temperature is likely to cause an increase in take-off distance to a height of 50 ft ....%, i.e. a factor of ....

19 Short, dry grass under 5 inches is likely to cause an increase in take-off distance to a height of 50 ft of ....%, i.e. a factor of ....

20 Long, dry grass between 5 and 10 inches is likely to cause an increase in take-off distance to a height of 50 ft ....%, i.e. a factor of ....

21 Short, wet grass under 5 inches is likely to cause an increase in take-off distance to a height of 50 ft of ....%, i.e. a factor of ....

22 Long, wet grass between 5 and 10 inches is likely to cause an increase in take-off distance to a height of 50 ft of ....%, i.e. a factor of ....

23 Soft ground or snow is likely to cause an increase in take-off distance to a height of 50 ft of at least ....%, i.e. a factor of at least ....

24 A 2% uphill slope is likely to cause an increase in take-off distance to a height of 50 ft of ....%, i.e. a factor of ....

25 A tailwind component of 10% of lift-off speed is likely to cause an increase in take-off distance to a height of 50 ft of ....%, i.e. a factor of ....

26 For Private flights, the CAA recommends that, after taking account of all relevant variables, a safety factor of .... be applied for take-off.

27 The measured take-off distance for an aeroplane at a given weight and flap setting extracted from a manual is 370 metres at sea level and 10°C. For this particular aeroplane type, the CAA has imposed a mandatory 5% increase in published distances. What is the recommended minimum take-off distance for the aeroplane at an aerodrome elevation 1,000 ft amsl; 2% upslope; a short grass surface that is wet; a temperature of +20°C; and a tailwind of 5 kt (lift-off speed is 50 kt)?

28 Measured take-off distance from the manual is 400 metres; take-off aerodrome elevation 1,000 ft; a wet, long-grass strip with 2% upslope; +20°C; tailwind component 5 kt (lift-off speed 50 kt). Mandatory CAA limitation: nil.

29 Clearway (must/need not) be a clear ground surface.

30 Stopway (must/need not) be an unobstructed ground surface.

31 Headwind (increases/decreases/does not affect) take-off distance.

32 Tailwind (increases/decreases/does not affect) take-off distance.

33 Tailwind (increases/decreases/does not affect) lift-off IAS.

34 Tailwind (increases/decreases/does not affect) lift-off GS.

35 Headwind (increases/decreases/does not affect) lift-off IAS

36 Headwind (increases/decreases/does not affect) lift-off GS.

37 Landing distance is measured from .... ft over the ground, power (off/on), to a stop.

38 Increased weights mean (increased/decreased) landing distances.

39 High elevations mean (increased/decreased) landing distance.

40 High temperatures mean (increased/decreased) landing distances.

41 Tailwind means (increased/decreased) landing distances.

42 Tailwind means (higher/lower/the same) IAS on approach.

43 Tailwind means (higher/lower/the same) GS on approach.

44 Wet and slippery runway surfaces mean (increased/decreased) landing distances.

45 Down-slope means (increased/decreased) landing distances.

46 Flap means (increased/decreased) approach speeds.

47 Use of flap means (shorter/longer) landing distances.

48 A 10% increase in aircraft weight is likely to cause an increase in landing distance from a height of 50 ft of ....%, i.e. a factor of ....

49 An increase of 1,000 ft in aerodrome elevation is likely to cause an increase in landing distance from a height of 50 ft of ....%, i.e. a factor of ....

50 An increase of 10°C in ambient temperature is likely to cause an increase in landing distance from a height of 50 ft of ....%, i.e. a factor of ....

51 Short, dry grass under 5 inches is likely to cause an increase in landing distance from a height of 50 ft of ....%, i.e. a factor of ....

52 Long, dry grass is likely to cause an increase in landing distance from a height of 50 ft of ....%, i.e. a factor of ....

53 Short, wet grass under 5 inches is likely to cause an increase in landing distance to a height of 50 ft of ....%, i.e. a factor of ....

54 Long, wet grass above 5 inches is likely to cause an increase in landing distance from a height of 50 ft of ....%, i.e. a factor of ....

55 Snow is likely to cause an increase in landing distance from a height of 50 ft of at least ....%, i.e. a factor of at least ....

56 A 2% downhill slope is likely to cause an increase in landing distance from a height of 50 ft of ....%, i.e. a factor of ....

57 A tailwind component of 10% of landing speed is likely to cause an increase in landing distance from a height of 50 ft of ....%, i.e. a factor of ....

58 For Private flights, the CAA recommends that, after taking account of all relevant variables, a safety factor of .... be applied for landing.

59 The measured landing distance from 50 ft for an aeroplane at a given weight extracted from a manual is 370 metres at sea level and 10°C. What is the recommended landing distance for the aeroplane at an aerodrome elevation 1,000 ft amsl, 2% downslope, a short grass surface that is wet, a temperature of +20°C, and a tailwind of 5 kt (landing speed is 50 kt)?

60 Performance data (are/are not) found in the Flight Manual and its associated CAA Supplement.

Exercises 32
En Route Performance

1 Flying for range is flying to achieve the best (distance over the ground/time in the air) for a given amount of fuel.

2 Another way of expressing 'flying for range' is to say that you want to achieve the (least/greatest) fuel burn-off for a given distance.

3 Flying for best range, the pilot wants to achieve the greatest number of (nautical miles/minutes in the air) for the given fuel.

4 Flying the aeroplane so that it can stay in the air for the longest time possible is called (endurance/range) flying.

5 To achieve best endurance, the fuel flows should be kept as (high/low) as possible for safe flight.

6 Fuel flow in a piston-engined aeroplane depends upon the power being produced, so for best endurance and lowest fuel flow you should choose a speed for (minimum/maximum) power.

7 When flying at a given airspeed, an aeroplane loaded to a gross weight of 2,000 lb will fly at (a greater/the same/a lesser) angle of attack compared to when it is loaded to a gross weight of 1,500 lb.

8 The power required to maintain cruising speed for a particular aeroplane when it is heavily laden is (the same as/greater than/less than) the power required when it is light.

Exercises 33

Weight and Balance

1 The weight that includes the weight of the airframe, engine, fixed equipment, unusable fuel, full oil is called the b.... e.... w...... .

2 The weight of the aeroplane plus pilot, passengers, baggage, cargo, ballast, but excluding only the usable fuel, is called the ....

3 The maximum allowable gross weight permitted for take-off is the m...... t...-o.. w...... .

4 Sometimes a high obstacle in the take-off flightpath or a short runway or some other performance consideration restricts the weight that you may take off at to something less than the structural MTOW. This reduced TOW is called a p.........-limited take-off weight.

5 The maximum permitted landing weight is called the m...... l...... w...... .

6 A short runway may not allow us to land at the MLW (structural), but at a p.........-l...... landing weight.

7 Landing weight = take-off weight minus b...-o.. .

8 List the items that must be weighed in determining the load of an aeroplane.

9 The turning effect or turning moment of a force depends on two things, its (magnitude/temperature) and its (pressure/moment arm).

10 The longer the moment arm from the centre of gravity the (greater/smaller) the turning effect of a given force.

11 The CG datum is used as a reference from which to measure moment arm. (True/False)?

12 The pilot has the legal responsibility to ensure that the aeroplane will be operated within the weight and balance limitations. (True/False)?

13 Calculate the moment of 250 lb of fuel in a fuel tank whose moment arm is 20 inches from the datum.

14 Calculate the moment of 30 imperial gallons of Avgas in a fuel tank whose moment arm is 802 inches from the datum. The specific gravity of Avgas is 072, so 1 imp. gallon weighs 72 lb.

15 A pilot would normally check the CG position of ....-... weight and .... weight prior to flight.

16 It is possible in some aeroplanes that full fuel tanks and a full passenger and baggage load would exceed the maximum weight limits. An appropriate solution would be to:

(a) operate over the maximum weight limit.

(b) reduce the fuel on board, even though it will be insufficient for the flight plus reserves.

(c) reduce the fuel on board, but to not less than that required for the flight plus reserves, and then, if necessary, off-load baggage and/or passengers.

(d) Off-load baggage and/or passengers, so that a full fuel load can be carried.

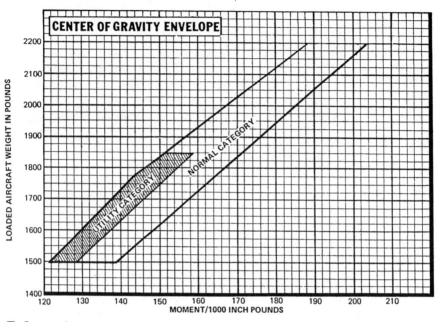

■ *Centre of gravity envelope*

The following questions refer to the centre of gravity envelope above

17 The combination(s) of weight and total moment which are acceptable for flight in the Normal Category are:

(a) 1,900 lb and 170,000 inch.pounds (or pound.inches).

(b) 1,900 lb and 180,000 inch.pounds.

(c) 1,640 lb and 180,000 inch.pounds.

(d) 1,640 lb and 138,000 inch.pounds.

(e) 1,640 lb and 130,000 inch.pounds.

(f) 2,125 lb and 196,000 inch.pounds.

18 The combination(s) of weight and total moment which are acceptable for flight in the Utility Category are:

(a) 1,900 lb and 170,000 inch.pounds (or pound.inches).

(b) 1,900 lb and 180,000 inch.pounds.

(c) 1,640 lb and 180,000 inch.pounds.

(d) 1,640 lb and 138,000 inch.pounds.

(e) 1,640 lb and 130,000 inch.pounds.

(f) 2,125 lb and 196,000 inch.pounds.

19 Having calculated the take-off weight and CG position, a pilot can calculate a zero fuel weight and CG position by subtracting the weight and moment of the (total usable fuel/estimated burn-off).

20 Having calculated the take-off weight and CG position, a pilot can calculate a landing weight and CG position by subtracting the weight and moment of the (total usable fuel/estimated fuel consumed).

Exercises 34

Wake Turbulence

1 The static air pressure beneath a wing is (greater than/less than) the static air pressure above the wing.

2 The air beneath a wing of an aeroplane in flight tends to leak around the wingtip and into the lower static pressure area above the wing. This leaves a trail of invisible w...... v......s behind.

3 These wingtip vortices can be very strong behind a heavy aeroplane flying slowly at a high a.... of a....., such as on take-off and landing.

4 Wingtip vortices tend to drift (up/down).

5 Wingtip vortices tend to (drift downwind/drift upwind/remain stationary over the ground, even in steady winds).

6 You should (disregard/avoid) wake turbulence behind a heavy jet that has just taken-off.

7 The most dangerous area for wake turbulence behind a heavy jet is (at the start of his take-off run/just past his point of rotation and on his climb-out).

8 Wake turbulence (is different to/the same as) 'jet blast'.

Exercises 35

Ground Effect

1 The better 'flyability' of an aeroplane near the ground or some other surface is called g..... e...... .

2 When an aeroplane is flying close to the ground the ground surface will restrict the airflow around the wings in a number of ways. The surface will restrict ..wash and ....wash and also restrict the formation of w...... vortices.

3 Ground effect will cause an increase in 'lifting ability'. The more technical name for this is c.......... of l.... .

4 Ground effect will not allow as great a formation of wingtip vortices as in 'free air' and therefore ground effect causes a reduction in i...... drag.

5 As an aeroplane climbs out of ground effect on take-off its climb performance will tend to (increase/decrease).

6 In ground effect the airspeed indicator and the altimeter (will/may not) read accurately.

Exercises 36

Windshear

1 Any change in the wind speed and/or the wind direction as you move from one point to another is called a w...sh... .

2 The effect of a windshear that causes an aeroplane to fly above the desired flightpath and/or to increase its speed is called o...shoot effect.

3 The effect of a windshear that causes an aeroplane to fly below the desired flightpath and/or to decrease its speed is called u....shoot effect.

4 If the initial effect of a windshear is reversed as the aeroplane travels further along its flightpath (say on approach to land), then the overall influence of the windshear on the aeroplane is called a windshear r....... effect.

Principles of Flight

Answers 1

The Forces Acting on an Aeroplane

1   weight
2   lift
3   thrust
4   drag
5   lift, thrust
6   greater

Answers 2

Weight

1   centre of gravity
2   wing loading = weight of the aeroplane/ wing area
3   15 lb/sq.ft

Answers 3

Aerofoil Lift

1   lift
2   boundary layer
3   streamline
4   turbulent
5   Bernoulli
6   in all directions
7   due to motion
8   constant
9   static +dynamic
10 decrease
11 increase
12 decrease
13 decreases
14 speed up
15 decrease
16 camber
17 mean camber line
18 chord line
19 chord
20 thickness
21 decreases
22 less than
23 lift

24 drag
25 total reaction, lift, drag
26 angle of attack
27 decrease, lift
28 increases
29 decreases
30 centre of pressure
31 moves forwards
32 rearwards
33 wing shape, angle of attack, air density (*rho*), velocity of airflow, wing area (*S*)
34 ability
35 coefficient of lift
36 dynamic pressure
37 $L = C_{Lift} \times \frac{1}{2}\ rho\ V\text{-}squared \times S$
38 angle of attack
39 increases
40 lower
41 will
42 zero
43 (c)
44 increases
45 90
46 angle of attack
47 increases
48 (a)

Answers 4

Drag

1   opposes
2   parallel to
3   thrust
4   thrust
5   parallel to, opposite to
6   induced, parasite
7   skin friction, form drag, interference drag
8   skin friction
9   skin friction
10 increases
11 separates, turbulent
12 delayed

13 form drag
14 interference drag
15 increases
16 induced drag
17 lower
18 lower, vortices
19 outwards towards the wingtip
20 inwards towards the root
21 vortices
22 high
23 high
24 low
25 low
26 (a)
27 high, washout
28 long span and a short chord
29 wingtip
30 low
31 high
32 at a speed where the parasite drag and induced drag are equal
33 thrust
34 induced drag, greater
35 parasite drag, greater
36 (c)
37 (a)

Answers 5

Lift/Drag Ratio

1 12:1
2 induced drag, 5:1
3 parasite, 6:1
4 15:1
5 most
6 minimum
7 minimum
8 (d)

Answers 6

Thrust from the Propeller

1 thrust
2 aerofoil
3 blade angle
4 twisted
5 hub
6 tip

7 propeller tip
8 thrust
9 rpm, airspeed
10 fine
11 coarse
12 power
13 yaw, rudder
14 roll left and yaw left
15 (a)
16 (b)

Answers 7

Stability

1 nose-down
2 nose-up
3 pitch down
4 tailplane, horizontal stabiliser
5 (b)
6 will
7 without
8 longitudinal, rolling
9 lateral, pitching
10 normal, yawing
11 tailplane
12 well forward
13 forward
14 CP is behind the CG, tailplane generates a downward force
15 (b)
16 large, vertical
17 dihedral
18 low
19 sideslip, yaw
20 roll
21 roll and yaw
22 forward
23 aft
24 is not

Answers 8

Control

1 elevator
2 lateral
3 down
4 up
5 (d)

6   fall

7   ailerons

8   longitudinal

9   left

10 go down

11 up

12 higher

13 higher, more

14 away from

15 adverse aileron yaw

16 differential ailerons, Frise-type ailerons

17 greater than

18 lowered, lesser

19 rudder

20 normal

21 increase, roll

22 rise

23 roll

24 (b)

25 increases

26 more

27 increases

28 elevator, rudder

29 true

30 (d)

31 elevator trim tab, elevator trim wheel

32 trim tabs

33 large

34 will

35 (a)

36 may, lateral

37 (a)

38 (a)

39 (b)

40 (b)

Answers 9

Flaps

1   increase

2   lower

3   lowers

4   lower

5   drag

6   lift, drag

7   less

8   steeper

9   lower

10 lower

11 better, lower

12 shortens

13 slower, shorter

14 (a)

15 (b)

16 decrease

17 delay

18 true

Answers 10

Straight and Level

1   is

2   lift, drag, weight and thrust

3   equal

4   equal

5   (b)

6 $L = C_{Lift} \times \frac{1}{2}\, rho\ V\text{-}squared \times S$

7   indicated airspeed

8   angle of attack

9   angle of attack, IAS, decrease

10 reduced

11 increased

12 high

13 low

14 low

15 high

16 lift

17 decrease

18 lower

19 lower

20 thrust

21 thrust

22 high

23 high

24 high

25 high

26 indicated airspeed

27 angle of attack

28 increase

29 increasing

Answers 11

Climbing

1 exceed
2 weight
3 drag
4 less
5 feet per minute
6 350 fpm
7 350 fpm
8 400
9 500 fpm
10 500 fpm
11 600 fpm
12 vertical speed indicator
13 drag
14 ceiling
15 better
16 worse
17 500 ft
18 best rate of climb speed
19 best-gradient (angle)
20 cruise-climb speed
21 yes
22 yes
23 (b)
24 worse
25 worse
26 worse than
27 (c)
28 flatter
29 flightpath relative to the ground

Answers 12

Descending

1 lift, drag, weight
2 is
3 lift and drag
4 true
5 steeper
6 shallower
7 increased
8 steeper
9 the same distance, higher airspeed
10 decrease
11 increase
12 6 mins
13 6 mins
14 increase
15 steeper
16 steeper
17 flatten
18 decrease
19 steepen
20 steepen
21 remain the same
22 over the ground
23 reduces

Answers 13

Turning

1 centripetal
2 lift
3 ailerons
4 greater than
5 angle of attack
6 lift, angle of attack, backward
7 lift/weight
8 greater than
9 2
10 balance
11 drag
12 power
13 angle of attack
14 higher than
15 overbank
16 overbank
17 is not
18 left
19 ailerons
20 elevators
21 rudder

Answers 14

Stalling

1 turbulent
2 static, lift
3 decreasing
4 lower
5 rearwards
6 control buffet

7 16°

8 angle of attack

9 $L = C_{Lift} \times \frac{1}{2}\ rho\ V\text{-}squared \times S$

10 angle of attack, indicated airspeed

11 angle of attack, indicated airspeed

12 airspeed-squared

13 square root of lift

14 stalling speed

15 weight, load factor

16 lower, lower

17 increase

18 increase

19 increased

20 greater

21 higher

22 increases

23 is increased

24 is increased

25 7%

26 41%

27 100%, i.e. stall speed is doubled

28 lift

29 more

30 higher

31 angle

32 the same

33 does not vary

34 less than

35 wing root

36 causes

37 (d)

38 lower

39 the same

40 (b)

41 (a)

42 increases (dropping wing), decreases (rising wing)

Airframe, Engines and Systems

Answers 15

The Airframe

1 spar
2 ribs
3 semi-monocoque
4 no
5 yes
6 (a)
7 refer to the text
8 refer to the text
9 should
10 exhaust manifold
11 carbon monoxide
12 OFF, increased

Answers 16

The Aeroplane Engine

1 induction or intake, compression, power, exhaust
2 inlet, cylinder
3 closed, closed
4 closed, closed
5 closed, open
6 top dead centre, bottom dead centre
7 valve lead
8 valve lag
9 before
10 after
11 valve overlap
12 increase
13 increase
14 compression
15 before
16 (d)
17 spark
18 spark, ignition
19 magneto, distributor
20 once
21 two
22 true
23 should

24 safety, combustion
25 true
26 will not
27 (c)
28 will not
29 (b)
30 (b)
31 low
32 (d)
33 impulse coupling
34 will, will
35 (b)
36 carbon monoxide
37 (c)
38 (a)

Answers 17

The Carburettor

1 carburettor
2 (c)
3 (d) Note: It is indirectly controlled by the throttle, which varies the butterfly valve position. This affects the airflow, but it is the airflow which directly controls the amount of fuel taken into the airstream.
4 is
5 fuel
6 air
7 butterfly valve
8 accelerator pump
9 (c)
10 idling jet
11 reduced, mixture control, red
12 (a)
13 (c)
14 full rich
15 power, fuel, spark plugs, carbon
16 cooling
17 high CHTs, detonation
18 idle cut-off or cut-out
19 does not leave
20 pre-ignition

21 carburettor ice
22 carburettor
23 carburettor heat
24 small
25 (c)
26 unfiltered
27 (a)
28 (c)

Answers 18

The Fuel System

1 pressure, vapour, prime, engine-driven
2 (c)
3 detonation
4 lead-fouling, spark plugs, eroded
5 should not
6 pre-ignition, detonation
7 lead
8 lead-fouling, detonation
9 first flight of the day, each re-fuelling
10 lowest
11 (a)
12 (a)
13 colour and smell
14 green
15 blue
16 Avgas – red; Avtur – black
17 (c)
18 refer to the text
19 refer to the text

Answers 19

The Oil System

1 temperatures, oil
2 true
3 (a)
4 may not
5 may
6 oil filter
7 oil filter bypass valve, is
8 oil-cooler
9 high temperature, low pressure
10 engine, seals
11 within 30 seconds

Answers 20

The Cooling System

1 fins
2 better
3 worse
4 higher
5 higher
6 higher
7 better
8 higher

Answers 21

Engine Handling

1 oil temperature gauge
2 may
3 sufficient
4 immediate landing
5 true
6 true
7 cooling
8 because the hot air is unfiltered

Answers 22

The Electrical System

1 alternator, generator
2 (d)
3 battery
4 alternator, battery
5 sulphuric
6 (a)
7 (c)
8 current in amps
9 battery, output, left
10 high
11 high, is
12 true
13 true
14 battery, alternator
15 voltage
16 fuses, circuit breakers
17 current
18 should not
19 true
20 should not
21 should, should

22 (b)

23 3 hours

24 (c)

25 is

26 (c)

27 ASI, altimeter and VSI are pitot-static
instruments and are not electrically powered
(although there may be an electrical pitot
heater to avoid icing); the gyroscopic instruments (AI, TC and HI) may be electrically
powered or powered from the vacuum
system – a typical arrangement is a vacuum-
powered AI and HI with an electrical TC;
the fuel quantity gauges and oil temperature
gauge (if fitted) will probably be electrically
powered; the rpm gauge is self-powered
directly off the engine.

Answers 23

The Vacuum System

1 true

2 below

3 gyroscopic

4 draws, gyro rotors

5 engine-driven

6 vacuum relief valve

7 (c)

8 low, low

9 may

10 high, high

11 (d)

12 engine-driven vacuum pumps and externally mounted venturi-tubes

Answers 24

Landing Gear, Tyres and Brakes

1 should

2 oil

3 further

4 is

5 To avoid rapid wearing of the seals during
taxiing and ground manoeuvres as the strut
telescopes in and out.

6 torque link, shimmy-damper

7 castoring

8 (a)

9 (b)

10 creep

11 (b)

12 need not

13 should

14 should

15 (c)

16 (c)

17 are not

18 will, will

19 (d)

20 should

Flight Instruments

Answers 25

Pressure Instruments

1 pitot
2 static
3 static vent
4 total pressure
5 pitot heater
6 should
7 could
8 dynamic
9 pitot, static
10 static
11 the same
12 true
13 false
14 (a)
15 (b)
16 is
17 QFE
18 QNH
19 (c)
20 never-exceed speed, red
21 low, white
22 low, green
23 normal operating limit speed, high speed end of the green arc
24 altimeter, vertical speed indicator, airspeed indicator
25 airspeed indicator

Answers 26

Gyroscopic Instruments

1 compass
2 AI, HI, TC
3 (b)
4 true
5 (b)
6 horizontal
7 vertical

Answers 27

The Magnetic Compass

1 (c)
2 variation
3 deviation
4 no
5 near the equator
6 undershoot
7 overshoot
8 north
9 refer to the text
10 (b)

Airworthiness and Performance

Answers 28

Airworthiness

1   Registration
2   Certificate of Airworthiness
3   true
4   must
5   no
6   must, need not
7   true
8   Flight Manual
9   (c)
10 (a) before the first flight of the day
11 yes
12 yes
13 (d), ANR (GEN)
14 (c)
15 (b)
16 (a)
17 yes
18 yes
19 yes
20 no
21 (c)
22 Flight Manual and CAA Supplement
23 (a)
24 refer to the text

Answers 29

Airframe Limitations

1   refer to the text
2   refer to the text
3   refer to the text
4   refer to the text
5   refer to the text
6   refer to the text
7   can
8   true
9   (b)
10 (a)
11 refer to the text

Answers 30

The Atmosphere

1   nitrogen, oxygen and water vapour
2   decrease
3   (c)
4   (b)
5   (a)
6   (b)
7   (a)
8   (a)
9   (c)
10 (a)
11 (c)
12 high
13 poorer
14 International Standard Atmosphere
15 1013.2 mb(hPa)
16 15
17 30
18 2
19 1012, 1011, 913
20 +11, +5, −5
21 59°F, °F = °C + 32
22 25°C, °C = (°F − 32)

Answers 31

Take-Off and Landing Performance

1   hard surface that is level and dry
2   increase
3   increase
4   increased
5   increases
6   9
7   18
8   5
9   10
10 should
11 9
12 18
13 (c)
14 increase

15 increase

16 20%, 1.2

17 10%, 1.1

18 10%, 1.1

19 20%, 1.2

20 25%, 1.25

21 25%, 1.25

22 30%, 1.3

23 at least 25%, at least 1.25

24 10%, 1.1

25 20%, 1.2

26 1.33

27 minimum recommended take-off distance = 370 × mandatory 105 × 1.1 × 1.1 × 1.25 × 1.1 × 1.2 × 1.33 = 1,032 metres

28 recommended take-off distance = 400 × 1.1 × 1.1 × 1.3 × 1.1 × 1.2 × 1.33 = 1,105 metres
Note the significant increase in distance when the various factors are applied. Good airmanship would suggest that a take-off in the opposite direction would be preferable, taking advantage of a downslope and a headwind.

29 need not

30 must

31 decreases

32 increases

33 does not affect

34 increases

35 does not affect

36 decreases

37 50, power off

38 increased

39 increased

40 increased

41 increased

42 the same

43 higher

44 increased

45 increased

46 decreased

47 shorter

48 10%, 1.1

49 5%, 1.05

50 5%, 1.05

51 20%, 1.2

52 30%, 1.3

53 30%, 1.3

54 40%, 1.4

55 at least 25%, at least 1.25

56 10%, 1.1

57 20%, 1.2

58 1.43

59 370 × 1.05 × 1.1 × 1.3 × 1.05 × 1.2 × 1.43 = 1,001 metres

60 are

Answers 32

En Route Performance

1 distance over the ground

2 least

3 nautical miles

4 endurance

5 low

6 minimum power

7 greater

8 greater than

Answers 33

Weight and Balance

1 basic empty weight

2 zero fuel weight

3 maximum take-off weight

4 performance

5 maximum landing weight

6 performance-limited

7 burn-off

8 refer to the text

9 magnitude, moment arm

10 greater

11 true

12 true

13 5,000 lb.in

14 216 lb × 802 in = 17,3232 lb.in

15 take-off weight, zero fuel weight

16 (c)

17 (a), (d), (f)

18 (d)

19 total usable fuel

20 estimated fuel consumed

Answers 34

Wake Turbulence

1 greater
2 wingtip vortices
3 angle of attack
4 down
5 drift downwind
6 avoid
7 point of rotation and climb out
8 different to

Answers 35

Ground Effect

1 ground effect
2 upwash, downwash, wingtip vortices
3 coefficient of lift
4 induced drag
5 decrease
6 may not

Answers 36

Windshear

1 windshear
2 overshoot effect
3 undershoot effect
4 windshear reversal effect

Index

re-stall buffet 144
rimary control systems 75
riming pump 194
ropeller 47–56
    blade terminology 47, 49
    constant speed propellers 53, 220
    efficiency 51
    forces on 50
    hand-swinging 219
    helical motion 48
    helical twist 49
    out-of-balance 217
    rotational velocity 48
    take-off effects 54
    thrust 47, 50, 105
    torque 50
    variable-pitch propellers 54, 220

Q

QFE 257
QNH 257, 304
    regional QNH 257

R

radial engines 165
range speed 112, 344
rate-1 turn 142
rate of bank 263
rate of climb 119
    indicator 258
rectified airspeed 294
refrigeration icing 187
refuelling 196
regional QNH 257
relative
    airflow 18
    effect on performance 317
    humidity 187, 302
    velocity 9
relay 229
rho (air density) 22, 247, 301
ribs 160
roll 63
    control 79
    followed by yaw 71
    yaw followed by roll 72
rudder 75, 160
    control 83, 87, 161
    power of 86
ruddervator 160
runway 309
    slope 309, 321, 336, 340
    surface 309, 320, 335

S

safety factor
    recommended for landing 337
    recommended for take-off 322
semi-monocoque construction 159
separation point 11
servo tab 89
shimmy damper 239
short take-off or landing aircraft 16
sideslip 67–73
simple flap 102
single-engine speed, on ASI 251
skidding in a turn 265
skin friction drag 28
    effects on boundary layer 10
slats 96, 103
slipping in a turn 139, 264
slipstream
    effect on rudder 84, 87
    effect on tailplane 87
slots 96, 103
slotted flap 102
solenoid 229
spark
    advance 173
    plugs 171
    timing 170
spars 159
specific gravity, of fuel and oil 351
speed
    limitations 86, 294, 295
    maximum endurance 113
    maximum range 112
    stability 114
    variation in level flight 107
spins
    and aileron use 154
    how spins develop 153
    instrument indications 155
spiral instability 72
split flap 102
spoilers 103
stabilator 78, 90
stability 57–73
    compared with controllability 62
    lateral 68
    lateral and directional 71
    longitudinal stability 65
    on the ground 73
    positive stability 62
    spiral instability 72
    sweepback, effect of 70